ZAGAT
2014

London
Restaurants

LOCAL EDITORS
Sholto Douglas-Home and Claire Coleman
STAFF EDITORS
Jill Emeny, Neil Fazakerley and Bill Corsello

Published and distributed by
Zagat Survey, LLC
76 Ninth Avenue
New York, NY 10011
T: 212.977.6000
E: feedback@zagat.com
www.zagat.com

ACKNOWLEDGMENTS

We're grateful to our local editors, Sholto Douglas-Home, a London restaurant critic for over two decades, and Claire Coleman, lifestyle journalist and all-round epicurean enthusiast. We also sincerely thank the thousands of people who participated in this survey – this guide is really "theirs."

We also thank Katie Carroll (editor), Lil C-G, Max, Fiz and Rebecca Coleman, Alex, Louis and Tallula Douglas-Home, John Godwin and Betty Marcus, as well as the following members of our staff: Danielle Borovoy (editor), Brian Albert, Sean Beachell, Maryanne Bertollo, Reni Chin, Larry Cohn, Nicole Diaz, Kelly Dobkin, Sarah Drinkwater, Jeff Freier, Alison Gainor, Michelle Golden, Justin Hartung, Marc Henson, Ryutaro Ishikane, Natalie Lebert, Mike Liao, Derek Lock, Vivian Ma, Molly Moker, James Mulcahy, Andrew Murphy, Polina Paley, Clara Rivera, Josh Siegel, Albry Smither, Amanda Spurlock, Scott Totman, Chris Walsh, Jacqueline Wasilczyk, Art Yagci, Sharon Yates, Anna Zappia and Kyle Zolner.

ABOUT ZAGAT

In 1979, we asked friends to rate and review restaurants purely for fun. The term "user-generated content" had yet to be coined. That hobby grew into Zagat Survey; 34 years later, we have loyal surveyors around the globe and our content now includes nightlife, shopping, tourist attractions, golf and more. Along the way, we evolved from being a print publisher to a digital content provider. We also produce marketing tools for a wide range of corporate clients, and you can find us on Google+ and just about any other social media network.

The reviews in this guide are based on public opinion surveys. The ratings reflect the average scores given by the survey participants who voted on each establishment, while the text is based on quotes from, or paraphrasings of, the surveyors' comments. Ratings and reviews have been updated throughout this edition based on our most recent survey results. Phone numbers, addresses and other factual data were correct to the best of our knowledge when published in this guide.

JOIN IN

To improve our guides, we solicit your comments – positive or negative; it's vital that we hear your opinions. Just contact us at **nina-tim@zagat.com**.

Contents

Ratings & Symbols

	Name	Symbols	Cuisine	Zagat Ratings			
				FOOD	DECOR	SERVICE	COST
Area, Address & Contact	**Tim & Nina's** ◑ *Burgers/Peruvian*			▽ 23	9	13	£15
	Brixton | Hotport St., SW9 8PS | 020-7123-4567 | www.zagat.com						
Review, surveyor comments in quotes	"Bang on trend" as ever, Nina and Tim Zagat's new venture serves up a "baffling" selection of "inexplicably addictive" Peruvian burgers in "wholly inappropriate" French brasserie surrounds; service is "not even average", but at least the bill is generally "cheap".						

Ratings

Food, Decor & **Service** are rated on a 30-point scale.

26 - 30 extraordinary to perfection

21 - 25 very good to excellent

16 - 20 good to very good

11 - 15 fair to good

0 - 10 poor to fair

▽ low response | less reliable

Cost

The price of dinner with a drink and service; lunch is usually 25% to 30% less. For unrated **newcomers,** the price range is as follows:

I £20 and below   E £41 to £60

M £21 to £40   VE £61 or above

Symbols

◑ serves after 11 PM

🚫 closed on Sunday

Ⓜ closed on Monday

🚫 cash only

Maps

Index maps show restaurants with the highest Food ratings and other notable places in those areas.

Phone

From outside the U.K., dial international code (e.g. 011 from the U.S.) +44, then omit the first zero of the listed number.

London at a Glance

WINNERS: The Waterside Inn in Bray earns the Survey's top ratings for Food and Service; in London, those honors go to **Yashin Sushi** and **The Ledbury. Sketch – The Lecture Room & Library** earns the top Decor rating, **The Woleseley** is voted Most Popular and **Masala Zone** ranks as the Most Popular chain.

SURVEY STATS:

- 1,290 restaurants covered
- 10,271 surveyors
- In our recent Dining Trends Survey, Londoners reported that they eat dinner out twice a week, spending £37.35 on average.
- Italian (23%) food still rules the roost as London's favourite cuisine, with Japanese in second place (17%), having pushed last year's runner up, French, into third place (14%).
- More people are reportedly now booking online (53%) than over the phone (39%).
- Eighty-five percent think it's ok in moderation or perfectly acceptable to take photos of your meal while at the table.

TRENDS: Big names from overseas continued to flock to London, like Hong Kong-based Alvin Leung, the maverick behind **Bo London,** and Spain's lauded Arzak family, who teamed up with the Halkin Hotel for **Ametsa with Arzak Instruction.** Keith McNally's New York trendsetter, **Balthazar,** and French chef Eric Chavot's **Brasserie Chavot** continued the renaissance of the classic French brasserie. Restaurateurs quickly unveiled offshoots of recent premieres, like Arkady Novikov's **Brompton Asian Brasserie** (a Novikov cousin) and Jason Atherton's **Little Social** and **Social Eating House** (siblings of **Pollen Street Social**). The gourmet fast-food juggernaut rumbles on, with **Bubbledogs, Chooks, Dirty Burger** and U.S. burger favourites **Five Guys** and **Shake Shack.** London's new skyscrapers host buzzed-about debuts, with **Duck & Waffle** and **SushiSamba** straddling three floors atop the Heron Tower, and **Aqua Shard, Hutong** and **Oblix** at The Shard.

HOT NEIGHBOURHOODS: Usually synonymous with top prices, Mayfair this year welcomed accessible newcomers like Argentinean **Zoilo** and burger haven **Patty & Bun.** There's fresh blood in similarly traditional Piccadilly with Peruvian **Coya** and steakhouse **MASH.** The gentrification of King's Cross continues with **Grain Store** and **Plum + Spilt Milk,** and there's a similar scene in Southwark with the arrival of **Story** and Spanish bodega **Bar Tozino.** Brixton Market's recent transformation into a gourmet destination continues, as hot spots like **French & Grace, KaoSarn** and **Mama Lan** were joined this year by seasonal British cuisine retreat **Salon.**

MOST SEARCHED ON ZAGAT.COM: Wagamama, Hakkasan, Hawksmoor, Gordon Ramsay, The Ledbury

London
10 September, 2013

Sholto Douglas-Home
Claire Coleman

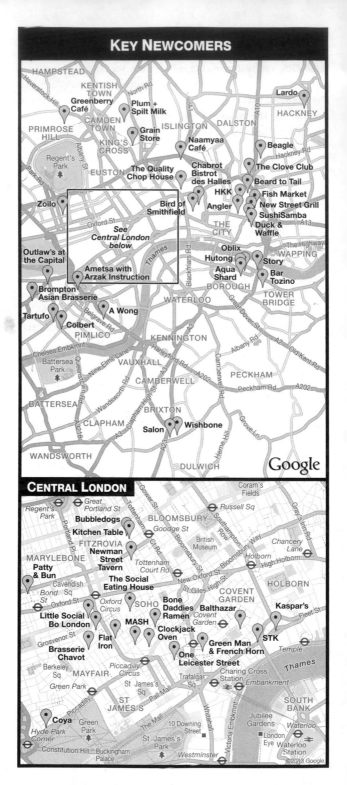

KEY NEWCOMERS

HAMPSTEAD
KENTISH TOWN
Greenberry Café
Plum + Spilt Milk
Lardo
HACKNEY
CAMDEN TOWN
PRIMROSE HILL
Grain Store
ISLINGTON
DALSTON
Regent's Park
KING'S CROSS
Naamyaa Café
Beagle
EUSTON
The Quality Chop House
Chabrot Bistrot des Halles
The Clove Club
Beard to Tail
Zoilo
Bird of Smithfield
HKK
Angler
Fish Market
New Street Grill
SushiSamba
Duck & Waffle
THE CITY
See Central London below
Oblix
Hutong
Story
Outlaw's at the Capital
Aqua Shard
Bar Tozino
WAPPING
Ametsa with Arzak Instruction
BOROUGH
TOWER BRIDGE
Brompton Asian Brasserie
WATERLOO
Tartufo
A Wong
Colbert
PIMLICO
KENNINGTON
Battersea Park
VAUXHALL
CAMBERWELL
PECKHAM
BATTERSEA
Salon
Wishbone
BRIXTON
CLAPHAM
WANDSWORTH
DULWICH

Google

CENTRAL LONDON

Coram's Fields
Regent's Park
Great Portland St
Bubbledogs
Kitchen Table
BLOOMSBURY
Russell Sq
FITZROVIA
Newman Street Tavern
British Museum
Chancery Lane
MARYLEBONE
The Social Eating House
Holborn
HOLBORN
Patty & Bun
Bond St
Little Social
Bo London
MASH
Bone Daddies Ramen
Balthazar
COVENT GARDEN
Kaspar's
SOHO
Clockjack Oven
STK
Brasserie Chavot
Flat Iron
Green Man & French Horn
One Leicester Street
MAYFAIR
Piccadilly Circus
Charing Cross Station
Thames
St James's Sq
Trafalgar Sq
Embankment
SOUTH BANK
Coya
Green Park
Pall Mall
Jubilee Gardens
Waterloo
Hyde Park Corner
The Mall
10 Downing Street
London Eye
Waterloo Station
Constitution Hill
Buckingham Palace
St James's Park
Westminster

©2013 Google

Key Newcomers

Our editors' picks among this year's arrivals. See full list at p. 197.

SEASONED RESTAURATEURS

Balthazar
Brasserie Chavot
Brompton Asian Brasserie
Colbert
Grain Store
Greenberry Café
Little Social
Naamyaa Café
Oblix
Outlaw's at the Capital

MEATY TREATS

Beard To Tail
Clockjack Oven
Flat Iron
MASH
Patty & Bun
STK
Wishbone
Zoilo

CONSUMMATELY CASUAL

A Wong
Beagle
Chabrot Bistrot des Halles
Green Man & French Horn
Lardo
Newman Street Tavern
One Leicester Street

The Quality Chop House
Salon

CITY SLICKERS

Angler
Duck & Waffle
Fish Market
HKK
New Street Grill
SushiSamba

INTERNATIONAL ARRIVALS

Ametsa with Arzak Instruction
Bar Tozino
Bo London
Coya
Hutong

BOLD AND IDIOSYNCRATIC

Aqua Shard
Bird of Smithfield
Bone Daddies Ramen
Bubbledogs
The Clove Club
Kaspar's
Kitchen Table
Plum + Spilt Milk
The Social Eating HouseStory
Tartufo

WHAT'S NEXT

Scheduled to debut soon after deadline were chicken-and-egg specialists **Whyte & Brown** in Soho, Japanese bun experts **Flesh & Buns** in Covent Garden and the colonial Indian–themed **Gymkhana** in Mayfair. Further on the horizon is the return of a landmark that closed in 1994, **Boulestin**, at a new site in St. James's. Other big names expanding their reach include Angela Hartnett (along with **Canteen**'s founders) at **Merchant's Tavern** in Shoreditch, Florence Knight back in the **Polpetto** kitchen at its new home in Berwick Street, a Gordon Ramsay collaboration with David Beckham, called **Union Street Cafe,** in Borough Market and Will Beckett (of **Hawksmoor**) doing his take on a low-key local, **Foxlow,** in Clerkenwell. Jason Atherton's empire building is set to continue as he takes over the Tower 42 site from Gary Rhodes, and Simon Rogan is working on a new venture after closing his lauded two-year pop-up, **Roganic.** The Shard hasn't finished opening new restaurants yet, with two new eateries planned at the Shangri-La.

Most Popular

This list is plotted on the map at the back of this book.

1. Wolseley | European
2. Hakkasan | Chinese
3. Hawksmoor | Steak
4. J. Sheekey | Seafood
5. Dinner by Heston | British
6. L'Atelier/Robuchon* | French
7. River Café | Italian
8. Alain Ducasse | French
9. Ivy* | British/European
10. Ledbury | French
11. Rest. Gordon Ramsay | French
12. Le Gavroche | French
13. Zuma* | Japanese
14. Clos Maggiore | French
15. Roka* | Japanese
16. Fat Duck (Bray) | British
17. Square | French
18. St. John | British
19. Pied à Terre | French
20. Pollen Street Social* | British
21. Bentley's | British/Seafood
22. Patara | Thai
23. Rules* | British
24. Chez Bruce | British/Med.
25. Nobu London* | Japanese
26. Ottolenghi | Bakery/Med.
27. Le Manoir/Quat (Great Milton) | French
28. Le Caprice | British/European
29. Arbutus | European
30. Brasserie Zédel* | French
31. Koffmann's* | French
32. Scott's | Seafood
33. Amaya | Indian
34. Belgo* | Belgian
35. Chutney Mary* | Indian
36. Bar Boulud | French
37. Savoy Grill* | British/French
38. Veeraswamy* | Indian
39. Delaunay | European
40. Burger & Lobster | American
41. Petrus* | French
42. Cinnamon Club | Indian
43. Franco Manca | Pizza
44. MEATliquor* | Burgers
45. Greenhouse* | French
46. Waterside Inn* | French
47. 10 Greek Street | European
48. La Petite Maison* | Med.
49. Marcus Wareing* | French
50. NOPI* | Asian/Mideastern
51. St. John Bread* | British
52. Zafferano* | Italian

MOST POPULAR CHAINS

1. Masala Zone | Indian
2. Wahaca | Mexican
3. Wagamama | Japanese
4. Gaucho | Argentinean/Steak
5. Jamie's Italian | Italian
6. Busaba Eathai | Thai
7. Pho | Vietnamese
8. Browns | British
9. Carluccio's | Italian
10. Byron | Burgers

Many of the above restaurants are among the London area's most expensive, but if popularity were calibrated to price, a number of other restaurants would surely join their ranks. To illustrate this, we have added two pages of Best Buys starting on page 17.

* Indicates a tie with restaurant above

Top Food

<u>29</u> Waterside Inn (Bray) | *French*

<u>28</u> Yashin Sushi | *Japanese*
Barrafina | *Spanish*
Gauthier Soho | *French*
Ledbury | *French*
Le Gavroche | *French*
Dinings | *Japanese*
Petrus | *French*
French Table | *French/Med.*
Square | *French*
Pitt Cue Co. | *BBQ*
Pied à Terre | *French*
L'Atelier/Robuchon | *French*
Chez Bruce | *British/Med.*
Rest. Gordon Ramsay | *French*
Fat Duck (Bray) | *British/Med.*
José | *Spanish*
Morgan M | *French*
Rasoi Vineet Bhatia | *Indian*

<u>27</u> Le Manoir/Quat
(Great Milton) | *French*

Babur | *Indian*
Alain Ducasse | *French*
Marcus Wareing | *French*
La Trompette | *French*
Harwood Arms | *British*
River Café | *Italian*
Jin Kichi | *Japanese*
Zuma | *Japanese*
Hunan | *Chinese/Taiwan.*
Honest Burgers | *Burgers*
Umu | *Japanese*
Zucca | *Italian*
Nobu London | *Japanese/Peru.*
Koffmann's | *French*
Pepper Tree* | *Thai*
Yauatcha | *Chinese*
Amaya | *Indian*
Club Gascon | *French*
Spice Village | *Indian*
Greenhouse | *French*

Top Decor

<u>28</u> Sketch/Lecture
Sketch/Parlour
Ritz

<u>27</u> Mosimann's
Bob Bob Ricard
Sketch/Gallery
Le Manoir/Quat (Great Milton)
Clos Maggiore
Waterside Inn (Bray)
SushiSamba

<u>26</u> Galvin Café/Chapelle
Les Trois Garçons
Apsleys
Petrus
Wapping Food
Brasserie Zédel

<u>26</u> Criterion
Alain Ducasse
Goring
Hélène Darroze

Top Service

<u>28</u> Waterside Inn (Bray)
Ledbury
Le Gavroche
Rest. Gordon Ramsay

<u>27</u> Mosimann's
Le Manoir/Quat (Great Milton)
Petrus
Marcus Wareing
Fat Duck (Bray)
Alain Ducasse

Pied à Terre
Goring
Oslo Court
Roux at The Landau

<u>26</u> Square
Apsleys
Koffmann's
Chez Bruce
Wilton's
Ritz

Excludes places with low votes

TOPS BY CUISINE

AMERICAN

25 Cut at 45 Park Lane
23 JW Steakhouse
   Spuntino
22 Sophie's
   Hoxton Grill

BBQ & BURGERS

28 Pitt Cue Co.
27 Honest Burgers
23 Burger & Lobster
   Barbecoa
   MEATliquor

BRITISH

28 Chez Bruce
   Fat Duck (Bray)
27 Harwood Arms
26 Dinner by Heston
   Wilton's

CHINESE

27 Hunan
   Yauatcha
26 Hakkasan
25 Min Jiang
   Kai Mayfair

EUROPEAN (MODERN)

26 Glasshouse
   Trinity
   Dabbous
   Texture
   Roux at The Landau

FISH 'N' CHIPS

26 Nautilus Fish
24 Golden Hind
   Rock & Sole Plaice
   North Sea
20 Geales

FRENCH

29 Waterside Inn (Bray)
28 Gauthier Soho
   Ledbury
   Le Gavroche
   Petrus

FRENCH BISTRO

25 Bistrot Bruno Loubet
   Galvin Bistrot
   Le Café/Marché
   Comptoir Gascon
24 Le Vacherin

FRENCH BRASSERIE

25 Angelus
24 Bellamy's
   Racine
23 Le Colombier
22 Le Café Anglais

INDIAN

28 Rasoi Vineet Bhatia
27 Babur
   Amaya
   Spice Village
26 Trishna

INTERNATIONAL

26 Mosimann's
   Viajante
25 Providores
   Modern Pantry
24 Caravan

ITALIAN

27 River Café
   Zucca
26 Apsleys
   Murano
25 Il Bordello

JAPANESE

28 Yashin Sushi
   Dinings
27 Jin Kichi
   Zuma
   Umu

LEBANESE

24 Yalla Yalla
   Ishbilia
23 Maroush
   Beirut Express
   Al Hamra

MEDITERRANEAN

28 French Table
26 La Petite Maison
   Ottolenghi
   Brawn
24 Eagle

MEXICAN

25 Lupita
24 Taqueria
23 Cantina Laredo
22 Tortilla
   Wahaca

PIZZA

- 26 Franco Manca
- 24 Princi London
- Oliveto
- Osteria Basilico
- 23 Portabello Rist.

SEAFOOD

- 26 Wilton's
- Nautilus Fish
- Scott's
- J. Sheekey
- 25 J. Sheekey Oyster Bar

SPANISH

- 28 Barrafina
- José
- 26 Morito
- Moro
- Fino

STEAK

- 27 Goodman
- 26 Santa Maria

- Hawksmoor
- Garufa/Garufin
- 25 Cut at 45 Park Lane

THAI

- 27 Pepper Tree
- 24 101 Thai Kitchen
- Patara
- Blue Elephant
- 23 Yum Yum

TURKISH

- 26 Antepliler
- 24 Kazan
- 23 Haz
- 22 Efes
- Tas

VEGETARIAN

- 24 Food for Thought
- 222 Veggie Vegan
- Vanilla Black
- Rasa
- 23 Gate

TOPS BY SPECIAL FEATURE

AFTERNOON TEA (NOT HOTELS)

- 25 Modern Pantry
- 24 Ladurée
- 23 Wolseley
- 22 Bob Bob Ricard
- 21 Sketch/Parlour

BREAKFAST

- 26 Ottolenghi
- Cinnamon Club
- 25 St. John Bread
- NOPI
- Roast

BRUNCH

- 26 Pizarro
- 25 Providores
- Modern Pantry
- 24 Caravan
- Le Caprice

BUSINESS LUNCH

- 28 Gauthier
- Ledbury
- Petrus

- Pied à Terre
- Rest. Gordon Ramsay

CHILD-FRIENDLY

- 28 Pitt Cue Co.
- 27 Harwood Arms
- 25 Opera Tavern
- 24 Caravan
- Tom's Deli

CREATIVE COCKTAILS

- 26 Hakkasan
- Hawksmoor
- Roka
- Cinnamon Club
- 20 Mishkin's

EXPERIMENTAL

- 28 Fat Duck (Bray)
- 26 Viajante
- Dabbous
- Texture
- 25 Hibiscus

GASTROPUBS

27 Harwood Arms
25 Anchor/Hope
24 Bull & Last
   Great Queen St.
   Eagle

HISTORIC PLACES

26 Mosimann's
24 Savoy Grill
   Rules
23 Bibendum
21 Simpson's/Strand

HOTEL DINING

29 Waterside Inn (Bray)
27 Le Manoir/Quat (Great Milton)
   Alain Ducasse (Dorchester)
   Marcus Wareing (Berkeley)
   Nobu London (Metropolitan)

LATE NIGHT

24 New Mayflower
23 Maroush
20 Duck & Waffle
19 Balans
18 Café Boheme

NOTABLE WINE LISTS

28 Gauthier
   Ledbury
   Le Gavroche
   Petrus
   French Table

OUTDOOR DINING

28 Ledbury
27 River Café
26 Scott's
24 Amaranto
23 Coq d'Argent

PEOPLE-WATCHING

28 Ledbury
   L'Atelier/Robuchon
27 River Café
   Zuma
   Nobu London

PRIVATE CLUBS

26 Mosimann's
25 Harry's Bar
23 George
   Adam St.
22 Arts Club

PRIVATE ROOMS

28 Square
27 Le Manoir/Quat (Great Milton)
   Alain Ducasse
   Zuma
   Greenhouse

ROMANTIC

29 Waterside Inn (Bray)
28 Rest. Gordon Ramsay
27 Alain Ducasse
26 Dinner by Heston
25 Clos Maggiore

SMALL PLATES

28 Dinings
   L'Atelier/Robuchon
27 Hunan
   Amaya
   Club Gascon

SUNDAY ROASTS

25 Goring
   Roast
   Anchor/Hope
24 Savoy Grill
   Bull & Last

TASTING MENUS

28 Gauthier
   Ledbury
   Le Gavroche
   Petrus
   Square

VIEWS

29 Waterside Inn (Bray)
27 Le Manoir/Quat (Great Milton)
   Nobu London
26 Dinner by Heston
25 Galvin at Windows

TOPS BY OCCASION

Some best bets in a range of prices and cuisines for these occasions.

CHRISTMAS LUNCH

- 22 Kettner's
- 21 Pizza East
- Novikov
- Quaglino's
- 17 Brasserie Zédel

CURING A HANGOVER

- 24 Koya
- 23 Paradise/Kensal Green
- 21 Riding House Café
- Fernandez & Wells
- Breakfast Club

DINNER WITH YOUR PARENTS

- 23 Quo Vadis
- 22 R.S.J.
- 18 Café des Amis
- Côte
- 17 Brasserie Zédel

FIRST DATES

- 22 Aurelia
- El Pirata
- Polpo
- 21 Maggie Jones's
- 18 Kensington Wine Rooms

GROUP BIRTHDAYS

- 22 Tas
- Masala Zone
- 21 Pizza East
- 20 Le Mercury
- 19 Made in Italy

MEET FOR A DRINK

- 28 L'Atelier/Robuchon
- 27 Zuma
- 26 Moro
- Hawksmoor
- Roka

NEW YEAR'S EVE

- 22 Oxo Tower
- Babylon
- 21 Paramount
- 20 Duck & Waffle
- Skylon*

OFFICE PARTIES

- 23 Coq d'Argent
- 22 Babylon
- Kettner's
- 21 Sketch/Gallery
- 19 Hush

TOPS BY LOCATION

BAYSWATER

- 25 Mandarin Kitchen
- 24 Hereford Road
- Halepi
- 23 Alounak
- 22 Royal China

BELGRAVIA

- 28 Petrus
- 27 Marcus Wareing
- Hunan
- Koffmann's
- Amaya

BELSIZE PARK/ HAMPSTEAD

- 27 Jin Kichi
- 26 Nautilus Fish
- 23 Woodlands
- 22 Artigiano
- Wells

BOROUGH/TOWER BRIDGE

- 28 José
- 27 Zucca
- 26 Pizarro
- 25 Magdalen
- Roast

BRIXTON/CLAPHAM

- 27 Honest Burgers
- Pepper Tree
- 26 Trinity
- Franco Manca
- 23 Abbeville

CAMDEN TOWN/ PRIMROSE HILL/ KENTISH TOWN

- 25 Odette's
- 24 Bull & Last
- 23 Carob Tree
- L'Absinthe
- Haché

CANARY WHARF

27 Goodman
26 Roka
24 Le Relais de Venise
23 Iberica
   Royal China

CHELSEA

28 Rest. Gordon Ramsay
   Rasoi Vineet Bhatia
25 Medlar
   Tom Aikens
   Chutney Mary

CHINATOWN

24 Haozhan
23 Golden Dragon
   Four Seasons Chinese
22 Tokyo Diner
21 Mr. Kong

CHISWICK

27 La Trompette
26 Franco Manca
25 Charlotte's Bistro
24 Le Vacherin
   Sam's Brasserie

CITY

27 Goodman
26 Hawksmoor
25 Rhodes Twenty Four
   L'Anima
   Café Spice Namasté

CLERKENWELL/FARRINGDON

28 Morgan M
27 Club Gascon
26 Morito
   Moro
   St. John

COVENT GARDEN

28 L'Atelier/Robuchon
26 Hawksmoor
   J. Sheekey
25 Moti Mahal
   J. Sheekey Oyster Bar

FITZROVIA

28 Pied à Terre
26 Hakkasan
   Dabbous
   Roka
   Fino

HAMMERSMITH

27 River Café
24 101 Thai Kitchen
23 Indian Zing
   Gate
22 Tortilla

HOLBORN

26 Garufin
24 Vanilla Black
   Shanghai Blues
23 Asadal
22 Amico Bio
   Bountiful Cow*

HOXTON/SHOREDITCH

26 Brawn
25 Song Que Café
   Eyre Brothers
24 Mien Tay
23 Busaba Eathai

ISLINGTON

26 Ottolenghi
   Antepliler
24 Akari
   Afghan Kitchen
   Trullo

KENSINGTON

28 Yashin Sushi
26 Ottolenghi
25 Kitchen W8
   Launceston Place
   Clarke's

KNIGHTSBRIDGE

27 Zuma
26 Dinner by Heston
25 Good Earth
24 Patara
   Rib Room

LADBROKE GROVE/NOTTING HILL

28 Ledbury
26 Ottolenghi
25 Assaggi
24 Dock Kitchen
   Tom's Deli

MARYLEBONE

28 Dinings
26 Atari-Ya Sushi Bar
   Trishna
   Texture
   Roux at The Landau

MAYFAIR

28 Le Gavroche
   Square
27 Alain Ducasse
   Umu
   Nobu London

PICCADILLY

26 Hawksmoor
25 Bentley's
24 Ritz
   Yoshino
   Ladurée

RICHMOND

26 Glasshouse
25 A Cena
24 Petersham Nurseries Café
   Bingham
23 Petersham

SOHO

28 Barrafina
   Gauthier Soho
   Pitt Cue Co.
27 Honest Burgers
   Yauatcha

SOUTH BANK/ SOUTHWARK/ WATERLOO

25 Anchor/Hope
23 Baltic
   Vapiano
   Oxo Tower Brasserie
22 Tortilla

SOUTH KENSINGTON

26 Star of India
25 L'Etranger
24 Patara
   Cambio de Tercio
   Rocca

SPITALFIELDS/ WHITECHAPEL

26 Hawksmoor
   Galvin Café/Chapelle
25 Tayyabs
   Lahore Kebab House
   St. John Bread

ST. JAMES'S

26 Wilton's
25 Sake No Hana
24 Le Caprice
23 Rowley's
   Matsuri

TOPS BY DESTINATION

A selection of the best bets in a range of prices and cuisines near these points of interest.

BRITISH MUSEUM

26 Garufin
24 Abeno
22 Hare & Tortoise
   Tas
19 Malabar Junction

BUCKINGHAM PALACE

25 Goring
   Sake No Hana
22 Noura
   Olivo
20 Bank Westminster

HYDE PARK

27 Nobu London
26 Dinner by Heston
   Texture
25 Min Jiang
24 Halepi

KING'S CROSS, ST. PANCRAS & EUSTON STATIONS

24 Caravan
   North Sea
23 Chutneys
22 Camino
19 Gilbert Scott

LIVERPOOL ST. STATION

26 Hawksmoor
   St. John
   Galvin Café a Vin
25 L'Anima
23 1901

PARLIAMENT

26 Cinnamon Club
25 Quirinale
21 Massimo
20 Bank Westminster
   Skylon*

PORTOBELLO MARKET

- 24 Osteria Basilico
- 23 E&O
- 22 Gail's
- 21 Daylesford Organic Café
  Pizza East

ROYAL ACADEMY

- 26 Hawksmoor
- 24 Le Caprice
- 23 Cecconi's
  Wolseley
- 20 Fortnum's Fountain

ROYAL ALBERT HALL

- 25 Launceston Place
  L'Etranger
  Min Jiang
  Zaika
- 21 Koi

ST. PAUL'S CATHEDRAL

- 23 Barbecoa
  Miyama

Coq d'Argent
- 22 Paternoster Chop House
- 20 Bread Street Kitchen

TOWER OF LONDON

- 25 Magdalen
  Café Spice Namasté
- 23 Le Pont de la Tour
- 22 Bodeans
- 17 Wagamama

TRAFALGAR SQUARE

- 22 Mint Leaf
  Terroirs
  Portrait
- 20 Albannach
- 19 Les Deux Salons

WEST END THEATRES

- 24 Ivy
- 23 Yming
- 22 Terroirs
  Hix
- 19 Les Deux Salons

Best Buys

Top-rated restaurants £25 and under

1. Pitt Cue Co. | *BBQ*
2. Honest Burgers | *Burgers*
3. Pepper Tree | *Thai*
4. Spice Village | *Indian*
5. Morito | *African/Spanish*
6. Satay House | *Malaysian*
7. Atari-Ya Sushi Bar | *Japanese*
8. Franco Manca | *Pizza*
9. Nautilus Fish | *Seafood*
10. Antepliler | *Turkish*
11. Tayyabs | *Pakistani*
12. Lahore Kebab House | *Pakistani*
13. Lupita | *Mexican*
14. Kaffeine | *Australian/Coffee*
15. Song Que Café | *Vietnamese*
16. Lantana | *Australian/Coffee*
17. Food for Thought | *Veg.*
18. Koya | *Japanese*
19. Rasa | *Indian/Vegetarian*
20. La Fromagerie | *Deli/Sandwiches*

BEST BUYS BY NEIGHBOURHOOD

BLOOMSBURY/FITZROVIA

25	Kaffeine
24	Lantana
	Yalla Yalla
	North Sea
	Banh Mi Bay

CHINATOWN

22	Tokyo Diner
21	Mr. Kong
	Leong's Legend
	Joy King Lau
20	New World

CITY

22	Bodeans
	Hare & Tortoise
	Tortilla
21	Chilango
20	Leon

CLERKENWELL/FARRINGDON

26	Morito
24	Rasa
22	Tas
	Gail's
	La Porchetta

COVENT GARDEN

24	Food for Thought
	Rock & Sole Plaice
23	Busaba Eathai
	Rossopomodoro
22	Tortilla

ISLINGTON

26	Antepliler
24	Afghan Kitchen
22	Tortilla
	Wahaca
	La Porchetta

SOHO

28	Pitt Cue Co.
27	Honest Burgers
24	Koya
	New Mayflower
	Taro

SOUTH BANK/SOUTHWARK/WATERLOO

23	Vapiano
22	Tortilla
	Wahaca
	Tas
20	Real Greek

SOUTH KENSINGTON

23	Beirut Express
22	Kulu Kulu Sushi
21	Fernandez & Wells
20	Comptoir Libanais
19	Byron

SPITALFIELDS/WHITECHAPEL

25	Tayyabs
	Lahore Kebab House
	Lupita East
22	Rosa's
	Pho

BEST BUYS BY CATEGORY

BAKERIES/COFFEE

- 25 Kaffeine
- 24 Lantana
- Princi London
- Flat White
- 22 Gail's

BYO

- 25 Lahore Kebab House
- 24 Food for Thought
- Golden Hind
- 22 Blue Legume
- 20 Comptoir Libanais

CHAINS

- 23 Busaba Eathai
- Rossopomodoro
- 22 Hare & Tortoise
- Tortilla
- Wahaca

CHEAP DATES

- 28 Pitt Cue Co.
- 26 Morito
- Franco Manca
- 24 Koya
- 22 Cây Tre

CHILD-FRIENDLY

- 28 Pitt Cue Co
- 24 Tom's Deli
- 23 Rossopomodoro
- 22 Bodeans
- Masala Zone

EARLY-BIRDS

- 26 Hawksmoor (£23)
- Trishna (£25)
- 25 Kitchen W8 (£22)
- Odette's (£17)
- L'Etranger(£22)

INDIAN

- 27 Spice Village
- 24 Rasa
- 23 Chutneys
- 22 Masala Zone
- 21 Sagar

JAPANESE

- 26 Atari-Ya
- 24 Koya
- Taro
- 23 Bento
- 22 Hare & Tortoise

LIGHT BITES

- 24 Yalla Yalla
- 22 Pho
- 21 Sagar
- 20 Comptoir Libanais
- Leon

PRE-THEATRE

- 28 Gauthier Soho (£18)
- 26 Cinnamon Club (£22)
- 25 Moti Mahal (£19)
- Theo Randall (£25)
- L'Autre Pied (£23)

PRIX FIXE LUNCH

- 28 French Table (£20)
- Rasoi Vineet Bhatia (£23)
- 27 Umu (£25)
- Koffmann's (£25)
- Amaya (£21)

TAKEAWAY

- 25 Lahore Kebab House
- 24 Rasa
- La Fromagerie
- Tom's Deli
- Princi London

RESTAURANT
DIRECTORY

	FOOD	DECOR	SERVICE	COST

The Abbeville British

23 | 20 | 21 | £32

Clapham | 67-69 Abbeville Rd., SW4 9JW | 020-8675-2201 |
www.theabbeville.com

It's "worth veering off the main Clapham track" for the "brilliant"
British fare at this "earthy" gastropub on a "gentrified street"; with its
"charming" vibe, moderate prices and "attentive" staff, it's a "great
place to eat, drink and hang out", especially for a "quiet date".

Abeno Japanese

24 | 16 | 21 | £28

Bloomsbury | 47 Museum St., WC1A 1LY | 020-7405-3211
Abeno Too Japanese
Covent Garden | 17-18 Great Newport St., WC2H 7JE | 020-7379-1160
www.abeno.co.uk

Witness "cookery theatre" starring "skilful chefs" preparing "excellent" okonomiyaki (pancakes with savoury toppings) and other
Japanese comfort food at the table grills of this duo in Bloomsbury and
Covent Garden; it can be "cramped", and no reservations are accepted, so expect "to queue most nights" – but at least the "quick",
"helpful" service and "fairly reasonable" prices balance the books.

The Abingdon European

21 | 18 | 20 | £38

Kensington | 54 Abingdon Rd., W8 6AP | 020-7937-3339 |
www.theabingdon.co.uk

A "cool Kensington crowd" crams into the booths of this "trusted local" for "consistently decent" Modern European gastropub fare;
"sweet" staff and an "excellent wine list" help keep things "convivial", even when it's "busy", and while it may be "a little overpriced
for a pub, you're paying for the location".

About Thyme ⊠ European

24 | 20 | 23 | £36

Victoria | 82 Wilton Rd., SW1V 1DL | 020-7821-7504 |
www.aboutthyme.co.uk

If you crave "incredible" Modern European dishes, "it's about time you
visited" this "crowd-pleasing" Victoria "gem"; the "tablecloth atmosphere" upstairs is "upmarket enough for clients", while downstairs
is where you get "the bistro effect" – but wherever you end up, the
service is generally "reliable" and the prices are wholly "reasonable".

NEW Acciuga Ⓜ Italian

– | – | – | E

Kensington | 343 Kensington High St., W8 6NW | 020-7603-3888 |
www.acciuga.co.com

Produce and recipes from Liguria and Piedmont are the specialities
of this narrow, low-lit and expensive trattoria on Kensington High
Street, decked out with linen-clad tables and an eclectic mix of wood
panelling and stylish monochromes; there's also a private dining
room that doubles as the cellar for an exclusively Italian wine list.

A Cena Italian

25 | 20 | 22 | £42

Richmond | 418 Richmond Rd., TW1 2EB | 020-8288-0108 |
www.acena.co.uk

"Fab cocktails get things off to a good start" at this "cracking" neighbourhood eatery over the river from Richmond, where the experi-

| | FOOD | DECOR | SERVICE | COST |

ence continues with "delicious" Northern Italian dishes comprised of "gorgeous" ingredients "handled with much care"; "ever-present owners" ensure "consistent service", so even though it's a "little expensive" "for regular use", for a "treat", it's "worth the price".

Adams Cafe ☒ *Moroccan/Tunisian* | 21 | 18 | 23 | £36 |

Shepherd's Bush | 77 Askew Rd., W12 9AH | 020-8743-0572 | www.adamscafe.co.uk

The "authentic Moorish ceramic tiles" of this "cafe by day" in Shepherd's Bush are the only clues to its evening alter-ego as a Moroccan-Tunisian bistro offering "super-value" "mix 'n' match" set menus starring "delicious couscous and tagines"; there's "excellent" service too, corresponding to the "relaxed" atmosphere.

Adam Street ☒ *British* | 23 | 21 | 22 | £50 |

Covent Garden | private club | 9 Adam St., downstairs, WC2N 6AA | 020-7379-8000 | www.adamstreet.co.uk

"Sophisticated, yet relaxed" (it *is* a private club after all, though anyone can book a table), this "intimate" subterranean "gem" "hidden away" off The Strand serves up "delicious" Modern British staples; while a few protest that it's "pricey", the "cool" setting (brick walls, vaulted ceilings) and "friendly" vibe lead to many a "lovely evening".

The Admiral Codrington *British/European* | 19 | 18 | 18 | £37 |

Chelsea | 17 Mossop St., SW3 2LY | 020-7581-0005 | www.theadmiralcodrington.co.uk

Ask the "smiling" staff for recommendations about the "sophisticated", "tempting" Modern British–European menu at this Chelsea gastropub; the atmosphere is always "buzzing", but in summer, the roof literally gets raised thanks to a retractable glass ceiling in the rear dining room, much to the delight of the "trendy crowd" filled with "boys named Harry and girls named Philippa".

Afghan Kitchen Ⓜ☞ *Afghan* | 24 | 14 | 17 | £19 |

Islington | 35 Islington Green, N1 8DU | 020-7359-8019

"Nourishing grub" like "phenomenal" lamb spinach and "homemade bread to die for" offers a "flavourful" introduction to Afghan cuisine at this "cosy", "friendly" Islington joint; "ridiculously cheap" prices, a "table-share policy" and no credit cards lend it the vibe of a "student cafe", but that doesn't stop it from getting "crowded" with all manner of people, so "prepare to queue".

Aglio e Olio ❶ *Italian* | 22 | 13 | 17 | £31 |

Chelsea | 194 Fulham Rd., SW10 9PN | 020-7351-0070

The homemade pasta, gnocchi and such are *"delizioso"*, the portions "plentiful" and the prices "reasonable" at this Chelsea Italian, so little wonder "young, glossy" types pile into its "narrow railway carriage"–like setting for "quick lunches" and "easy weekday dinners"; staff can be "glum" and the acoustics a touch "noisy", but still, somehow "no one wants to leave" (indeed, there's probably "going to be a wait" for a table).

	FOOD	DECOR	SERVICE	COST

Akari ☑ *Japanese*
24 | 19 | 21 | £32

Islington | 196 Essex Rd., N1 8LZ | 020-7226-9943 |
www.akarilondon.co.uk

"Buckets of hot noodles, warm salmon rice balls, garlicky greens" and other "wonderful Japanese small plates" make "a welcome change from the usual sushi" at this "affordable" Essex Road izakaya set in a Victorian pub; the tables, which are "a bit close together", are "always packed" – and serviced by "staff whose friendliness would melt the heart" of any Islingtonite.

Alain Ducasse at The Dorchester ☒☑ *French*
27 | 26 | 27 | £115

Mayfair | The Dorchester | 53 Park Ln., W1K 1QA | 020-7629-8866 |
www.alainducasse-dorchester.com

"Top class in every respect" – from the "complex", "heavenly" New French cuisine prepared "with a twist" to the "discreet", "incomparable service" – is the word on celebrity chef Alain Ducasse's Dorchester outpost, which provides an "elegant" atmosphere for a "quiet business lunch" or a "dress-up" dinner; although some comment that prices are "in the stratosphere" (especially on the "impressive wine list"), many concur it's "worth every penny"; P.S. jackets are required.

Alba ☒ *Italian*
22 | 19 | 24 | £44

City | 107 Whitecross St., EC1Y 8JH | 020-7588-1798 |
www.albarestaurant.com

"Charming" and "attentive but never overbearing" staff deliver "excellent" Italian cuisine at this casual option for a quick meal near the Barbican in the City; what's more, there's a "wonderful list of slightly unusual wines" from Italy, which adds to the wholly "great atmosphere".

Albannach *Scottish*
20 | 20 | 19 | £41

Charing Cross | 66 Trafalgar Sq., WC2N 5DS | 020-7930-0066 |
www.albannach.co.uk

"Exiled Scots" missing "shortbread and Irn-Bru" make their way to this antler-bedecked Charing Cross dining room for "a dram" from the "extensive whisky list" and a wee haggis from the "fairly priced" menu, all delivered by "well-dressed staff"; a word of warning: the bar below can get "noisy at night" so get a "table upstairs after 7 PM" if you're not in a party mood.

The Albion *British*
22 | 23 | 19 | £30

Islington | 10 Thornhill Rd., N1 1HW | 020-7607-7450 |
www.the-albion.co.uk

"Take foreign visitors" to this "chilled" Islington gastropub to "change their view of British cooking", as the traditional menu is not only "well prepared", it lists "options for even the fussiest eater", not to mention a Sunday lunch with "fantastic Yorkshire puds"; what's more, it's a spot for all seasons, with a Georgian bar that's especially "cosy" in winter and a "fantastic beer garden" for "balmy summer evenings".

	FOOD	DECOR	SERVICE	COST

Al Duca ☒ Italian   22 | 17 | 19 | £41

St. James's | 4-5 Duke of York St., SW1Y 6LA | 020-7839-3090 | www.alduca-restaurant.co.uk

This "charming" terra-cotta-hued St. James's Italian stands out with an all-day menu that boasts "unmistakably old-world flavour", plus "interesting wines" and "excellent value for the area"; it also bene-fits from "personable" service that's "prompt without being rushed".

Al Hamra ● Lebanese   23 | 16 | 20 | £38

Mayfair | 31-33 Shepherd Mkt., W1J 7PT | 020-7493-1954

Brasserie Al Hamra ☒ Lebanese

Mayfair | 52 Shepherd Mkt., W1J 7QU | 020-7493-1068
www.alhamrarestaurant.co.uk

"Reliable" and "reasonably priced", this Lebanese duo sits on either side of Shepherd Market and is "always jammed" with diners "graz-ing" on "wave after wave" of "mouth-watering" mezze and more, all washed down with "excellent" wines from the region; if you don't like "cramped" quarters, go in summer and ask the mostly "pleas-ant" staff to seat you outside.

A Little of What You Fancy Ⓜ British   22 | 17 | 18 | £34

Dalston | 464 Kingsland Rd., E8 4AE | 020 7275 0060 | www.alittleofwhatyoufancy.info

Fans of this "quirky", "no-frills" "hole-in-the-wall" that "epitomises the cool Dalston lifestyle" have taken a fancy to its "delicious" all day British fare; "variable service" and prices that belie its "shoe-string production values" vex a few, but overall it's a "welcome little place" that "fits in nicely with what the local clientele is after".

Alloro ☒ Italian   22 | 19 | 20 | £56

Mayfair | 19-20 Dover St., W1S 4LU | 020-7495-4768 | www.alloro-restaurant.co.uk

"One of Mayfair's best-kept secrets", this "handy" Italian draws business types and "special-day" celebrants with a "tremendous wine list" and "well-executed" fare whose prices equal "nice value" for the location; "spot-on service" and a "comfortable" setting fur-ther its reputation as a "sure bet".

Almeida French   22 | 21 | 22 | £40

Islington | 30 Almeida St., N1 1AD | 020-7354-4777 | www.almeida-restaurant.co.uk

At this "posh" Islington New French "convenient" for the Almeida Theatre, "consistently strong" bistro fare is dished out in a "refined" room; "smooth" service and a "splendid" wine list add to the "winning formula", while pre- and post-show menus offer "exceptional value".

Alounak ● Persian   23 | 15 | 17 | £26

Bayswater | 44 Westbourne Grove, W2 5SH | 020-7229-4158
Olympia | 10 Russell Gdns., W14 8EZ | 020-7603-1130

The queue "reaches out onto the road sometimes" for the "large portions" of "reliable" Persian food dished out at this duo in Bayswater and Olympia; the decor is "basic", and "service can be slow", but it's "gentle on your wallet" (helped by BYO with no corkage), and "good value for money".

Al Sultan ● *Lebanese*   22 | 16 | 20 | £36

Mayfair | 51-52 Hertford St., W1J 7ST | 020-7408-1155 | www.alsultan.co.uk

"Great smells" herald the "tasty hummus, kibbeh, falafel" and other "excellent mezze" doled out in "hearty portions" at this long-time Mayfair Lebanese; ok, so the "dull, dark" decor is probably in need of a "major uplift", but it's "good value", and you can get in and out "quick".

Al Waha *Lebanese*   22 | 15 | 18 | £32

Bayswater | 75 Westbourne Grove, W2 4UL | 020-7229-0806 | www.alwaharestaurant.com

"Unless you have a Lebanese grandmother tucked away some-where", this "family-friendly" Bayswater local is the closest you'll get to "fabulous, home-style" cooking, with a "multitude of choices for all palates", from "tasty lamb" to "great vegetarian" dishes; the "cramped" setting is "not for a special occasion", but it is "reliable" for "excellent value" and "friendly service".

Alyn Williams at The Westbury Ⓩ *European*   23 | 19 | 23 | £78

Mayfair | Westbury Hotel | 37 Conduit St., W1S 2YF | 020-7078-9579 | www.alynwilliams.co.uk

In Mayfair's Westbury Hotel "talented" chef Alyn Williams employs "welcoming" staff to serve "inventive" Modern European cuisine – in-cluding an "incredible-value" tasting menu – in what aesthetes deem a "wonderfully decorated" modern room; for oenophiles, there's also an eight-seat wine salon with a specially designed menu.

Amaranto ● *Italian*   24 | 23 | 25 | £64

Mayfair | Four Seasons Hotel London at Park Ln. | Hamilton Pl., Park Ln., W1J 7DR | 020-7319-5206 | www.fourseasons.com

"Outstanding" hospitality sets the tone at this "stylish", "pricey" Italian in Mayfair's Four Seasons Hotel at Park Lane, where "tasty" fare is "well presented" in a "beautiful", scarlet-hued room; there's also a garden dining area ripe for a "summer rendezvous", a "lovely" bar specialising in Italian wines and a lounge serving afternoon tea.

Amaya ● *Indian*   27 | 24 | 23 | £64

Belgravia | Halkin Arcade | Motcomb St., SW1X 8JT | 020-7823-1166 | www.amaya.biz

"Sleek and chic", this Belgravia "oasis" takes an "intellectual ap-proach" to the "rich fabric of Indian cuisine", producing "beautifully presented", "mouth-watering" dishes "designed for sharing"; prices are "high-end", but most agree it's "fairly priced", taking into ac-count the overall "attention to detail" and "efficient service".

Amerigo Vespucci Ⓩ *Italian*   23 | 18 | 22 | £44

Canary Wharf | 25 Cabot Sq., E14 4QA | 020-7513-0288 | www.amerigovespucci.co.uk

"Almost a tradition" after 18-plus years in "business-lunch" territory, this "casual" Canary Wharf venue cooks up "excellent" renditions of

Italian standards accompanied by a "solid" wine list and equally solid service, all at the "right price"; there's also an alfresco bar and dining terrace.

NEW Ametsa with Arzak Instruction _Spanish_

- | - | - | VE

Belgravia | The Halkin by Como | Halkin St., SW1X 7DJ | 020-7333-1234 | www.ametsa.co.uk

Spanish chef Elena Arzak and her father Juan Mari's successful San Sebastian–based restaurant has been re-created for Londoners at the swish Halkin Hotel in Belgravia, where the high-end Basque cuisine is prepped with innovative techniques and plated up with precision; design aficionados may be tickled by the sight of 7,000 spice-filled test tubes hanging from the ceiling.

Amico Bio _Italian/Vegetarian_

22 | 17 | 18 | £23

Farringdon | 44 Cloth Fair, EC1A 7JQ | 020-7600-7778 🛇
NEW Holborn | 43 New Oxford St., WC1A 1BH | 020-7836-7509
www.amicobio.co.uk

Vegetarians find "nirvana for the taste buds" at this Italian, meat-free trattoria (with branches in Holborn and Farringdon) where the daily changing menu makes use of "really good olive oil", "proper cheese" and organic produce grown on the family farm; "friendly" service and a "cosy", "homely" atmosphere complete the picture; P.S. afternoon tea with Prosecco is served on weekdays at the Barbican branch (booking essential).

Anchor & Hope _British_

25 | 17 | 19 | £37

Waterloo | 36 The Cut, SE1 8LP | 020-7928-9898

"Fantastic", "reasonably priced" British fare is the stock-in-trade of this Waterloo gastropub; its "comfy" ambience and "friendly, unhurried" service also earn kudos, though impatient types decry "having to queue" for a taste of the ever-changing menu (reservations are taken only for Sunday lunch).

Andrew Edmunds _European_

24 | 22 | 23 | £43

Soho | 46 Lexington St., W1F 0LW | 020-7437-5708 | www.andrewedmunds.com

If you're not "gazing into someone's eyes" across a "small" candlelit table, you'll be "sharing smug smiles with the complete strangers seated inches away from you" at this "snug", "romantic" Soho bistro for foodies in the know; while the Modern Euro menu is "always changing", expect "sumptuous", "delicious" "comfort food" that's "not as pricey as you'd think it would be", complemented by "great-value" wines recommended by "friendly, well-informed" staff.

Angels & Gypsies _Spanish_

25 | 22 | 23 | £35

Camberwell | Church Street Hotel | 29-33 Camberwell Church St., SE5 8TR | 020-7703-5984 | www.angelsandgypsies.com

While "the name doesn't readily conjure up Spain", the "fresh produce on the counter", whole hams and "tasty", "innovative tapas" do at this "beautifully styled" venue in a Latin-themed Camberwell hotel; "amazing wines by the glass" come at an "attractively fair markup", matching the "not-overpriced" food bill, and "friendly, efficient" staff only "add to the charm".

Angelus *French*
25 | 20 | 24 | £53

Paddington | 4 Bathurst St., W2 2SD | 020-7402-0083 | www.angelusrestaurant.co.uk

"Expertly prepared" "French classics" "with a twist" (like the "out-of-this-world" foie gras crème brûlée) are complemented by "great wines" at this "cosy" Paddington brasserie; the "lovely" chandelier-lit interior and "excellent" service make it "ideal for couples on a cold winter's night", but be prepared – apart from the "brilliant lunchtime set-menu deal", such "quality" comes at an "expensive" price.

NEW Angler ☒ *British/Seafood*
- | - | - | VE

City | South Place Hotel | 3 South Pl., 7th fl., EC2M 2AF | 020-3215-1260 | www.anglerrestaurant.com

Huge windows offer views over the City at this seventh-floor Modern Brit in the South Place Hotel, where a mirrored ceiling and black-and-white striped chairs are highlights of the decor; the fish-focused menu changes daily, and many selections from the 250-strong wine list are available by the glass; P.S. in warm weather, a terrace offers cocktails and light bites.

The Anglesea Arms *British*
21 | 17 | 18 | £30

Shepherd's Bush | 35 Wingate Rd., W6 0UR | 020-8749-1291 | www.anglesea-arms.com

Though the "edited menu" "varies daily", you can always count on "well-sourced ingredients" and "grub with panache" at this "up-scale" (yet affordable) British gastropub in Shepherd's Bush; it works as well for "cosy winter evenings" as it does "outdoor summer lunches with the dogs at your feet", but whatever the season, it's "rammed" on Sundays with a "yummy mummy crowd", so if you're after "a quieter evening", go midweek.

Annabel's ●☒ *British/French*
21 | 23 | 23 | £81

Mayfair | private club | 44 Berkeley Sq., W1J 5QB | 020-7629-1096 | www.annabels.co.uk

"Ageing rockers with arm candy", "wannabe Kates and Pippas" and those who've been "regulars for 30 years" converge at this "pictur-esque, dignified" members-only Mayfair "institution" with "money oozing out of its antique paintings and ceilings"; the "expensive" Classic French–Traditional British fare is "reliable" and served in a "regal" manner, but truly, it's the "social show" and the "old-world clubby charm" that's the draw.

Annie's *British*
23 | 23 | 23 | £35

Barnes | 36-38 White Hart Ln., SW13 0PZ | 020-8878-2020
Chiswick | 162 Thames Rd., W4 3QS | 020-8994-9080
www.anniesrestaurant.co.uk

"Belly-busting portions" of "tasty", "non-fancy" Modern British fare make this pair – "by the glorious Thames" in Chiswick and in the "leafy green" depths of Barnes – "fantastic value"; "beautiful", somewhat "bohemian decor" and "personable", "efficient" staff ensure it's a "home from home" type of local that's as "comfortable" "for a night out with friends" as it is for brunch.

Antepliler *Turkish* `26` `20` `21` `£25`

Islington | 139 Upper St., N1 1QP | 020-7226-5441 | www.anteplilerrestaurant.com

"When you can't get to Istanbul", this moderately priced Upper Street spot offers the next best thing in the form of "wonderful Turkish pizzas", "smoky, flavoursome" kebabs, "delicious mezze and never-ending bread and salad"; a few aesthetes complain that "the decor is a bit in your face", but "friendly, attentive service" elevates the experience to "a cut above the usual".

Antonio's Ristorante *Italian* `23` `20` `22` `£31`

Islington | 137 Upper St., rear, N1 1QP | 020-7226-8994 | www.antoniosristorante.co.uk

If you discover somewhere "off the beaten track" is "packed, even on a Monday night", you know it's something "special" – and this "easy-going Italian" in Islington fits the description, with its "excellent-value" menu of "wonderfully prepared" dishes; another draw is the "engaging, efficient" service, adding to the "warm" ambience; P.S. for a lighter bite with a drink or two, there's an antipasti bar on the first floor.

Apsleys *Italian* `26` `26` `26` `£76`

Belgravia | The Lanesborough | Hyde Park Corner, SW1X 7TA | 020-7333-7254 | www.lanesborough.com

"A swirling circle" of staff makes you "feel spoilt" at this "sedate", "romantic" Italian in The Lanesborough, where "sensational" savouries and "thrilling desserts" "seriously impress", as do the "fantastic wine list" and "exquisite" "ballroom" setting with glass ceilings, "extravagant" chandeliers and "well-spaced tables"; perhaps unsurprisingly, the price of this level of "refinement" is "very expensive", unless you come for the "excellent-value" set lunch.

Aqua Kyoto 🗷 *Japanese* `22` `25` `20` `£61`

Soho | 240 Regent St., W1B 3BR | 020-7478-0540 | www.aqua-london.com

"London needs more" roof terraces like the "fantastic" one that this Soho Japanese shares with its neighbour, Aqua Nueva, and the view from the "beautiful" interior is no less "amazing", keeping the place "packed and buzzing" with a "chic crowd" no matter what the weather; furthermore, staff are usually "sweet" as they serve the "expensive" though "delicious sushi".

Aqua Nueva 🗷 *Spanish* `21` `25` `19` `£56`

Soho | 240 Regent St., W1B 3BR | 020-7478-0540 | www.aqua-london.com

"From the charging bull at the entrance to the thousands of dangling wooden beads", the "stylish" decor of this Oxford Circus Spaniard "impresses", and that's before you've seen the "amazing" views from the roof bar and terrace (open till 2 AM) it shares with its sibling, Aqua Kyoto; indeed, "it's all about the atmosphere" here, though there are some "nice" tapas on offer, "overpriced" though they may be (and accompanied by sometimes "snooty" service).

NEW Aqua Shard *British*

| - | - | - | E |

Tower Bridge | The Shard | 31 St. Thomas St., 31st fl., SE1 9RY | 020-7478-0540 | www.aquashard.co.uk

Whether viewed from one of the main dining room's peacock print banquettes or from the bar (home of the signature gin-and-tea cocktail), the panoramic vistas from this all-day, upscale Modern Brit on the 31st floor of The Shard should impress; budgeters can opt for the set-price lunch menu, which like the rest of the offerings, transforms traditional ingredients into innovative creations such as green-pea custard, tea jelly and confit salmon.

Arbutus *European*

| 24 | 19 | 23 | £50 |

Soho | 63-64 Frith St., W1D 3JW | 020-7734-4545 | www.arbutusrestaurant.co.uk

"Creative", "hearty", "refined bistro classics" that often make use of "unfavoured cuts" of meat are now something of a "trend", but it was this "minimalist", "convivial" Soho Modern European that was one of the first on the scene; "constant attention to detail" from "friendly, professional" staff, wine served by the carafe and prices deemed "reasonable considering the high standard" (especially the "complete steal" of a weekday lunch) have fans returning "again and again".

Archipelago ⊠ *International*

| 22 | 24 | 23 | £49 |

Fitzrovia | 110 Whitfield St., W1T 5ED | 020-7383-3346 | www.archipelago-restaurant.co.uk

Adorned with trinkets and geegaws from foreign lands, this "picturesque" spot whisks you "around the world without leaving" Fitzrovia; the global tour continues with an "exotic" International menu featuring "quirky" meats like crocodile, zebra and alpaca – "not cheap" but suitable to "impress someone" on a "special occasion".

Artigiano *Italian*

| 22 | 20 | 20 | £43 |

Belsize Park | 12 Belsize Terr., NW3 4AX | 020-7794-4288 | www.etruscarestaurants.com

Belsize Park locals are "happy" to have this light and airy Italian, whose menu is "solid", "dependable" and filled with "fantastic" pastas; so even though the prices seem a bit "inflated" to a few, the place remains a "neighbourhood standby", particularly due to "nice staff".

The Arts Club *European*

| 22 | 25 | 21 | £61 |

Mayfair | private club | 40 Dover St., W1S 4NP | 020-7499-8581 | www.theartsclub.co.uk

Since 1896, the likes of Dickens, Liszt and Whistler have been congregating at this "sophisticated" private club in Mayfair, and even today it's still one of the "hottest" spots in town, "teeming with famous faces"; a "tasty", "pricey", fish-heavy European menu, "relaxing" ambience and "friendly" service are further inducements – that is, "if you can get a member to invite you".

	FOOD	DECOR	SERVICE	COST

Asadal *Korean*
23 | **17** | **19** | **£32**

Holborn | 227 High Holborn, WC1V 7DA | 020-7430-9006 | www.asadal.co.uk

"Melt-in-the-mouth" barbecue "cooked at your table" and "feisty bibimbop" are the stars of the "yummy", affordable Korean menu at this "dark", subterranean spot with "a super-convenient location next to Holborn tube"; what's more, if you're not familiar with the "delightfully different" cuisine, "attentive" staff can guide you.

Asia de Cuba ❶ *Asian/Cuban*
23 | **23** | **20** | **£58**

Covent Garden | St. Martins Lane Hotel | 45 St. Martins Ln., WC2N 4HX | 020-7300-5588 | www.stmartinslane.com

"Lively" and "social", this "ultramodern", "upscale" dining room on the ground floor of the St. Martins Lane Hotel offers up a "delightful fusion" of Asian and Cuban cuisines, made into "creative" dishes "designed to be shared family-style" (though probably "not on a quiet date") and paired with "drinks that overflow with character"; "helpful, friendly" staff and an "expensive" bill are more reasons why it suits "a special occasion"; P.S. the Mexican donuts are "a must".

Assaggi ⧄ *Italian*
25 | **18** | **24** | **£63**

Notting Hill | 39 Chepstow Pl., 1st fl., W2 4TS | 020-7792-5501

"Irrespective of what you choose" at this "casual" Notting Hill Italian, "it will be cooked beautifully" and "worth every penny"; "personable service" is led by an "exceptional" maître d', and although it's "hard to get a table", devotees assure it's "worth persevering".

Atari-Ya Sushi Bar *Japanese*
26 | **13** | **21** | **£25**

Marylebone | 20 James St., W1U 1EH | 020-7491-1178
Hendon | 31 Vivian Ave., NW4 3UX | 020-8202-2789
Ealing | 1 Station Parade, W5 3LD | 020-8896-3175 Ⓜ
Swiss Cottage | 75 Fairfax Rd., NW6 4EE | 020-7328-5338 Ⓜ
www.atariya.co.uk

As it's an offshoot of a chain of fishmongers, it's fitting that this Japanese chainlet's "made-to-order" sushi-orientated eats are "super fresh" and "succulent"; "reasonable" prices befit the "simple" settings, which get a boost from "welcoming" staff.

Aubaine *French*
18 | **19** | **17** | **£34**

Marylebone | Selfridges | 400 Oxford St., 2nd fl., W1A 1AM | 020-7318-3738
Mayfair | 31 Dover St., W1S 4ND | 020-7368-0955
St. James's | 4 Heddon St., W1B 4BS | 020-7440-2510
Kensington | 37-45 Kensington High St., W8 5ED | 020-7368-0950
South Kensington | 260-262 Brompton Rd., SW3 2AS | 020-7052-0100
www.aubaine.co.uk

This "bright, buzzing" all-day cafe chain delivers "solid", "standard" French bistro fare to "ladies who lunch", as well as "great people-watching" ("when the sun shines", diners "fight for the outside tables" at some branches); to sum up, it's an "efficient and generally pleasant" option, despite the "mediocre service" and that niggling feeling that it's "too expensive for what it is".

| | FOOD | DECOR | SERVICE | COST |

Aurelia ● *Mediterranean* 22 | 20 | 19 | £60
Mayfair | 13-14 Cork St., W1S 3NS | 020-7409-1370 |
www.aurelialondon.co.uk

The "terrific" dishes are meant for sharing at this "stylish" Mayfair
Mediterranean whose "attractive clientele" chooses between a
"chic, buzzing" upstairs and a "quieter, more serious" downstairs
dining room; advocates assure that you'll have a "charming"
experience – "but at a price".

Aurora *European* ▽ 24 | 22 | 23 | £51
Soho | 49 Lexington St., W1F 9AP | 020-7494-0514 |
www.aurorasoho.co.uk

Dark red walls and dripping candles in wine bottles make for a
"cosy", "romantic" setting at this "charming" Soho European with a
garden that's "a fantastic bonus" in summertime; "friendly, attentive staff" proffer a "frequently changing" menu, that's not only
"quite good", but also "great value" for money (sometimes "difficult
to find in the Theatre District").

Automat ● *American* 19 | 20 | 18 | £38
Mayfair | 33 Dover St., W1S 4NF | 020-7499-3033 |
www.automat-london.com

Its "hipster glory days might be over", but "Mayfair's beautiful people"
still say this all-day diner "hits the spot" for "uncomplicated American
comfort food" like burgers, fries, pancakes and mac 'n' cheese, despite
what a few deem "slightly bonkers pricing"; some reckon service can
be "surly", but all "love the decor", both in the "train car" simulacrum
with "intimate booths" and the "light, bright and airy" conservatory.

Avenue ●⊠ *British* 20 | 20 | 20 | £49
St. James's | 7-9 St. James's St., SW1A 1EE | 020-7321-2111 |
www.theavenue-restaurant.co.uk

On St. James's Street, "where there aren't a lot of dining options",
this "spacious", "trendy" Modern Brit is "the pick of the litter" for
"business dining" – or so say "loud lads on expense accounts" and
their guests "from out of town"; indeed, it can get "ridiculously
noisy" the later it gets, so it's a good thing there are "smart" staff to
keep everything in line.

NEW A Wong ⊠ *Chinese* - | - | - | M
Victoria | 70 Wilton Rd., SW1V 1DE | 020-7828-8931 | www.awong.co.uk

Andrew Wong has given his father's Chinese in Victoria a culinary
makeover, with a short, reasonably priced menu that celebrates
China's diverse regional cooking traditions in the evenings and dim
sum at lunchtime; the space has been refurbished also, with a modern
aesthetic, bare wooden tables and views into the kitchen.

Babbo *Italian* 21 | 20 | 20 | £70
Mayfair | 39 Albermarle St., W1S 4JQ | 020-3205-1099 |
www.babborestaurant.co.uk

"Heart-warming" dishes with "a few surprise twists" and a wine list
that's "extensive and expensive" (like the food menu) are the draws

at this "warm, quaint" Mayfair Italian; "attentive", "friendly staff" (whose pictures adorn the walls) add to the "relaxed" vibe, "perfect" for a "business lunch" or "first date"; P.S. "nothing to do with the New York spot" of the same name.

Babur ● Indian 27 | 22 | 26 | £32

Honor Oak | 119 Brockley Rise, SE23 1JP | 020-8291-2400 | www.babur.info

With "delicately spiced" dishes featuring atypical meats like quail, venison, rabbit and mackerel on its "reliably good", "high-quality" menu, fans claim this long-standing, moderately priced Honor Oak Indian stands "head-and-shoulders above" many of its ilk; service is "attentive and friendly", while the interior of floor-to-ceiling glass and exposed brick adds to the "pleasant" experience.

Babylon British 22 | 25 | 22 | £60

Kensington | Roof Gdns. | 99 Kensington High St., 7th fl., W8 5SA | 020-7368-3993 | www.roofgardens.com

"Finding a garden on the roof is an added wow-factor bonus" at this "romantic" seventh-floor dining room on Kensington High Street, where "the pleasure of eating under trees" and among the flamingoes on warmer days makes the "lovely" Modern British menu and "well-chosen wine list" that bit "more exotic and interesting"; it's "expensive", but "friendly staff" help make it a "special" experience; P.S. diners can buy entry to the sister private club below on Friday and Saturday night.

Baker & Spice Bakery/Mediterranean 21 | 17 | 14 | £25

Belgravia | 54-56 Elizabeth St., SW1W 9PB | 020-7730-5524
Chelsea | 47 Denyer St., SW3 2LX | 020-7225-3417
St. John's Wood | 20 Clifton Rd., W9 1SU | 020-7289-2499
www.bakerandspice.uk.com

"Knockout pastries", "wonderful breads" and "well-prepared salads" are the draws at this "gourmet" Mediterranean bakery/cafe chainlet; given that service can range from "charming" to "inattentive" to downright "sociopathic", most do takeaway, but whether you dine in or out, be prepared to pay the relatively "stratospheric" prices that earn it the nickname "Baker & Mortgage".

Balans British 19 | 18 | 19 | £30

Soho | 60-62 Old Compton St., W1D 4UG | 020-7439-2183 ●
Stratford | Westfield Stratford City | 2 Stratford Pl., E20 1EN | 020-8555-5478 ●
Earls Court | 239 Old Brompton Rd., SW5 9HP | 020-7244-8838 ●
Kensington | 187 Kensington High St., W8 6SH | 020-7376-0115 ●
Shepherd's Bush | Westfield Shopping Ctr. | Ariel Way, lower ground fl., W12 7GA | 020-8600-3320

Balans Café ● British

Soho | 34 Old Compton St., W1 4TS | 020-7439-3309
www.balans.co.uk

Whether you're "watching the world and his well-groomed dog go past" at the "cramped, camp" Soho mother-ship cafe (open nearly 24/7) or dining in one of its "jovial" offshoots, you're assured an "enter-

| | FOOD | DECOR | SERVICE | COST |

taining" time at this "reliable" Brit; "efficient" staff deliver everything from all-day breakfasts "guaranteed to beat a hangover" to "wicked cocktails" that'll assuredly give you one, all at "reasonable prices".

Balcon *British/French*   ▽ 23 | 27 | 24 | £45
St. James's | Sofitel St. James | 8 Pall Mall, SW1Y 5NG | 020-7968-2900 | www.thebalconlondon.com
Luxurious, "lovely decor" and high ceilings at this "calm" all-day Sofitel St. James dining room form the backdrop for "quality" French Brasserie-Modern Brit fare; the service is "great", and while the prices are high, the pre-theatre menu is "excellent value".

Bali Bali ● *Indonesian*   20 | 16 | 20 | £24
Covent Garden | 150 Shaftesbury Ave., WC2H 8HL | 020-7836-2644 | www.balibalirestaurant.com
"Friendly" staff " deliver a wide variety" of "tasty" Indonesian dishes including "staples such as beef rendang" at this "unpretentious" Covent Garden spot; its "excellent-value" set menus make it a place to "visit before or after the theatre" or for lunch, whether with a "group" or *à deux*.

NEW Balthazar *French*   ▽ 19 | 26 | 22 | £56
Covent Garden | The Flower Cellars Bldg. | 4-8 Russell St., WC2B 5HZ | 020-3301-1155 | www.balthazarlondon.com
It's the "buzzy" atmosphere at this "crowded" Covent Garden French brasserie from restaurateur Keith McNally – complete with red leather banquettes and a bottle-stacked bar like the New York original – that makes for an "enjoyable evening"; some who've found the pricey eats "average" conclude that it must be more "about the experience than the food" here, but service is decent, and it "gets the ambience right".

Baltic *E European*   23 | 22 | 22 | £39
Southwark | 74 Blackfriars Rd., SE1 8HA | 020-7928-1111 | www.balticrestaurant.co.uk
While mostly Polish, the "hearty" menu at this "bare, white-walled" Southwark "barn" with a large skylight "hops through the Baltic States like an Iron Curtain InterRailer", showcasing "scrumptious" "ingredients and preparations you won't see much outside their home nations"; the "buzzy" adjacent cocktail bar stocks "a multitude of different vodkas" and "reasonable prices" seem to come straight from the Eastern Bloc.

Bam-Bou ●Ⓩ *Asian*   22 | 22 | 20 | £45
Fitzrovia | 1 Percy St., W1T 1DB | 020-7323-9130 | www.bam-bou.co.uk
Set in a three-storey townhouse, this "high-end" Pan-Asian is a "date-night favourite" among the Fitzrovia set, who kick things off with "great cocktails" in the top-floor bar before moving on to the "lushly decorated" dining rooms below; "spice combinations ranging from subtle to strong" mean there's something to suit all tastes (ask "helpful" staff for suggestions), and while it's "not the cheapest", most feel it's "a treat worth spending a bit more on".

	FOOD	DECOR	SERVICE	COST

Banana Tree *SE Asian*
21 | 17 | 19 | £22

Soho | 103-109 Wardour St., W1F 0UQ | 020-7437-1351
Hampstead | 237-239 West End Ln., NW6 1XN | 020-7431-7808
Islington | 412-416 St. John St., EC1V 4NJ | 020-7278-7565
Clapham | 75-79 Battersea Rise, SW11 1HN | 020-7228-2828
Bayswater | 21-23 Westbourne Grove, W2 4UA | 020-7221-4085
Maida Vale | 166 Randolph Ave., W9 1PG | 020-7286-3869
www.bananatree.co.uk

"Huge portions" of "big-flavoured" Southeast Asian fare, including "classics", "imaginative" dishes and the "exceptional" Legendary Rendang ("legendary for a reason"), come for "very reasonable prices" at this chain; there's almost "always a queue", but "sweet" and "speedy" staff keep things moving – nevertheless, the "long communal tables" tend to be "hectic", so it's "better for refuelling than romancing".

Banh Mi Bay 🖪 *Vietnamese*
24 | 17 | 19 | £12

Bloomsbury | 4-6 Theobald's Rd., WC1X 8PN | 020-7831-4079
Fitzrovia | 21 Rathbone St., W1T 1NF | 020-3609-4830 |
www.banhmibay.co.uk

At lunchtime, Bloomsbury "office workers" reckon it's "worth the wait" for the "to-die-for" baguettes, "huge" bowls of pho (perfect "on a cold, wintry day") and other "wonderfully filling" Vietnamese food served at this "cheap and cheerful" caff; there's "not a lot of room" and "not much atmosphere", so most grab something to go, even though "in-house service is quick"; P.S. a Fitzrovia branch is open for takeouts only.

Bank Westminster & Zander Bar 🖪 *European*
20 | 24 | 20 | £46

Westminster | 45 Buckingham Gate, SW1E 6BS | 020-7630-6644 |
www.bankrestaurants.com

In a "sunlit room with huge windows" framing "spectacular views" of a "wonderful" courtyard, this European provides a "pleasant" place for Westminster workers to "entertain clients" over a "good range" of "well-cooked" dishes, all brought by "attentive" staff; there's also plenty of praise for the "cool" bar.

Barbecoa *BBQ*
23 | 23 | 21 | £53

City | 20 New Change Passage, EC4M 9AG | 020-3005-8555 |
www.barbecoa.com

A "meat lover's paradise" sums up this "lively", "unpretentious" City BBQ joint from Jamie Oliver; besides "excellent" ribs, steak and more, it boasts "unsurpassed views" of St. Paul's Cathedral plus "cool, relaxed" service, so most deem it "well worth visiting"; P.S. there's an on-site butchery too.

Bar Boulud *French*
24 | 21 | 23 | £54

Knightsbridge | Mandarin Oriental Hyde Park | 66 Knightsbridge, SW1X 7LA | 020-7201-3899 | www.barboulud.com

Daniel Boulud's London version of his New York original downstairs in the Mandarin Oriental Hyde Park is "all-round first class", with a "varied", "creative" French menu – including "killer burgers" – served in an "elegant, casual", "buzzy" setting with a charcuterie counter and bar; despite "expense-account" prices, fans claim it's "worth it" to dine "among the beau monde".

Barcelona Tapas *Spanish* | 22 | 17 | 21 | £38 |

City | 24 Lime St., EC3M 7HR | 020-7929-2389 🗷
Spitalfields | 15 St. Botolph St., EC3A 7DT | 020-7377-5111 🗷
Dulwich | 481 Lordship Ln., SE22 8JY | 020-8693-5111 ●
www.barcelona-tapas.com

A "massive menu" of "tasty" tapas complemented by an "extensive" list of "brilliant" wines makes this Spanish chainlet work for anything from a "quick" dinner to a "family get-together"; "generous portions" boost its value, as do the "friendly" staff, some with just the "right lack of English vocabulary to complete the air of authenticity".

Barrafina *Spanish* | 28 | 19 | 23 | £42 |

Soho | 54 Frith St., W1D 4SL | 020-7813-8016 | www.barrafina.co.uk

"Stellar" Spanish nibbles, including the "freshest seafood", are prepared in front of you and served with "wines to impress" at this "intimate", no-reservations tapas bar in Soho; generally there's a queue (though it may be shorter for seats at the counter), but fans assure it's "well worth" the "crazy" wait and costs that can "add up".

Barrica 🗷 *Spanish* | 25 | 19 | 22 | £37 |

Fitzrovia | 62 Goodge St., W1T 4NE | 020-7436-9448 | www.barrica.co.uk

This Fitzrovia tapas bar is appreciated not only for its "lovely and unusual" small plates and "fabulous" range of Spanish wines and sherries, but also for its "airy", "laid-back atmosphere" and fairly "gentle tabs" (especially in comparison to "pricier neighbours"); add in "knowledgeable" service, and some say it's "right up there with Goodge Street's best".

Barshu *Chinese* | 23 | 16 | 13 | £35 |

Soho | 28 Frith St., W1D 5LF | 020-7287-8822 | www.bar-shu.co.uk

"Like it hot?" – you'll be "blown away" by the "fabulous, fiery" Sichuan fare this traditionally decked-out Soho spot serves up for moderate prices; indeed, the heat is "not for the faint-hearted", though you might be left "cold" by "abrupt" service (to be fair, "some staff are fine").

NEW Barsito Ⓜ *Spanish* | - | - | - | M |

Clapham | 57 Venn St., SW4 0BD | 020-7627-4000 |
www.barsito.co.uk

Clapham gets a taste of Barcelona with this tiny tapas bar where you perch on a stool, take your pick from the day's reasonably priced blackboard specials and watch as the chef whips them up in the galley-style kitchen; a Spanish-focused wine list adds to the sense that you're closer to Las Ramblas than the High Street, as does warm-weather outdoor seating on the pedestrian-friendly street, where barrels are used as tables.

	FOOD	DECOR	SERVICE	COST

NEW Bar Tozino M *Spanish* — | — | — | M

Tower Bridge | Maltby St., SE1 3PA | no phone |
www.bartozino.com

Vintage and provenance are the focus of the jamon, which hangs from
the ceiling and then gets carved from the bone right in front of diners
at this small, dark, no-reservations Spanish bodega whose blackboard menu features an array of tapas; a sensibly priced list of cava
and sherry helps to keep it perennially packed.

Ba Shan *Chinese* 24 | 18 | 17 | £32

Soho | 24 Romilly St., W1S 5AH | 020-7287-3266 |
www.bashanlondon.com

"If you don't like spice", this Soho Sichuan, an offshoot of Barshu,
"probably isn't for you"; however, heat-lovers call it "mecca", cram-
ming into the "small nooks" of the "cosy", traditionally outfitted dining room where "fluctuating" though often "willing" staff ferry fare
that's "a world apart" from what you often find in Chinatown – and
"worth" the slight "extra cost".

NEW Beagle *British* — | — | — | M

Hoxton | 397 Geffrye St., E2 8HZ | 020-7613-2967 |
www.beaglelondon.co.uk

Named after an old steam locomotive that once rattled over-
head, this laid-back Hoxton restaurant-bar offers a moderately
priced, daily changing, grill leaning Modern British menu; re-
claimed railway sleeper flooring and exposed brick arches form
the shell of the earthy decor, and there's also a large alfresco
space on the pedestrian-friendly street.

NEW Beard To Tail *British/Steak* — | — | — | M

Shoreditch | 77 Curtain Rd., EC2A 3BS | 020-7729-2966 |
www.beardtotail.co.uk

After a successful stint as a pop-up, this Modern Brit gets itself a permanent base in a former warehouse in Shoreditch, where chef Dan
Thrippleton (ex Hix group) serves a midpriced, meat-heavy menu
along with craft beers and bourbon-based cocktails; a blue-and-grey
palette with exposed brickwork nods to the venue's industrial heritage.

Beirut Express ● *Lebanese* 23 | 14 | 18 | £21

Marylebone | 112-114 Edgware Rd., W2 2DZ | 020-7724-2700
South Kensington | 65 Old Brompton Rd., SW7 3JS |
020-7591-0123
www.maroush.com

The "same menu, prices and good food as Maroush" (same owners)
are offered at this "value"-priced Lebanese duo on Edgware Road
and in South Kensington; service is decent, whether you pop in for a
quick takeaway snack or a sit-down meal.

Beiteddine ● *Lebanese* ▽ 26 | 18 | 26 | £37

Belgravia | 8 Harriet St., SW1X 9JW | 020-7235-3969 |
www.beiteddinerestaurant.com

"Excellent" staff who "make you feel welcome" serve up "brilliant" mezze and the signature mixed-grill platter at this "quiet"

Belgravia Lebanese, where prices seem "cheap" compared to the place's "posher" neighbours.

Belgo *Belgian*   21 | 17 | 18 | £27

Covent Garden | 50 Earlham St., WC2H 9LJ | 020-7813-2233
Holborn | 67 Kingsway, WC2B 6TD | 020-7242-7469
Chalk Farm | 72 Chalk Farm Rd., NW1 8AN | 020-7267-0718
Clapham | 44-48 Clapham High St., SW4 7UR |
020-7720-1118 ●
www.belgo-restaurants.co.uk

"Piping hot and delicious" plates of "plump" mussels served with frites, along with an "extensive" selection of bottled beers and ciders, are what keep this "congenial" Belgian chainlet "buzzing"; staff, who are dressed in monk's robes at the Covent Garden branch, "seem to enjoy what they're doing", and "for a quick bite", the lunchtime and early evening deals are "good value for money".

Bellamy's ☒ *French*   24 | 23 | 24 | £62

Mayfair | 18 Bruton Pl., W1J 6LY | 020-7491-2727 |
www.bellamysrestaurant.co.uk

This "serene", "clublike" Mayfair brasserie and oyster bar serves "reliable, indulgent" Classic French cuisine; it's predictably "expensive", but that's no issue for its "upscale clientele", who also appreciate that "dedicated", "friendly" staff seem to "value" their patronage.

The Belvedere *British/French*   21 | 24 | 21 | £62

Holland Park | Holland Park | off Abbotsbury Rd., W8 6LU |
020-7602-1238 | www.belvedererestaurant.co.uk

Surrounded by "beautiful grounds" with "peacocks screeching", this "romantic", tri-tiered Holland Park "landmark" offers "good people-watching" alongside "well-executed" Modern British–New French fare that "never fails to impress"; "polished service" is a boon, while the "wonderful-value" set lunch mitigates the "high-end" prices.

Benares *Indian*   25 | 24 | 24 | £65

Mayfair | 12 Berkeley Sq., W1J 6BS | 020-7629-8886 |
www.benaresrestaurant.com

Chef-owner Atul Kochar's "sophisticated", expensive Mayfair venue (now into its second decade) offers a "sublime", "spicy" menu whose "modern twists" "take Indian cuisine to another level"; plaudits are also earned for the "beautiful bar" (though some feel the cocktail prices might "nearly cause bankruptcy") and "friendly", "refined" service.

Bengal Clipper ● *Indian*   ▽ 21 | 17 | 20 | £39

Tower Bridge | Cardamom Bldg. | 31 Shad Thames, SE1 2YR |
020-7357-9001 | www.bengalclipper.co.uk

For "reasonably priced" Indian cuisine that's often "better than a typical neighbourhood tandoori", fans stop by this venue near Tower Bridge; service is "friendly", however, the setting's "not charming", "despite the nice touch of having a piano player" Tuesday–Saturday evenings.

Benihana *Japanese* 20 | 1(

City | Grange Hotel St. Paul | 10 Godliman St., EC4V 5AJ | 02
Piccadilly | 37 Sackville St., W1S 3DQ | 020-7494-2525
Chelsea | 77 King's Rd., SW3 4NX | 020-7376-7799
www.benihana.co.uk

"Tantalising teppanyaki" is "prepared in front of you" by chefs who "love what they do" at this "entertaining" Japanese chainlet; it's "fantastic for kids" ("the onion volcano trick" "never ceases to delight"), but "theatrics" aside, a number of surveyors feel it's "expensive for what you get", and the "decor's a little dull" too; P.S. "don't wear your best" – the "hibachi leaves a lingering impression".

Bentley's *British/Seafood* 25 | 22 | 23 | £62

Piccadilly | 11-15 Swallow St., W1B 4DG | 020-7734-4756 |
www.bentleys.org

"Well-prepared" British seafood and a "decent selection of wines" are the hallmarks of chef-owner Richard Corrigan's "old-school" Piccadilly "standby" featuring an upstairs dining room and a downstairs bar where "oh-so-many varieties of oysters" get "shucked right in front of you"; it can be "pricey", but such is the cost of "refinement and class".

Bento *Japanese* 23 | 15 | 19 | £25

Camden Town | 9 Parkway, NW1 7PG | 020-7482-3990 |
www.bentocafe.co.uk

"Local kids" tuck into a "diverse selection" of "wonderful speciality rolls" and "great-value-for-money bento lunch deals" at this Camden sushi spot with an "unassuming environment" (some call it "dull"); there's "good service at all times", but often a "mad rush" at midday, which you might avoid by grabbing a takeaway.

Bevis Marks ☒ *International/Kosher* 23 | 22 | 22 | £49

Spitalfields | 3 Middlesex St., E1 7AA | 020-7247-5474 |
www.bevismarkstherestaurant.com

"Delicious" "traditional Jewish dishes" are "spiced up" for "locals", "tourists" and "business"-types at this "gourmet" kosher spot in Spitalfields, which also prepares other International fare; service is well received, and during the daytime in particular, the modern art deco setting benefits from a "good atmosphere".

Bibendum *French* 23 | 23 | 23 | £63

South Kensington | Michelin Hse. | 81 Fulham Rd., SW3 6RD |
020-7581-5817 | www.bibendum.co.uk

South Ken's Michelin House plays host to this "charming" first-floor dining room where "attentive" staff (who go "above and beyond") proffer "terrific" New French cuisine in an "elegant" room with high ceilings and stained glass; despite high prices, most "couldn't be happier", deeming it an "all-round" performer.

Bibendum Oyster Bar *French/Seafood* 23 | 21 | 20 | £47

South Kensington | Michelin Hse. | 81 Fulham Rd., SW3 6RD |
020-7589-1480 | www.bibendum.co.uk

For a "stylish, elegant" meal of "divine oysters" "paired with a suitable wine" or "a glass of bubbly" in South Kensington, pop into this French bistro with "beautiful art deco tiled mosaics" in the "unique" former Michelin tyre factory; it's "less formal" than Bibendum upstairs, but "there's no reduction in service" and a moderate discount in price.

Big Easy *American* `21` `19` `19` `£30`
Chelsea | 332-334 King's Rd., SW3 5UR | 020-7352-4071 | www.bigeasy.uk.com

"American expats" "craving" a taste of "the Deep South" are rewarded with "awesome" portions of "messy wings", ribs and "other meaty delights" plus "seafood combos with oysters, shrimps and crab claws" at this "friendly", slightly "kitschy" King's Road diner; nightly live bands amp up the "fantastic" atmosphere, while regular "all-you-can-eat" promotions keep costs down, which is why it's "always packed".

Bill's Produce Store *British/Deli* `19` `20` `18` `£23`
Covent Garden | St. Martin's Courtyard | 13 Slingsby Pl., WC2E 9AB | 020-7240-8183
Soho | 36-44 Brewer St., W1F 92B | 020-7287-8712
Islington | 9 White Lion St., N1 9PD | 020-7713-7272
NEW **Richmond** | 1-3 Hill Rise, TW10 6UQ | 020-8948-0768
Wimbledon | 20 Hartfield Rd., SW19 3TA | 020-8947-8285
www.bills-website.co.uk

A "midpriced", "quirky chain for the Whole Foods generation", this "relaxed, informal" cafe and shop has "teens and twentysome-things" tucking into "hearty", "simple", "well-prepared" British food; the service is "bubbly" and "welcoming", and the "unusual but nicely decorated" interior features shelves "stacked with syrups and a few homemade goods" for sale.

Bincho ● *Japanese* `23` `19` `18` `£33`
Soho | 16 Old Compton St., W1D 4TL | 020-7287-9111 | www.bincho.co.uk

"They'll grill almost anything" at this yakitori-style Soho Japanese whose "tasty" charcoal-cooked small plates are served at long wooden tables; at first glance it appears "cheap and cheerful", but "beware", you have to order two of each item, "so you can easily spend a fortune"; P.S. the basement sake bar boasts London's reportedly largest selection of Japanese whiskies.

The Bingham *British/European* `24` `22` `22` `£61`
Richmond | Bingham Hotel | 61-63 Petersham Rd., TW10 6UT | 020-8940-0902 | www.thebingham.co.uk

"Superb", "imaginative" Modern British–European cuisine is complemented by a "huge wine list" at this "idyllic" setting in a "fantastic boutique hotel" on the Richmond riverbank ("wonderful at sunset"); "charming service" is the order of the day, as is an "expensive" bill, though there's a set lunch that's "excellent value".

NEW Bird of Smithfield ● *British* `-` `-` `-` `E`
Farringdon | 26 Smithfield St., EC1A 9LB | 020-7559-5100 | www.birdofsmithfield.com

After years at the helm of The Ivy, chef Alan Bird lands at this Georgian townhouse in Farringdon where fans of his high-end

Modern British cooking can tuck into their favourites in a classically styled, Harris Tweed-clad dining room; elsewhere in the five-storey building, you'll find a lounge bar, a private dining floor with a chef's table, a roof terrace overlooking Smithfield Market and The Birdcage, an intimate live music venue.

Bistrot Bruno Loubet *French*

25 | 20 | 21 | £54

Clerkenwell | The Zetter | 86-88 Clerkenwell Rd., EC1M 5RJ | 020-7324-4455 | www.bistrotbrunoloubet.com

Bruno Loubet's French bistro cooking is "adventurous enough to be interesting" and downright "brilliant" thanks to an "amazing combination of ingredients, flavours and creativity" at the "master" chef's Clerkenwell spot in the "super-cool" Zetter Hotel; "warm" service from "well-informed" staff complements the "bright and airy" dining room's "laid-back atmosphere", and best of all, it's "priced well for the quality".

Bistrotheque *French*

21 | 22 | 19 | £44

Bethnal Green | 23-27 Wadeson St., E2 9DR | 020-8983-7900 | www.bistrotheque.com

"Anything goes" at this "minimalist New York loft-style" Bethnal Green hangout (big sister to Shrimpy's), where a "hipster clientele" of "artists, photographers" and "fashion" types convene over "well-thought-out" French bistro fare; though service is sometimes "surly", it's often "attentive" and "friendly", which helps mollify those who feel it's "overpriced for what it is"; P.S. a private dining room is available downstairs.

NEW Bistro Union *British*

- | - | - | M

Clapham | 40 Abbeville Rd., SW4 9NG | 020-7042-6400 | www.bistrounion.co.uk

A quintessentially British menu, including moderately priced brunch and bar snacks (pork scratchings, pickled quails eggs, and sausage and sage puffs), is the signature of this informal neighbourhood eatery and sister of Trinity in nearby Clapham Old Town (from local boy, Adam Byatt); a nostalgic air pervades the front bar area with its chemistry lab stools and bell jars, plus there's a main dining area at the rear and some tables out on the front terrace.

Black & Blue *Steak*

19 | 17 | 18 | £33

Fitzrovia | 37 Berners St., W1T 3NJ | 020-7436-0451 🖂
Marylebone | 90-92 Wigmore St., W1 3RD | 020-7486-1912
Borough | Borough Mkt. | 1-2 Rochester Walk, SE1 9AF | 020-7357-9922
NEW Waterloo | 1 Mepham St., SE1 8RL | 020-7928-9131
Notting Hill | 215-217 Kensington Church St., W8 7LX | 020-7727-0004
www.blackandbluerestaurants.com

"Stonking sides" accompany "huge, juicy" burgers and "reliable" steaks at this meaty chain; though somewhat "uninspiring", the interiors featuring black leather banquettes and marble tables are "functional" and "comfortable" enough, and service is mostly "quick and polite", so while it might be "nothing to go out of your way for", it's "a good fallback" for an "affordable" meal.

| | FOOD | DECOR | SERVICE | COST |

Blakes ● *International* ⬛ 20 | 22 | 20 | £76

South Kensington | Blakes Hotel | 33 Roland Gdns., SW7 3PF | 020-7370-6701 | www.blakeshotels.com

Its "beautifully stylish" black, "windowless" setting is "as dark as Nosferatu's eyeliner", and that's why this "intimate" South Kensington hotel international is an "old standby" for "illicit" "rendezvous" and discreet "business meetings"; for some, the "excessive pricing" and slightly "frosty" service don't match up to the setting, but others plead "don't change anything".

Bleeding Heart 🅱 *British/French* 23 | 21 | 22 | £51

Farringdon | 4 Bleeding Heart Yard, off Greville St., EC1N 8SJ | 020-7242-8238

Bleeding Heart Tavern 🅱 *British/French*

Farringdon | 19 Greville St., EC1N 8SJ | 020-7242-2056 www.bleedingheart.co.uk

These eateries in a "secluded" Farringdon courtyard include a "romantic", pricey Modern French restaurant joined with a "little" bistro dishing out "unpretentious" Gallic dishes in a "rustic" interior and on a patio, plus a "cosy, relaxed" tavern (open from 7 AM) serving "reasonably priced" British fare; all boast "excellent wines" and "lovely service".

Bluebird *British* 20 | 22 | 20 | £45

Chelsea | 350 King's Rd., SW3 5UU | 020-7559-1000 | www.bluebird-restaurant.co.uk

Given its former life as a 1920s garage, this "trendy" Modern Brit is an appropriate "pit stop" for King's Road shoppers to refuel, offering a "delightful" menu in the large first-floor restaurant, a glass of wine and a "light" meal on the patio or a treat from the on-site retail shop; the adjacent bar's "vibrant scene" is another aspect that keeps the whole endeavour "popular", despite sometimes "stressed" service and "pricey" costs.

Blue Elephant *Thai* 24 | 25 | 22 | £53

Chelsea | The Boulevard, Imperial Wharf, SW6 2UB | 020-7751-3111 | www.blueelephant.com

Inspired by a Bangkok palace, this "sumptuous" and "beautiful" Imperial Wharf Thai pleases with its "mouth-watering" dishes and the "legendary" all-you-can-eat Sunday brunch – featuring everything from "seafood cooked in front of you to traditional noodle dishes"; service is usually "attentive", and considering the "expensive" bill, some feel it's "worth it" for a "treat".

Blue Legume *Mediterranean* 22 | 20 | 18 | £20

Islington | 177 Upper St., N1 1RG | 020-7226-5858

Stoke Newington | 101 Stoke Newington Church St., N16 0UD | 020-7923-1303

Crouch End | 130 Crouch Hill, N8 9DY | 020-8442-9282 www.thebluelegume.co.uk

"Generous portions" of "hearty", "reliable" Mediterranean fare (including some "excellent" veggie options) are what's on offer at this "lovely" chainlet of all-day cafes; it's "enjoyable for all the family" and prices are moderate, particularly if you opt for the "good-value" set menu.

Blueprint Café *European*   `22` `21` `20` `£41`

Tower Bridge | Design Museum | 28 Shad Thames, SE1 2YD |
020-7378-7031 | www.blueprintcafe.co.uk

The Design Museum's "smart" cafe offers an "imaginative" Modern European menu featuring seasonal ingredients and "reasonably priced" prix fixe deals; service is "charming" and the "huge" windows offer "stunning" views of Tower Bridge and the Thames.

Bob Bob Ricard ⚅ *International/Russian*   `22` `27` `24` `£59`

Soho | 1 Upper James St., W1F 9DF | 020-3145-1000 |
www.bobbobricard.com

"What's not to love?" ask fans of this "gorgeous", "old-world" Soho spot with "Orient Express"-style decor, complete with banquettes, brass rails and a 'push for champagne' button at every table; the "helpful" on-board team, all dressed in pink tuxedos, serve an "original" English-meets-Russian menu that spans everything from burgers to caviar – just "don't go if you're on a budget, it would spoil the fun".

Bocca di Lupo *Italian*   `25` `19` `21` `£45`

Soho | 12 Archer St., W1D 7BB | 020-7734-2223 | www.boccadilupo.com

Gelupo *Italian*

Soho | 7 Archer St., W1D 7AU | 020-7287-5555 | www.gelupo.com

For "lively, seasonal cooking" including "superb" homemade pasta, this "reasonably priced" Soho Italian "lives up to the hype", and its sister gelateria is "well worth crossing the street" for; staff who are usually "knowledgeable" and "attentive" patrol the "buzzy" setting, for which it's wise to "book in advance", because it "fills up fast" (though some seats at the bar are available for walk-ins).

Bodeans *American/BBQ*   `22` `17` `19` `£23`

City | 16 Byward St., EC3R 5BA | 020-7488-3883
Soho | 10 Poland St., W1F 8PZ | 020-7287-7575
Clapham | 169 Clapham High St., SW4 7SS | 020-7622-4248
Fulham | 4 Broadway Chambers, SW6 1EP | 020-7610-0440
www.bodeansbbq.com

"Meat lovers" crave the "epic portions" of burnt ends, pulled pork, ribs and jerk chicken – all "served with a smile" – at this "good-value" American BBQ chainlet; as it shows U.S. football and baseball on giant TVs, it can get "super busy" and "noisy", but that's all part of the "happy, cheerful" package.

Boisdale ⚅ *British/Scottish*   `22` `22` `20` `£53`

City | Swedeland Ct. | 202 Bishopsgate, EC2M 4NR |
020-7283-1763
Canary Wharf | Cabot Pl. W., E14 4QT | 020-7715-5818 ☽
Belgravia | 15 Eccleston St., SW1W 9LX | 020-7730-6922
www.boisdale.co.uk

"Sozzled with the spirit of Scotland", this "post-box-red", tartan-bedecked Belgravia "old boys' club" and its City and Canary

Wharf cousins ply fans with "quality" steaks and other "pricey" Traditional British fodder plus a "marvellous" whisky supply; a "renowned" cigar selection (and smokers' terrace), "superb" nightly live jazz and the occasional bagpiper compensate for occasionally "slapdash" service.

NEW Bo London ● ⊠ *Chinese* — — — VE

Mayfair | 4 Mill St., W1S 2AX | 020-7493-3886 | www.bolondonrestaurant.com

Hong Kong–based chef Alvin Leung introduces his maverick approach to traditional Chinese recipes, available in pricey dim-sum lunch and fixed-price dinner menus, at this Mayfair venue; highlights of the dark, minimalist decor include granite, metal and marble.

Bombay Brasserie ● *Indian* 23 22 21 £47

South Kensington | Courtfield Rd., SW7 4QH | 020-7370-4040 | www.bombaybrasserielondon.com

A South Ken "favourite", this "opulent" Indian offers "a last look at the empire in its faded glory", with "reliable" fare in "spacious" digs that can be "a bit hushed during the week"; however, some feel it's slightly "overpriced", notwithstanding the "incredible-value" weekend brunch.

Bombay Palace ● *Indian* 24 19 20 £48

Paddington | 50 Connaught St., W2 2AA | 020-7723-8855 | www.bombay-palace.co.uk

"Astonishing" flavours abound in the "superb Indian food" prepared at this Paddington branch of an international chain; prices may be a bit "high" for the genre, but they do include "attentive", "accommodating" service and a contemporary, modern setting.

Bonds *British* ∇ 22 21 19 £52

City | Threadneedles Hotel | 5 Threadneedle St., EC2R 8AY | 020-7657-8088 | www.bonds-restaurant.co.uk

Set within a City banking hall–turned–boutique hotel, this spot with high ceilings, white walls, wood and well-spaced tables serves "high-quality" British fare from dawn till dinner (breakfast only at weekends); "attentive" service is a plus, but it all comes at a "rather expensive" price.

NEW Bone Daddies Ramen *Japanese* ∇ 21 16 15 £24

Soho | 30-31 Peter St., W1F 0AR | 020-7287-8581 | www.bonedaddiesramen.com

Possessing "an air of Soho hipsterism", this no-reservations joint dishes up bowls of "tasty" ramen alongside a selection of Japanese snacks; it's "more of a quick bite type of place" than somewhere to linger, with "brisk, attentive" service and a "buzzing" atmosphere; P.S. there are "bibs or hair ties available if you need them".

Books for Cooks ⊠ Ⓜ *International* ∇ 25 17 20 £21

Notting Hill | 4 Blenheim Crescent, W11 1NN | 020-7221-1992 | www.booksforcooks.com

Eat surrounded by over 10,000 "wonderful" recipe tomes at this "cosy" International cafe/test kitchen at the back of a "sweet, slightly scruffy" Notting Hill cookbook store; it's only open for lunch and you have to "get there before they run out" of the usually "excellent" daily changing dishes, which are often crafted by "visiting cooks doing demonstrations" and usually sold at moderate prices.

Boqueria *Spanish*

FCOD	DECOR	SERVICE	COST
-	-	-	M

Brixton | 192 Acre Ln., SW2 5UL | 020-7733-4408 | www.boqueriatapas.com

Named after the iconic Barcelona market, this Brixton taperia seeks to emulate its namesake with a selection of moderately priced tapas (both traditional and innovative), sherries, cavas and wines; sit at the bar or in the larger dining room beyond, where Spanish staff wind their way through closely packed wooden tables; P.S. a cafe next door serves daytime snacks, churros and hot chocolate.

The Botanist ● *British*

18	18	15	£41

Chelsea | 7 Sloane Sq., SW1W 8EE | 020-7730-0077 | www.thebotanistonsloanesquare.com

Leaving their "Bentleys, Maseratis and other exotic rides" outside, a "hip Chelsea crowd" hangs out at this "light, airy" Sloane Square spot "more for the happening bar" than the adjacent all-day dining room, where breakfast is the "most reliable" option and the rest of the midpriced Modern British offerings are "fine" though "without surprises"; so "come here for the scene", but when it gets busy, "be prepared to be looked over" by the "rushed" staff.

Boundary *French*

23	23	21	£54

Shoreditch | 2-4 Boundary St., E2 7DD | 020-7729-1051 | www.theboundary.co.uk

Supporters say the "well-made" French fare is "worth every pound" at this "sophisticated" basement dining room in Sir Terence Conran's same-named hotel ("in the middle of trendyville Shoreditch"), which manages to be "airy" despite having "no natural light"; also on offer are a cafe-cum-grocery, called Albion, and an "amazing" rooftop bar that's a "must-go when it's hot".

Bountiful Cow ⊠ *Steak*

22	15	18	£31

Holborn | 51 Eagle St., WC1R 4AP | 020-7404-0200 | www.thebountifulcow.co.uk

"Great-quality" steaks and "big" burgers are "cooked just the way you want" by flamboyant chef-owner Roxy Beaujolais at this spot with a virtually "hidden" Holborn location; the publike decor is a bit "drab", but the more the "Malbec flows", the less those seem to matter.

Bradley's *British/French*

22	17	20	£45

Swiss Cottage | 25 Winchester Rd., NW3 3NR | 020-7722-3457 | www.bradleysnw3.co.uk

"Personable" staff deliver chef-owner Simon Bradley's "solid", "interesting" French-accented Modern British cuisine alongside a "short, well-chosen wine list" at this Swiss Cottage site; if the "small" digs are looking "a little tired", at least the prices are "reasonable" due to the set lunch, dinner and "pre-Hampstead Theatre" menus.

	FOOD	DECOR	SERVICE	COST

Brasserie Blanc *French* | 18 | 18 | 18 | £38 |

Fitzrovia | 8 Charlotte St., W1T 2LS | 020-7636-4975
City | 1 Watling St., EC4M 9BP | 020-7213-0540 🅢
City | 60 Threadneedle St., EC2R 8HP | 020-7710-9440 🅢
City | Trinity Sq., EC3N 4AA | 020-7480-5500 🅢
Covent Garden | Covent Garden Piazza | 35 The Market, WC2E 8RF |
020-7379-0666
Holborn | 119 Chancery Ln., WC2A 1PP | 020-7405-0290 🅢
Waterloo | 9 Belvedere Rd., SE1 8YL | 020-7202-8470 ●
www.brasserieblanc.com

Raymond Blanc's burgeoning nationwide chain is "reliable" for French brasserie fare, a "decent" wine list and "polite" service; so, some find it "nothing extraordinary", but most deem it a "good standby", with a "pleasant" ambience and "reasonable" prices.

NEW Brasserie Chavot *French* | - | - | - | E |

Mayfair | 41 Conduit St., W1S 2YF | 020-7016-6740 |
www.brasseriechavot.com

After making his name at the Capital Hotel in the early 2000s (and a subsequent stint in Florida), Eric Chavot returns to London with this glossy French brasserie in Mayfair; the high-end Gallic fare pays homage to his Southwestern French roots while using ingredients sourced from specialist producers from around the British Isles.

Brasserie Zédel ● *French* | 17 | 26 | 20 | £34 |

Soho | 20 Sherwood St., W1F 7ED | 020-7734-4888 |
www.brasseriezedel.com

There's "masses of buzz and considerable wow factor" in this Wolseley sibling's "glamourous", "cavernous" Soho basement setting, which is "reminiscent of a luxe deco cruise ship" (and augmented by a cabaret-cum-cocktail bar and street level cafe); even if the "classic" French Brasserie fare "doesn't quite live up" to the setting, at least it's "cheaper than one might think", with "efficient" service as a bonus; P.S. reservations not required, so it's "great for pre- or post-theatre".

Brawn *British/Mediterranean* | 26 | 20 | 22 | £35 |

Shoreditch | 49 Columbia Rd., E2 7RG | 020-7729-5692 |
www.brawn.co

"Overlooked grapes and ingredients" are celebrated at this "simple, stylish" Shoreditch sibling of Terroirs, whose "wonderful" British and Mediterranean small-plates menu includes an "all-things-pork" section and an "interesting" wine list that highlights natural and bio-dynamic options; "über-cool" staff, "super-fair" prices and a "fantastic" set lunch on Sundays complete the picture.

Bread Street Kitchen *European* | 20 | 23 | 20 | £47 |

City | 10 Bread St., EC4M 9AJ | 020-7592-1616 |
www.breadstreetkitchen.com

"Floor-to-ceiling windows" and "exposed beams" give this "huge", "airy" City space from Gordon Ramsay an "NYC vibe"; the "safe" Modern European menu offers "all-day dining" options "just right for a

client lunch", but even the "strong, fruity" cocktails don't quite dull the
sense that you're "paying a lot of bread" for "portions that verge on
mean", not to mention variable (though "well-intentioned") service.

Breakfast Club *American/British* | 21 | 20 | 17 | £17 |

Soho | 33 D'Arblay St., W1F 8EU | 020-7434-2571
Hoxton | 2-4 Rufus St., N1 6PE | 020-7729-5252
Spitalfields | 12-16 Artillery Ln., E1 7LS | 020-7078-9633
Islington | 31 Camden Passage, N1 8EA | 020-7226-5454
NEW **Clapham** | 5-9 Battersea Rise, SW11 1HG | 020-8078-9630
www.thebreakfastclubcafes.com

"Hipsters" cite the "amazing-value" grub at this "funky" cafe chain
specialising in "huge" breakfasts, ranging from "healthy", "delicious"
smoothies to "heart-attack-on-a-plate" full Englishes and American-
style brunch; "waits at weekends" are the norm both before getting
a table and after, when it "often takes a long time to get your food"
from "friendly", "good-looking", "tight-jeaned" staff; P.S. in the City,
"ask to see 'The Mayor'" for access through a fridge to the secret
cocktail bar downstairs.

NEW BRGR.CO *Burgers* | - | - | - | M |

Soho | 187 Wardour St., W1F 8ZB | 020-7920-6480 | www.brgr.co
Designer burgers plus classic American diner fare like hot dogs and
shakes are all served in hefty portions at this Soho eatery, which is
the first international outpost of a Lebanese mini chain; it's a boisterous, crowded place and accepts no reservations (except for large
groups at the weekend).

Brindisa, Tapas *Spanish* | 23 | 17 | 19 | £34 |

Soho | 46 Broadwick St., W1F 7AF | 020-7534-1690
Borough | Borough Mkt. | 18-20 Southwark St., SE1 1TJ | 020-7357-8880
Brindisa, Casa *Spanish*
South Kensington | 7-9 Exhibition Rd., SW7 2HE | 020-7590-0008
NEW Brindisa, Tramontana *Spanish*
Shoreditch | 152 Curtain Rd., EC2A 3AT | 020-7749-9961
www.brindisa.com

The "excellent ingredients" "shine" at this "effortlessly spot-on"
Spanish tapas chainlet, which also offers a "great wine list"; the casual
setting gets "crowded" ("be prepared to wait"), but "staff remain
calm" and "friendly"; P.S. only some locations take reservations.

NEW Brompton Asian | - | - | - | E |
Brasserie *Asian/European*
Knightsbridge | 223-225 Brompton Rd., SW3 2EJ | 020-7225-2107 |
www.bromptonasianbrasserie.co.uk

This Knightsbridge brasserie from Russian restaurateur Arkady
Novikov starts the day with Modern European-style breakfasts before moving onto an upscale Asian lunch-and-dinner menu that covers sushi, salads and spicy wok creations; a bright, glass-wrapped
dining room with an open kitchen sits above an intimate cocktail
lounge, while the neighbouring Grocer offers quick bites and gourmet provisions to go from morning until 9 PM.

	FOOD	DECOR	SERVICE	COST

Brompton Bar & Grill *British/European*   20 | 19 | 21 | £43

Knightsbridge | 243 Brompton Rd., SW3 2EP | 020-7589-8005 |
www.bromptonbarandgrill.com

"Charming" staff who "remember their regulars" make even tourists
"feel like locals" at this bright, art-bedecked Knightsbridge brasserie,
where the "solid" British menu with Modern European touches is "a bit
pricey" but leaves most feeling "stuffed and content"; furthermore,
there's a "lively" bar scene fuelled by "awesome absinthe cocktails".

Browns *British*   19 | 20 | 19 | £36

City | 8 Old Jewry, EC2R 8DN | 020-7606-6677 🚫
Covent Garden | 82-84 St. Martin's Ln., WC2N 4AG | 020-7497-5050
Mayfair | 47 Maddox St., W1S 2PG | 020-7491-4565
Victoria | 2 Cardinal Walk, SW1E 5AG | 020-7821-1450
Canary Wharf | Hertsmere Rd., E14 8JJ | 020-7987-9777
Islington | 9 Islington Green, N1 8DU | 020-7226-2555
Tower Bridge | Butlers Wharf Bldg. | 35 Shad Thames, SE1 2YG |
020-7378-1700
www.browns-restaurants.com

Providing a "homely atmosphere at any time of year", a "solid",
"straightforward" British menu and "quick in-and-out" service, this
"comfortable, family-friendly" national chain is a "reliable" choice
for an "easy-on-the-pocket" meal; depending on the location and
time, the atmosphere can oscillate from "quiet" to "lively and a bit
noisy", but most agree it's always a "useful standby".

Brumus *European*   ▽ 22 | 23 | 21 | £41

St. James's | Haymarket Hotel | 1 Suffolk Pl., SW1Y 4HX |
020-7470-4007 | www.firmdalehotels.com

At this recently revamped, all-day European in St. James's "funky"
Haymarket Hotel, guests and theatregoers enjoy "high-quality cooking" and "great-value set meals"; while service is usually "efficient", at
peak times you may have to "wait a while", so consider the bar, offering
"fine" tapas; P.S. "delicious scones" are the highlights of afternoon tea.

NEW Bubbledogs 🚫Ⓜ *Hot Dogs*   ▽ 18 | 19 | 20 | £37

Fitzrovia | 70 Charlotte St., W1T 4QG | 020-7637-7770 |
www.bubbledogs.co.uk

"Where else can you get good hot dogs with champagne?" than at
this "innovative", "reasonably priced" Charlotte Street concept with
"counter-type stool seating", "lovely" staff and "long queues" ("you
can't book"); even those who reckon they're "too old" for such a
"novelty" suggest you try it "at least once".

NEW Buddha-Bar ☀ *Asian*   - | - | - | E

Knightsbridge | 145 Knightsbridge, SW1X 7PA | 020-3667-5222 |
www.buddhabarlondon.com

The former Chicago Rib Shack in Knightsbridge has been transformed into this outpost of the snazzy international chain serving
high-end Pan-Asian fare that caters as much to exotic palates as it
does to Western tastes; inside, the dark, opulent space is bedecked
with Oriental lanterns and crystal Chinese dragons.

	FOOD	DECOR	SERVICE	COST

Buen Ayre *Argentinean* | 25 | 16 | 21 | £40

Hackney | 50 Broadway Mkt., E8 4QJ | 020-7275-9900 |
www.buenayre.co.uk

"Massive portions" of "perfectly cooked" Argentinean beef are best
"washed down with a hearty Malbec" from the "decent" wine list at
this "relaxed", "reasonably priced" *parrilla* in Hackney; despite the
"cramped", "brightly lit" quarters, it's "deservedly full" of diners who
"take their steak seriously", so "booking is a must".

The Bull & Last *British* | 24 | 18 | 21 | £41

Kentish Town | 168 Highgate Rd., NW5 1QS | 020-7267-3641 |
www.thebullandlast.co.uk

Expect "Scotch eggs to die for" and other "tempting" offerings on an
"imaginative" seasonal menu at this "high-calibre" Traditional British
gastropub with "top-end" prices and an "unpretentious" interior opposite Hampstead Heath in Kentish Town; booking is "essential",
especially at weekends when crowds swamp the place and occasionally "strain" the normally "helpful" service (upstairs is "quieter"); P.S. in summer, you can reserve an "awesome picnic hamper"
to take away.

Bumpkin *British* | 19 | 19 | 18 | £38

Stratford | Westfield Stratford City | 105-106 The Street, E20 1EN |
020-8221-9900
Chelsea | 119 Sydney St., SW3 6NR | 020-3730-9344 ●
Notting Hill | 209 Westbourne Park Rd., W11 1EA | 020-7243-9818 ●
South Kensington | 102 Old Brompton Rd., SW7 3RD | 020-7341-0802 ●
www.bumpkinuk.com

This "cute, rustic" bistro chainlet done out in "homey designer-
shabby" style doles out "reliable", "tasty" Modern Brit dishes, often
with an "organic" bent; if a few are "underwhelmed" due to what
they deem "pricey" bills for "ordinary" offerings, most are won over
by the "warm ambience" and "laid-back but efficient service".

Buona Sera ● *Italian* | 20 | 18 | 20 | £26

Clapham | 22-26 Northcote Rd., SW11 1NX | 020-7228-9925
Chelsea | 289A King's Rd., SW3 5EW | 020-7352-8827

"Families" and "groups of girls keen to catch up" populate these
"friendly" Chelsea and Clapham trattorias presenting "solid", "good-
value" pizza and Italian "staples"; the settings are "not flashy",
though "attentive" service and a "lively" vibe help to "bring the place
to life"; P.S. kids love the "novelty of climbing up ladders to dine" at
the King's Road branch.

Burger & Lobster *American* | 23 | 19 | 21 | £33

NEW **City** | Bow Bells Hse. | 1 Bread St., EC4M 9HH | 020-7248-1789 ⊠
NEW **Farringdon** | 38-42 St. John St., EC1M 4DL | 020-7490-9230 ⊠
Mayfair | 29 Clarges St., W1J 7EF | 020-7409-1699
Soho | 36 Dean St., W1D 4PS | 020-7432-4800
www.burgerandlobster.com

"Expect a long wait", as it's "always packed" and there are no reservations at this "effective" American chainlet with a "simple proposi-

tion": a choice of two "mouth-wateringly good" lobster dishes or a "delicious" burger with chips and a salad, all "good value for money"; service can be "hurried but friendly", and despite "unfussy" decor, the atmosphere is usually "lively".

Busaba Eathai *Thai*

| 23 | 20 | 19 | £24 |

Bloomsbury | 22 Store St., WC1E 7DF | 020-7299-7900
Covent Garden | 44 Floral St., WC2E 9DA | 020-7759-0088
Marylebone | 8-13 Bird St., W1U 1BU | 020-7518-8080
Leicester Square | 35 Panton St., SW1Y 4EA | 020-7930-0088
Soho | 106-110 Wardour St., W1F 0TR | 020-7255-8686
Shoreditch | 319 Old St., EC1V 9LG | 020-7729-0808
Stratford | Westfield Stratford City | 2 Stratford Pl., E20 1GL | 020-8221-8989
Chelsea | 358 King's Rd., SW3 5UZ | 020-7349-5488
Shepherd's Bush | Westfield Shopping Ctr. | Ariel Way, lower ground fl., W12 7GA | 020-3249-1919
www.busaba.com

"Well-executed Thai favourites" made from "quality" ingredients and served in "stylish" dark-wood, incense-fragranced surroundings mean fans "make no apologies for loving" this "reasonably priced", no-reservations chain; "don't be put off by the queues", as the "brisk but friendly" staff usually find spots at one of the shared tables "fast".

The Butcher & Grill *British*

| 20 | 18 | 19 | £34 |

Battersea | 39-41 Parkgate Rd., SW11 4NP | 020-7924-3999
Wimbledon | 33 High St., SW19 5BY | 020-8944-8269 Ⓜ
www.thebutcherandgrill.com

With a "butcher at the front and restaurant in the back", "carni-vores" are well catered for at this "large", casual Traditional British pair in Wimbledon and Battersea; "generous portions" and "value" prices mean it's "great for families", and as for the quality, while many feel that the "basics" are "done well", others say they "need improvement", just like sometimes "indifferent" service.

Butlers Wharf Chop House *British/Steak*

| 23 | 20 | 22 | £43 |

Tower Bridge | Butlers Wharf Bldg. | 36 Shad Thames, SE1 2YE | 020-7403-3403 | www.chophouse.co.uk

"Fabulous" British "classics" like roast beef with Yorkshire pudding (and of course charcoal-grilled steaks) are paired with a "fantastic wine selection" and "formal" though "friendly" service at this all-day venue; with "amazing views" of Tower Bridge (from the alfresco or window tables) thrown in, it's the sort place to "take an out-of-towner and watch their jaw drop" – "even those on a budget", who should check out the "superb-value" bar menu.

Byron ● *Burgers*

| 19 | 15 | 19 | £19 |

Covent Garden | 33-35 Wellington St., WC2E 7BN | 020-7420-9850
Leicester Square | 24-28 Charing Cross Rd., WC2H 0DT | 020-7557-9830
Canary Wharf | Cabot Pl. E., E14 4QT | 020-7715-9360
Islington | 341 Upper St., N1 0PB | 020-7704-7620
Greenwich | Greenwich Promenade, East Pavilion, SE10 9HT | 020-8269-0800

(continued)

Byron

Bayswater | 103 Westbourne Grove, W2 4UW | 020-7243-4226
Chelsea | 300 King's Rd., SW3 5UH | 020-7352-6040
Kensington | 222 Kensington High St., W8 7RG | 020-7361-1717
Shepherd's Bush | Westfield Shopping Ctr. | Ariel Way, mezzanine, W12 7GF | 020-8743-7755
South Kensington | 75 Gloucester Rd., SW7 4SS | 020-7244-0700
www.byronhamburgers.com
Additional locations throughout London

This "relaxed", U.S.-style hamburger chain's menu might be "simple", but there are "endless" toppings that allow you to customize the "cracking burgers", complemented by "impressive" milkshakes; fronted by "genuine", "accommodating" staff, it's a hit with "happy families at weekends", while weekday evenings often see a post-work crowd drop by for a "quick bite" and a craft beer or two.

Cabana *Brazilian*   21 | 18 | 19 | £27

Holborn | 7 Central St. Giles Piazza, WC2H 8AB | 020-7632-9630
Stratford | Westfield Stratford City | Montfichet Rd., E20 1GL | 020-8536-2650
NEW Shepherd's Bush | Westfield White City | Westfield, 1054-1055 Ariel Way, W12 7GB | 020-3249-1920
www.cabana-brasil.com

"Something different" comes in the form of "yummy" Brazilian barbecue plus "delish" sides and salads at this "funky", "colourful" chain; service is typically "attentive", prices are relatively "inexpensive" and "tasty" cocktails like caipirinhas "complete the experience".

Café Boheme ● *French*   18 | 20 | 17 | £34

Soho | 13-17 Old Compton St., W1D 5JQ | 020-7734-0623 | www.cafeboheme.co.uk

"Always packed" with an "interesting bohemian crowd", this zinc-barred, mosaic-floored, all-day Soho bistro serves traditional, moderately priced French fare that "won't disappoint"; live music at weekends, pavement seating "perfect for people-watching" and "amazing" cocktails (served, like the food, until 2.30 AM) help fuel the "great vibe".

Café des Amis ● *French*   18 | 17 | 18 | £38

Covent Garden | 11-14 Hanover Pl., WC2E 9JP | 020-7379-3444 | www.cafedesamis.co.uk

For a "quick pre-theatre meal" "away from the crowds" of Covent Garden, ticket-holders "heartily recommend" this "relaxed" French "standby", despite a bill that is "perhaps a bit overpriced"; what's more, service is mostly "attentive even when the restaurant is busy" and particularly in the "cosy" downstairs wine bar, where "lighter" options are offered.

Cafe East ⊅ *Vietnamese*   24 | 8 | 13 | £16

Surrey Quays | 100 Redriff Rd., SE16 7LH | 020-7252-1212
It may be in "the middle of a car park" in Surrey Quays, but when it comes to "delicious" pho, this Vietnamese spot is "the real deal",

and "the number of diners show it"; if you can look past the "simplistic setting and slightly lacklustre service", it's "worth a visit", not least because it's "affordable"; P.S. cash only.

Café Japan ⓜ *Japanese*   26 | 14 | 21 | £32

Golders Green | 626 Finchley Rd., NW11 7RR | 020-8455-6854
"Large slices" of "cracking sushi and sashimi" are accompanied by "obscure Japanese beers" at this "well-priced" Golders Green cafe where the setting is "modest" and the "welcome" is "warm"; just be sure to "go early or make reservations", because "word is out" among "young North Londoners", hence it's "always crowded".

Café Med *Mediterranean*   19 | 17 | 20 | £34

St. John's Wood | 21 Loudoun Rd., NW8 0NB | 020-7625-1222 | www.cafemed.co.uk
When St. John's Wood "locals" "can't be bothered to cook", they turn to this "reliable neighbourhood stalwart" for "tasty" "home-style" Mediterranean meals at the "right price"; highlights of the "casual" setting include "outdoor seating for warm evenings", "a blazing fire" in winter and "helpful staff" the whole year round.

Cafe Pacifico ❶ *Mexican*   20 | 17 | 19 | £28

Covent Garden | 5 Langley St., WC2H 9JA | 020-7379-7728 | www.cafepacifico-laperla.com
Reflecting on the last 30 years, this "fun, noisy" Covent Garden cantina has been serving up "big portions" of "tasty" Mexican fare at prices that "won't give your wallet a belting"; but it's the "fantastic atmosphere", fuelled by "hot music", a "great choice of tequila" and "prompt" service, that really make it a such a "popular" "hangout".

Café Spice Namasté ⓧ *Indian*   25 | 20 | 23 | £40

City | 16 Prescot St., E1 8AZ | 020-7488-9242 | www.cafespice.co.uk
Chef-owner Cyrus Todiwala's moderately priced City stalwart offers a "real tour of the Indian palate", with "excellent ingredients" and "distinctive flavours", "sometimes with a twist"; although not everyone is enamoured with the decor, "good service" compensates.

Caffe Caldesi *Italian*   18 | 15 | 16 | £38

Marylebone | 118 Marylebone Ln., W1U 2QF | 020-7487-0753 | www.caldesi.com
"Well located" for "the ladies who lunch", this "cosy" Italian "in a little lane off the main Marylebone drag" specialises in "nicely prepared" Tuscan plates, just like its "joy" of a cousin in Bray; however, some feel that it "should be better" given the "posh" prices, recommending you stick to "the bar area downstairs, which is supposedly a bit cheaper than upstairs".

Cambio de Tercio *Spanish*   24 | 18 | 19 | £51

South Kensington | 163 Old Brompton Rd., SW5 0LJ | 020-7244-8970 | www.cambiodetercio.co.uk
This "classy" South Ken haunt impresses with its "delicious" Spanish food, particularly the "stand-out" "sweet and juicy" eight-hour roasted tomatoes; even though the "bill mounts up pretty quickly",

the "friendly service" and "bright, fun" setting (the "flamboyant" decor may be "an acquired taste") seem to keep it "quite busy with locals".

Camden Brasserie *European* | 23 | 18 | 20 | £35

Camden Town | 9-11 Jamestown Rd., NW1 7BW | 020-7482-2114 | www.camdenbrasserie.co.uk

A "second home" to locals, this "friendly" Camden "landmark" serves up "reliable" Modern European brasserie fare – including "huge bowls of frites" – suitable for "quick, easy meals"; some quibble that although "they try with the wallpaper" (resembling shelves of books), the decor is slightly "lacking", in contrast to the service, which is "efficient".

Camino *Spanish* | 22 | 20 | 19 | £35

NEW **City** | 15 Mincing Ln., EC3R 7BD | 020-7841-7335 **Ⓢ**
City | 33 Blackfriars Ln., EC4V 6EP | 020-7125-0930 **Ⓢ**
Canary Wharf | 28 Westferry Circus, E14 8RR | 020-7239-9077
King's Cross | 3 Varnishers Yard, Regents Quarter, N1 9FD | 020-7841-7331
www.camino.uk.com

Hispanophiles find this "atmospheric" Spanish tapas chainlet "usually packed" with people sampling the "yummy" small plates and "incredible" wines; the "noise level" is a bit of a "drawback" for some, but most just focus on the "helpful" service, "decent pricing", "brilliant" weekend brunch and, at Westferry Circus, "buzzy fun" on the deck in summer.

Canela *Brazilian/Portuguese* ∇ | 21 | 18 | 19 | £21

Covent Garden | 33 Earlham St., WC2H 9LS | 020-7240-6926 | www.canelacafe.com

Drawing on the flavours of Portugal and Brazil, this Covent Garden eatery is a "fun and easy" option for a relatively "cheap" meal; the "cosy" setting is notable for a glass-fronted cabinet in which desserts are temptingly displayed.

Canteen *British* | 18 | 17 | 16 | £27

Marylebone | 55 Baker St., W1U 8EW | 0845-686-1122
Canary Wharf | Park Pavilion | 40 Canada Sq., E14 5FW | 0845-686-1122
Spitalfields | 2 Crispin Pl., E1 6DW | 0845-686-1122
South Bank | Royal Festival Hall | Belvedere Rd., SE1 8XX | 0845-686-1122
www.canteen.co.uk

A "basic selection" of Traditional British "comfort food and school dinner–style desserts" is dished up in a "modern", "communal" "cafeteria setting with table service" at this "casual" chainlet; however, a number of respondents "like the idea more" than the experience, citing staff who "vary" ("upbeat" vs. "unfriendly") and the fact that it "seems odd to be paying [relatively speaking] lots for childhood staples".

Cantina del Ponte *Italian* ∇ | 19 | 19 | 20 | £46

Tower Bridge | Butlers Wharf Bldg. | 36 Shad Thames, SE1 2YE | 020-7403-5403 | www.cantinadelponte.co.uk

Fans of this rustic Thameside Italian claim that it's "hard to criticise" – maybe because of its "terrific views over Tower Bridge" and its "great location" which boasts outdoor seating in the summer; "on-the-ball" staff serve the "hearty, satisfying" fare which is also available in "great-value" set menus at lunchtime.

Cantina Laredo ● *Mexican*   23 | 19 | 21 | £34

Covent Garden | St. Martin's Courtyard | 10 Upper St. Martin's Ln., WC2H 7PU | 020-7420-0630 | www.cantinalaredo.co.uk
"When you need your Mexican fix", this light and bright Covent Garden cantina charges to the rescue with "upmarket, tastefully prepared" dishes starring "excellent guacamole made fresh at the table"; "pricey top-shelf" tequila can bump up the bill, and normally "wonderful service" can go "to pot when it's busy", but drink enough "amazing margaritas" and you won't care.

Cantina Vinopolis ⧄ *International*   ▽ 19 | 22 | 19 | £35

South Bank | Vinopolis Museum | 1 Bank End, SE1 9BU | 020-7940-8333 | www.cantinavinopolis.com
After a "relaxing day" at Bankside wine museum Vinopolis, tipplers "retreat" to the "lovely surroundings" of this International eatery with vaulted ceilings; the "locally sourced" grub offered up by "accommodating" staff is "delicious" enough (and "good value" if you stick to the set menu), but you really "come here for the wines" – and they "do not disappoint".

Cape Town Fish   23 | 19 | 21 | £34
Market *International/Seafood*

Soho | 5-6 Argyll St., W1F 7TE | 020-7437-1143 | www.capetownfishmarket.co.uk
If you're angling for "top-quality fish" in "the heart of the West End", this large, slick, neon-lit Soho diner vends a "wide variety" of "wonderful tasting" International seafood dishes with "South African flair", all brought to table by "friendly" staff; an "extensive sushi" selection comes via conveyor belt at the bar (where "creative cocktails" are crafted), while all of the wares are "value for money".

Caraffini ●⧄ *Italian*   22 | 18 | 24 | £46

Chelsea | 61-63 Lower Sloane St., SW1 8DH | 020-7259-0235 | www.caraffini.co.uk
"Long-time repeat customers" are "welcomed" by "charming" staff at this "reliable" Chelsea Italian with "old-world ambience" and a "sunny terrace"; the "delicious", "comforting classics" and "good selection of wines" are all "reasonably priced", guaranteeing that it remains "hard to get into", so "make sure to make reservations".

Caravaggio ⧄ *Italian*   19 | 18 | 18 | £45

City | 107-112 Leadenhall St., EC3A 4DP | 020-7626-6206 | www.etruscarestaurants.com
Set in a high-ceilinged former City banking hall, this upscale Italian gets nods for its "attentive" service, "lovely" food and "great" wine list; it does have critics who pan it for being "old-fashioned" and "ordinary" – however, for a "reliable" "business" meal, most attest that you "won't go wrong".

	FOOD	DECOR	SERVICE	COST

Caravan *International*
24 | 22 | 19 | £27

Clerkenwell | 11-13 Exmouth Mkt., EC1R 4QD | 020-7833-8115 | www.caravanonexmouth.co.uk
NEW King's Cross | Granary Bldg. | 1 Granary Sq., N1C 4AA | 020-7101-7661 | www.caravankingscross.co.uk

There's an "urban industrial feel" to this "versatile" cafe-diner duo with branches in Exmouth Market and a "converted warehouse" in Kings Cross, both offering a moderately priced International menu that includes "amazing" brunches and "beautifully presented" small plates; although the service "isn't anything to write home about", the "cool" "buzz" draws people back "again and again".

Carluccio's *Italian*
16 | 15 | 16 | £27

Bloomsbury | 1 The Brunswick, WC1N 1AF | 020-7833-4130 ◐
Bloomsbury | 8 Market Pl., W1W 8AG | 020-7636-2228 ◐
Farringdon | 12 W. Smithfield, EC1A 9JR | 020-7329-5904
Marylebone | St. Christopher's Pl., W1U 1AY | 020-7935-5927 ◐
Islington | 305-307 Upper St., N1 2TU | 020-7359-8167
Wandsworth | 537-539 Garratt Ln., SW18 4SR | 020-8947-4651
Putney | Putney Wharf, SW15 2JQ | 020-8789-0591
Chelsea | 236 Fulham Rd., SW10 9NB | 020-7376-5960
Ealing | 5-6 The Green, W5 5DA | 020-8566-4458
NEW Waterloo | Waterloo Station, Balcony, SE1 7LY | 020-7928-2702 ◐
www.carluccios.com
Additional locations throughout London

This "relaxed", "child-friendly" Italian chain with a "decent" menu of "simple" dishes may offer "no surprises", but it's "reliable" for everything from "business breakfasts" to weekend lunches, and "well priced" too; perhaps because it's generally "crowded", service is sometimes "slow", though staff are at least "cheerful".

Carob Tree Ⓜ *Greek/Mediterranean*
23 | 17 | 23 | £33

Kentish Town | 15 Highgate Rd., NW5 1QX | 020-7267-9880

"Loyal" Kentish Town locals make it "hard to get a table" at this "bustling", "rustic" Greek-focused Mediterranean featuring "delicious homemade" mezze alongside an "impressive" choice of "first-class" fish in a "smart but austere" space; "attentive", "friendly" service is the norm, and as for the bill, it's usually "reasonable".

NEW Casa Negra ◑ *Mexican*
- | - | - | M

Shoreditch | 54-56 Great Eastern St., EC2A 3QR | 020-7033-7360 | www.casanegra.co.uk

Behind a mysterious black facade in Shoreditch, this midpriced Mexican offers a mix of traditional and original dishes; the dark, wood-panelled room has rudimentary tables and quirky fold-away chairs, while the kitchen is home to a large communal table.

Cassis Bistro *French/Mediterranean*
22 | 20 | 21 | £52

South Kensington | 232 Brompton Rd., SW3 2BB | 020-7581-1101 | www.cassisbistro.co.uk

"If you're a lady who lunches or you just want to masquerade as one", patronise this "relaxed, elegant", "Mediterranean-chic" South

Kensington bistro specialising in "delicious" Provençal plates; though a handful of respondents bemoan "ear-splitting noise" ("turn the music down!"), most of the criticism is aimed at the "overpriced wine list" – good thing there's "attentive service" to "smooth" things out.

Caviar House & Prunier *Seafood* | 23 | 22 | 19 | £74 |

Piccadilly | 161 Piccadilly, W1J 9HS | 020-7409-0445 | www.caviar-house.ch

"Luxurious snacks" to "re-energise the soul" is how surveyors describe the caviar-centric seafood offered at this sleek, glass-fronted Piccadilly spot where "everything is superb", including "attentive service"; it's expectedly "expensive" (and "worth every penny"), so maybe it's best to "let someone take you".

Cây Tre *Vietnamese* | 22 | 14 | 15 | £25 |

Soho | 42-43 Dean St., W1, 4PZ | 020-7317-9118 | www.caytresoho.co.uk
Hoxton | 301 Old St., EC1V 9LA | 020-7729-8662 | www.vietnamesekitchen.co.uk

"Exotic, intriguing, mouth-watering tastes" of Vietnam provide "filling" sustenance at this "excellent-value" eatery in Hoxton and its newer Soho offshoot; it's "worth the queue" as long as you "focus on the food" rather than the "indifferent, rushed" staff, "lack of decor" and "noisy atmosphere".

Cecconi's ● *Italian* | 23 | 21 | 22 | £60 |

Mayfair | 5 Burlington Gdns., W1S 3EP | 020-7434-1500 | www.cecconis.co.uk

"You'll feel fabulous as you step through the doors" of this all-day Italian "scene" in Mayfair, where the "corner tables with wall-to-wall velvet" are tops for "people-watching", but the bar where "you don't need a reservation" runs a close second; "old-school" staff are "on top of everything" as they ferry the fare, which is as "delicious" as it is "expensive" (a contingent calls it "overpriced").

Cellar Gascon ●▣ *French* | ▽ 23 | 21 | 20 | £52 |

Farringdon | 59 W. Smithfield, EC1A 9DS | 020-7600-7561 | www.clubgascon.com

Southwest-focused French "nibbles of the highest quality" take centre stage at this "cosy" "informal" "little brother" of Club Gascon (also in Farringdon); things can get "loud" as the place fills up – and people partake in the "wonderful" wine selection – yet the atmosphere remains remarkably "civilised".

Ceviche ● *Peruvian* | ▽ 27 | 20 | 20 | £33 |

Soho | 17 Frith St., W1D 4RG | 020-7292-2040 | www.cevicheuk.com

"Fresh, tangy and exciting food" involving marinated raw fish and "succulent beef" create an "intense" flavour "fiesta" at this "buzzy, little", moderately priced Soho space that "sticks strongly to its Peruvian theme"; a "plethora of pisco drinks" help pass the time while you're waiting for a table, and once installed, service can be "a wee bit chaotic", but staff are "friendly".

	FOOD	DECOR	SERVICE	COST

Chabrot Bistro des Amis *French*   20 | 16 | 23 | £49

Knightsbridge | 9 Knightsbridge Green, SW1X 7QL | 020-7225-2238 |
www.chabrot.co.uk

At this "tiny" two-storey bistro "just a diamond's throw" from
Knightsbridge's multimillion-pound flats, "friendly, professional"
staff serve up "traditional" French bistro dishes with "satisfying flavours" and a "wine list to match"; it's "not cheap", but it's "good
value" for the well-heeled locals.

NEW Chabrot Bistrot des Halles ⧄ *French* – | – | – | E

Farringdon | 62-63 Long Ln., EC1A 9EJ | 020-7796-4550 |
www.chabrot.com

On the edge of Smithfield Market in Farringdon, this expensive
French bistro proffers an earthy, meat-dominated menu of sharing
starters and robust regional dishes; scarlet brushed-velvet banquettes, simple wooden tables and evocative monochrome photography give it a cosy, comfy feel.

Cha Cha Moon *Chinese*   18 | 17 | 16 | £19

Soho | 15-21 Ganton St., W1F 9BN | 020-7297-9800 |
www.chachamoon.com

"Squeeze" around a communal table and "watch your noodles being
pulled in the open kitchen" at this bamboo-ceilinged Chinese eatery
in Soho; though there are complaints of "forgetful" service, most applaud the "tasty", "quickly prepared" grub – which everyone agrees
is "a steal for London".

Chakra *Indian*   ▽ 23 | 21 | 22 | £46

Notting Hill | 157-159 Notting Hill Gate, W11 3LF | 020-7229-2115 |
www.chakralondon.com

Fans herald this Notting Hill Indian as a "triumph", praising its "light,
refreshing" cuisine and quality service; though the sophisticated
setting replete with tufted leather walls and banquettes is matched
by upscale pricing, there's still value to be found, namely at the all-
you-can-eat weekend lunches.

Champor-Champor *Malaysian*   22 | 21 | 20 | £45

Tower Bridge | 62-64 Weston St., SE1 3QJ | 020-7403-4600 |
www.champor-champor.com

"Flavourful" fusion cuisine is "masterfully prepared" at this "intimate", somewhat "expensive" Malaysian in Tower Bridge which has
a "quirky, eclectic" interior decorated with souvenirs from far-flung
lands; if you can snare it, romantics "highly recommend the candlelit balcony for two", but at any table, "friendly" staff help shape
a "memorable" experience.

The Chancery ⧄ *European*   ▽ 24 | 20 | 22 | £50

Holborn | 9 Cursitor St., EC4A 1LL | 020-3589-2096 |
www.thechancery.co.uk

"Perfect for client entertaining", this "tiny", "lovely" Modern European
"hidden" in the Holborn backstreets boasts "formal service" that
"runs like a well-oiled machine" as it ferries fare that "impresses

with technique and flavour"; tables that are "small and close to-gether" ruffle some feathers, but "affordable" prix fixes for both lunch and dinner invariably please.

Chapters All Day Dining *European*   24 | 20 | 23 | £45
Blackheath | 43-45 Montpelier Vale, SE3 0TJ | 020-8333-2666 | www.chaptersrestaurants.com

"On a nice day, it's hard to get a better location" than the alfresco area "looking out over the Heath", but the "elegant, modern" interior is its own draw at this all-day Blackheath Modern European where the fare is "superb", especially the "cut-above" Josper oven-cooked meats; "it's not the cheapest", but with "personable" service thrown into the mix, fans are "more than happy to pay the price".

Charlotte's Bistro ◑ *European*   25 | 21 | 24 | £42
Chiswick | 6 Turnham Green Terr., W4 1QP | 020-8742-3590
Charlotte's Place ◑ *European*
Ealing | 16 St. Matthew's Rd., W5 3JT | 020-8567-7541
www.charlottes.co.uk

"Beautifully set on the common" in Ealing and by Turnham Green tube, these "gems" provide "fabulous", "seasonal, locally sourced" Modern European cuisine, "fantastic cocktails" and "friendly, knowledgeable" service in "smart" settings; most people find "great value for money" here, but "if the price seems a little high" to you, there are "cost-conscious" set menus for both lunch and dinner.

Cheyne Walk Brasserie *French*   20 | 21 | 17 | £59
Chelsea | 50 Cheyne Walk, SW3 5LR | 020-7376-8787 | www.cheynewalkbrasserie.com

"After a pleasant walk through a quiet section of Chelsea", the "airy" dining room of this "neighbourhood gem" makes a "romantic date destination", thanks to river views and an "impressive" French menu that includes "delicious" meats cooked on the "open wood-fired oven" (you'll smell "plenty of rosemary"); if there's one criticism, it's the "high prices", but at least service is mostly "friendly".

Chez Bruce *British/Mediterranean*   28 | 22 | 26 | £63
Wandsworth | 2 Bellevue Rd., SW17 7EG | 020-8672-0114 | www.chezbruce.co.uk

It's "well worth the fight to get a table" at chef Bruce Poole's upscale Wandsworth dining room, which makes the most of "quality" ingredients to create an "elegant" British-Mediterranean set menu that "never disappoints"; it's all delivered in "professional" fashion, epitomised by the "star sommelier" who will lead you through the "tremendous" wine list (which comes at a "reasonable mark-up"); P.S. if your budget won't stretch, try the "far, far cheaper" weekday lunch, "a great deal".

Chez Gérard ⓩ *French*   - | - | - | E
City | 64 Bishopsgate, EC2N 4AW | 020-7588-1200 | www.chezgerard.co.uk

This longstanding City steak-frites specialist (no longer a chain after the sale of the other branches) has been spruced up, and its reason-

| | FOOD | DECOR | SERVICE | COST |

ably expensive French menu has been augmented by a set-price 'steak express' option (also served at the bar at lunchtime); besides the airy, high-ceilinged dining room, there's a macho-ish basement bar with a globe-trotting wine list.

NEW **Chicken Shop** ● *Chicken*   – | – | – | I

Kentish Town | 79 Highgate Rd., NW5 1TL | 020-3310-2020 | www.chickenshop.com

Sitting below the Kentish Town outpost of Pizza East, this no-bookings rotisserie joint offers free-range chicken – served in quarter, half or whole portions – plus a choice of four simple sides and three puddings; the look is part-American diner (bar seating, Formica tables, red-and-white chequered floor) and part-farmhouse kitchen.

Chilango *Mexican*   21 | 16 | 19 | £12

City | 142 Fleet St., EC4A 2BP | 020-7353-6761 ⑤
City | 32 Brushfield St., E1 6AA | 020-3246-0086
City | 64 London Wall, EC2M 5TP | 020-7628-7663 ⑤
Holborn | 76 Chancery Ln., WC2A 1AA | 020-7430-1231 ⑤
Islington | 27 Upper St., N1 0PN | 020-7704-2123
www.chilango.co.uk

Even the famished "struggle to finish the huge burritos" at this "trendy" Mexican chain that "hits the spot" for a lunchtime treat or a "post-pub snack" with "well-priced", "design-your-own" options "packed with flavour"; "super-speedy" staff get you "quickly" in and out of the "practical" settings or you can just take away instead.

China Tang ● *Chinese*   21 | 24 | 21 | £70

Mayfair | The Dorchester | 53 Park Ln., W1K 1QA | 020-7629-9988 | www.dorchesterhotel.com

Underneath The Dorchester Hotel, this "exquisite" space evokes a "chic" "private club" in "'20s Shanghai", where "tuxedoed staff" serve "international business types" and their "well-dressed" dates "upscale", "excessively expensive" Cantonese fare; "duck in some manner is a must", but the "dim sum is just as good", as are "divine cocktails" at the "packed bar".

Chisou *Japanese*   23 | 18 | 21 | £48

Mayfair | 4 Princes St., W1B 2LE | 020-7629-3931
Chiswick | 1-4 Barley Mow Passage, W4 4PH | 020-8994-3636 ⑤ Ⓜ
Knightsbridge | 31 Beauchamp Pl., SW3 1NU | 020-3155-0005
www.chisourestaurant.com

"Deluxe, reliable sushi" is "surprisingly good value" at this "relaxed" Japanese chainlet with decor that's "nothing memorable" yet sufficiently "functional"; a notable "business-lunch" option, it's also a "busy" dinner destination thanks in part to the "knowledgeable" staff and a "sommelier with a great command of the sake list".

Chiswell Street Dining Rooms ● *British*   ∇ 22 | 24 | 22 | £46

City | 56 Chiswell St., EC1 4SA | 020-7614-0177 | www.chiswellstreetdining.com

The owners of The Botanist and The Gun are behind this "charming" dining room in the City (close to the Barbican), with "beautiful" green-and-white decor, "friendly" staff and all-day Modern British fare; it's "good for breakfast", "buzzy at lunchtime" and suitable for "business dinners" too, but a bit "pricey".

NEW Chooks *American*

— | — | — | I

Muswell Hill | 43 The Broadway, N10 3HA | 020-8444-5383 | www.chooks.me

The brainchild of Gideon Joffe, son of the founders of the Giraffe chain, this no-reservations American diner in Muswell Hill offers fried or grilled chicken by the quarter, half or whole along with other U.S. comfort foods, including ribs, burgers and cheesecake; the stripped-back space has a casual vibe and retro styling, with neon lights and vintage chairs; P.S. there's also a brunch and a kids menu.

Chor Bizarre ● *Indian*

25 | 22 | 21 | £39

Mayfair | 16 Albemarle St., W1S 4HW | 020-7629-9802 | www.chorbizarre.com

"Flea-market treasures" create an "exotic", "whimsical" environment for "highly spiced", "scrumptious" Indian delicacies at this "cosy" Mayfair offshoot of the New Delhi institution; service can be "slow", but staff are wholly "warm", and thankfully the whole experience is "not too stressful on the wallet".

Christopher's *American/Steak*

— | — | — | E

Covent Garden | 18 Wellington St., WC2E 7DD | 020-7240-4222 | www.christophersgrill.com

Well into its third decade, this expensive Covent Garden steakhouse sports an art deco-style look in its airy first floor dining room where the varied American menu is flush with surf n' turf classics (prime steaks and Maryland crab cakes), while the ground floor Martini Bar serves an all-day menu of snacks and salads; there's also a private room for parties.

Chuen Cheng Ku ● *Chinese*

20 | 10 | 14 | £22

Chinatown | 17 Wardour St., W1D 6PJ | 020-7437-1398 | www.chuenchengku.co.uk

"Dumplings that look like clouds" and other "delicious dim sum" delivered on trolleys supplement Cantonese specialties like "melt-in-your-mouth crispy duck" at this Chinatown "stalwart"; staff vacillate between "polite" and "curt", and the "scruffy" surroundings look "about 100 years old", but most grievances are forgiven in light of the "modest prices".

Churchill Arms *Thai*

21 | 20 | 17 | £19

Kensington | 119 Kensington Church St., W8 7LN | 020-7727-4242 | www.fullers.co.uk

With its "old English" "boozer" setting, "decorated with Churchill memorabilia" and "hanging baskets" that "spill over with flowers and foliage", this Kensington pub proffers an "unexpected" menu rife with "scrumptious", "spicy" Thai plates at "economical" prices; "fast" (and "friendly") staff facilitate the "high turnover" necessary to service all those "standing at the bar" "waiting for a table", so don't expect to linger over your meal.

	FOOD	DECOR	SERVICE	COST

Chutney Mary ● *Indian*   25 | 23 | 22 | £48
Chelsea | 535 King's Rd., SW10 0SZ | 020-7351-3113 |
www.chutneymary.com
"Artfully prepared", "flavoursome" food and "well-made" cocktails
served in "large, colourful" environs characterise this "sophisticated, upmarket" King's Road Indian, "not your typical curry house
by any means"; the service is "friendly and efficient", which when
coupled with the "relaxed atmosphere" explains why many "can't
wait" to return.

Chutneys ● *Indian/Vegetarian*   23 | 16 | 19 | £20
Euston | 124 Drummond St., NW1 2PA | 020-7388-0604 |
www.chutneyseuston.co.uk
The "fantastic" all-you-can-eat vegetarian buffet (which even "includes a sweet") is a major draw at this "inexpensive" Indian in bi-
level Euston digs; the decor may be average, but the "friendly",
"helpful" staff are well regarded by some.

Ciao Bella ● *Mediterranean*   23 | 18 | 21 | £26
Bloomsbury | 86-90 Lamb's Conduit St., WC1N 3LZ | 020-7242-4119 |
www.ciaobellarestaurant.co.uk
"Always packed-to-the-rafters", this Bloomsbury trattoria provides
"massive portions" of "yummy" Med fare served by "fast", "friendly"
staff in an "entertaining family atmosphere"; a wine list that "exceeds
expectations" and a "resident pianist" that entertains nightly add to
the "charm", but its best aspect may be the "not-expensive" bill.

Cigala *Spanish*   20 | 16 | 19 | £38
Bloomsbury | 54 Lamb's Conduit St., WC1N 3LW | 020-7405-1717 |
www.cigala.co.uk
If you're planning on indulging in the "lovely tapas" and "hearty" paella at this "hyped" Spanish destination in Bloomsbury, "get there
early, as it fills up quickly"; a few can "only afford these prices once
in a while", but some "reasonable" varieties can be found among the
"excellent" wine and brandy selection, and a "warm welcome" is
part of the deal.

Cigalon 🗷 *French*   ▽ 22 | 22 | 21 | £49
Holborn | 115 Chancery Ln., WC2A 1PP | 020-7242-8373 |
www.cigalon.co.uk
"Robust flavours" from Provence abound at this "intimate", "bright"
skylit venue "in the heart of the legal district" in Holborn, where the
"well-executed" fare is complemented by a wine list that also "flies the
flag" for the region; with the added advantages of "excellent service",
"reasonable" à la carte prices and "bargain" set menus, it's no wonder supporters peg it as "an option for any time and any occasion".

Cinnamon Club 🗷 *Indian*   26 | 25 | 23 | £62
Westminster | Old Westminster Library | 30-32 Great Smith St.,
SW1P 3BU | 020-7222-2555 | www.cinnamonclub.com
"There's a real sense of drama" about this former library in
Westminster converted into a "posh" Indian, offering "original"

dishes, "cooked with real passion"; during a parliament session, expect to find "politicos" and "lobbyists" appreciating the "exemplary" service, whether in the dining room or in the book-lined entrance bar where the cinnamon Bellini is a "wonderful" way to kick things off.

Cinnamon Kitchen ●🗷 *Indian* | 24 | 21 | 21 | £42 |

City | 9 Devonshire Sq., EC2M 4WY | 020-7626-5000 |
www.cinnamon-kitchen.com

"Tucked away in a tranquil corner of the City" under the Devonshire Square atrium, this "stylish", "upscale" offshoot of the Cinnamon Club "brilliantly reinterprets" Indian "classics"; service is generally "attentive", while the downstairs terrace shakes up some "creative" cocktails – although watch your step, some suggest "they are stronger than usual".

Circus ●🗷Ⓜ *Asian* | 18 | 23 | 18 | £46 |

Covent Garden | 27-29 Endell St., WC2H 9BA | 020-7420-9300 |
www.circus-london.co.uk

"Fire-eating acrobats in sequins" "prance down the long table" and "voluptuous lovelies gyrate in hoops mere feet from you" at this "quirky" "opulent Tom Dixon–designed" Covent Garden "cabaret" where a team of "great" staff deliver Pan-Asian plates; the "food is good, but definitely not the main event", which is why some deem it "pricey for what you get" – notwithstanding the "awesome cocktails".

Citrus *Italian* | 21 | 19 | 19 | £41 |

Piccadilly | Park Lane Hotel | 112 Piccadilly, W1J 7BX | 020-7290-7364 |
www.citrusrestaurant.co.uk

"Decent", "fancy" Italian cuisine is served in an "informal" atmosphere at this Piccadilly hotel dining room with a "convenient" location "across from Green Park"; what's more, it's "surprisingly affordable" given the "posh minimalist decor" featuring black-and-white-portraiture wallpaper by Fornasetti, "brilliant" alfresco seating and "above-average" service.

Clarke's *British* | 25 | 18 | 23 | £61 |

Kensington | 124 Kensington Church St., W8 4BH | 020-7221-9225 |
www.sallyclarke.com

"Wonderfully selected" "farm-to-table" ingredients are whipped into "complex flavours" at this "relaxed", "reliable" Kensington Modern Brit "star" where chef-owner Sally Clarke usually "can be seen behind the stoves"; also to be found in the bi-level setting are "understated elegance" in the decor, "efficient" staff and a "decent wine list", adding up to a "sophisticated" experience whose "loyal following" feels it's "worth every pound – and you'll spend lots of them".

NEW Clockjack Oven 🗷 *American/Chicken* | - | - | - | M |

Soho | 14 Denman St., W1D 7HJ | 020-7287-5111 |
www.clockjackoven.com

Perch at the bar and you'll spot the Tudor-style spit-roasting device that gives this industrial-style, slate-floored Soho American its name; otherwise, grab a non-reservable spot at one of the communal blonde wood tables to sample sensibly priced free-range chicken, sourced from Brittany then rotisseried and served in a sub, a salad or solo.

C London ● *Italian* | 23 | 21 | 22 | £73 |

Mayfair | 23-25 Davies St., W1K 3DE | 020-7399-0500 | www.crestaurant.co.uk

"The paparazzi outside" this "famous" Davies Street Italian confirm that it's still a "hotspot" for "people-watching" a "diverse" "parade" of "hedge-fund managers", "*X Factor*" contestants and the like; the "smart", "vibrant" setting boasts "a lot of character" and "charming" staff, and as for the food, it "pleases" – as it should do for being so "extravagantly priced".

Clos Maggiore *French* | 25 | 27 | 24 | £57 |

Covent Garden | 33 King St., WC2E 8JD | 020-7379-9696 | www.closmaggiore.com

"Romantics" attracted to this "magical" Modern French close to the Covent Garden theatre belt find the "lovely atmosphere", open fireplace and garden room "charming" and the service "efficient"; the "elaborate" menu of "excellent" food and wine (the latter including many half bottles) can be "expensive", but the prix fixe, available at lunch and pre-theatre, is "superb value".

NEW The Clove Club ⧉ *British* | - | - | - | E |

Shoreditch | Shoreditch Town Hall | 380 Old St., EC1V 9LT | 020 7729-6496 | www.thecloveclub.com

Isaac McHale (of the Young Turks collective and formerly of The Ledbury and Noma) serves Modern British cuisine conjured from unusual U.K.-sourced ingredients at this Shoreditch crowd-funded project; in the simple, high-ceilinged, wood-heavy main restaurant, the open kitchen sends out a pricey set tasting menu, while the adjacent bar offers up a more moderately priced selection of sharing plates.

Club Gascon ⧉ *French* | 27 | 22 | 23 | £71 |

Farringdon | 57 W. Smithfield, EC1A 9DS | 020-7600-6144 | www.clubgascon.com

"Innovative, well-presented" dishes make Pascal Aussignac's slice of Southwest France in Farringdon a "true standout", and the tasting menu paired with "excellent", "unusual" wines is a real "delight"; "accommodating" service and a "romantic" environment help make it a "great place for a special night or celebration", all for a price that's "decent considering the quality".

Cocomaya *Bakery* | ∇ 24 | 21 | 17 | £16 |

King's Cross | 35 Connaught St., W2 2AF | 020-7706-2883
Bayswater | 3 Porchester Pl., W2 2BS | 020-7706-2770
Knightsbridge | 186 Pavilion Rd., SW1X 0BJ | 020-7730-8395
www.cocomaya.co.uk

This "lovely, homely" bakery chainlet is the kind of place parents pop in for an "after drop-off coffee and after-school cake with the kids", or even a "delicious" "light lunch or afternoon tea"; the seating areas are "small", so a few just stop by to grab some "to-die-for chocolates".

	FOOD	DECOR	SERVICE	COST

NEW Colbert ● *French* ▽ 17 | 19 | 19 | £47

Chelsea | 50-52 Sloane Sq., SW1W 8AX | 020-7730-2804 |
www.colbertchelsea.com

Feeling "like it's been there forever", this somewhat pricey French
newcomer in Chelsea is a suitable "place for meeting friends" with
its "lovely decor", featuring walls jammed with images of Gallic heritage, and service that's "attentive without hovering"; although the
"revolving menu" may "not be the most innovative", for "casual food"
and a "little slice of Paris on Sloane Square", it's "worth a visit";
P.S. "book well ahead for peak times".

Como Lario ● *Italian* 21 | 16 | 22 | £51

Belgravia | 18-22 Holbein Pl., SW1W 8NL | 020-7730-2954 |
www.comolario.co.uk

"Jovial staff" clearly "want you to enjoy yourself" at this perennially
"packed", 40-plus-year-old Belgravia eatery pairing "excellent"
Northern Italian eats with "drinkable house wine"; whilst somewhat
"cramped", the "cheery atmosphere" makes it a "keeper" for an "informal" "evening with friends", though it is a bit pricey.

Comptoir Gascon 🅱🅼 *French* 25 | 20 | 21 | £44

Farringdon | 63 Charterhouse St., EC1M 6HJ | 020-7608-0851 |
www.comptoirgascon.com

"All the imagination" and "excellent taste" of Club Gascon is offered
at "a better price" at this "lovely little" French "bistro relative", also
in Farringdon; "simply decorated with tables tightly packed", the
"intimate" setting benefits from "charming" staff who are as
"knowledgeable" about chef Pascal Aussignac's fare as they are the
"great" wine selection, making it all in all "a real joy to eat here".

Comptoir Libanais *Lebanese* 20 | 16 | 15 | £20

Marylebone | 65 Wigmore St., W1U 1PZ | 020-7935-1110
NEW Soho | 59 Broadwick St., W1F 9QH | 020-7434-4335 ●
Stratford | Westfield Stratford City | 2 Stratford Pl., E20 1EN |
020-8811-2222
Shepherd's Bush | Westfield Shopping Ctr. | Ariel Way, balcony,
W12 7GE | 020-8811-2222
South Kensington | 1-5 Exhibition Rd., SW7 2HE | 020-7225-5006 🅱
www.lecomptoir.co.uk

"Groaning plates of mezze" and other "delicious" Lebanese staples
are "washed down with mint tea or fresh smoothies" at this "funky"
chain; though the "colourful" decor strikes some as "Formica heaven"
and the "slow" service can be "a letdown", shoppers seeking
"respite" – financial and otherwise – reckon it's "terrific".

Constancia *Argentinean/Steak* 25 | 20 | 21 | £36

Tower Bridge | 52 Tanner St., SE1 3PH | 020-7234-0676 |
www.constancia.co.uk

"As soon as you walk in, you start salivating at the smell of the char-
coal grill" at this "cosy" steakhouse near Tower Bridge, where "attentive" staff deliver "fabulous Argentinean steaks", "great sides"
and "superb" South American wines; the "laid-back" setting is as

	FOOD	DECOR	SERVICE	COST

"right for a romantic dinner" as it is "comfortable for big groups", and best of all, it "knocks the spots off some" of its "pricier" competitors.

Copita ☒ *Spanish*   ▽ 24 | 21 | 19 | £28

Soho | 26 D'Arblay St., W1F 8EP | 020-7287-7797 | www.copita.co.uk
"Clever combinations", "excellent ingredients" and "strong punches of flavour" abound in the "varied" Spanish tapas at this "loud" Soho sibling of Barrica that's "appropriately priced" for being so "casual"; the "small seating area" can only be booked for lunch, so in the evening, the "cool" clientele passes waiting time at the bar with a glass of wine or sherry from the "simple" list.

Coq d'Argent *French*   23 | 23 | 22 | £58

City | 1 Poultry, EC2R 8EJ | 020-7395-5000 | www.coqdargent.co.uk
From early morning until night, this "rooftop hub" is "packed" with "City high fliers" "expensing" "reliable", "well-presented" Classic French fare and quaffing "excellent" cocktails; it may seem "a bit pricey" for those without business accounts, but the package includes "smashing views", a "gorgeous" garden terrace and "professional service".

Corner Room *European*   ▽ 29 | 25 | 26 | £32

Bethnal Green | Town Hall Hotel | Patriot Sq., E2 9NF | 020-7871-0460 | www.townhallhotel.com
"Inspiring", "delicious" European dishes with "inventive" "flair" leave diners "in awe" of chef Nuno Mendes at this "small", "informal" venture in the same Bethnal Green hotel as his Viajante; it's "off the beaten path" for many, and the "no-reservations policy" at dinner (lunch is bookable) irks some, but with such "thoughtful" service and "economical prices", fans conclude it's "well worth the detour and the wait".

Corrigan's Mayfair *British*   25 | 23 | 24 | £75

Mayfair | Grosvenor Hse. | 28 Upper Grosvenor St., W1K 7EH | 020-7499-9943 | www.corrigansmayfair.com
"Business" types and "special-night-out" celebrants converge on Richard Corrigan's "gentleman's club"–like Modern Brit in the Grosvenor House for "beautifully prepared", "decadent" "gastronomic delights"; "solicitous" service is delivered by smartly attired staff, but the whole experience comes at a "frightening" cost that may compel you to "take the bus home when you get the bill"; P.S. "the chef's table private dining package is particularly excellent".

Côte *French*   18 | 17 | 19 | £28

City | 26 Ludgate Hill, EC4M 7DR | 020-7236-4399
Covent Garden | 17-21 Tavistock St., WC2E 7PA | 020-7379-9991
Covent Garden | 50-51 St. Martin's Ln., WC2N 4EA | 020-7379-9747
Soho | 124-126 Wardour St., W1F 0TY | 020-7287-9280
Highgate | 2 Highgate High St., N6 5JL | 020-8348-9107
NEW **Blackheath** | 15-16 Royal Parade, SE3 0TL | 020-8852-9548
Bayswater | 98 Westbourne Grove, W2 5RU | 020-7792-3298
Chiswick | 50-54 Turnham Green Terr., W4 1QP | 020-8747-6788
(continued)

(continued)

Côte

Ealing | 9-10 The Green, High St., W5 5DA | 020-8579-3115
Fulham | 45-47 Parsons Green Ln., SW6 4HH | 020-7736-8444
www.cote-restaurants.co.uk
Additional locations throughout London

It may "never set the world on fire", but this "solid" French brasserie chain is "consistent in its quality", presenting "well-executed" standards and "decent" wines; service is "friendly", and even if you don't opt for the fixed price menus, the "reasonable" bill at the end often seems like "good value".

Cottons *Caribbean*   22 | 19 | 20 | £29

Clerkenwell | 70 Exmouth Mkt., EC1R 4QP | 020-7833-3332 |
www.cottons-restaurant.co.uk
Chalk Farm | 55 Chalk Farm Rd., NW1 8AN | 020-7485-8388 |
www.cottonscamden.co.uk

If you're "feeling homesick for the islands", this "family-friendly" pair in Clerkenwell and Chalk Farm takes you back via "yummy" Caribbean dishes with "a modern twist" plus a "fantastic selection of rums"; "great prices" keep it "crowded", and for those who've been saddled with "slow service" (it's "prompt" only sometimes), regulars suggest you tune into the "laid-back" island vibe of the bar.

The Cow *British*   22 | 15 | 17 | £33

Notting Hill | 89 Westbourne Park Rd., W2 5QH | 020-7221-0021 |
www.thecowlondon.co.uk

"Push past the crowds" of hip Notting Hill types at this "cultish" pub to find a "small upstairs dining room" serving "well-prepared" British food that "changes daily depending on what fresh meats are available" ("everything from steak to squirrel to pigeon"); some feel that the "food may be an afterthought" downstairs (where the menu is "smaller"), so they focus on the "great beer selection".

NEW Coya ●☒ *Peruvian*   ▽ 24 | 23 | 17 | £67

Piccadilly | 118 Piccadilly, W1J 7NW | 020-7042-7118 |
www.coyarestaurant.com

An "extensive" menu featuring "different", "delicious" Peruvian flavours from an "accomplished" chef "presented in small portions to share" at this "loud, glitzy" basement on Piccadilly (same ownership as Zuma); although the "lovely bar" is often "crowded" with "beautiful" people, with the right credentials, you can seek out the quieter private members' lounge on the ground floor, but beware, "everything is expensive".

Crazy Bear *Thai*   20 | 24 | 19 | £52

Fitzrovia | 26-28 Whitfield St., W1T 2RG | 020-7631-0088
Covent Garden | private club | 17 Mercer St., WC2H 9QJ |
020-7520-5450 ☒
www.crazybeargroup.co.uk

With all the "opulence" of an "over-the-top Dubai hotel", the "baroque-meets-Gothic" decor of this "loungey" Covent Garden (members only) and Fitzrovia Thai duo "impresses" "first dates" and "out-of-towners"; it's "a bit on the pricey side" and service is "inconsistent" (though often "helpful"), but the menu's "great variety" is appreciated, with both "traditional" and "adventurous dishes", plus "nibbles and creative drinks"; P.S. the Mercer St. branch also houses a sushi bar, while Whitfield St. has live jazz on Wednesdays.

Crazy Homies *Mexican* | 18 | 19 | 15 | £29 |

Notting Hill | 125-127 Westbourne Park Rd., W2 5QL | 020-7727-6771 | www.crazyhomieslondon.co.uk

A "hipster" crowd frequents this "tiny", "kitsch" Notting Hill "dive", which offers up "filling" Mexican fare backed by a "loud" soundtrack; it's certainly not the prices (that some deem "too high for what it is") or the staff (who can be "downright rude") that attracts regulars – it's the "rocking range" of tequilas and "wicked" margaritas that "knock your socks off".

Criterion Restaurant ● *European* | 21 | 26 | 21 | £53 |

Piccadilly | 224 Piccadilly, W1J 9HP | 020-7930-0488 | www.criterionrestaurant.com

"The sheer opulence of the gold mosaic ceilings" and marble walls is "reason enough to visit" this "sumptuous" neo-Byzantine Piccadilly "haven"; and though the "magical" surroundings are "not quite matched" by the Modern European dishes, they're "alright" nonetheless, and "well presented" by "polite" staff – but "on the expensive side", so consider opting for the "bargain" pre-theatre menu.

Cut at 45 Park Lane *American/Steak* | 25 | 21 | 22 | £87 |

Mayfair | 45 Park Ln. | 45 Park Ln., W1K 1PN | 020-7493-4554 | www.45parklane.com

Chef-restaurateur Wolfgang Puck's London outpost in the boutique Park Lane hotel offers a "to-die-for" American steakhouse menu rife with "tender, flavoursome" cuts and "clever" starters; though "expensive", many find it "worth it", especially with such a "posh" setting filled with works by Damien Hirst.

Dabbous ●⊠Ⓜ *European* | 26 | 19 | 24 | £60 |

Fitzrovia | 39 Whitfield St., W1T 2SF | 020-7323-1544 | www.dabbous.co.uk

Foodies flock to this much "hyped" Fitzrovia venue to "savour smart, ingenious combinations" of "cutting-edge" Modern European cuisine from the kitchen of chef Ollie Dabbous; "knowledgeable and attentive" staff keep things "relaxed", while the decor sports an "industrial" edge; P.S. "plan at least six months in advance".

Daphne's ● *Italian* | 22 | 21 | 21 | £56 |

Chelsea | 112 Draycott Ave., SW3 3AE | 020-7589-4257 | www.daphnes-restaurant.co.uk

Over twenty years on, this "smart", "stylish" Chelsea Italian with "charming service" is a "must" for "ladies who lunch" and "famous" people; indeed, while the "upmarket" fare is "reliable", it "isn't the point here" – you're paying "expensive" prices for the "buzzy" atmosphere and "great people-watching" (try for "a table near the windows").

FOOD	DECOR	SERVICE	COST

Daylesford Organic Café *International* | 21 | 20 | 16 | £29 |

Belgravia | Daylesford Organic Store | 44 Pimlico Rd., SW1W 8LP | 020-7881-8060
Notting Hill | 208-212 Westbourne Grove, W11 2RH | 020-7313-8050
www.daylesfordorganic.com

"Divine" "straight-from-the-farm" produce fills the "healthy" International fare presented (often in a "slow" manner) at this pair of "glamourous" all-day cafes in Notting Hill and Belgravia; they're "jam packed" at weekends, when "yummy mummies" and "beautiful Europeans" "browse" the organic groceries at the adjacent shop before settling in for "virtuous" bits of "heaven" – and "the prices reflect the altitude".

Dean Street Townhouse ● *British* | 22 | 23 | 20 | £49 |

Soho | Dean Street Townhse. | 69-71 Dean St., W1D 3SE | 020-7434-1775 | www.deanstreettownhouse.com

A "buzzy" atmosphere is created by a "young" crowd at this "smart", "clubby" Soho hotel dining room serving "well-executed", "satisfying" British comfort food; "reliable" staff are on hand, and although it's certainly "upscale", most feel that the prices are, "on balance, fair"; P.S. there's also a bar and a small terrace.

Defune *Japanese* | 25 | 15 | 20 | £70 |

Marylebone | 34 George St., W1U 7DP | 020-7935-8311

"Elegant" preparations of "superb sushi" will "blow you away", as will the "super-expensive" prices at this "quiet", "understated" Marylebone Japanese; don't come "looking for atmosphere", but do feel free to "stay all night", because it's "easy to secure a table" and the staff "won't throw you out".

Dehesa *Italian/Spanish* | 25 | 20 | 23 | £42 |

Soho | 25 Ganton St., W1F 9BP | 020-7494-4170 | www.dehesa.co.uk

"Graze" your way through "inventive", "seasonal" Spanish-Italian tapas and "outstanding charcuterie" at this "slick", "lively-verging-on-noisy" Salt Yard sibling "close to Carnaby Street" in Soho; it's quite "small", but staff do their best to be "speedy" – and diners can sample the "fabulous" wine list while they wait.

The Delaunay ● *European* | 21 | 26 | 24 | £49 |

Covent Garden | 55 Aldwych, WC2B 4BB | 020-7499-8558 | www.thedelaunay.com

A "nostalgia fest" of "exquisite linen" tablecloths and "polished silver" forms the backdrop at this "elegant" Wolseley sibling in Covent Garden, which follows a similar "formula" of "excellent" service and "well-prepared" European comfort food, including possibly "more schnitzel choices than anywhere this side of Vienna"; whether entertaining business associates, dining post-theatre or brunching at weekends, many agree that it's an "impressive" experience worth "splashing out" for.

Del'Aziz *African/Mediterranean* | 20 | 21 | 17 | £26 |

Southwark | Blue Fin Bldg. | 5 Canvey St., SE1 9AN | 020-7633-0033

| | | FOOD | DECOR | SERVICE | COST |

(continued)

Del'Aziz

Tower Bridge | Bermondsey Sq. | 11 Bermondsey Sq., SE1 3UN | 020-7407-2991
Clapham | 55-57 The Pavement, SW4 0JQ | 020-7498-9128
Fulham | 24-32 Vanston Pl., SW6 1AX | 020-7386-0086
Swiss Cottage | Swiss Cottage Leisure Ctr. | Adelaide Rd., NW3 3NF | 020-7586-3338
www.delaziz.co.uk

You "can't go wrong" at this midpriced chain of all-day deli/bar/cafes delivering "reliable, tasty" Mediterranean mezze, mains and sweets (meringues, cakes) in environs decked out like a North African bazaar (and often just as "busy"); service is generally "friendly", and entertainment can include live music and belly dancing at different branches.

Delfino ⓩ *Italian*　　　　　　20 | 14 | 18 | £40

Mayfair | 121 Mount St., W1K 3NW | 020-7499-1256 | www.finos.co.uk

It's a "basic proposition", but for "filling" Italian eats and "awesome pizza" at prices that, for Mayfair anyway, are "reasonable", this trattoria in a Victorian building ticks a lot of boxes; though the "tight" setting is "always busy", staff manage to make you "feel loved", even if you're just buying takeaway.

The Diner　*American*　　　　18 | 18 | 15 | £20

Covent Garden | 190 Shaftesbury Ave., WC2H 8JL | 020-3551-5225 ●
Soho | 18 Ganton St., W1F 7BU | 020-7287-8962 ●
Shoreditch | 128-130 Curtain Rd., EC2A 3AQ | 020-7729-4452 ●
Camden Town | 2 Jamestown Rd., NW1 7BY | 020-7485-5223
Islington | 21 Essex Rd., N1 2SA | 020-7226-4533
Kensal Green | 64-66 Chamberlayne Rd., NW10 3JJ | 020-8968-9033
NEW **South Kensington** | 105 Gloucester Rd., SW7 4SS | 020-7244-7666 ●
www.goodlifediner.com

A "feel-good destination" for "family get-togethers" or "hungover Sundays", this "value" chain "captures the feel and decor of a proper American diner", with "standard" "comfort food" and "thick milkshakes" that "hit the spot if you're in need of a touch of gluttony"; if "hipster staff seem to forget they're at work sometimes", maybe they're just in sympathy with the "laid-back atmosphere".

Dinings ⓩ *Japanese*　　　　28 | 13 | 21 | £64

Marylebone | 22 Harcourt St., W1H 4HH | 020-7723-0666 | www.dinings.co.uk

Every morsel is "exquisite" at this "creative" Japanese that dishes up food with "innovative twists" in an "unassuming", "subterranean bunker" in Marylebone; the lunchtime prix fixe is "superb value", but "if your wallet dares", opt for the à la carte to experience the full range of the menu, and get stuck into the "good selection of sake".

	FOOD	DECOR	SERVICE	COST

Dinner by Heston Blumenthal British | 26 | 24 | 26 | £91 |

Knightsbridge | Mandarin Oriental Hyde Park | 66 Knightsbridge, SW1X 7LA | 020-7201-3833 | www.dinnerbyheston.com

Heston Blumenthal's "famous techniques, combined with an homage to Britain's culinary past", result in "impeccably prepared", "visually stunning", "other-worldly" creations at this "chic, modern" dining room with a glass-walled kitchen and views of Hyde Park in the Mandarin Oriental; service is "exceptional", and while the prices are "sky high", the set lunch offers "amazing value".

NEW Dirty Burger ● Burgers | - | - | - | I |

Kentish Town | 79 Highgate Rd., NW5 1TL | 020-3310-2010 | www.eatdirtyburger.com

In a corrugated iron shed in Kentish Town, hungover students queue alongside suits to order bargain-priced breakfasts or the eponymous patty with cheese at this no-frills, American burger joint; if there's no space at the communal wooden table, the nearby Heath is an alternative picnic spot.

Dishoom Indian | 23 | 22 | 20 | £27 |

Covent Garden | St. Martin's Courtyard | 12 Upper St. Martin's Ln., WC2H 9FB | 020-7420-9320
NEW Shoreditch | 7 Boundary St., E2 7JE | 020-7420-9320
www.dishoom.com

Start your day with an "Indian twist on breakfast" at this pair of reasonably priced cafes in Covent Garden and Shoreditch, whose "fun, modern" takes on subcontinental "street food" continue with "well-spiced", "tapas"-sized lunches and dinners, all washed down with "lovely lassis"; it's a "big hit" with groups, who enjoy the "fantastic", "vintage"-inspired decor as well as watching the cooks in the open kitchen; P.S. evenings are no reservations except for parties of six or more.

Dock Kitchen European | 24 | 22 | 24 | £45 |

Ladbroke Grove | Wharf Bldg., Portobello Dock | 344 Ladbroke Grove, W10 5AH | 020-8962-1610 | www.dockkitchen.co.uk

In the "immaculate open kitchen" of this "beautifully appointed" venue atop the Tom Dixon showroom on the canal in Ladbroke Grove, "risk-taking" chef-owner Stevie Parle creates Modern Euro fare showcasing "innovative flavour combinations and a dedication to seasonality", all delivered by "attentive", "friendly staff"; some moan that it's "a bit pricey", but still, it's "cheaper" than Parle's alma mater, the River Cafe.

Dockmaster's House 🏠 Indian   ∇ | 22 | 22 | 19 | £40 |

Canary Wharf | 1 Hertsmere Rd., E14 8JJ | 020-7345-0345 | www.dockmastershouse.com

Set in a "superb", "imposing" Georgian building in Canary Wharf that was a 19th-century customs house, this venue offers a "refreshingly different take on Indian cuisine" – and the results are "fantastic"; staff are mostly "accommodating" and the prices are reasonable, so it's just a "shame it's a bit out of the way" for many.

| | FOOD | DECOR | SERVICE | COST |

The Don ☒ *European* | 23 | 21 | 22 | £53 |

City | The Courtyard | 20 St. Swithins Ln., EC4N 8AD | 020-7626-2606 |
www.thedonrestaurant.co.uk

Whether it's the "sophisticated" main dining room with its "monumental paintings" or the "noisier downstairs" with its "vaulted ceilings" and cheaper prices, this "charming" City Modern European in the circa-1798 Sandeman's port warehouse is a "discreet" option that's "good for business or pleasure"; "skilful cooking" and "understated elegance" are evident in the food, which is delivered via "reliable" service and enhanced by an array of "excellent" sherries and wines.

Donostia *Spanish* | ∇ 24 | 18 | 18 | £40 |

Marylebone | 10 Seymour Pl., W1H 7ND | 020-3620-1845 |
www.donostia.co.uk

"Traditional" Basque tapas are imbued with "sophistication" at this "smart" Marylebone joint where you can sit at the marble bar with a glass of "reasonably priced wine" and be tended to by generally "friendly", "attentive" staff; some go as far as saying it's "like a trip back home" to San Sebastian.

Dorchester – The Grill *British* | 25 | 24 | 26 | £76 |

Mayfair | The Dorchester | 53 Park Ln., W1K 1QA | 020-7629-8888 |
www.dorchesterhotel.com

"Formal" yet "not stuffy", this "fantastic" all-day grill in The Dorchester pairs a "civilised", "clubby" setting of Scottish murals and tartan with "terrific" Modern British food, plus "superb" "traditional" Sunday lunches starring "roast beef carved at table"; it's "quite expensive", but "considering what you get" – including "welcoming", "exact" service – it's really "not badly priced", whether for "business" or a "special treat".

Downtown Mayfair ● *Italian* | 21 | 22 | 21 | £74 |

Mayfair | 15 New Burlington Pl., W1S 2HX | 020-3056-1001 |
www.downtownmayfair.com

Like its "trendy" cousin, C London, this new off–Savile Row Italian is a "place to be seen" in Mayfair – indeed, there's "wonderful people-watching" in the warm setting adorned with walnut, leather and chandeliers; and similar to the Davies Street original, the service is "attentive" and the food is usually "great", though cost-calculators suspect you pay "three times more" than the usual for it.

The Draft House *International* | 20 | 19 | 19 | £24 |

Fitzrovia | 43 Goodge St., W1T 1TA | 020-7323-9361 ☒
Dulwich | 21 Lordship Ln., SE22 8EW | 020-8299-3511
Tower Bridge | 206-208 Tower Bridge Rd., SE1 2UP |
020-7378-9995
Battersea | 74-76 Battersea Bridge Rd., SW11 3HE |
020-7228-6482
Clapham | 94 Northcote Rd., SW11 6QW | 020-7924-1814
www.drafthouse.co.uk

"Worth it for the beer selection alone", this "informal", "convivial" gastropub chain also houses a "small" menu of "well-executed" international eats, including a choice of "rhyming burgers" (yolk, poke and smoke – and "they're all good"); there's a "decent Sunday lunch" too, plus "great service" and affordable prices every day.

Dragon Castle Chinese   ▽ 22 | 13 | 14 | £27

Kennington | 100 Walworth Rd., SE17 1JL | 020-7277-3388 | www.dragon-castle.com

A "wide range" of Cantonese delicacies including "fabulous dim sum" is doled out in "generous" portions at this "large" "culinary oasis" just "a five-minute walk from Elephant & Castle station"; service can be "comically brusque", but bills cause such a "little dent to the wallet", "it's worth just ignoring the staff and tucking right in".

NEW Duck & Waffle ● British   20 | 24 | 17 | £46

City | Heron Tower | 110 Bishopsgate, 40th fl., EC2N 4AY | 020-3640-7310 | www.duckandwaffle.com

"An exhilarating glass elevator ride up 40 floors" delivers you to Heron Tower's all-day, all-night British diner, which is surrounded by floor-to-ceiling windows that provide "breathtaking" "panoramic" vistas; the menu of "classics with a twist" includes the signature confit duck leg on a waffle (a "must have"), and although it's "not particularly cheap" overall, most acknowledge that "given the location" you "wouldn't expect it to be".

Ducksoup European   21 | 17 | 17 | £38

Soho | 41 Dean St., W1D 4PY | 020-7287-4599 | www.ducksoupsoho.co.uk

With a daily changing, handwritten menu of "ingredient-driven" European small plates and a similar approach to the natural-focused wine list, "there's always something fresh" to try at this "narrow" Soho bistro; those weary of "queuing for a table" (no reservations) or jostling with other people at the "crowded bar" seek solace in the "killer customer-controlled vinyl playlist".

The Duke of Cambridge British   22 | 19 | 20 | £26

Islington | 30 St. Peter's St., N1 8JT | 020-7359-3066 | www.sloeberry.co.uk

"Even if you don't care" that this "comfortable", rustic Islington "classic" bills itself as Britain's first and only certified organic gastropub, you'll appreciate the "terrific" Modern British cuisine, not to mention the "reasonable prices"; it's the sort of place where staff "recognise you on a return visit" – no wonder the crowd seems so "friendly".

The Duke of Sussex British/Spanish   22 | 20 | 21 | £28

Chiswick | 75 S. Parade, W4 5LF | 020-8742-8801 | www.thedukeofsussex.co.uk

"Classic British dishes" with "great twists" and "hearty" Spanish tapas make this "inviting" Chiswick gastropub with art deco chandeliers a bit different than most; "helpful staff" wait on "locals" enjoying a "romantic night" out, a "lazy" lunch or a warm-weather repast in the "large beer garden at the back" ("great if you're with the kids"), while delivering "excellent value" at all times.

	FOOD	DECOR	SERVICE	COST

The Eagle *Mediterranean* | 24 | 16 | 18 | £27 |

Clerkenwell | 159 Farringdon Rd., EC1R 3AL | 020-7837-1353
The "original" gastropub, and "still one of the best, at least in terms of food", this "rambunctious" Clerkenwell boozer presents "hearty", "superb-quality" Med fare with Iberian influences; "thankfully, the decor and service aren't what set the trend", though "watching the chefs do their magic" in the open kitchen is "fun".

E&O *Asian* | 23 | 21 | 19 | £52 |

Notting Hill | 14 Blenheim Crescent, W11 1NN | 020-7229-5454 | www.rickerrestaurants.com
"Creative" Pan-Asian dishes "delight the palate" at this "smooth" Notting Hill "scene" that's "buzzy all day" (thanks in part to the "bargain" lunch deal) and flat-out "noisy at night" when "beautiful people" and the "occasional star" flood the "trendy bar" for "wonderful cocktails"; service is "young" and "upbeat", and as for the cost, it's "slightly pricey, but money well spent".

Ed's Easy Diner *American* | 19 | 20 | 20 | £19 |

Mayfair | Sedley Pl. | 14 Woodstock St., W1C 2AG | 020-7493-9916
Leicester Square | London Trocadero Ctr. | 19 Rupert St., W1D 7PA | 020-7287-1951
Soho | 12 Moor St., W1D 5NG | 020-7434-4439 ◑
Euston | The Piazza | Euston Station, NW1 2DY | 020-7388-6967
NEW Wandsworth | Southside Shopping Ctr. | Garratt Ln., SW18 4TS | 020-8874-5634
www.edseasydiner.co.uk
"Ravenous" "tourists and teens" scoff "standard diner fare" like burgers, chili dogs and fries plus "amazing milkshakes" that are "meals in themselves" at this "kitsch", "'50s-style" "slice of Americana"; "friendly staff" skirt round rooms bedecked with chrome, neon, red-vinyl counter stools, "loads of memorabilia" and jukeboxes, and though to some it's all "a little cheesy", at least the prices are "fair".

Efes ◑🗷 *Turkish* | 22 | 16 | 22 | £36 |

Fitzrovia | 80-82 Great Titchfield St., W1W 7QT | 020-7636-1953 | www.efesrestaurant.co.uk

Efes 2 ◑ *Turkish*

Marylebone | 175-177 Great Portland St., W1W 5PJ | 020-7436-0600 | www.efes2.co.uk
"Succulent" lamb kebabs and other "wonderful" grill-heavy Turkish fare come in "good portions" and for "the right price" at this "reliable" pair of separately owned eateries in Fitzrovia and Marylebone; as a result, the traditionally outfitted digs are "always crowded" with punters who appreciate the staff's "charm" and, in Great Portland Street, those of the nightly belly dancer.

805 ◑ *African* | 24 | 19 | 20 | £26 |

Peckham | 805 Old Kent Rd., SE15 1NX | 020-7639-0808 | www.805restaurant.com
The Old Kent Road in Peckham might not strike you as the best "place to go to reminisce about" Africa, or even to get your "first

taste" of its cuisine, but that it is, thanks to this light, airy, "peaceful environment" that serves up "marvellous" renditions of West African dishes; affordable prices for "large portions" are further incentives, as is the "good" service.

Eight Over Eight *Asian*
23 | 21 | 20 | £50

Chelsea | 392 King's Rd., SW3 5UZ | 020-7349-9934 | www.rickerrestaurants.com

"Sophisticated" types inhabit this "cool" minimalist E&O sister located "in the heart of Chelsea", where a "vibrant menu" of "tasty" Pan-Asian "bites" is complemented by "delicious cocktails"; it's "not the cheapest" of destinations, but at least it's "predictable" (in a good way), with "attentive, welcoming service" and a "buzzing" atmosphere virtually guaranteed.

NEW Electric Diner ◑ *American/French*
– | – | – | M

Notting Hill | 191 Portobello Rd., W11 2ED | 020-7908-9696 | www.electricdiner.com

This all-day, no-reservations Franco-American diner in Notting Hill presents a midpriced menu devised by U.S. chef Brendan Sodikoff, who pairs the likes of fried bologna sandwiches and cheeseburgers with some unusual beers and cocktails; highlights of the brick-walled dining room include red-leather banquettes and a bar; P.S. it also sells hot doughnuts and coffee (from 8 AM) in the foyer of the adjacent Electric Cinema.

Elena's L'Etoile ⊠ *French/Italian*
20 | 17 | 17 | £46

Fitzrovia | 30 Charlotte St., W1T 2NG | 020-7636-1496 | www.elenasletoile.co.uk

"From the moment you enter to the moment you leave, the whole experience is joy" declare advocates of this "charming" Fitzrovia "page from the past", whipping up "decent" "old-school" Franco-Italian fare; though modernists moan that it "feels rather tired" for being so "pricey", for most, the "slightly worn" scarlet-hued decor and "venerable staff only add to its timeless quality".

El Gaucho *Argentinean/Steak*
23 | 20 | 22 | £48

Chelsea | Chelsea Farmers Mkt. | 125 Sydney St., SW3 6NR | 020-7376-8514
South Kensington | 30 Old Brompton Rd., SW7 3DL | 020-7584-8999 ◑
www.elgaucho.co.uk

"Sizzling", "reliable" steaks shipped from the Pampas are accompanied by a "good selection of wines" at these "casual", "well-run" Argentinean steakhouses in Chelsea and South Ken, both decked out in "over-the-top" "cowboy decor", the latter dinner-only during the week; though it's a bit "pricey", the portions are "large", which causes hungry types to exclaim that they "cannot wait to go back".

Elistano *Italian*
∇ 21 | 16 | 19 | £41

Chelsea | 25-27 Elystan St., SW3 3NT | 020-7584-5248 | www.elistano.com

"Lovely, especially in summer" when pavement tables are available, this sleek, modern Italian is a "recommended meeting place" in

Chelsea; pizzas, pastas and other "simple" dishes do a "great" job of staving off hunger, and it's reasonably priced for the location.

Elk in the Woods *International* | 21 | 22 | 18 | £27 |

Islington | 37-39 Camden Passage, N1 8EA | 020-7226-3535 | www.the-elk-in-the-woods.co.uk

"Seriously cool wallpaper", antlers and mirrors comprise the "quirky", "eccentric" and somehow "soothing decor" at this "informal" spot "tucked in Camden Passage" in Islington, while "big, tasty" dishes fill the affordable all-day International menu; "relaxed" staff provide the "friendly service" – no wonder it's "always on the right side of busy".

El Parador *Spanish*   ∇ | 25 | 13 | 20 | £28 |

Camden Town | 245 Eversholt St., NW1 1BA | 020-7387-2789 | www.elparadorlondon.com

There's a "folksy feel" to this Camden Spaniard in "a storefront setting", where the "brilliant", "reasonably priced" tapas menu "changes frequently, yet always seems to leave your favourite dish available", a boon for "repeat visitors"; if some find the decor a bit "uninspiring", they concede that the back garden offers a "great escape".

El Pirata ●◿ *Spanish* | 22 | 18 | 20 | £40 |

Mayfair | 5-6 Down St., W1J 7AQ | 020-7491-3810 | www.elpirata.co.uk

El Pirata Detapas *Spanish*

Bayswater | 115 Westbourne Grove, W2 4UP | 020-7727-5000 | www.elpiratadetapas.co.uk

"On a dull winter day", you can practically "feel the Spanish sun on your back" at this pair in Bayswater and Mayfair, where "friendly" staff serve a "great selection of tasty tapas"; sure, it can be a bit "crowded" and "noisy", but with such "great value", especially via the fixed-price menus, most just say "bravo"; P.S. "if you can't get a table", sit at the "well-stocked" bar.

The Empress *British*   ∇ | 23 | 20 | 21 | £38 |

Hackney | 130 Lauriston Rd., E9 7LH | 020-8533-5123 | www.theempressofindia.com

Just outside "leafy Victoria Park", this "reliable" 19th-century Hackney gastropub delivers "fantastic" Modern British dishes from a chef who "clearly cares about quality and presentation"; everything's "served promptly" at the "well-spaced tables" by "friendly staff", and as you'd expect from a boozer, there's a "good beer selection" too.

Empress of Sichuan *Chinese* | 21 | 16 | 16 | £32 |

Chinatown | 6 Lisle St., WC2H 7BG | 020-7734-8128 | www.restaurantprivilege.co.uk

"Spicy-as-you-like Sichuan cooking" is the speciality of this "yummy" Chinatown spot; some confess to being "put off" by the "mediocre" service and "average" surrounds, especially those for whom the bill "ended up being a little more expensive" than they "would have liked", but on the plus side, the portions are "ample".

	FOOD	DECOR	SERVICE	COST

The English Pig ⚠ *British* — ▽ 20 | 15 | 16 | £39
Westminster | 4 Millbank, SW1P 3JA | 020-7600-9707 |
www.theenglishpig.co.uk

An "original concept" venture in Westminster, where the Modern
British menu – "concentrating on all the bits of the pig" – stars "melt-
in-the-mouth 21-hour roast pork belly", augmented with "creative
desserts and delicious drinks"; most don't come for the decor, or the
service, which are both unremarkable, though prices are fairly moderate; P.S. closed on weekends.

Enoteca Turi ⚠ *Italian* — 25 | 18 | 23 | £51
Putney | 28 Putney High St., SW15 1SQ | 020-8785-4449 |
www.enotecaturi.com

"Superb", "modern" takes on Italian classics are matched by a "large
but not intimidating wine list" at this spot "over the bridge in Putney",
where "professional", "friendly service" makes up for decor that
some deem "a little dated"; so, despite "pricey" costs, there's "value
for money" here, thus locals "would rather keep it a secret".

The Enterprise *British* — 21 | 22 | 22 | £40
Chelsea | 35 Walton St., SW3 2HU | 020-7584-3148 |
www.theenterprise.co.uk

"One of the most convivial" spots in Chelsea, this "fancy local" is often
"tourist free" but "always busy with investment/Sloane Ranger types"
and other "wealthy people" enjoying "haute" (read: "not cheap")
Modern British gastropub grub and some "unique specials"; bookings are only taken for weekday lunches, so if you come for dinner,
"arrive early or have a few drinks at the bar" while you wait.

Esarn Kheaw *Thai* — ▽ 23 | 9 | 16 | £25
Shepherd's Bush | 314 Uxbridge Rd., W12 7LJ | 020-8743-8930 |
www.esarnkheaw.com

"Rich and delicious" Thai tastes are available for "reasonable
prices" at this Shepherd's Bush venue; the green surroundings are
"rather tired", service is so so, and it's "off the beaten track" for
many, but that "doesn't seem to deter people" – some even say it's
"worth travelling to".

Espelette *French* — ▽ 25 | 27 | 28 | £66
Mayfair | The Connaught | Carlos Pl., W1K 2AL | 020-7107-8861 |
www.the-connaught.co.uk

"Fantastic" staff ferry chef Hélène Darroze's "delightful, refined"
Classic French cuisine at this "stunning" glass conservatory in The
Connaught; devotees "could eat here every night and every day"
(starting with breakfast), but the "ethereal afternoon tea is the highlight", so "take gran, charm her – and let her pay" the "expensive" bill.

Eyre Brothers ⚠ *Portuguese/Spanish* — 25 | 20 | 22 | £47
Shoreditch | 70 Leonard St., EC2A 4QX | 020-7613-5346 |
www.eyrebrothers.co.uk

Fortunately it's "rustic Spanish and Portuguese" plates (including
Ibérico ham that "has to be tasted to be believed") that are "bold

and have attitude", not the "approachable" staff, at this "classy" "low-lit" "dark-wood" dining room in a Shoreditch backstreet; it can be "a touch pricey", so for something a bit cheaper, go for tapas at the bar, home to a wine list that is "an Iberian education" in itself.

Fairuz ● Lebanese
22 | 12 | 17 | £31

Marylebone | 3 Blandford St., W1U 3DA | 020-7486-8108 | www.fairuz.uk.com

"Big portions" of "tasty" Lebanese dishes fill the "small" handmade tables at this "cosy" Marylebone eatery with no frills in the decor department; regulars appreciate that they're "never rushed" by "polite" staff, but they're most impressed by the "excellent value".

The Fat Duck 🗷Ⓜ British
28 | 23 | 27 | £244

Bray | High St., Berkshire, SL6 2AQ | 016-2858-0333 | www.thefatduck.co.uk

"The experience is pure theatre" at chef Heston Blumenthal's "temple" to "food entertainment" in the village of Bray (about an hour from London), where the "inspiring", "mind-blowing", "truly inventive" Modern British dishes (all on a fixed-price menu) "aren't just about taste, but also sight, smell, sound and texture"; service is "impeccable", and while the "hefty" cost makes it "a once in a lifetime" treat for some, it is "exquisite – and great fun" to boot.

Feng Sushi Japanese
19 | 14 | 17 | £29

Canary Wharf | Billingsgate Mkt. | Trafalgar Way, E14 5ST | 020-7537-9160
Chalk Farm | 1 Adelaide Rd., NW3 3QE | 020-7483-2929
Hampstead | 280 West End Ln., NW6 1LJ | 020-7435-1833
Borough | 13 Stoney St., SE1 9AD | 020-7407-8744
South Bank | Royal Festival Hall | Festival Terr., SE1 8XX | 020-7261-0001
Chelsea | 218 Fulham Rd., SW10 9NB | 020-7795-1900
Kensington | 24 Kensington Church St., W8 4EP | 020-7937-7927
Notting Hill | 101 Notting Hill Gate, W11 3JZ | 020-7727-1123
www.fengsushi.co.uk

Eco-conscious types "commend" this "functional" midrange Japanese sushi chain for the "emphasis it puts on sustainably sourced fish", available in "attractively presented" "basics" as well as some "interesting" dishes that "change seasonally"; though "friendly", service can be "not the speediest", and with "no atmosphere" taken into consideration, it's perhaps "better suited to takeaway".

Fernandez & Wells Sandwiches/Spanish
21 | 19 | 20 | £23

Covent Garden | Somerset Hse. | The Strand, WC2R 1LA | 020-7420-9408
Soho | 16 St. Anne's Court, W1F 0BF | 020-7494-4242 🗷
Soho | 43 Lexington St., W1F 9AL | 020-7734-1546
Soho | 73 Beak St., W1F 9SR | 020-7287-8124
NEW South Kensington | 8 Exhibition Rd., SW7 2HF | 020-7589-7473
www.fernandezandwells.com

"Superb coffee" and "brilliant" wines wash down "fantastic" sandwiches, "beautiful" cheeses and meats and "lovely" cakes at this "informal", Spanish-style cafe/tapas chain; the Soho branches are a bit "small", but all benefit from "charming" staff, "relaxed" atmospheres and reasonable prices.

Ffiona's ☒ *British*
23 | 19 | 24 | £38

Kensington | 51 Kensington Church St., W8 4BA | 020-7937-4152 | www.ffionas.com

"Long-standing regulars" head for this "quirky", "cosy" Kensington bistro for "ffabulous" traditional British "comfort food" that's "reasonably priced"; decor is bright, with plenty of natural light, but the "star attraction" is "one-of-a-kind" owner Ffiona Reid-Owen, who delivers a "warm welcome" and "guides you to the best dishes of the day".

Fifteen *British*
- | - | - | M

Shoreditch | 15 Westland Pl., N1 7LP | 020-3375-1515 | www.fifteen.net

At Jamie Oliver's split-level Shoreditch venture, seasonal British sharing plates are prepared by young chefs from underprivileged backgrounds and their professional mentors; a cocktail and snacks menu are served in the relaxed bar area, and prices are moderate throughout.

Fino ◑☒ *Spanish*
26 | 21 | 22 | £53

Fitzrovia | 33 Charlotte St., W1T 1RR | 020-7813-8010 | www.finorestaurant.com

"Phenomenal" "upscale tapas" as well as "more-substantial" "full-flavoured" Spanish dishes are "elegantly presented" with "friendly flair" at this "boisterous", "glamourous underground" locale on Charlotte Street in Fitzrovia; when it comes to drinks, the "exceptional" Iberian wine list intrigues, but it's the "array of sherries" that "bewilders" – just watch out, as everything quickly "adds up to a fine bill" (however, it's "worth it").

Fish *Seafood*
23 | 17 | 19 | £35

Borough | Borough Mkt. | Cathedral St., SE1 9AL | 020-7407-3803 | www.fishkitchen.com

"If the fish were any fresher, it would be flapping about on the plate" muse supporters of this "light and airy" Borough Market spot where the "great array" of "professionally prepared" dishes comes via "friendly" service; a few find the "hubbub" "too noisy" and the cost "too expensive for what it is", so they stick to the takeaway stand outside for "super delish" fish 'n' chips.

NEW The Fish &
- | - | - | M

Chip Shop *British/Seafood*

Islington | 189 Upper St., N1 1RQ | 020-7704-2074 | www.thefishandchipshop.uk.com

Staffed by alumni from J. Sheekey and Caprice, this posh Islington fish and chippy focuses on sustainably sourced seafood, served over the counter as takeaway or in a wood-panelled, Victorian-esque dining room; midpriced homemade savelous, curried chips, fish pie, lobster rolls and seasonal specials round out the offerings.

NEW Fish Market ☒ *Seafood* — | — | — | M

City | The Old Bengal Warehouse | 16b New St., EC2M 4TR |
020-3503-0790 | www.fishmarket-restaurant.co.uk

This all-day seafood spot in the handsome Old Bengal Warehouse
development offers City diners a casual, moderately priced option
for raw and cooked fish offerings, along with an 80-strong English
wine list; the space exudes the look and spirit of a traditional British
seaside cafe, with white tiled and teal-hued walls, basic classroom-
style chairs and a large terrace out front.

FishWorks *Seafood* 20 | 16 | 18 | £38

Marylebone | 89 Marylebone High St., W1U 4QW | 020-7935-9796
Piccadilly | 7-9 Swallow St., W1B 4DE | 020-7734-5813
Richmond | 13-19 The Square, TW9 1EA | 020-8948-5965
www.fishworks.co.uk

The premise of this seafood chainlet is "simple" – you pick your catch
from the on-site fishmonger's "great range", and it's cooked "as you
like", with "tasty" results; sticklers for value say "it's more expensive
than one expects" given the "no-frills" environment and "hit-and-
miss" service, but for many, it's a "reasonable restaurant" all around.

NEW Five Guys ● *Burgers* — | — | — | I

Covent Garden | 1 Long Acre, WC2E 9BD | 020-7240-2057 |
www.fiveguys.co.uk

On the corner of St Martin's Lane and Long Acre sits the first non-U.S.
outlet of this revered burger chain, where inexpensive burgers, hot
dogs and over 100 soft-drink options are doled out among red-and-
white chequerboard tiles and red upholstered booths; it's no reservations, but you can pre-order your lunch online to avoid queuing.

500 *Italian* 25 | 18 | 22 | £33

Archway | 782 Holloway Rd., N19 3JH | 020-7272-3406 |
www.500restaurant.co.uk

"Wonderful", "well-sourced" Italian cuisine with "seasonal menu
changes" – not to mention "attentive service" and "great value" – make
this "tiny, family-run" trattoria in Archway, not far from Highgate, "a
must-try"; despite the "unpromising" location, "word has spread
far", so "book ahead" or risk being "disappointed".

NEW Flat Iron *Steak* — | — | — | I

Soho | 17 Beak St., W1 9RW | no phone | www.flatironsteak.co.uk

As a former pop-up gone permanent, this tiny, exposed-brick, Soho
steak place with enamel crockery and meat cleaver cutlery ticks all the
zeitgeist boxes; the choice is basically limited to flat iron (aka feather
blade) steak, served at an inexpensive fixed price with a handful of
sauces and sides, like beef dripping chips; P.S. no reservations.

Flat White ⌂ *Australian/Coffeehouse* 24 | 17 | 20 | £9

Soho | 17 Berwick St., W1F 0PT | 020-7734-0370 |
www.flatwhitecafe.com

This "easy-to-miss" Australian-influenced cafe in Soho is a "good
source" of "well-made" coffees, including the eponymous flat white;

if you need more sustenance, the "too-cool-for-school" staff can rustle up pastries and a small number of reasonably priced sandwiches and salads, although eating in can be a "bit of a squeeze".

Flemings Grill *European*   ▽ 21 | 19 | 22 | £59

Mayfair | Flemings Hotel | 7-12 Half Moon St., W1J 7BH | 020-7499-0000 | www.flemings-mayfair.co.uk

"Under the radar" in a Mayfair hotel set in six Georgian townhouses, this plush, dark "hideaway" delivers "expensive", "quality" European fare to those in the know; indeed, it's "often uncrowded" (and "quiet"), which can make it feel like you have staff who "really seem to care that you're having a great time" all to yourself; P.S. there's a value-priced pre-theatre prix fixe.

Food for Thought ⊅ *Vegetarian*   24 | 12 | 19 | £13

Covent Garden | 31 Neal St., WC2H 9PR | 020-7836-0239 | www.foodforthought-london.co.uk

The "constantly changing", "fulfilling" menu of "big" stews and "hefty" bakes, pies and quiches has made this Covent Garden vegetarian a "staple" for decades; "helpful", "friendly" staff tackle the crowds at lunchtimes ("prepare to queue"), and although it's "not a place to dwell" due to "lack of space", at least it's "reasonably cheap".

Fortnum's Fountain *British*   20 | 19 | 20 | £35

Piccadilly | Fortnum & Mason | 181 Piccadilly, W1A 1ER | 020-5602-5694 | www.fortnumandmason.com

Tourists and shoppers seeking an "oasis from the fray of Piccadilly" retire to this "serene", "light and airy" all-day parlour in Fortnum & Mason, where staff with "old-style manners" bring "reliable, well-prepared" British fare, "excellent" "traditional high tea" and "wonderful ice cream sundaes"; "there's no quibble about the cost – it's affordable".

Four Seasons Chinese ● *Chinese*   23 | 11 | 14 | £28

Chinatown | 12 Gerrard St., W1D 5PR | 020-7494-0870
Chinatown | 23 Wardour St., W1D 6PW | 020-7287-9995
Bayswater | 84 Queensway, W2 3RL | 020-7229-4320
www.fs-restaurants.co.uk

"It's difficult not to over-indulge" on the "impressive array" of starters at this Cantonese chainlet, but "addicts" urge you to focus your attention on the "great" house speciality of crispy duck pancakes; service may be "brusque" and decor "not much better", but in light of the moderately priced food, some insist those are "not problems".

Fox & Grapes *British*   20 | 19 | 21 | £33

Wimbledon | 9 Camp Rd., SW19 4UN | 020-8619-1300 | www.foxandgrapeswimbledon.co.uk

"With such headlining pedigree" (Hibiscus' Claude Bosi is executive chef), Wimbledon diners "expect great things" of this "typical"-looking gastropub in the middle of the Common; lucky for them, the Modern Brit menu is "hearty" and "high quality", with "courteous" service and reasonable prices that make the place "just right" for a "casual" meal, as well as a "standby for a drink".

	FOOD	DECOR	SERVICE	COST

Foxtrot Oscar *British* | 19 | 18 | 20 | £45 |

Chelsea | 79 Royal Hospital Rd., SW3 4HN | 020-7352-4448 |
www.gordonramsay.com

"Improved since its early days", this "unpretentious" Chelsea venue
from the Gordon Ramsay stable serves "tasty" Traditional British
"schoolboy" fare in a "compact" (some say "cramped") setting overseen by "smiley", "attentive" staff; it may be a "tad pricey" for a bistro, but still, it's much cheaper than the celeb chef's nearby flagship.

Franco Manca *Pizza* | 26 | 17 | 21 | £15 |

Stratford | Westfield Stratford City | 2 Stratford Pl., E20 1ES |
020-8522-6669
Brixton | 4 Market Row, SW9 8LD | 020-7738-3021
NEW Clapham | 76 Northcote Rd., SW11 6QL | 020-7924-3110
Chiswick | 144 Chiswick High Rd., W4 1PU | 020-8747-4822
www.francomanca.co.uk

What fans rhapsodise is the "best pizza outside Naples" – with "divine" sourdough bases topped with "carefully sourced", "intensely
flavoured" ingredients, then "blistered" in a wood-burning oven – is
the highlight of the "concise" menu at this "affordable" mini
chain; the "friendly" service "quickly" disperses the "long queue"
(only Chiswick takes reservations), and while you wait, you can sample the "organic" wines and "interesting" beers on offer.

Franco's ⊠ *Italian/Mediterranean* | 22 | 20 | 22 | £53 |

St. James's | 61 Jermyn St., SW1Y 6LX | 020-7499-2211 |
www.francoslondon.com

"Reliable" Italian-Mediterranean fare is served from breakfast to
dinner at this "sophisticated" St. James's spot whose "bright" 1940s-
inspired interior is always "buzzy", whether with the "lunchtime
high-finance crowd" or the "pre-theatre" and "media-types" who
meander in later; service is generally "friendly and attentive" – just
what you'd expect given the "big price tag".

Frankie's *Italian* | 17 | 17 | 20 | £37 |

Fulham | Chelsea Football Club Complex | Stamford Bridge, Fulham Rd.,
SW6 1HS | 020-7957-8298 | www.frankies-chelsea.org
Knightsbridge | 3 Yeoman's Row, SW3 2AL | 020-7590-9999 |
www.frankies-knightsbridge.org

Many punters praise chef Marco Pierre White and jockey Frankie
Dettori's duo at Stamford Bridge ("wide-screen TVs showing football") and in Knightsbridge ("glitter balls hanging from the ceiling")
for "friendly" service and "quality", "reasonably priced" Italian
dishes; others however, finding everything "just adequate", suggest
that it "up its game" – with a "bit of sparkle and effort, it could be really quite good".

Frederick's ●⊠ *British/European* | 23 | 22 | 22 | £50 |

Islington | 106 Camden Passage, N1 8EG | 020-7359-2888 |
www.fredericks.co.uk

During the day it's strictly "business", while at night, "romantics"
drink at the "buzzy" bar before retiring to the "smart" dining room,

"beautiful conservatory" or, in summer, "attractive garden" at this "pleasant" Islington haunt where the Modern British–European fare is "well executed" and served with "class"; unless you nab a "great-value" lunch or pre-theatre prix fixe, the prices are "expensive", though "worth it".

French & Grace ⏺🚫🅸🅼 *British/Mideastern* <u>-</u> <u>-</u> <u>-</u> <u>I</u>
Brixton | Brixton Mkt. | 19 Brixton Village Mkt., SW9 8PR | no phone | www.frenchandgrace.co.uk
Former supper club hosts Rosie French and Ellie Grace swapped their sitting room for this permanent spot in Brixton Village Market, where in an open, larder-style kitchen, they craft affordable dishes fusing Modern British and Middle Eastern cooking; a short list of beers and wines is available for those dining in, but if you don't want to wait for one of the few tables, you can queue for a takeaway.

The French Table 🅼 *French/Mediterranean* <u>28</u> <u>24</u> <u>26</u> <u>£52</u>
Surbiton | 85 Maple Rd., KT6 4AW | 020-8399-2365 | www.thefrenchtable.co.uk
Chef-owners Eric and Sarah Guignard's "smart", "bright" Surbiton "gem" is "no longer a secret", as evidenced by the foodies who flock from all over for the "imaginative", "fantastic" French-Mediterranean cuisine; "knowledgeable", "friendly" staff and prices that, while "expensive", are ultimately "good value" for the overall "quality" help explain why it's "worth the trek" from Central London.

Frontline 🅂 *British* ▽ <u>23</u> <u>23</u> <u>19</u> <u>£37</u>
Paddington | 13 Norfolk Pl., W2 1QJ | 020-7479-8960 | www.frontlineclub.com
"Foreign war correspondents" on their "way to Heathrow" join civvies at this "cosy, comfortable", "high-ceilinged" Traditional British dining room that's decorated with "striking" photography and located underneath the private Paddington club of the same name; "delicious", "reasonably priced" dishes made from organic ingredients give a good send-off, as do the "obliging" staff.

Gaby's ⏺ *Jewish/Mideastern* <u>23</u> <u>14</u> <u>20</u> <u>£15</u>
Leicester Square | 30 Charing Cross Rd., WC2H 0DB | 020-7836-4233
"Fantastic falafel and hummus, proper salt beef sandwiches" and other similarly "comforting" Jewish–Middle Eastern grub have been served since 1965 at this "gem of the West End" near Leicester Square; and although "the decor's never been up to much", "the service keeps you coming back" for "a quick bite before the theatre or cinema", or simply when you're "hungry" and "skint".

Gail's *Bakery* <u>22</u> <u>16</u> <u>18</u> <u>£16</u>
Clerkenwell | 33-35 Exmouth Mkt., EC1R 4QL | 020-7713-6550
Soho | 128 Wardour St., W1 8ZL | 020-7287-1324
Hampstead | 64 Hampstead High St., NW3 1QH | 020-7794-5700
Crouch End | 48 The Broadway, N8 9TP | 020-8348-6323
Clapham | 64 Northcote Rd., SW11 6QL | 020-7924-6330
Chelsea | 341 Fulham Rd., SW10 9TW | 020-7352-8842
Chiswick | 282-284 Chiswick High Rd., W4 1PA | 020-8995-2266

(continued)

Gail's

Notting Hill | 138 Portobello Rd., W11 2DZ | 020-7460-0766
Queen's Park | 75 Salusbury Rd., NW6 6NH | 020-7625-0068
St. John's Wood | 5 Circus Rd., NW8 6NX | 020-7722-0983
www.gailsbread.co.uk
Additional locations throughout London

Fans are "addicted" to the "scrumptious cakes" and "mouth-watering savouries" at this all-day bakery/cafe chain, despite the feeling that they're a relatively "expensive indulgence"; though service is often "friendly", it can also be "indifferent", so entertain yourself by squeezing into the "tight communal tables" and listening to the "amazing conversations" of the "daily crush of mums" (with babies) who keep it "crowded".

NEW Gail's Kitchen *European*   - | - | - | M

Bloomsbury | Myhotel Bloomsbury | 11-13 Bayley St., WC1B 3HD |
020-7323-9694 | www.gailskitchen.co.uk

High-end bakery outfit Gail's runs this new all-day cafe attached to a modern Bloomsbury hotel, where the midpriced Modern European menu skews toward small plates and bread-heavy recipes and features daily specials displayed on a wooden deli-counter; the bright, casual setting has cage-wire chairs, oak and steel tables and a wine list that includes half carafes.

Gallipoli *Turkish*   21 | 22 | 21 | £24

Islington | 102 Upper St., N1 1QN | 020-7359-0630
Islington | 107 Upper St., N1 1QN | 020-7226-5333
Islington | 120 Upper St., N1 1QP | 020-7359-1578
www.cafegallipoli.com

"There's something to be said" for a place with three locations (of "varying casualness") on the same Islington street; all are "lovely", "cluttered and noisy", with "efficient" staff who are "anxious to please" as they "stuff you in like sardines" for "tasty Turkish" eats at "incredibly reasonable prices".

Galvin at Windows *French*   25 | 25 | 25 | £67

Mayfair | London Hilton on Park Ln. | 22 Park Ln., 28th fl., W1K 1BE |
020-7208-4021 | www.galvinatwindows.com

"Glorious views" of Hyde Park and way beyond, "original", "excellent" New French cuisine from chef-patron Chris Galvin and "attentive, informative" service make the Hilton Park Lane's 28th-floor restaurant a "fantastic all-round" option for an "enjoyable lunch", high-end "biz dinner" or "romantic date"; P.S. "don't forget to check out the cocktail bar next door".

Galvin Bistrot de Luxe *French*   25 | 22 | 23 | £55

Marylebone | 66 Baker St., W1U 7DJ | 020-7935-4007 |
www.galvinrestaurants.com

"Still going strong, despite the competition", this "polished French brasserie" in Marylebone from brothers Chris and Jeff Galvin continues to impress with its "excellent", "classic" French dishes accompanied by a "very good" wine list; the "sophistication" of the

	FOOD	DECOR	SERVICE	COST

place is evident in the "professional" waiters, who "spoil" diners and ensure a "slick experience" all-round.

Galvin La Chapelle *French* | 26 | 26 | 24 | £64 |

Spitalfields | St. Botolph's Hall | 35 Spital Sq., E1 6DY | 020-7299-0400

Galvin Café a Vin *French*

Spitalfields | 35 Spital Sq., E1 6DY | 020-7299-0404
www.galvinrestaurants.com

An "awesome dining experience from top to bottom", this "grand" setting in a Victorian former school chapel on Spital Square offers a "taste explosion" in the form of chef/brothers Chris and Jeff Galvin's "outstanding", "expensive" New French fare; "welcoming service" adds to its reputation as a "real treat" for a quick City lunch (which can be "great value") or to "take time entertaining clients and friends"; P.S. the adjacent Cafe a Vin has a heated terrace for "unforgiving weather".

Ganapati *Indian* | ∇ 26 | 19 | 24 | £28 |

Peckham | 38 Holly Grove, SE15 5DF | 020-7277-2928 |
www.ganapatirestaurant.com

"Not your typical" curry house, this Peckham place pulls in locals with "brilliant", sometimes "spicy" South Indian snacks that are "cooked and served by people who know how to do it"; its "rustic, casual" setting is "quite small and popular", so booking is recommended.

Garufa *Argentinean/Steak* | 26 | 17 | 21 | £39 |

Highbury | 104 Highbury Pk., N5 2XE | 020-7226-0070 |
www.garufa.co.uk

NEW Garufin 🗷 *Argentinean/Steak*

Holborn | 25-27 Theobald's Rd., WC1X 8SP | 020-7430-9073 |
www.garufin.co.uk

Steak and other "amazing" comfort foods are the stars of the menu at this pair of Argentinean parrillas in a ground-floor cafe with a basement restaurant in Holborn and with street-view windows in Highbury; "friendly" service, a wine list packed with Argentine Malbecs and bare-brick-and-wood decor complete the picture.

The Gate *Vegetarian/Vegan* | 23 | 18 | 20 | £34 |

Islington | 370 St. John St., EC1V 4NN | 020-7278-5483
Hammersmith | 51 Queen Caroline St., W6 9QL | 020-8748-6932 🗷
www.thegaterestaurants.com

"Knowledgeable" staff are "happy to serve you at your own pace" at this "reasonably priced" veggie-vegan with branches in Hammersmith and Islington; "creative", "well-presented" dishes leave the "bohemian" types" that frequent the duo "begging for more"; P.S. at time of publication, the Hammersmith branch was closed for refurbishment and set to reopen later this year.

Gaucho *Argentinean/Steak* | 22 | 20 | 20 | £59 |

City | 1 Bell Inn Yard, EC3V 0BL | 020-7626-5180 🗷
City | 5 Finsbury Ave., EC2M 2PG | 020-7256-6877 🗷
Farringdon | 93 Charterhouse St., EC1M 6HL | 020-7490-1676 🗷
Holborn | 125-126 Chancery Ln., WC2A 1PU | 020-7242-7727 🗷

(continued)

Gaucho

Piccadilly | 25 Swallow St., W1B 4QR | 020-7734-4040 ◖
Canary Wharf | 29 Westferry Circus, E14 8RR | 020-7987-9494
Hampstead | 64 Heath St., NW3 1DN | 020-7431-8222
Tower Bridge | 2 More London Riverside, SE1 2AP | 020-7407-5222
Richmond | The Towpath, TW10 6UJ | 020-8948-4030
Chelsea | 89 Sloane Ave., SW3 3DX | 020-7584-9901
www.gauchorestaurants.com
Additional locations throughout London

Carnivores applaud the "quality" Argentinean steaks at this "brilliantly conceived" chain that attempts to "break away from the traditional mold" with cow-hide furnishings and a "sexy", "nightclubby" vibe; some detect "creeping" prices, but the "variety and selection of wine" gets the thumbs up, and service is generally "professional" and "quick".

Gauthier Soho ⑤ *French*

28	23	26	£65

Soho | 21 Romilly St., W1D 5AF | 020-7494-3111 |
www.gauthiersoho.co.uk

Chef-owner Alexis Gauthier's "creative, delicate" New French cuisine is served by "enthusiastic" staff who treat diners "like kings" at this "unique" Soho townhouse, which offers set menus of up to five courses; the "understated but beautiful", "low-lit" rooms create a "seductive" mood, while the "incredible-value" lunch sets it "apart from the crowd" (at other times, it's pricey).

The Gay Hussar ⑤ *Hungarian*

21	20	22	£41

Soho | 2 Greek St., W1D 4NB | 020-7437-0973 | www.gayhussar.co.uk

"Steeped in fascinating heritage", this "atmospheric" Soho spot from 1953 presents "glorious" pictures of "patrons past" as a backdrop for "solid", "old-school" Hungarian meals like "hearty goulash" and other "filling" fare washed down with Bull's Blood wine; indeed, you'll eat "extremely well for relatively little", and you'll get "friendly service" in the bargain.

Gaylord *Indian*

21	19	21	£40

Fitzrovia | 79-81 Mortimer St., W1W 7SJ | 020-7580-3615 |
www.gaylordlondon.com

"Imaginative cuisine from the subcontinent" is what's on offer at this "solid", long-time Fitzrovia Indian whose "interesting variety includes lots of fish"; it's "always busy", but "generously spaced" tables in the "traditionally decorated" dining room means it never feels cramped, while "friendly staff" ensure everyone is comfortable.

Gazette *French*

20	21	18	£31

Balham | 100 Balham High Rd., SW12 9AA | 020-8772-1232
Battersea | 79 Sherwood Ct., Chatfield Rd., SW11 3UY | 020-7223-0999
www.gazettebrasserie.co.uk

"Locals count themselves lucky" to have this pair of brasseries decked out in "typically French" fashion "on their doorstep" in Balham and Battersea, as the "classic" cuisine is "delightful" and "good value for money" too; "sweet" service helps to keep it a "lovely place to chill out", whether in the "romantic" interior, or on the "nice" patio in Sherwood Court.

Geales *Seafood*

| 20 | 14 | 18 | £32 |

Chelsea | 1 Cale St., SW3 3QT | 020-7965-0555
Notting Hill | 2 Farmer St., W8 7SN | 020-7727-7528
www.geales.com
"Serious about fish 'n' chips, 'n' good at it too" affirm champions of these "poshed-up" chippies in Notting Hill (since 1939) and Chelsea (2010), where the "delectable" seafood and sides are "fairly priced" and served alongside "some pleasant wines"; service can be "accommodating", while the "classic black-and-white settings" are definitely "a bit snug", though "welcoming" nonetheless.

George ⓩ *European*

| 23 | 22 | 25 | £70 |

Mayfair | private club | 87-88 Mount St., W1K 2SR | 020-7491-4433 | www.georgeclub.com
"George delivers a first-class product at breakfast, lunch and dinner" say members of this "well-run" private club in Mayfair, which employs "discreet, thoughtful" staff to proffer its Modern European menu; affiliates choose the Hockney-bedecked dining room, the high-energy downstairs bar or the patio ("don't mind the traffic noise"), all reportedly "worth every pound" – and many are needed.

The Giaconda Dining Rooms ⓩ Ⓜ *European*

| 23 | 14 | 20 | £45 |

Soho | 9 Denmark St., WC2H 8LS | 020-7240-3334 | www.giacondadining.com
The "no-man's-land between Covent Garden and Oxford Street" harbours this Soho "secret", a "modest setting"–cum–"fine-dining experience" with an "excellent husband-and-wife team" at the helm and "complex", "imaginative" Modern European food on the menu; what's more, it's "good value for money", particularly when factoring in the "great" wine list that includes a "decent selection of half bottles".

The Gilbert Scott *British*

| 19 | 24 | 20 | £63 |

King's Cross | St. Pancras Renaissance Hotel | Euston Rd., NW1 2AR | 020-7278-3888 | www.thegilbertscott.co.uk
"In terms of decor, you couldn't ask for more" from the "drop-dead gorgeous setting" of this British restaurant in the St Pancras Renaissance Hotel – it's "simply beautiful", with "cavernous" proportions and Victorian features; chef Marcus Wareing's "competent" "classics" can be "pricey", although the set lunch is an "enjoyable, affordable" option; P.S. the adjacent cocktail bar is a similarly "stunning" affair.

Gilgamesh ◕ *Asian*

| 19 | 24 | 17 | £49 |

Camden Town | Stables Mkt. | Chalk Farm Rd., NW1 8AH | 020-7482-5757 | www.gilgameshbar.com
In this "cavernous" setting in Camden's Stables Market, "fantastic", "opulent decor" featuring "stunning woodwork" sets the scene for the "different" Pan-Asian creations of chef Ian Pengelley – which fans find "tasty" but others feel "fall short" considering the "amazing atmosphere" and "pricey" cost; some take issue with "variable

staff" too, yet it's still a magnet for "dates" and "large groups", enticed in part by the "memorable" cocktails.

Giovanni's of Covent Garden ●🛇🖾 *Italian* ▽ 23 | 19 | 21 | £39

Covent Garden | 10 Goodwin's Ct., WC2N 4LL | 020-7240-2877 | www.giovannislondon.co.uk

The owner "makes you feel like a member of the family", while his "friendly", "attentive staff" deliver "wonderful" "old-school" Italian at this "cosy" Covent Garden "jewel"; open until late, it's "the perfect after-theatre dinner spot".

The Glasshouse *European* 26 | 21 | 25 | £56

Richmond | 14 Station Parade, TW9 3PZ | 020-8940-6777 | www.glasshouserestaurant.co.uk

Kew's "laidback" sister of La Trompette exudes "star quality" with an expensive, fixed priced Modern European menu that's "incredible from the amuse bouche to the dessert", as well as an "impressive" wine list and "a consistently high level of service"; even if the "noisy acoustics" of the light-filled space ruffle some feathers, overall, it "delivers" for "any occasion".

Golden Dragon ● *Chinese* 23 | 15 | 16 | £31

Chinatown | 28-29 Gerrard St., W1D 6JW | 020-7734-1073 | www.goldendragonlondon.com

"Massive portions" of "tasty" dim sum and other "reliable" Chinese fare is the "cheap" deal at this "traditional" Chinatown establishment with a "wide-ranging menu" and "hectic" "school-canteen" atmospherics; service is "not necessarily a strong point", but at least there's plenty of room for "family parties" in the "spacious" environs.

The Golden Hind 🖾 *Seafood* 24 | 11 | 18 | £18

Marylebone | 73 Marylebone Ln., W1U 2PN | 020-7486-3644

Over 100 years in business, this "cheap and cheerful" Marylebone fryer serves "large" portions of "quality" fish 'n' chips alongside "equally tasty" steamed seafood in a "basic" environment; "fast" service and a money-saving BYO policy (there's a wine shop round the corner) mean it's "always packed", so make sure you book ahead.

Goldmine ● *Chinese* ▽ 25 | 8 | 14 | £32

Bayswater | 102 Queensway, W2 3RR | 020-7792-8331

"If you can bear the crowds" of "large groups" at this Bayswater Chinese, you'll be rewarded with its "amazing" signature roast duck, the star among "a fairly standard range" of "more-than-acceptable" Cantonese dishes; you'll also have to endure "sometimes surly service" and no-frills decor, but you won't need to spend much money.

The Good Earth *Chinese* 25 | 19 | 22 | £44

Mill Hill | 143-145 The Broadway, NW7 4RN | 020-8959-7011
NEW **Wandsworth** | 11 Bellevue Rd., SW17 7EG | 020-8682-9230
Knightsbridge | 233 Brompton Rd., SW3 2EP | 020-7584-3658
www.goodearthgroup.co.uk

An "innovative", "eclectic" Chinese menu (including "lots of vegetarian choices") and "friendly" service ensure this chainlet is "always busy"; though fairly "pricey", fans insist it's "excellent value" for money, thus "well worth a visit"; P.S. takeaway and "quick delivery" are also available.

Goodman ☒ *Steak*
27 | 21 | 24 | £60

City | 11 Old Jewry, EC2R 8DU | 020-7600-8220
Mayfair | 26 Maddox St., W1S 1QH | 020-7499-3776
Canary Wharf | Discovery Dock E. | 3 S. Quay, E14 9RU | 020-7531-0300
www.goodmanrestaurants.com

"Simply cooked", "flavoursome" steaks, including fillets "so tender" they "might be cut with a spoon", form the menu at this "stylish", "fairly expensive" chainlet; staff are "welcoming" and "friendly", and while fans suggest it's "great for business lunches", it's a dinner destination too thanks in part to the "good wine list".

Gopal's of Soho ● *Indian*
▽ 19 | 11 | 19 | £32

Soho | 12 Bateman St., W1D 4AH | 020-7434-0840 | www.gopalsofsoho.co.uk

"You may not be surprised, but you won't be disappointed" at this "reasonably priced", "old reliable" Soho Indian; many people "prefer takeaway", perhaps because they find the environs "a bit tired", but those who opt to eat in are catered for by "ever-so-polite" staff; P.S. late hours make it an "after-theatre" go to.

The Goring Dining Room *British*
25 | 26 | 27 | £73

Victoria | Goring Hotel | 15 Beeston Pl., SW1 0JW | 020-7396-9000 | www.goringhotel.co.uk

"Prepare to be pampered" at this "outstanding hotel dining room" "a stone's throw from Buckingham Palace", where "long-standing staff" deliver "superb Traditional British cuisine" (served as set-price menus) and "excellently curated" wines; the "classic setting" is a "model of elegant restraint", though "not as stuffy as you might think", as evidenced by the "free-form" Swarovski chandeliers; in sum, it's the "quintessential high-end experience", complete with a royally "pricey" bill.

Gourmet Burger Kitchen *Burgers*
18 | 11 | 15 | £18

Soho | 15 Frith St., W1D 4RE | 020-7494-9533
Spitalfields | 5 Horner Sq., E1 6EW | 020-7422-0052
NEW Islington | N1 Ctr. | 9 Parkfield St., N1 0PS | 020-7354-9134
Dulwich | 121 Lordship Ln., SE22 8HU | 020-8693-9307
Tower Bridge | 2A Tower Pl., EC3R 5BU | 020-7929-2222
Clapham | 44 Northcote Rd., SW11 1NZ | 020-7228-3309
Clapham | 84 Clapham High St., SW4 7UL | 020-7627-5367
South Bank | Soho Wharf, Clink St., SE1 9DG | 020-7403-2379
Fulham | 49 Fulham Broadway, SW6 1AE | 020-7381-4242
Notting Hill | 160 Portobello Rd., W11 2EB | 020-7243-6597
www.gbk.co.uk
Additional locations throughout London

At this "unpretentious" burger chain, the "cheap and cheerful" menu offers "plenty of variety", with "large", "cooked-just-right" patties and "delicious" drinks like the "super-indulgent Oreo milkshake"; with its "semi-self-service concept" (overseen by "friendly" staff) and "somewhat sparse", "neutral" setting, it's "not one for a romantic evening", but it is a "safe bet" for a "quick bite".

NEW Grain Store *International*   `-` `-` `-` `E`

King's Cross | Granary Square, 1-3 Stable St., N1C 4AB | 020-7324-4466 | www.grainstore.com

The team behind the Zetter Townhouse and Bistrot Bruno Loubet spread their wings at this spacious, expensive King's Cross restaurant and bar, where chef Bruno Loubet's International concoctions give a starring role to vegetables, often in unusual combos; the casual-chic, exposed brick wall setting has no obvious delineation between kitchen and dining and spreads out into Granary Square; P.S. expect some experimental savoury mixes on the cocktail list.

Granger & Co. *Australian/International*   `19` `19` `16` `£39`

Notting Hill | 175 Westbourne Grove, W11 2SB | 020-7229-9111 | www.grangerandco.com

"Interesting, well-prepared", Australian-influenced International fare and a pervading "Notting Hill buzz" account for the "queues around the block" at this moderately priced all-day dining room; service runs the gamut from "attentive" to "slow" (especially when its "super busy"), but overall it's a "comfortable, welcoming place to spend time".

The Grazing Goat *British*   `20` `20` `20` `£40`

Marylebone | Public House & Hotel | 6 New Quebec St., W1 7RQ | 020-7724-7243 | www.thegrazinggoat.co.uk

In the "no-man's land" between Edgware Road and Oxford Street, this "relaxed" (though occasionally "noisy") all-day country-house-style gastropub, with eight hotel rooms above, offers "tasty" Traditional British "classics" to mostly "younger patrons"; "decent wines" and "friendly staff" add to surveyors' "satisfaction", and the prices are "ok" too.

NEW The Great British *British*   `-` `-` `-` `M`

Mayfair | 14 N. Audley St., W1K 6WE | 020-7741-2233 | www.eatbrit.com

This all-day Mayfair eatery serves a moderately priced, classic British menu that includes everything from no-nonsense breakfast fry-ups to roast dinners and afternoon tea; there's an earthy simplicity to the narrow, wood-panelled space, which includes alfresco tables in the handsome portico of the building next door.

Great Queen Street *British*   `24` `16` `21` `£36`

Covent Garden | 32 Great Queen St., WC2B 5AA | 020-7242-0622

Comfort food seekers tuck into "out-of-this-world" soups, "meaty" mains and other "hearty" food from an "ever-changing" menu of British "classics" at this "friendly" Covent Garden gastropub; although there are "fancier" places, fans argue it possesses the "right amount of homeliness", all at prices that "won't deplete your wallet".

	FOOD	DECOR	SERVICE	COST

NEW Greenberry Café *International* | - | - | - | M |

Primrose Hill | 101 Regent's Park Rd., NW1 8UR | 020-7483-3765 | www.greenberrycafe.co.uk

Morfudd Richards, the woman behind former Islington icon Lola's, is now in this light, bright Primrose Hill cafe offering up midpriced all-day comfort food based on International recipes and local ingredients; unusual ice creams made onsite round out the offerings.

Green Cottage *Chinese* | ▽ 25 | 13 | 19 | £23 |

Finchley | 9 New College Pde., NW3 5EP | 020-7722-5305

"Always buzzing" with a "loyal, local clientele", this Finchley Chinese churns out "straight-forward", "well-executed" oriental dishes; "friendly" staff extend a "warm welcome", and the "decent-size" portions present "good value for money".

The Greenhouse Ⓩ *French* | 27 | 25 | 26 | £87 |

Mayfair | 27 Hay's Mews, W1J 5NY | 020-7499-3331 | www.greenhouserestaurant.co.uk

Chef Arnaud Bignon is "a master of taste" declare fans of this "superb", upscale French dining room in Mayfair, where the "depth of vintages" on the huge wine list is also applauded; the "beautiful" room (with "lots of space between the tables"), "quiet ambience" and high level of service works equally well for "business meetings" as it does for "romantic" encounters.

NEW Green Man & French Horn Ⓩ *French* | ▽ 21 | 20 | 22 | £38 |

Covent Garden | 54 St. Martin's Ln., WC2N 4EA | 020-7836-2645 | www.greenmanfrenchhorn.co

"Friendly" staff ply you with "tasty, traditional" French fare with an accent on "all things Loire valley" at this "good-value", rustic St Martin's Lane bistro; it's a suitable pre- or post-theatre pit stop, especially for oenophiles as, like its siblings Soif, Brawn, etc., the "well-thought-out" wine list, heavy on natural cuvées, is as much a draw as the grub.

Green's Restaurant & Oyster Bar Ⓩ *British/Seafood* | 21 | 19 | 22 | £59 |

City | 14 Cornhill, EC3V 3ND | 020-7220-6300
St. James's | 36 Duke St., SW1Y 6DF | 020-7930-4566
www.greens.org.uk

Conjuring up the feel of a "gentleman's club" with mahogany panelling, leather banquettes and "impeccable service", this "dependable" St. James's venue and its City cousin offer a "quintessential old-school" Traditional British experience as well as "splendid seafood" that's "not painful to the purse" ("for the quality"); the setting's "general hush" is ideal for "private conversation", while the bar might be a bit livelier, with its martinis and oysters that "never fail".

Greig's ● *Steak* | ▽ 21 | 20 | 21 | £48 |

Mayfair | 26 Bruton Pl., W1J 6NG | 020-7629-5613 | www.greigs.com

"Huge" "dependable" steaks are served up by staff who "care about making you welcome" at this dining room with "old-fashioned" wood panelling, stained glass and a "superb" Mayfair location "near Berkeley Square"; however, critics find it too "expensive" for being what they deem simply "average".

The Groucho Club *British*   18 | 17 | 19 | £48

Soho | private club | 45 Dean St., W1D 4QB | 020-7439-4685 | www.thegrouchoclub.com

Members of this "exclusive" Soho private club say "don't expect the debauchery that made the place famous", but do count on "expensive", "well-cooked" Modern Brit dishes served alongside a "good wine list" in a brasserie, dining room and several bar areas; so even if it's "not in its heyday", it's "still cool" – and "more about seeing and being seen" among "showbiz" types than anything else.

Grumbles *British/French*   ∇ 19 | 16 | 22 | £30

Pimlico | 35 Churton St., SW1V 2LT | 020-7834-0149 | www.grumblesrestaurant.co.uk

Pay little attention to its name, as there are few grouses about this low-key Pimlico stalwart serving "typical bistro"-style fare from a British-French menu; even though the digs are "cramped", there's a "nice old-fashioned feel" to the place, plus service is "attentive" and prices "fairly reasonable".

Guinea Grill ☒ *Steak*   24 | 19 | 22 | £56

Mayfair | 30 Bruton Pl., W1J 6NL | 020-7499-1210 | www.theguinea.co.uk

"Old-school in the best sense", this "darkly lit" steakhouse behind a same-named pub in a "charming" Mayfair mews has "been around forever" (1952), plying locals and their "foreign guests" with "luscious", "cooked-to-perfection steaks" and "wonderful" savoury pies; the prices are a tad "crazy" and seating is a bit "cramped", but much is forgiven thanks to staff who "make you feel that you are welcome".

The Gun *British*   23 | 22 | 21 | £41

Canary Wharf | 27 Coldharbour, E14 9NS | 020-7515-5222 | www.thegundocklands.com

"Cosy up inside by the log fire in winter" and enjoy Thames views from the "wonderful terrace" in summer at this "old-world" Canary Wharf "escape" offering "reliable" Modern British gastropub fare (including "an incredible Sunday roast"), plus a "solid wine list" and "friendly service"; despite being "a little pricey", "romantics" are drawn in droves, so "you definitely need to reserve a table at busy times".

Haandi *Indian*   21 | 15 | 20 | £33

NEW **Knightsbridge** | 136 Brompton Rd., SW3 1HY
Knightsbridge | 7 Cheval Pl., SW7 1EW | 020-7823-7373
www.haandi-restaurants.com

"On a quiet side street steps from Harrods", the original Cheval Place branch of this "friendly" Indian duo (the second is on the Brompton Road) might be "overlooked because of its hard-to-find entrance", but those who venture inside discover "tasty", sometimes "unusual" dishes; it's "not fancy", but then neither are the prices; P.S. it's part of a small chain with locations in Kampala and Nairobi.

	FOOD	DECOR	SERVICE	COST

Haché *Burgers* | 23 | 19 | 20 | £22 |

NEW **Shoreditch** | 147-149 Curtain Rd., EC2A 3QE | 020-7739-8396
Camden Town | 24 Inverness St., NW1 7HJ | 020-7485-9100
Clapham | 153 Clapham High St., SW4 7SS | 020-7738-8760
Chelsea | 329-331 Fulham Rd., SW10 9QL | 020-7823-3515
www.hacheburgers.com

There's "always a queue out the door" at this "quirky", "new wave" burger chainlet, which fans say is "a cut above" due to its "interesting, original" patties, which come in either a ciabatta or brioche, with a range of "exciting" toppings; it may be "nothing fancy", but the "great atmosphere", "friendly" staff and "decent" prices make it "worth a pit stop if you're hungry".

Hakkasan ◑ *Chinese* | 26 | 25 | 22 | £68 |

Fitzrovia | 8 Hanway Pl., W1T 1HD | 020-7927-7000
Mayfair | 17 Bruton St., W1J 6QB | 020-7907-1888
www.hakkasan.com

This "super sexy" Cantonese with locations in Fitzrovia and Mayfair marries "to-die-for", "innovative" cuisine with a "vibrant", "clublike atmosphere" designed for "people-watching"; although it's "pricey", many find it "worth every pretty penny", especially with such "friendly, prompt" service.

Halepi ◑ *Greek* | 24 | 15 | 21 | £38 |

Bayswater | 18 Leinster Terr., W2 3ET | 020-7262-1070 |
www.halepi.co.uk

"My big fat Greek favourite!" exclaim "regulars" who delight in the "huge portions" of "affordable", "lip-smacking" Hellenic cuisine served in "efficient" fashion at this "buzzing, informal" Bayswater "stalwart"; the interior "could do with a little smartening up" and it's "so cramped, sardines would be upset", but that's "part of the charm".

Haozhan ◑ *Chinese* | 24 | 15 | 19 | £32 |

Chinatown | 8 Gerrard St., W1D 5PJ | 020-7434-3838 |
www.haozhan.co.uk

"Exotic twists" abound on the "well-executed" Chinese menu, which includes a number of "destination dishes" and prices that are a "fraction of the cost" of some other "high-end" competitors, at this minimalist Chinatown "find"; the "service may not be as sophisticated as the food", but it "means well", and it's "swift" to boot.

NEW **The Happenstance** *European* | - | - | - | M |

City | 1A Ludgate Hill, EC4M 7AA | 0845-468-0104 |
www.thehappenstancebar.co.uk

On a corner spot by St. Paul's Cathedral in the City, this all-day, accessibly priced Modern European's dining, drinking and deli spaces all reflect an industrial-chic style featuring monochrome and steel, mingled with exposed bricks.

Harbour City ◑ *Chinese* | 19 | 13 | 15 | £24 |

Chinatown | 46 Gerrard St., W1D 5QH | 020-7439-7859
"Delicious" dim sum and other "quality" dishes take diners "back to the days of the old Chinatown" at this Cantonese spot where it's all

about "no fuss, good food"; there might be "not much space between the tables and chairs" and service is merely "ok", yet all three of its "pleasant" floors are almost always "busy".

Hare & Tortoise *Japanese*   22 | 16 | 17 | £22

Bloomsbury | 11-13 Brunswick Ctr., WC1N 1AF | 020-7278-9799
City | 90 New Bridge St., EC4V 6JJ | 020-7651-0266 🗷
Putney | 296-298 Upper Richmond Rd., SW15 6TH | 020-8394-7666
Ealing | 38-39 Haven Green, W5 2NX | 020-8810-7066
Kensington | 373 Kensington High St., W14 8QZ | 020-7603-8887
www.hareandtortoise.co.uk

"The queues are testament" to the "tasty" Japanese eats (including sushi, tempura and noodle soups) to be found at this "no-frills" chain; furthermore, the "quick", "lovely staff", "friendly" atmosphere and "affordable" prices make it "well worth" the wait for a table.

Harry's Bar ●🗷 *Italian*   25 | 24 | 25 | £87

Mayfair | private club | 26 S. Audley St., W1K 2PD | 020-7408-0844 |
www.harrysbar.co.uk

"The chauffeur-driven Bentleys waiting outside" tell you all you need to know about "the rich and famous" clientele who are members of this "beautiful" private club in Mayfair, where "personalised service" conveys "excellent Italian-influenced cuisine"; by all means "beg, borrow, steal or bribe your way in", just make sure "someone else is paying" – it's so "wildly expensive", there must be "gold in the food".

The Harwood Arms *British*   27 | 21 | 23 | £45

Fulham | Walham Grove, SW6 1QP | 020-7386-1847 |
www.harwoodarms.com

You'll "never be able to eat shop-bought Scotch eggs again" after sampling the "triumphant" versions whipped up at this "next-level" Fulham gastropub where the entire Modern British menu is "phenomenal", especially the "to-die-for game dishes", all at prices so "reasonable" you can "bring the whole family along"; "friendly" staff work the "rustic, airy" digs, which are "deservedly popular" – and downright "packed" "when Chelsea are playing" (always "book ahead").

Hawksmoor *Steak*   26 | 21 | 23 | £58

City | Guildhall | 10 Basinghall St., EC2V 5BQ |
020-7397-8120 🗷
Covent Garden | 11 Langley St., WC2H 9JG | 020-7420-9390
NEW **Piccadilly** | 5A Air St., W1J 0AD | 020-7406-3980 ●
Spitalfields | 157A Commercial St., E1 6BJ | 020-7426-4850
www.thehawksmoor.com

"Tender" cuts of meat are what this "brilliant all-round" steakhouse chainlet is "all about", with "incredible" cocktails and "knowledgeable", "down-to-earth" service adding to its merits; some suggest the atmosphere is reminiscent of a "secret nightclub" or "gentleman's club", and despite "steep" prices, fans assure it's "worth every pound"; P.S. all branches have seafood on the menu, and it's a particular focus at the new Air Street link.

	FOOD	DECOR	SERVICE	COST

Haz ● *Turkish* · · · · · · · · · · · · · · · 23 | 20 | 21 | £28

City | 112 Houndsditch, EC3A 7BD | 020-7623-8180 🖫
City | 34 Foster Ln., EC2V 6HD | 020-7515-9467
City | 6 Mincing Ln., EC3M 3BD | 020-7929-3173
City | 9 Cutler St., E1 7DJ | 020-7929-7923
www.hazrestaurant.co.uk

Sprinkled around the City, this "busy" chain of cafe/bistros produces "reliable" Turkish eats from a "varied", moderately priced menu; if some are "not overly keen" on the "bland" decor and "canteen-style" tables, at least the "attentive" service is appreciated.

Hedone 🖫 Ⓜ *European* · · · · · · · · · 23 | 21 | 22 | £72

Chiswick | 301-303 Chiswick High Rd., W4 4HH | 020-8747-0377 |
www.hedonerestaurant.com

"London needs more people like" Mikael Jonsson, the "discerning" Swedish chef-owner who prepares "fascinating" Modern Euro set menus paired with "excellent wines recommended by the sommelier" at this "expensive" Chiswick venue; bare-brick walls, an open kitchen and a ceiling decorated with caveman-style images sets the scene.

Hélène Darroze at the · · · · · · · · · 25 | 26 | 25 | £114
Connaught 🖫 Ⓜ *French*

Mayfair | Connaught | Carlos Pl., W1K 2AL | 020-7107-8880 |
www.the-connaught.co.uk

The Connaught's "stylish" dining room presents "classic" "first-class haute" French cuisine from "one of Paris's great chefs", supported by "well-paired wines by the glass"; if some find it generally very expensive, all agree lunch is "good value", and service is "exemplary" too – "pampering you all the way".

Hereford Road *British* · · · · · · · · · · 24 | 19 | 21 | £49

Bayswater | 3 Hereford Rd., W2 4AB | 020-7727-1144 |
www.herefordroad.org

This Notting Hill "gem" wins plaudits for the "fabulous, simple execution" of its "interesting" Modern British menu, not to mention "fantastic wine list" and "divine" cheese selection; the "cosy, inviting" setting in a former Victorian butcher's shop features an open kitchen to "enjoy the choreography" behind the stoves, while praise also goes to the "friendly" service and "reasonable" pricing.

Herman ze German *German/Hot Dogs* ∇ 23 | 13 | 18 | £11

Charing Cross | 19 Villiers St., WC2N 6NE | 020-7839-5264 |
www.herman-ze-german.co.uk

In Charing Cross, this low-cost German eatery serves up "excellent" bratwurst and "space-age fries cooked with hot air rather than oil"; and with a basic set up, it's a "quick-and-easy", "grab-and-walk" option for local office lunchers and pre-party revellers.

Hibiscus 🖫 *French* · · · · · · · · · · · 25 | 22 | 24 | £85

Mayfair | 29 Maddox St., W1S 2PA | 020-7629-2999 |
www.hibiscusrestaurant.co.uk

The "flavours and elegance" of chef-owner Claude Bosi's "exquisite" French cooking make some view this discreet Mayfair venue as an "expensive" "pearl"; although some suggest that "a bit more colour" on the pale, wood-panelled interiors "could do no harm", at least most are satisfied with the "friendly", "professional" service.

High Road Brasserie *European*　　22 | 21 | 17 | £44

Chiswick | High Road Hse. | 162-166 Chiswick High Rd., W4 1PR | 020-8742-7474 | www.highroadhouse.co.uk

To the delight of "Nappyland" trendies, "you don't have to be a member to enjoy" this "lovely, bright" and "efficient" Modern European brasserie underneath Nick Jones' Chiswick hotel and private club; in fact, they say they could eat the "reliable", "frequently changing" fare "every night and still want to come in for lunch", which along with the "reasonable prices", explains why it's "always packed".

Hi Sushi *Japanese*　　22 | 20 | 18 | £29

Covent Garden | 27 Catherine St., WC2B 5JS | 020-7836-9398
Camden Town | 28 Jamestown Rd., NW1 7BY | 020-7482-7088
www.hisushi.net

"A great selection" of "fresh and delicious" Japanese fare is "quickly delivered" at this chainlet with branches in Covent Garden and Camden (both with "pleasant" decor); but it's "fantastic value for money" that's the real draw, with "big portions" (e.g. ramen bowls that are "Godzilla-sized"), "bargain bento boxes" and an "all-you-can-eat sushi" option.

Hix *British*　　22 | 19 | 20 | £54

Soho | 66-70 Brewer St., W1F 9UT | 020-7292-3518 | www.hixsoho.co.uk

Chef-owner Mark Hix's "trendy" Soho destination turns out British cuisine that is sometimes "simple", sometimes "daring", always "bang-on" and "rather expensive"; "service is easy and knowing", while the "slick", "contemporary art"–bedecked setting can be rather "noisy" – but that sort of "bustling" atmosphere appeals to its "hipster" habitués, especially the "cool downstairs bar", a "late-night" "scene unto itself" complete with "mad-scientist barmen and great alchemic cocktails".

Hix Mayfair *British*　　25 | 24 | 24 | £63

Mayfair | Brown's Hotel | 30-34 Albemarle St., W1S 4BP | 020-7518-4004 | www.thealbemarlerestaurant.com

Artwork by Tracey Emin, Michael Landy, Bridget Riley and more give this "traditional" Brown's Hotel dining room a "fantastic" "contemporary twist", though the "quality" victuals from the Hix stable are "classic British" (they're "expensive" too); "polished" staff glide between the "well-spaced" tables (hurrah, "you can hear" your companions!) and make sure diners "feel very well looked after".

Hix Oyster & Chop House *British/Steak*　　24 | 21 | 24 | £55

Farringdon | 36-37 Greenhill's Rents, EC1M 6BN | 020-7017-1930 | www.hixoysterandchophouse.co.uk

When "the decor's so simple", "the place must have a lot of confidence in its food", and that confidence is not misplaced at Mark Hix's Traditional Brit set in a former Smithfield sausage factory, where "hearty portions" of "wonderful" steakhouse classics are offered alongside "delicious seafood" ("on the expensive side" but "reasonable for the location"); it's "always full", so if you "drop in without a reservation", see if "intelligent staff" can seat you at the bar, home to "impressive" wines.

NEW HKK ⊠ *Chinese*　　　　　- | - | - | VE

City | Broadgate W., 88 Worship St., EC2A 2BE | 020-3535-1888 | www.hkklondon.com

The master restaurateurs at Hakkasan Group have conjured up this new and very expensive Chinese fine-dining experience in the City, where the bespoke banquet-style Cantonese tasting menu is designed to challenge even the most sophisticated of foodies; a range of cocktails, wines, fresh juices and teas can be matched with each course (which run to eight at lunch, 15 at dinner), all presented in a setting laced with ancient Oriental symbols.

Honest Burgers *Burgers*　　　27 | 20 | 23 | £15

NEW Soho | 4A Meard St., W1F 0EF | 020-3609-9524
Brixton | Brixton Mkt. | 12 Brixton Village Mkt., SW9 8PR | 020-7733-7963 ⊅
www.honestburgers.co.uk

Fans claim "you can taste every element" of the "juicy, flavoursome" patties served at this "inexpensive" pair of "straight-forward", "friendly" burger joints; some jest "bring a sleeping bag or pitch a tent", because both the Brixton original and the Soho offshoot are "tiny", and the no-bookings policy means queues are inevitable.

Honey & Co ⊠ *Mideastern*　　　- | - | - | M

Fitzrovia | 25A Warren St., W1T 5LZ | 020-7388-6175 | www.honeyandco.co.uk

A husband-and-wife team who worked at Ottolenghi and NOPI are behind this affordable all-day Warren Street Middle Eastern cafe; the colourful salads, pastries and mezze that line the windows are available to eat in the compact space as well as to take away.

Hot Stuff *Indian*　　　▽ 25 | 11 | 25 | £17

Vauxhall | 17-19 Wilcox Rd., SW8 2XΛ | 020-7720-1480 | www.welovehotstuff.com

Trusting foodies feel the Indian food made at this spot "tucked away" in a Vauxhall side street is so universally "fragrant and richly flavoured", they "don't even look at the menu", instead asking the "lovely staff" to "bring what they recommend"; the already "superb value" is bolstered by BYOB, and due to a recent expansion, the once "tiny premises" is now double the size.

Hoxton Grill ● *American*　　　22 | 20 | 20 | £35

Shoreditch | Hoxton Hotel | 81 Great Eastern St., EC2A 3HU | 020-7739-9111 | www.hoxtongrill.com

"Good-value" American cuisine featuring "amazing" steaks and "solid" "comfort food" (wings, burgers) is dished out all day by "friendly" staff to punters who pack the red-leather banquettes at this "lovely", "cosy", bare-brick diner in the Hoxton Hotel; at night, it's a "trendy" destination where the "post-work crowd" can down "great martinis" until 2 AM, and It's a notable brunch spot too, thanks in part to "cracking Bloody Marys".

Hoxton Square ● *Tex-Mex*   16 | 17 | 15 | £28

Hoxton | 2-4 Hoxton Sq., N1 6NU | 020-7613-0709 | www.hoxtonsquarebar.com

"Hip" Hoxton residents go to this "cool" Tex-Mex–themed bar and restaurant with "plenty of space to spread out" and "people-watch" while listening to live bands or DJs; the "food isn't amazing, but the atmosphere makes up for it", and for just a reasonably priced, "quick bite", it's "decent".

Hunan ⌧ *Chinese/Taiwanese*   27 | 13 | 21 | £58

Belgravia | 51 Pimlico Rd., SW1W 8NE | 020-7730-5712 | www.hunanlondon.com

"Relax and let the chef" whip up a selection of Chinese and Taiwanese "tapas"-style dishes to suit your preferences (just tell him things like "what you don't like and how spicy you want your food") at this "family-run" Belgravia eatery with an "interesting" "no-menu" concept; service is "friendly" and generally "quick", and while "there isn't really any decor" to note, "you don't care once you start eating".

Hush *European*   19 | 20 | 19 | £46

Holborn | 95-97 High Holborn, WC1V 6LF | 020-7242-4580 | www.hushbrasseries.com
Mayfair | 8 Lancashire Ct., W1S 1EY | 020-7659-1500 | www.hush.co.uk ⌧

"When the wife is shopping on Bond Street", "jet-setting hedge funders" make their way to this virtually "hidden" brasserie (with a similar new Holborn offshoot) for "solid" Modern Euro cuisine – "affordable" for Mayfair – or just a cocktail in the "plush" first-floor bar; service "strikes the balance between warm and formal" whether inside or out In the "cobbled" courtyard, just "lovely in the summer".

NEW Hutong *Chinese*   - | - | - | E

Tower Bridge | The Shard | 31 St. Thomas St., 33rd fl, SE1 9RY | 020-7478-0540 | www.aquahutong.co.uk

The panoramic view from this Chinese spot on the 33rd floor of the Shard (Europe's tallest building) isn't the only thing demanding attention – the decor is equally eye-catching, with its red lanterns, billowing silk curtains and hand-carved wooden panels; lamb marinated three times over a 24-hour period is a highlight of the expensive Northern Chinese-focused menu, while dim sum is the star at lunch.

Iberica *Spanish*   23 | 21 | 21 | £42

Marylebone | 195 Great Portland St., W1W 5PS | 020-7636-8650
Canary Wharf | 12 Cabot Sq., E14 4QQ | 020-7636-8650
NEW Iberica La Terraza *Spanish*
Canary Wharf | Cabot Sq., E14 EQQ | 020-7636-8650
www.ibericalondon.co.uk

From "quality" classic tapas to more "inventive" creations ("try the chorizo lollipops"), every bite at this "affordable" Spanish chainlet is "something to savour"; while the "wide selection" of wines and cocktails and "relaxed ambience" encourage "chilling out", the "friendly" waiters can make things "quick" if you're pressed for time.

Ikeda ☒ *Japanese*   26 | 13 | 21 | £69

Mayfair | 30 Brook St., W1K 5DJ | 020-7629-2730 | www.ikedarestaurant.co.uk

"Wow" exclaim fans who claim you could "order anything on the menu" and "be happy" at this small but "spectacular" Mayfair Japanese where both sushi and hot dishes are presented by kimono-clad waitresses; despite decor that "probably hasn't changed since it opened", most find the "very expensive" costs justified because there's always a "surprise" to be found.

Il Baretto *Italian*   23 | 18 | 18 | £53

Marylebone | 43 Blandford St., W1U 7HF | 020-7486-7340 | www.ilbaretto.co.uk

"Lively basement dining" is the deal at this spot "next to Baker Street" tube, where "reliable Italian" cuisine comes in "pleasant" surrounds via "variable" service (though regulars rate it "mostly good"); a number of surveyors say "the bill turns out to be a little more expensive than you expected", though there's some "great value" to be found, namely in the pizzas; P.S. the "cosy ground-floor bar" is its own draw.

Il Bordello *Italian*   25 | 19 | 25 | £33

Wapping | 81 Wapping High St., E1W 2YN | 020-7481-9950

"Come hungry" to this moderately priced Italian in Wapping, because the portions of "finger-licking good" pizzas and pastas are "large" (you might wish you "hadn't eaten the day before"); a setting with white walls and brown leather chairs and well-rated service are other aspects that have respondents declaring "every time is a pleasure".

Il Convivio ☒ *Italian*   23 | 20 | 22 | £49

Belgravia | 143 Ebury St., SW1W 9QN | 020-7730-4099 | www.etruscarestaurants.com

"Beautifully presented" pastas that are "delicious down to the last detail" and an extensive wine list make this Belgravia Italian a "reliable" (if "pricey") choice; the "welcoming" service and "cosy", "civilised" vibe inside a Georgian house are fitting for a "romantic meal", while the set-price menu is "sensible" for a "quiet business lunch".

Il Portico ☒ *Italian*   19 | 16 | 24 | £44

Kensington | 277 Kensington High St., W8 6NA | 020-7602-6262 | www.ilportico.co.uk

Even "fussy" types approve of this "old-fashioned", "family-run" Kensington Italian, which has been dishing up "decent portions" of regional eats "cooked with heart and soul" since the '60s; it's "kid-friendly" too, with "gracious" staff who treat guests "like regulars", compensating for "crowded, cramped" conditions; P.S. booking is wise for dinner.

	FOOD	DECOR	SERVICE	COST

Imli Street *Indian*
22 | 17 | 18 | £29

Soho | 167-169 Wardour St., W1F 8WR | 020-7287-4243 |
www.imli.co.uk

An "Indian with lots of spin", this Soho cafe attracts a loyal following
with its "flavourful", "interesting" subcontinental "tapas-style"
dishes; it's often "a bit crowded", so it's good for "people-watching",
but most encouragingly, it all comes "at a decent price".

Imperial China ● *Chinese*
21 | 18 | 18 | £34

Chinatown | 25 Lisle St., WC2H 7BA | 020-7734-3388 |
www.imperial-china.co.uk

Hop across a footbridge to this "elegant" "oasis of calm in frantic
Chinatown" to feast on "generous helpings" of "moreish" dim sum
and a "wide choice" of Cantonese mains whose "price is fair considering the quality"; though a few complain of "long queues", "helpful,
efficient" staff keep things moving.

Imperial City ☒ *Chinese*
∇ 22 | 20 | 21 | £42

City | Royal Exchange, EC3V 3LL | 020-7626-3437 |
www.orientalrestaurantgroup.co.uk

With its dramatic arched dining room and "great location" in the
basement of the Royal Exchange, this "pricey" Chinese is an "old favourite" among the City crowd, especially for "business lunches";
what's more, the "wonderful" aromatic duck and other "tasty" dishes
are matched by equally commendable service.

Inamo ● *Asian*
19 | 22 | 17 | £40

St. James's | 4-12 Regent St., SW1Y 4PE | 020-7484-0500 |
www.inamo-stjames.com
Soho | 134-136 Wardour St., W1F 8ZP | 020-7851-7051 |
www.inamo-restaurant.com

Order via your "innovative" "computerised table" then play "clever"
video games while you wait for the "tasty" Asian-fusion dishes to be
delivered (usually "quickly") at these "funky", "kitschy" spots in
Soho and St. James's; however, many say the "novelty wears off"
when the "minuscule" portions arrive, followed by a "substantial"
bill – but perhaps it's "worth the experience" "at least once".

Indian Zing *Indian*
23 | 19 | 21 | £40

Hammersmith | 236 King St., W6 0RF | 020-8748-5959 |
www.indianzing.co.uk

"Modern takes on traditional Indian food" bring "real pizzazz" to this
"relaxed", upscale "gem" "tucked away" in Hammersmith, a white-
tablecloth affair with a "strong wine list" and prices that are only
slightly "expensive"; "charming", "attentive" staff are another
reason fans feel it's "worth a trip" from afar, particularly for the
"fabulous lunch deal".

Indigo *European*
23 | 22 | 22 | £43

Covent Garden | One Aldwych Hotel | 1 Aldwych, WC2B 4RH |
020-7300-0400 | www.onealdwych.com

Whether you stop by for the "excellent" weekend brunch or a "pre-
theatre dinner", you'll find "pleasant" staff at this "comfortable",

"contemporary" Modern European overlooking the "beautiful lobby bar" in Covent Garden's One Aldwych Hotel – and it's "not too expensive for the location"; most say that the "noise level is manageable", arguing it adds to the "brilliant atmosphere", while those who find it "overwhelming" recommend a seat a little further back.

Ishbilia ● *Lebanese* | 24 | 14 | 18 | £42 |

Belgravia | 8-9 William St., SW1X 9HL | 020-7235-7788 | www.ishbilia.com

An "upmarket" Belgravia stalwart serving "above-standard" Lebanese "staples", this spot leaves some "feeling like they are back in the Middle East"; the bi-level interior features a basement mezze bar with banquette seating, plus there's a pavement terrace surrounded by shrubs and "jovial" service throughout.

Ishtar ● *Turkish* | 20 | 17 | 19 | £29 |

Marylebone | 10-12 Crawford St., W1U 6AZ | 020-7224-2446 | www.ishtarrestaurant.com

"After shopping on Marylebone High Street", fuel up on "fantastic" charcoal-cooked dishes at this "busy" Turk boasting "affordable" prices and a "warm welcome" from "helpful" staff; simple chandeliers and red drapes in the "casual" space provide the backdrop for "stunning" live music and belly dancing that make for "a complete evening out" at the weekend, though it's "generally a fun place to be" at any time.

The Ivy ● *British/European* | 24 | 22 | 24 | £69 |

Covent Garden | 1-5 West St., WC2H 9NQ | 020-7836-4751 | www.the-ivy.co.uk

"Knowledgeable, efficient" staff treat everyone "like A-listers" at this upmarket Covent Garden "institution" serving "well-cooked and -presented" Modern Brit-Euro dishes; post-theatre diners "might sit next to one of the greats" if they're lucky, but either way it's "a fun experience if you can get in", and "worth every penny"; P.S. the attached private members club is invitation only.

Jamie's Italian *Italian* | 20 | 19 | 19 | £33 |

City | 38 Threadneedle St., EC2R 8AY | 020-3005-9445 | www.jamieoliver.com Ⓢ

Covent Garden | St. Martin's Courtyard | 11 Upper St. Martin's Ln., WC2H 9FB | 020-3326-6390 | www.jamieoliver.com ●

Canary Wharf | 2 Churchill Pl., E14 5RB | 020-3002-5252 | www.jamieoliver.com

Stratford | Westfield Stratford City | 147 The Street, E20 1EN | 020-3535-8063 | www.jamieoliver.com ●

Islington | North Retail Angel Bldg. | 403 St. John St., EC1V 4AB | 020-3435-9915 | www.jamieoliver.com

NEW **Greenwich** | 17-19 Nelson Rd., SE10 9JB | 020-3667-7087 | www.jamiesitalian.com

Shepherd's Bush | Westfield Shopping Ctr. | Ariel Way, W12 7GB | 020-8090-9070 | www.jamieoliver.com

"More please, Jamie!" enthuse fans of the eponymous Mr. Oliver's "fun and lively" chain where "generous portions" of "classic", "value-

| | FOOD | DECOR | SERVICE | COST |

for-money" Italian fare are dished out by "young, enthusiastic" staff; there's sometimes a "wait" for a table, but for a "fun night out with friends" or family, it "ticks all the boxes".

Jin Kichi 🅼 *Japanese*
| 27 | 13 | 21 | £43 |

Hampstead | 73 Heath St., NW3 6UG | 020-7794-6158 |
www.jinkichi.com

The "exquisitely delicious" yakitori skewers and "exceptionally prepared and presented" sushi at this family-run Hampstead Japanese ("which hasn't changed for years") are "affordable" despite the high "quality"; service is "attentive" and "friendly", and although it's "often difficult to get a table" due to the "cosy" "minimalist" layout, most agree it's "worth the wait".

Joe Allen ❶ *American*
| 19 | 19 | 19 | £39 |

Covent Garden | 13 Exeter St., WC2E 7DT | 020-7836-0651 |
www.joeallen.co.uk

A "stalwart of theatre darlings" ("lawks, how those luvvies can screech sometimes") thanks to its late hours and "handy" Covent Garden location, this "too-busy cellar" plastered with show posters offers "good-value", "appetising" American eats (try the "not-so-secret" off-menu burger) provided by "friendly" staff; those who claim that, menuwise, "the world has moved on" may be missing the point: "you don't go for the food – it's an experience".

ᴺᴱᵂ Joe's Southern Kitchen *American*
| - | - | - | M |

Covent Garden | 34 King St., WC2E 8JD | 020-7240-4008

Slow cooked ribs, mac 'n' cheese, collard greens, cornbread and a signature beer-can chicken (theatrically carved tableside on a specially designed trolley) are highlights of the distinctive, hearty Louisiana-style menu offered at this moderately priced, Southern U.S. diner in Covent Garden; spread out over three floors in a converted warehouse, the setting features bare brick walls and simple steel-topped tables.

José *Spanish*
| 28 | 21 | 25 | £36 |

Tower Bridge | 104 Bermondsey St., SE1 3UB | 020-7403-4902 |
www.josepizarro.com

This moderately priced Tower Bridge tapas bar presents "outstanding", "delicious" dishes and an "extensive" wine-and-sherry list that have some supporters cheering it's "the closest thing to the real deal outside of Spain"; the "adorable", "welcoming" setting is "quite small" with just a "few tables", so it "pays to turn up early" (no reservations).

Joy King Lau ❶ *Chinese*
| 21 | 11 | 15 | £23 |

Chinatown | 3 Leicester St., WC2H 7BL | 020-7437-1133 |
www.joykinglau.com

Feel the "joy" of "dim sum goodness" at this "reliable", four-storey Cantonese "standby", a destination for Chinatown locals who like the "extensive", "cheap" menu (there's dinner too) and "prompt" service; just ignore the "no-frills" ambience, and you'll find "great value".

J. Sheekey ● *Seafood*

FOOD	DECOR	SERVICE	COST
26	22	24	£62

Covent Garden | 28-35 St. Martin's Ct., WC2N 4AL | 020-7240-2565 | www.j-sheekey.co.uk

"If you're in the mood for seafood" this Covent Garden eatery ("perfectly located" for theatre-goers) is "still the standard" thanks to "just-out-the-water" catches that are "well-cooked and -presented" by "professional" staff; perch at the bar "watching the world walk by", or sink into the "opulent leather" seats at the "closely packed" tables in one of the dark, wood-panelled dining areas; P.S. "make your reservations well in advance".

J. Sheekey Oyster Bar ● *Seafood*

25	22	24	£48

Covent Garden | 33-34 St. Martin's Ct., WC2N 4AL | 020-7240-2565 | www.j-sheekey.co.uk

If its "big sister" "next door is fully booked", or you're after a more "casual" (yet still "sophisticated") "bite pre- or post-theatre", try this "stylish", "intimate" Covent Garden spot serving "sampler" portions of J. Sheekey's "fabulous seafood" plus "incredible oysters" at a U-shaped bar; "smart" staff service surroundings that can feel "a bit squashed", though few mind being in such close proximity to the "theatrical luvvies" who frequently drop in.

Julie's Ⓜ *British*

18	22	18	£48

Holland Park | 135 Portland Rd., W11 4LW | 020-7229-8331 | www.juliesrestaurant.com

The "perfect spot for a romantic dinner", this "pretty" Holland Park stalwart with a maze of "multiple rooms" (including an indoor garden-style area) has been "pleasing" both locals and the jet set since 1969; though critics feel the "expensive" British menu "hasn't evolved", the multinational wine list, "special atmosphere" and "likelihood of seeing someone famous" compensate.

Juniper Dining Ⓜ *International*

▽ 28	20	26	£34

Highbury | 100 Highbury Park, N5 2XE | 020-7288-8716 | www.juniperdining.co.uk

"Generous" portions of "simply brilliant" seasonally changing International fare are delivered by "friendly" staff at this "relaxed" neighbourhood bistro in Highbury; and with "excellent value for money" (including the "very good" wine list), no wonder locals call it "everything you wish for in a restaurant".

JW Steakhouse *American/Steak*

23	20	22	£57

Mayfair | Grosvenor Hse. | 86 Park Ln., W1K 7TL | 020-7399-8460 | www.jwsteakhouse.co.uk

"A little bit of the USA" comes to Mayfair via this "spacious" steakhouse in the Grosvenor House hotel that "gets most of the details right", offering "excellent" steaks ("amazing" cheesecake too) in "doggy bag"–worthy portions; service earns good marks as well, and even those hoping for more "buzz" say that overall it "lives up to expectations" (and prices).

	FOOD	DECOR	SERVICE	COST

Kaffeine *Australian/Coffeehouse* | 25 | 19 | 24 | £9 |

Fitzrovia | 66 Great Titchfield St., W1W 7QJ | 020-7580-6755 |
www.kaffeine.co.uk

You may be "tempted to ask for the recipes" at this "friendly" Antipodean cafe, an "oasis" near Oxford Circus presenting "tasty" sandwiches, salads, quiches and cakes alongside its "excellent" coffees; even though it "appears to be busy all the time", it's nevertheless a "great place to hang out" and "catch up on some work".

Kai Mayfair *Chinese* | 25 | 22 | 23 | £66 |

Mayfair | 65 S. Audley St., W1K 2QU | 020-7493-8988 |
www.kaimayfair.co.uk

"Each meal is an event" at this Mayfair "gourmet Chinese" offering "exquisite" fare distinguished by "unique presentations" and "inventive" twists; an "impressive wine list", "knowledgeable" staff and a "chic", but "cosy" setting add to its appeal – just "be prepared to pay for such quality" (or try the set lunch menu).

KaoSarn ⊄ *Thai* | - | - | - | I |

Brixton | Brixton Village Mkt., SW9 8PR | 020-7095-8922 Ⓜ
NEW **Battersea** | 110 St. John's Hill, SW11 1SJ | 020-7223-7888

At this duo of small, family-run BYO cafes – one on the Coldharbour Lane edge of bustling Brixton Village Market and the other in Battersea – a short menu of low-cost Thai dishes is swiftly served in understated surroundings; there's an alfresco area at the Brixton location that stays open even in cooler weather, when blankets are supplied.

NEW Kaspar's Seafood Bar & | - | - | - | VE |
Grill at The Savoy *European/Seafood*

Covent Garden | The Savoy Hotel | The Strand, WC2R 0EU |
020-7420-2111 | www.kaspars.co.uk

This expensive, all-day, seafood-focused Modern Euro dining room at the Savoy specializes in caviar, oysters and other shellfish as well as classic grills and salads; along with Thames views, the space is dominated by an art deco raw bar, which is surrounded by hanging glass shards; P.S. the place is named after the hotel's sculpted cat, who's placed at tables of 13 to ward off bad luck.

Kazan *Turkish* | 24 | 21 | 22 | £34 |

Victoria | 93-94 Wilton Rd., SW1V 1DW | 020-7233-7100 |
www.kazan-restaurant.com

"Traditional with a modern hint" is one take on this "beautiful" Victoria Turk offering "well-prepared Ottoman fare", including "mouthwatering" mezze and many choices for "lamb lovers"; add "accommodating" service plus "good value", and it's a true "Turkish delight".

Kensington Place *British* | 20 | 17 | 18 | £47 |

Notting Hill | 201-209 Kensington Church St., W8 7LX | 020-7727-3184 |
www.kensingtonplace-restaurant.co.uk

This "airy", big-windowed Notting Hill Gate institution has a "new spring in its step", with "fresh, bright" decor to go with its "dependable" Modern British menu, including "lovely" fish from its next-door market; fans also laud its "friendly" service and "value for money", but the "young crowd" that keeps it "bustling" can make it "noisy" too.

The Kensington Wine Rooms   European | 18 | 18 | 19 | £40 |
Kensington | 127-129 Kensington Church St., W8 7LP | 020-7727-8142

The Fulham Wine Rooms ● European
Fulham | 871-873 Fulham Rd., SW6 5HP | 020-7042-9440
www.greatwinesbytheglass.com

This sleek Kensington and Fulham wine bar/restaurant duo pleases both sippers and nibblers with its "inspired" list of bottles, "fab by-the-glass selection" (dispensed by Enomatic machines) and "unfussy" Modern European small plates; "polite" staff and "fair prices" (which extend to the "amazingly good-value classes and tastings") help make it "a real find".

Kentish Canteen   International | ∇ 22 | 19 | 19 | £26 |
Kentish Town | 300 Kentish Town Rd., NW5 2TG | 020-7485-7331 | www.kentishcanteen.co.uk

Kentish Town's "little gem", this "upmarket modern diner" employs "smiling" staff to serve its "wide range" of "unpretentious", "honestly priced" meals from an International menu; the "enticing, quirky decor" extends to banquettes and photo-montage murals, plus there's a "particularly cool" basement bar.

Kenza ☒ Lebanese/Moroccan | ∇ 24 | 27 | 22 | £39 |
City | 10 Devonshire Sq., EC2M 4YP | 020-7929-5533 | www.kenza-restaurant.com

"Watch belly dancers boogie" at this "decadent" and "a bit pricey" Lebanese-Moroccan basement in the City, where "carved wooden walls" add to an "exotic environment"; the dishes, which are brought to the table in stages, are "high quality", and while service can be sometimes "forgetful", it doesn't detract from the "fantastic atmosphere".

Kettner's   European | 22 | 23 | 21 | £44 |
Soho | 29 Romilly St., W1D 5HP | 020-7734-6112 | www.kettners.com

A "lovely, wonky building" houses this "legendary" 1867 brasserie whose "dark-wood panelling" and "tasteful private dining rooms" provide a "grown-up", "old Soho" backdrop for "satisfying" European classics at "reasonable prices"; service has "charm", and while "the Champagne Bar is the main attraction" for those wishing to "see and be seen", it's all "memorable", especially "when the pianist is playing" (Tuesdays–Saturdays).

Khan's ● Indian | 20 | 13 | 17 | £23 |
Bayswater | 13-15 Westbourne Grove, W2 4UA | 020-7727-5420 | www.khansrestaurant.com

"Don't expect delicate china" at this "no-frills" Bayswater "oldie" "packed" with diners craving a taste of "what Indians eat at home": "delicious", "hearty" dishes to "dream about"; service is "variable", and some find the "no-alcohol" policy "annoying", but "try the mango lassi" and "be charmed" by the "authentic" experience – not to mention the "cheap" prices.

	FOOD	DECOR	SERVICE	COST

Kiku *Japanese*

24 | 15 | 20 | £54

Mayfair | 17 Half Moon St., W1J 7BE | 020-7499-4208 | www.kikurestaurant.co.uk

"Marvel at the intense flavours" and "great diversity" at this Japanese destination in Mayfair, where "friendly" staff "guide your journey", from "top-class sushi" to tempura and shabu-shabu; "basic decor" means the "atmosphere could be better", but "bargain" set lunches earn praise, while the "high standard" makes "pricey" dinners "worth it".

NEW Kitchen Table 🗷 🖾 *European*

- | - | - | E

Fitzrovia | 70 Charlotte St., W1T 4QG | no phone | www.kitchentablelondon.co.uk

Behind a leather curtain at the back of Bubbledogs, Charlotte Street's ode to the frankfurter, you'll find this U-shaped bar where just 19 diners gather in two nightly sittings (Tuesday–Saturday) to watch chef James Knappett and his team create a daily changing tasting menu of European small plates based on premium ingredients; wine pairings come from Sandia Chang who, like Knappett (they're husband and wife), has worked at the famed likes of Noma in Copenhagen and Per Se in New York.

Kitchen W8 *European*

25 | 19 | 22 | £54

Kensington | 11-13 Abingdon Rd., W8 6AH | 020-7937-0120 | www.kitchenw8.com

Kensington's "well-heeled residents" have a "real gem" on their doorstep, this "refined", "exceptionally good" Modern European that's "just the right side of adventurous"; the dining room is "lovely" (though some say the acoustics are "not conducive to quiet conversations"), and service is "friendly and efficient".

Koffmann's *French*

27 | 23 | 26 | £65

Belgravia | The Berkeley | Wilton Pl., SW1X 7RL | 020-7235-1010 | www.the-berkeley.co.uk

"Long may Mr. Koffmann continue" proclaim supporters of the legendary chefs' "first-class" French cuisine (the signature morel-stuffed pig's trotters are "supremely well prepared") at this "quiet, elegant" three-tiered dining room in Belgravia's Berkeley Hotel; "professional", "attentive" staff contribute to the "unforgettable dining experience", which includes a "more than fair-priced set lunch".

Koi *Japanese*

21 | 21 | 20 | £55

Kensington | 1 Palace Gate, W8 5LS | 020-7581-8778

To admirers, this "pricey", three-level Kensington Japanese "feels like a special night out" thanks to its "solid" selection of food, "nicely designed" setting (complete with low tables) and "beautiful" crowd; a dissenting faction sees it differently ("average", "limited" selection), but they're outvoted.

Kopapa *International*   22 | 16 | 18 | £31

Covent Garden | 32-34 Monmouth St., WC2H 9HA | 020-7240-6076 |
www.kopapa.co.uk

"Don't be fooled by the cafe-like appearance" of this "casual", all-
day eatery in Covent Garden – chef Peter Gordon's "artistic", "inventive" International menu of small and large plates is generally "on
point" and "always interesting, even when it near-misses"; views on
cost vary ("good value" vs. "a bit high for what you get") and it can
be "noisy" with "slow" service, but most simply "love" it.

Koya ● *Japanese*   24 | 17 | 19 | £22

Soho | 49 Frith St., W1D 4SG | 020-7434-4463 | www.koya.co.uk
The "hearty" udon (served hot or cold) is "packed with flavour" at
this "affordable" Soho Japanese, which also offers blackboard specials plus small plates such as "crispy, light" tempura and a "palate-
cleansing seaweed salad"; the "cosy" interior means there can be
"long queues" at peak times, although devotees assure "the wait
is worth it".

K10 🗷 *Japanese*   ▽ 22 | 16 | 19 | £26

City | 20 Copthall Ave., EC2R 7DN | 020-7562-8510 | www.k10.com
Lunching workers are "spoilt for choice" at this reasonably priced all-
day City Japanese where "to-die-for" lamb chops and "melt-in-your-
mouth" teriyaki compete with "high-quality" sushi; even though it's
"always busy", the "friendly" staff manage to "greet you with a smile".

Kulu Kulu Sushi 🗷 *Japanese*   22 | 11 | 17 | £22

Covent Garden | 51-53 Shelton St., WC2H 9JU | 020-7240-5687
Soho | 76 Brewer St., W1F 9TX | 020-7734-7316
South Kensington | 39 Thurloe Pl., SW7 2HP | 020-7589-2225
"They keep it simple and the standard high" at this "bare-bones"
Japanese conveyor-belt chainlet, which rolls out a "great selection" of
"fresh", "no-frills" sushi and cooked dishes that are "usually worth trying"; cost-calculators conclude that "cheap prices sooth any ruffled
culinary feathers", while "courteous service" gets the thumbs-up.

La Bodega Negra ● *Mexican*   ▽ 17 | 20 | 20 | £41

Soho | 16 Moor St., W1D 5NH | 020-7758-4100
Soho | 9 Old Compton St., W1D 5JF | 020-7758-4100
www.labodeganegra.com

"Pretty decor" and "noisy music" add to the "*très* cool" vibe at this
"buzzy" Soho Mexican (from the team behind Eight Over Eight, E&O
et al.), conjoined twins with an evening-only basement restaurant/
bar on one side and a chilled all-day cafe and taqueria on the other;
some call the "simple" eats "treats" and others call them "pricey for
what you get", but at least service is "quick"; P.S. "be warned – no
bookings, and it can get busy".

La Bouchée *French*   24 | 18 | 21 | £37

South Kensington | 56 Old Brompton Rd., SW7 3DY | 020-7589-1929
"In a part of town that needs more no-fuss" restaurants, this "quaint,
cosy" neighbourhood bistro located in South Kensington fits the bill,

with "old-school", "delicious" "French country food" that's "done right" and "superb for the price"; if there's one criticism, regulars say it's that the environment seems "a bit old and dark", but "friendly" service and "interesting people-watching" make amends.

La Brasserie ❶ *French*   20 | 21 | 18 | £41

South Kensington | 272 Brompton Rd., SW3 2AW | 020-7581-3089 |
www.labrasserielondon.com

"Don't change it" plead devotees of this all-day South Ken "institution", a "family" "staple for brunch, coffee or an easy dinner" featuring "good-value", "satisfying" French dishes with "English twists"; in addition, "lovely staff" and a "true brasserie feel" with pleasing "buzz" ensure a "fun atmosphere".

L'Absinthe Ⓜ *French*   23 | 19 | 23 | £39

Primrose Hill | 40 Chalcot Rd., NW1 8LS | 020-7483-4848 |
www.labsinthe.co.uk

What really sets this Primrose Hill bistro apart is its "passionate" staff who "make you feel seriously welcome" as they present the "tasty", "good value" French "comfort food"; "cosy" surrounds "transport you to a smart cafe in rural France", and if you long to take a piece home with you, some "sensibly priced wines" are available in the attached shop.

Ladurée *Bakery/Sandwiches*   24 | 20 | 18 | £28

Covent Garden | Covent Garden Piazza | 1 The Market, WC2E 8RA |
020-7240-0706
Piccadilly | 71-72 Burlington Arcade, W1J 0QX | 020-7491-9155
Knightsbridge | Harrods | 87-135 Brompton Rd., ground fl., SW1X 7XL |
020-3155-0111
www.laduree.fr

Although most go for the "scrumptious", "super-light" macarons, there are other "sweet treats" plus "tasty, small" sandwiches to tempt at this French cafe chainlet, located in tourist-friendly spots around town; service is "informative", and even if it's relatively "pricey", it's "always a treat for the senses".

La Famiglia ❶ *Italian*   20 | 17 | 21 | £46

Chelsea | 7 Langton St., SW10 0JL | 020-7351-0761 |
www.lafamiglia.co.uk

"Inviting", "old-world service" and a "hearty" menu that "delivers quality every time" make this "lively neighbourhood" Chelsea Italian "beyond family friendly", despite prices that are "not cheap"; being so "popular", the "homey" interior "can be noisy", just like the large, covered year-round rear garden.

La Fromagerie Café *Deli/Sandwiches*   24 | 19 | 16 | £25

Marylebone | 2-6 Moxon St., W1U 4EW | 020-7935-0341
Highbury | 30 Highbury Park, N5 2AA | 020-7359-7440
www.lafromagerie.co.uk

"Bagging" a wooden bench for the "fabulous", "rustic" Modern European "lunchy things" at this "cramped" cheesemonger (with a cafe and deli) in Marylebone is "pretty darn challenging", and the

Highbury sibling "only has six seats, so best head there off-peak"; what has "cheese lovers in rapture" are the "state-of-the-art" temperature-controlled rooms, with their "impressive selections" for tasting and to take home.

La Genova ⑤ *Italian* 　　23 | 18 | 25 | £50

Mayfair | 32 N. Audley St., W1K 6ZG | 020-7629-5916 | www.lagenovarestaurant.com

It may look "fairly inconspicuous" from outside, but step into this Mayfair Italian and you're "transported back" to the old country thanks to its "simple" but "excellent" "traditional" cusine (special praise goes to the "fresh pasta") and "attentive" staff led by a "memorable" host/owner; maybe the decor "could be better", but the ambience is "warm" and prices are "extremely reasonable", at least for this neighbourhood.

Lahore Kebab House *Pakistani* 　　25 | 11 | 17 | £20

Whitechapel | 2-10 Umberston St., E1 1PY | 020-7481-9737 ◐
Streatham | 668 Streatham High Rd., SW16 3QL | 020-8679-9980
www.lahore-kebabhouse.com

"Expect long queues to get in" this "cracking" Whitechapel BYO with a "loud, large and laddish" Streatham sibling, both specialising in "amazing" Pakistani cooking featuring "excellent grilled meats" and plenty of "hot and spicy" dishes; many surveyors say the "crude", "cafeteria-like" environments "need updating", although nobody complains about the "cheap-as-chips" prices and "fast, efficient service".

Lamberts Ⓜ *British* 　　▽ 28 | 23 | 25 | £39

Balham | 2 Station Parade, Balham High Rd., SW12 9AZ | 020-8675-2233 | www.lambertsrestaurant.com

"Seasonal British cuisine" is "expertly cooked" and served by "fantastic" staff (who always extend a "warm welcome"), at this "absolute treat" in Balham; "striking the perfect balance between sumptuous and homely", the "elegant" environs include an alfresco area at the front, but best of all, it's "remarkable value", hence "a popular place for all and sundry".

Langan's Brasserie ◐ *British/French* 　　21 | 20 | 21 | £56

Mayfair | Stratton Hse. | Stratton St., W1J 8LB | 020-7491-8822 | www.langansrestaurants.co.uk

"Despite all the new kids on the block", this "epitome of an English brasserie" near Green Park has "been around forever" but is still "buzzing" thanks to "dependable" Traditional British–French cooking and "unstuffy" service that "makes everyone feel welcome"; some critics find it "slightly pricey", but in all other respects, it "should never change".

L'Anima ⑤ *Italian* 　　25 | 22 | 22 | £65

City | 1 Snowden St., EC2A 2DQ | 020-7422-7000 | www.lanima.co.uk

"Always full of people in suits", this "polished", "sophisticated" spot near Liverpool Street Station lures the "business" set with a "gutsy", "assured" regional Italian menu served by "efficient" staff; the white "minimalist" setting is debatable ("ethereal" for some, too "clinical" for others), while the price point is flat-out "expensive" – notwithstanding the "good"-value set lunch.

Lantana *Australian/Coffeehouse*   24 | 21 | 20 | £19

Fitzrovia | 13 Charlotte Pl., W1T 1SN | 020-7637-3347 | www.lantanacafe.co.uk

"Aussies treat breakfast like the English treat their tea", which is why this "small", "reasonably priced" Antipodean cafe in Fitzrovia has a "loyal" morning "fan base", who come for "tasty" savouries, "great" brownies and "excellent" coffee; "happy baristas", a "casual" ambience and magazines and newspapers "dotted around" complete the picture; P.S. open until early evening.

La Petite Maison *Mediterranean*   26 | 21 | 22 | £70

Mayfair | 54 Brooks Mews, W1K 4EG | 020-7495-4774 | www.lpmlondon.co.uk

"Simple" flavours that "characterise the French Riviera" dominate an "original", "excellent" Mediterranean sharing-style menu at this "buzzy" location in a discreet Mayfair mews, flush with local residents; "attentive" staff add to its appeal, and while it's "expensive" and "hard to get into", its "worth it".

La Porchetta *Pizza*   22 | 16 | 19 | £22

Bloomsbury | 33 Boswell St., WC1 3BP | 020-7242-2434 🛇
Clerkenwell | 84-86 Rosebery Ave., EC1R 4QY | 020-7837-6060
Chalk Farm | 74-77 Chalk Farm Rd., NW1 8AN | 020 7267 6822
Islington | 141-142 Upper St., N1 1QY | 020-7288-2488
Muswell Hill | 265 Muswell Hill Broadway, N10 1DE | 020-8883-1500 ◑
Stroud Green | 147 Stroud Green Rd., N4 3PZ | 020-7281-2892
www.laporchetta.net

"Giant" thin-crust pizzas and other "tasty" Italian fare served in "generous portions" at painless prices equal "solid value" at these "vibrant" standbys; a "fun", "informal" atmosphere, "child-friendly" attitude and "jovial" (if "not always the best") service further boost their appeal, but be prepared for some "noisy" birthday celebrations.

La Porte des Indes *Indian*   22 | 25 | 19 | £49

Marylebone | 32 Bryanston St., W1H 7EG | 020-7224-0055 | www.laportedesindes.com

"The interior designer deserves a medal" for the "exotic", "over-the-top" setting (complete with waterfall, palm trees and more) at this "huge", "upscale" Marylebone Indian that provides a "fab" backdrop for "celebrating groups"; the "interesting, French-influenced" fare is a "cut above" the norm, and though service "could be tightened up a bit", it's "charming", so all in all it's "worth a visit".

La Poule au Pot *French*   22 | 20 | 19 | £51

Belgravia | 231 Ebury St., SW1W 8UT | 020-7730-7763 | www.pouleaupot.co.uk

"Unbeatable for a date", this "been-there-forever" Belgravia French bistro oozes Gallic "charm" with its "ancient farmhouse decor" and "sumptuous" dishes like "*magnifique*" coq au vin; what's "cosy" to some feels a bit "cramped" to others and service can be "spotty", but given the "smashing wine selection" you may not notice; P.S. there's "no better place" in summer than the "wonderful terrace".

NEW Lardo *Italian/Pizza* — | — | — | M

Hackney | 197-205 Richmond Rd., E8 3NJ | 020-8985-2683 | www.lardo.co.uk

This all-day spot in Hackney's Arthaus complex serves a midpriced, seasonally changing menu of wood-fired pizzas, house-cured charcuterie and Italian small plates alongside a Euro-centric wine list; an oven decorated like an oversized disco ball dominates the industrial-chic space, where fashionable locals perch at the bar or crowd round one of the wooden tables in the back.

Las Iguanas *Pan-Latin* 21 | 20 | 20 | £27

Spitalfields | 1 Horner Sq., E1 6AA | 020-7426-0876
Stratford | Westfield Stratford City | 2 Stratford Pl., E20 1ET | 020-8522-4445
Greenwich | O2 Arena | Peninsula Sq., SE10 0DS | 020-8312-8680
South Bank | Royal Festival Hall | Belvedere Rd., SE1 8XX | 020-7620-1328
www.iguanas.co.uk

Expect a "happy", "lively atmosphere" at this burgeoning Pan-Latin chainlet with a handful of "prime locations" in London (and many more outside the capital); "good-quality" cooking and "excellent cocktails" keep it "heaving with people" at weekends, while staff are surprisingly "quick" "considering how jostled they are"; P.S. "special promotions" add to its "great-value" reputation.

L'Atelier de Joël Robuchon *French* 28 | 25 | 26 | £84

Covent Garden | 13-15 West St., WC2H 9NE | 020-7010-8600 | www.joelrobuchon.co.uk

"Prepare to be awed" by Joël Robuchon's Modern French cuisine at this "expensive" Covent Garden venue; "stylish", "sublime" small plates are served at the counters (plus a few tables) in the ground-floor L'Atelier, more "traditional" but equally "fantastic" meals are served in La Cuisine upstairs, and "amazing" cocktails are crafted in the rooftop bar, while a "slick", "sophisticated" ambience pervades throughout.

Latium 🖪 *Italian* 25 | 18 | 25 | £51

Fitzrovia | 21 Berners St., W1T 3LP | 020-7323-9123 | www.latiumrestaurant.com

"Long may she reign" proclaim subjects of this "great-value" Italian "treasure" just north of Oxford Street, where the "sophisticated" dishes are "well executed" with notable "attention to detail"; "refined" service and a "low-key" ambience ensure a "memorable" experience, whether dining with a date, friends or business clients.

La Trompette *French* 27 | 21 | 24 | £58

Chiswick | 5-7 Devonshire Rd., W4 2EU | 020-8747-1836 | www.latrompette.co.uk

The "impeccably prepared" Modern Euro-New French cuisine "never disappoints" at this "upmarket" yet "casual and relaxed" Chiswick sibling of Chez Bruce; respondents also praise the "slick service", particularly the "knowledgeable sommelier" with whom it's "worth discussing" the "exceptional-value" wine list.

Launceston Place *British*   25 | 24 | 24 | £65

Kensington | 1 Launceston Pl., W8 5RL | 020-7937-6912 | www.launcestonplace-restaurant.co.uk

Fans of this "beautiful" Kensington townhouse say it's the "ideal environment" for chef Tim Allen's "inventive", "modern" and somewhat pricey British cuisine, which is only presented in prix fixe menus; expect a "hospitable welcome" from the host and "good wine pairings" from the sommelier; P.S. the "set lunch is a bargain".

L'Autre Pied *European*   25 | 20 | 24 | £60

Marylebone | 5-7 Blandford St., W1U 3DB | 020-7486-9696 | www.lautrepied.co.uk

When you want "high-level", "inventive" gastronomy, but "can't handle putting on the Louboutins", this Marylebone sibling of Pied à Terre boasts a Modern European menu with similar "panache" and an "interesting" wine list, all "exceptional value for money"; the chefs' "confidence" extends to "well-trained" front-of-house staff who patrol the "casual", "unpretentious" setting.

L'Aventure ☒ *French*   25 | 18 | 22 | £52

St. John's Wood | 3 Blenheim Terr., NW8 0EH | 020-7624-6232 | www.laventure.co.uk

It's "been around forever", yet this "charming", circa-1979 St. John's Wood bistro remains "worth a visit" for "delicious" French fare that's "great value"; "excellent" staff "treat you like family (in a good way)", but be warned, the "tiny" dimensions mean "you might play footsie with the wrong neighbour" – unless you nab a spot on the patio in summer.

Le Boudin Blanc *French*   24 | 19 | 21 | £52

Mayfair | Shepherd Mkt. | 5 Trebeck St., W1J 7LT | 020-7499-3292 | www.boudinblanc.co.uk

"As French as you can get", this "lively" Shepherd Market "throwback" supplies "rustic country" "classics" and a "varied wine list" in a "charming" setting equipped with "mismatched furniture" and mostly "friendly" service; though critics cite somewhat "expensive" prices and "tightly packed" tables, most say it's "worth it" for an experience that's the "real deal".

Le Café Anglais *French*   22 | 21 | 21 | £55

Bayswater | Whiteleys Shopping Ctr. | 8 Porchester Gdns., W2 4DB | 020-7221-1415 | www.lecafeanglais.co.uk

"Clever", "well-prepared" French fare is served amid "great big windows, swish banquettes" and "lovely art deco" decor suggesting a "vintage ocean liner" at chef-owner Rowley Leigh's "airy" brasserie atop Whiteleys shopping centre on Queensway; adding to the "pleasurable experience" are "friendly", "efficient" staff, "fairly priced" wines and a "contented buzz" from the customers.

| | FOOD | DECOR | SERVICE | COST |

Le Café du Marché ☒ French
FOOD 25 | DECOR 23 | SERVICE 23 | COST £50

Farringdon | 22 Charterhouse Sq., EC1M 6AH | 020-7608-1609 |
www.cafedumarche.co.uk

"Tops for many years and keeping it up", this "charming" Smithfield
"gem" "justifies its reputation" for "memorable" French bistro cuisine
with its choice of a two or three-course, prix fixe menu; furthermore,
the "comfortable armchair"–like atmosphere (the piano playing is a
"nice touch") and "superb" service inspire "lots of bonhomie" while
still staying "sharp enough for business lunches" and dinners.

Le Caprice ● British/European
24 | 22 | 24 | £64

St. James's | Arlington Hse. | Arlington St., SW1A 1RJ | 020-7629-2239 |
www.le-caprice.co.uk

A "glamourous" spot to "see and be seen", this St. James's "classic
that never disappoints" is run with "precision and flair" by a "superb" crew proffering "fine", "expensive" Modern British-Euro fare;
the "bright, friendly ambience" is well suited for "after the theatre"
("when most restaurants are going to sleep"), and when it comes to
dining alone, "sitting at the bar is one of the joys of London".

Le Cercle ☒Ⓜ French
24 | 22 | 22 | £57

Chelsea | 1 Wilbraham Pl., SW1X 9AE | 020-7901-9999 |
www.lecercle.co.uk

"It's easy to miss this great little find" (an offshoot of Club Gascon) in
a basement off Sloane Square, proffering "sophisticated", "inventive"
New and Southwestern French small plates; the "well-chosen, often-
surprising" wine list adds to the "pleasant" if "expensive" experience.

Le Colombier French
23 | 20 | 23 | £56

Chelsea | 145 Dovehouse St., SW3 6LB | 020-7351-1155 |
www.lecolombier-sw3.co.uk

Oozing "lots of charm", this "classic" French brasserie in Chelsea
provides "simple", "old-school" dishes "made to perfection" and accompanied by a "comprehensive" wine list; "friendly" staff service
the crowd of "refined locals", who appreciate pricing that's "surprisingly reasonable for its location".

The Ledbury French
28 | 25 | 28 | £91

Notting Hill | 127 Ledbury Rd., W11 2AQ | 020-7792-9090 |
www.theledbury.com

"The techniques wielded are spectacular" on chef Brett Graham's
"masterful" New French menu, which is "immaculately presented"
by "fantastic" staff at this "classy" Notting Hill dining room; you'll
need to bring "big money", but many feel it's nonetheless "value for
what you get", and the "phenomenal" wine list puts it further into
the "special-occasion" league.

Le Deuxième ● European
22 | 19 | 21 | £44

Covent Garden | 65 Long Acre, WC2E 9JH | 020-7379-0033 |
www.ledeuxieme.com

"Mouth-watering" Modern European fare, "pleasant staff" and an
"extensive wine list" are all boons, but the real blessing of this

"smart" venue is that it's "reasonably priced for Covent Garden"; "business friendly" by day, it's known as a "handy" option pre- or post-theatre, so those looking for a quieter, less "cramped" repast opt for the "tranquil period" when the curtain's up.

Le Gavroche ☒ French   28 | 25 | 28 | £105

Mayfair | 43 Upper Brook St., W1K 7QR | 020-7408-0881 | www.le-gavroche.co.uk

"Gifted" chef Michel Roux Jr. presents a "culinary extravaganza" of "beautifully presented" French "classics" at this "sophisticated", "expensive" Mayfair dining room; an "extensive" wine list and "exceptional, professional" staff who "can't do enough for you" add to its reputation as a "consistently outstanding" legend that's "worth saving up for".

Le Manoir aux Quat'Saisons French   27 | 27 | 27 | £120

Great Milton | Le Manoir aux Quat'Saisons Hotel | Church Rd., OX44 7PD | 01844-278-881 | www.manoir.com

"The attention to detail is incredible" at chef-owned Raymond Blanc's "delightful" hotel and restaurant – "the place to go" in the Oxfordshire countryside to "be spoilt" with "exceptional" New French cuisine and "top-notch" service; "beautiful grounds" and gardens (where you can "see the vegetables and herbs used in the cooking") are more reasons why it's "well worth" the "long ride from London" and very expensive prices.

Le Mercury ❶ French   20 | 17 | 19 | £25

Islington | 140 Upper St., N1 1QY | 020-7354-4088

NEW Le Mercury (Deuxieme) French

Islington | 154-155 Upper St., N1 1RA | 020-7704-8516 www.lemercury.co.uk

Offering "old-school charm on the cheap", this "buzzing", "candlelit" New French duo in Islington have a "chilled-out feel", "functional" service and "simple", "nicely done" cuisine, making them a "great standby", especially before or after a show at the nearby Almeida Theatre.

Lemonia Greek   21 | 18 | 21 | £35

Primrose Hill | 89 Regent's Park Rd., NW1 8UY | 020-7586-7454 | www.lemonia.co.uk

A "perfect neighbourhood taverna" sums up this Primrose Hill Greek that "still gets it right after all these years" thanks to "simple", "reliably good" food, "friendly" service from "longtime staff" and a "convivial" "local vibe", complete with occasional "celeb-spotting"; yes, it can be "noisy" and "packed" ("book ahead"), but "terrific value" is the payoff.

Leon Mediterranean   20 | 17 | 18 | £14

City | 12 Ludgate Circus, EC4M 7LQ | 020-7489-1580 ☒
City | 86 Cannon St., EC4N 6HT | 020-7623-9699 ☒
Covent Garden | 73-76 The Strand, WC2R 0DE | 020-7240-3070
Marylebone | 275 Regent St., W1B 2HB | 020-7495-1514

(continued)

(continued)
Leon
Soho | 35 Great Marlborough St., W1F 7JE | 020-7437-5280
Canary Wharf | Cabot Pl. W., promenade, E14 4QS | 020-7719-6200
Spitalfields | 3 Crispin Pl., E1 6DW | 020-7247-4369
Hendon | Brent Cross Shopping Ctr. | Prince Charles Dr., NW4 3NB |
020-8457-9300
Southwark | Blue Fin Bldg. | 7 Canvey St., SE1 9AN | 020-7620-0035
www.leonrestaurants.co.uk

"This is what fast(er) food should be" declare fans of this eat-in/
takeaway chain, a "shining light" that dishes up "flavourful", "healthy"-
minded Mediterranean fare in "casual" environs; it can be "a struggle
to find a seat" at peak hours, but service is "friendly" and prices "affordable", making it a "go-to" for many.

Leon De Bruxelles *Belgian*   19 | 17 | 17 | £40
Covent Garden | 24 Cambridge Circus, WC2H 8AA | 020-7836-3500 |
www.leon-de-bruxelles.co.uk

Musseling into London's limited ranks of Belgian eateries, this
Cambridge Circus offshoot of a Brussels-born chain provides "large
portions" of "consistent" moules frites and other favourites, accompanied by "all varieties" of beer; leather banquettes, marble tables,
"courteous" service and moderate prices complete the picture.

Leong's Legend *Taiwanese*   21 | 16 | 13 | £23
Chinatown | 26-27 Lisle St., WC2H 7BA | 020-7734 3380
Chinatown | 4 Macclesfield St., W1 6AX | 020-7287-0288 |
www.leongslegend.com

"Those who know their Taiwanese food" frequent this Chinatown
duo offering "unusual dim sum", "proper soup dumplings" and
other "flavoursome", "authentic" food; service can vary from
"friendly" to "brusque", but the "dark" decor is "decent" and prices
are "cheap" enough.

Le Pont de la Tour *French/Seafood*   23 | 22 | 21 | £58
Tower Bridge | Butlers Wharf Bldg. | 36 Shad Thames, SE1 2YE |
020-7403-8403 | www.lepontdelatour.co.uk

The "high-quality", fish-focused French menu and "superb" views
over Tower Bridge and the City from the riverside terrace of this "bit
pricey" Butlers Wharf venue make it "a must for tourists" "strolling
along the Southbank"; it's "quite a romantic setting" due to the art
deco-inspired dining room, and for larger groups, there's a wine cellar that fits the bill.

Le Relais de Venise   24 | 18 | 19 | £34
l'Entrecôte *French/Steak*
City | 5 Throgmorton St., EC2N 2AD | 020-7638-6325 | 🎟
Marylebone | 120 Marylebone Ln., W1U 2QG | 020-7486-0878
Canary Wharf | 18-20 Mackenzie Walk, E14 4PH |
020-3475-3331
www.relaisdevenise.com

The "reliable" outposts of this moderately priced, no-reservations
French import serve a "simple" set menu comprising a "tangy"

salad followed by "divine" steak with a side of "thin, flavourful" frites; service is "fast and efficient" (some suggest it can be "a bit snappy"), but be prepared for a "long" queue for a table at peak times.

L'Escargot ●🅳🄎 *French* | 25 | 23 | 22 | £60 |

Soho | 48 Greek St., W1D 4EF | 020-7439-7474 | www.lescargotrestaurant.co.uk

"Dine among Chagalls, Miros" and mirrors at this longtime "Soho haunt" (est. 1927), with "outstanding" Classic French cuisine and a "slightly formal, but very welcoming" atmosphere; if some cite "expense-account" pricing, others say it delivers real "value" (especially via the set lunch, pre-and-post-theatre menus).

Les Deux Salons *French* | 19 | 21 | 18 | £46 |

Covent Garden | 40-42 William IV St., WC2N 4DD | 020-7420-2050 | www.lesdeuxsalons.co.uk

"Looking the part" of a "grand, old-school cafe", this "bustling" sibling of Arbutus and Wild Honey near Trafalgar Square is "worth a visit" for its "hearty", "well-executed" French fare with some "witty retakes on well-loved favourites", plus a "wonderful wine list"; if sceptics claim it's "nothing wow-worthy", with "hit-and-miss" service, "serious theatregoers" call it an "oasis" thanks to the "amazing-value" pre-show prix fixe.

Les Trois Garçons 🄎 *French* | 23 | 26 | 21 | £61 |

Shoreditch | 1 Club Row, E1 6JX | 020-7613-1924 | www.lestroisgarcons.com

"Eccentric and memorable", this Shoreditch Classic French set in a Victorian-era pub dazzles with its "opulent", "original" decor – complete with "evening bags hanging from the ceiling" and taxidermy on the walls – and if the food isn't quite as impressive, it's nevertheless "done well"; maybe service can vary and prices aren't cheap, but it makes for a "truly unique" experience.

L'Etranger *French/Japanese* | 25 | 18 | 23 | £65 |

South Kensington | 36 Gloucester Rd., SW7 4QT | 020-7584-1118 | www.etranger.co.uk

The "excellent" Franco-Japanese fusion menu earns plaudits of "wow" at this "expensive" South Kensington neighbourhood haunt where the wines and "knowledgeable" sommelier team are also "impressive"; the "dark" decor is not to everyone's taste, yet the place is quite "buzzy at dinner".

Le Vacherin *French* | 24 | 22 | 21 | £52 |

Chiswick | 76-77 S. Parade, W4 5LF | 020-8742-2121 | www.levacherin.com

"Can't be faulted" say supporters of the "reliable" French cooking and "fantastic Parisian atmosphere" at this "charming", "quiet" bistro just "off the main track" in Chiswick; "unobtrusive service" and a "fab wine list" bolster the feeling that, though prices are a "bit on the expensive side", "what you get is definitely worth paying for".

	FOOD	DECOR	SERVICE	COST

Light House *International*
24 | 21 | 24 | £41

Wimbledon | 75-77 Ridgway, SW19 4ST | 020-8944-6338 | www.lighthousewimbledon.com

"A great little find in Wimbledon Village", this "underrated" "local stalwart" offers an "interesting, keenly priced" International menu and generally "spot-on" service that's "quick to correct any concerns"; maybe the "minimalist" setting could use "a designer's touch" and some detect "no wow factor", but most leave "pleased".

Lima 🖻 *Peruvian*
▽ 23 | 16 | 22 | £62

Fitzrovia | 31 Rathbone Pl., W1T 1JH | 020-3002-2640 | www.limalondon.com

"Start with a pisco sour" and then get stuck into some "fantastic" ceviche and other "interesting" Peruvian dishes crafted from unusual ingredients (e.g. Amazon citrus, boniato, cochayuyo) at this "high-end" (and commensurately priced) venue in Fitzrovia; working against a backdrop of brightly coloured South American art, staff seem "genuinely excited" about what they're doing, helping to make an evening here an "experience worthy of attention".

Little Bay ❶ *European*
21 | 19 | 21 | £21

Farringdon | 171 Farringdon Rd., EC1R 3AL | 020-7278-1234
Kilburn | 228 Belsize Rd., NW6 4BT | 020-7372-4699 ⊟
www.little-bay.co.uk

Culture fiends "can't get enough" of this Modern European bistro chainlet, because the "quirky", "eclectic" "candles-in-wine-bottles" decor is "like being on a stage set" (and at weekends in Farringdon, there's even a live opera performance); what's more, the "varied" menu is "value for money", and the wines are similarly "reasonably priced".

Little Italy ❶ *Italian*
21 | 19 | 19 | £44

Soho | 21 Frith St., W1D 4RN | 020-7734-4737 | www.littleitalysoho.co.uk

"For a quick bite after work or before a show", or a "romantic meal if you can get tucked away upstairs", this Italian in Soho fits the bill with grub that's "relatively basic" though "not cheap"; the later it gets, the more "loud" and clublike it becomes – that is, "you can dance" to "fantastic music" until the "wee small" hours (4 AM).

𝗡𝗘𝗪 Little Social 🖻 *French*
- | - | - | E

Mayfair | 5 Pollen St., W1S 1NE | 020-7870-3730 | www.littlesocial.co.uk

Opposite Jason Atherton's original Pollen Street Social in Mayfair, this spin-off serves French bistro-style food in a Parisian environment with dark red banquettes, hardwood chairs and vintage picture frames; at lunchtime, there are prix fixe menus at moderate (for the area) prices while an à la carte menu takes over in the evening.

Locanda Locatelli *Italian*
25 | 22 | 24 | £71

Marylebone | Hyatt Regency London – The Churchill | 8 Seymour St., W1H 7JZ | 020-7935-9088 | www.locandalocatelli.com

Well-heeled visitors to this upscale Marylebone hotel dining room may jest that "the bread basket alone would make a great meal", but if you stopped there you'd miss out on Giorgio Locatelli's "exquisitely prepared", "beautifully presented", "creative" Italian food; it may be "a little quiet for some", but most just appreciate the "plush environment" with all the "trimmings", including "gracious", "attentive" staff.

Locanda Ottoemezzo 🗷 *Italian* ▽ 25 | 18 | 22 | £53

Kensington | 2-4 Thackeray St., W8 5ET | 020-7937-2200 | www.locandaottoemezzo.co.uk

Though "more expensive than it looks" – with "quirky wooden benches, plastic chairs" and "cool movie decor" paying "tribute" to Fellini's *8 ½* – this "intimate" Kensington Italian "doesn't disappoint" thanks to dishes that are "as excellent as the service"; P.S. "upstairs next to the window is recommended".

Loch Fyne *Seafood* 22 | 18 | 18 | £35

City | Leadenhall Mkt. | 77-78 Gracechurch St., EC3V 0AS | 020-7929-8380 🗷

Covent Garden | 2-4 Catherine St., WC2B 5JS | 020-7240-4999 www.lochfyne.com

"Fish lovers" say that these "buzzy" outposts of the national chain "never fail" for "simply presented" seafood at "fair prices" – even if the setting is as "colourless as your office canteen" and service is "variable"; Covent Garden is "good before the theatre", while the business-oriented City venue is unsurprisingly "popular at lunchtime".

NEW The Lockhart ●Ⅿ *American* - | - | - | E

Marylebone | 22-24 Seymour Pl., W1H 7NL | 020-3011-5400 | www.lockhartlondon.com

In a bright, airy setting with wooden floorboards and china antlers, this Marylebone dining room prepares poshed-up versions of Southwestern US dishes, such as hush puppies, mac 'n' cheese and meaty mains, using seasonal British ingredients; to accompany are wines, cocktails and an extensive tequila and mezcal selection, and everything's priced toward the expensive end.

Lotus Floating Restaurant Ⅿ *Chinese* 22 | 18 | 19 | £28

Canary Wharf | Inner Millwall Dock | 9 Oakland Quay, E14 9EA | 020-7515-6445 | www.lotusfloating.co.uk

With a location that "takes some finding" "in the heart of the docks" at Canary Wharf, this is "a great place for a special occasion", serving "fantastic" dim sum lunches and dinners that hail from all across China; "lovely decor", including authentic Asian prints, and "chatty" staff add to the "superb experience".

Lucio *Italian* 20 | 16 | 19 | £52

Chelsea | 257-259 Fulham Rd., SW3 6HY | 020-7823-3007 | www.luciorestaurant.com

Owner Lucio Altana is the "perfect host" at his "romantic" namesake Chelsea venue, a "happy find" for "quality" Italian cuisine; though some wish for "more menu creativity" and find the "wine list on the pricey side", it remains a "popular" "neighbourhood choice", thanks in part to "charming service" and an "excellent-value lunch".

	FOOD	DECOR	SERVICE	COST

Lucky 7 *American* ‖ 18 ‖ 17 ‖ 14 ‖ £24 ‖
Notting Hill | 127 Westbourne Park Rd., W2 5QL | 020-7727-6771 |
www.lucky7london.co.uk
When you want to "soothe that Sunday morning hangover" or "stuff
your face like a real American", this "classic '50s diner" in Notting
Hill fits the bill with "fabulous burgers, fries and super milkshakes";
staff "could try harder" – and may "make you share" booth seating
with another party – but at least prices are moderate.

Lupita *Mexican* ‖ 25 ‖ 19 ‖ 20 ‖ £25 ‖
Charing Cross | 13-15 Villiers St., WC2N 6ND | 020-7930-5355
NEW Lupita East *Mexican*
Spitalfields | 60-62 Commercial St., E1 6LT | 020-3141-6000
www.lupita.co.uk
"A tasty take on Mexico City cuisine", this duo in Charing Cross and
Spitalfields lures locals with "big portions" of tacos and other "cheap
and cheerful street food"; a "great lunch stop", it's also "brill after
work", because the "highly recommended" margaritas have a "kick".

Lutyens Restaurant, Bar & ‖ 23 ‖ 22 ‖ 22 ‖ £60 ‖
Private Rooms ⊠ *European/Scandinavian*
City | 85 Fleet St., EC4 1AE | 020-7583-8385 |
www.lutyens-restaurant.com
"Lots of suits" populate the "starched white tables" at Sir Terence
Conran's upscale Fleet Street Brasserie, where "pleasant" staff oversee a "well-prepared" Modern European-Scando menu and "decent
wine list"; open all day, the "formal" environment transitions from "a
convenient breakfast spot" to working lunch mecca to "buzzy" bar –
perhaps because "there isn't that much competition nearby".

Made in Camden *European* ‖ ∇ 24 ‖ 16 ‖ 21 ‖ £31 ‖
Chalk Farm | The Roundhouse | Chalk Farm Rd., NW1 8EH |
020-7424-8495 | www.madeincamden.com
The distinctive "colour and atmosphere of Camden" is evident in every corner of this "enjoyable" Chalk Farm eatery, whose "delicious"
European menu lists "traditional dishes alongside more unusual
offerings", all of which are "reasonably priced"; "friendly, efficient
service" is another reason advocates "adore" it, and given its
location – attached to the Roundhouse performing-arts centre – it's
especially "ideal for pre-theatre".

Made in Italy ● *Pizza* ‖ 19 ‖ 16 ‖ 16 ‖ £30 ‖
Marylebone | 50 James St., W1U 1HB | 020-7224-0182
Soho | 14 Old Compton St., W1D 4TH | 020-0011-1214
Chelsea | 249 King's Rd., SW3 5EL | 020-7352-1880
www.madeinitalygroup.co.uk
"Young, pretty people" come in "groups" to this King's Road Italian
"neighbourhood spot", because its "satisfying" "thin-crust pizza"
sold by the metre is "made to share"; although the "haphazard" service "could be better" and "tables are tight", it all comes at "a reasonable price"; P.S. the consensus is the Marylebone and Soho
offshoots are a "notch below the original on all fronts".

	FOOD	DECOR	SERVICE	COST

Magdalen ⌧ European
	25	20	23	£51

Tower Bridge | 152 Tooley St., SE1 2TU | 020-7403-1342 |
www.magdalenrestaurant.co.uk

"Imaginative", "ever-changing" Modern European cuisine is "cooked
with craft and heart" to "stunning" effect at this "easy-to-find secret" near Tower Bridge; factor in "gracious", "unrushed service", a
"carefully selected wine list" and prices that are "high without being
exorbitant", and no wonder surveyors call it a "place to impress";
P.S. the set lunch menu is "a steal".

Maggie Jones's British
	21	23	22	£38

Kensington | 6 Old Court Pl., W8 4PL | 020-7937-6462 |
www.maggie-jones.co.uk

If you're hankering for British fare, check out this Kensington "comfort-
food" haven where "wholesome", "generous portions" come for
"reasonable prices"; "quirky" "farmhouse decor" with "wonderful
booths and ancient candles spewing wax" creates a "rustic", "country
feel", and though a few find it all too "retro", most deem it a "warm",
"welcoming" place for a "quiet" meal, and it's "romantic to boot".

Ma Goa Indian
	22	15	20	£33

Putney | 242-244 Upper Richmond Rd., SW15 6TG | 020-8780-1767 |
www.ma-goa.com

Putney punters "swing by" for a "quick, cheap meal" at this "family-
owned and -operated" Indian specialising in "interesting, delicious
Goan food" ("the pork vindaloo is particularly brilliant") served by
"accommodating staff"; the "good value" extends from the two-
courses-for-£10 menu to the "terrific" Sunday buffet.

Malabar ◑ Indian
	20	17	20	£34

Notting Hill | 27 Uxbridge St., W8 7TQ | 020-7727-8800 |
www.malabar-restaurant.co.uk

"There's no need to travel" to India for "tasty" subcontinental food, because this "modern", midpriced "gem" prepares dishes with "great
care" and "exact spicing", right in Notting Hill; and with "lots of repeat
customers", the "friendly" staff "must be doing something right".

Malabar Junction Indian
	19	17	19	£29

Bloomsbury | 107 Great Russell St., WC1B 3NA | 020-7580-5230 |
www.malabarjunction.com

Focusing on "impressive" South Indian dishes, this moderately
priced Bloomsbury eatery clearly benefits from "chefs who are
proud of their work"; diners who appreciate that they're "not
rushed" mark it as "one to repeat", particularly for lunch when
there's a prix fixe "deal".

Mama Lan ⊄ Chinese
	-	-	-	I

Brixton | Brixton Village Mkt. | Coldharbour Ln., SW9 8PR | no phone
NEW **Clapham** | 8 The Pavement, SW4 0HY | no phone
www.mamalan.co.uk

Ning Ma re-creates the snacks stall that her mother and grandfather
ran in Beijing at these two compact South Londoners, the original in

Brixton Village Market and another by Clapham Common tube station; diners perch on brightly coloured stools, eat the inexpensive likes of noodle soups, salads and dumplings (the latter made by hand before their eyes) and sip on herbal tea, Tsing Tao beer or wine; P.S. no reservations and cash only.

Mandalay *Burmese*
▽ 24 | 14 | 22 | £18

Marylebone | 444 Edgware Rd., W2 1EG | 020-7258-3696 |
www.mandalayway.com

It may have "bright lights", "no decor" and "not much atmosphere" to speak off, but this Edgware Road option is, in fact, a "gem", producing "mind-blowing" Burmese food and offering it at "non-London-like prices"; "friendly, helpful service" is another reason it's "well worth a visit if you're keen to try something different".

Mandarin Kitchen ⚫ *Chinese/Seafood*
25 | 15 | 19 | £39

Bayswater | 14-16 Queensway, W2 3RX | 020-7727-9012

"Even with a reservation", diners can expect to "queue out the door" for the "famous", "fantastic" lobster noodles at this "temple to the crustacean gods" within a recently revamped "nightclub look-alike" in Bayswater; foodies feel that the quality of other items on the Chinese menu "varies", but the "price is right" across the board, and the service "decent".

Mangal Ocakbasi ⚫🍴 *Turkish*
- | - | - | I

Dalston | 10 Arcola St., E8 2DJ | 020-7275-8981 |
www.mangal1.com

"Meat lovers" suggest "don't let the back alley location or the simple decor put you off" this Dalston Turk, because its charcoal-grilled dishes – including "juicy" chicken kebabs and "crispy" ribs – are "seriously amazing"; indeed, some say it's even worth "driving miles" for, especially since it's so reasonably priced.

Mango Tree *Thai*
20 | 19 | 18 | £46

Victoria | 46 Grosvenor Pl., SW1X 7EQ | 020-7823-1888 |
www.mangotree.org.uk

While Victoria businesspeople call it "a place to bring a client for lunch", in the evening this "massive" Thai site becomes "way beyond buzzy" (indeed, "you'd think you were standing on a Heathrow runway"); whatever the hour, the food is "decent" if comparatively "expensive" and the service swings between "attentive" and "nonexistent" – cocktails, on the other hand, are generally "brilliant".

Manicomio *Italian*
18 | 16 | 17 | £46

City | 6 Gutter Ln., EC2V 8AS | 020-7726-5010 🖂
Chelsea | 85 Duke of York Sq., SW3 4LY | 020-7730-3366
www.manicomio.co.uk

Expect "reliable" cooking at this Chelsea Italian, where you can "watch the world go by" from the "sunny terrace", or its City offspring, an "oasis around St. Paul's"; though word is the "service is not as attentive as it should be", somehow they can "get you in, fed and out in an hour", making it a "solid" option for a "getaway lunch";

P.S. "classy takeaway" is offered in both the City venue and the deli attached to the Chelsea iteration.

Mao Tai ❶ *Asian* ▽ 25 | 23 | 24 | £51

Fulham | 58 New King's Rd., SW6 4LS | 020-7731-2520 | www.maotai.co.uk

It's "a treat to eat" at this sleek, "stylish" and "pricey" Fulham Pan-Asian with a menu that presents "lots of choice", including dim sum; staff who "know what they're doing" also oversee the "extensive" selection of wines and "amazing cocktails", the latter alone "worth going for".

Marco Pierre White Steak & Alehouse *Steak* 23 | 21 | 19 | £56

City | East India Hse. | 109-117 Middlesex St., E1 7JF | 020-7247-5050 | www.mpwsteakandalehouse.org

A combination of "swanky" and "rustic" describes this expensive City Steakhouse from the eponymous celeb chef, who provides meat lovers with "quality food" – and "not just good steak", there's also pork belly and fish on the menu; the "big, buzzy, bright room" makes a "great place for dinner" as well as lunch, so "no wonder it's always rammed".

Marcus Wareing at The Berkeley ⓔ *French* 27 | 25 | 27 | £107

Belgravia | The Berkeley | Wilton Pl., SW1X 7RL | 020-7235-1200 | www.marcus-wareing.com

"Bravo!" applaud admirers of this "elegant" dining room in Belgravia's Berkeley Hotel, where chef Marcus Wareing's "sublime" New French cuisine – "impressive and delightful in equal measure" – is proffered by "knowledgeable", "professional" staff; "well-matched" wines are also on offer, and while the prices are high end, many consider the set lunch a "bargain".

Mark's Club ❶ⓔ *British/French* ▽ 21 | 26 | 27 | £92

Mayfair | private club | 46 Charles St., W1J 5EJ | 020-7499-2936 | www.marksclub.co.uk

If you "get an invitation" to this private Mayfair club, take it and revel in its "old English" country house look, "superb" service and "very exclusive air"; the "classic" British-Franco cooking is "great", and as for the prices, members sniff "if you have to ask how much it costs, you can't afford to eat here".

Maroush ❶ *Lebanese* 23 | 16 | 19 | £28

Marylebone | 1-3 Connaught St., W2 2BH | 020-7262-0222
Marylebone | 21 Edgware Rd., W2 2JE | 020-7723-0773
Marylebone | 4 Vere St., W1G 0DG | 020-7493-5050
Marylebone | 68 Edgware Rd., W2 2JE | 020-7224-9339
Knightsbridge | 38 Beauchamp Pl., SW3 1NU | 020-7581-5434
www.maroush.com

The "wonderful variety" of Lebanese "street treats" produced at this "buzzing" "fair"-priced chain around Marylebone and Knightsbridge makes it a "favourite place to gorge"; although seating is "tight"

| | FOOD | DECOR | SERVICE | COST |

(there are often "people queuing"), the "polite" staff ensure a "reasonable" turnaround time.

Masala Zone *Indian*   22 | 20 | 21 | £22

Covent Garden | 48 Floral St., WC2E 9DA | 020-7379-0101
Soho | 9 Marshall St., W1F 7ER | 020-7287-9966
Camden Town | 25 Parkway, NW1 7PG | 020-7267-4422
Islington | 80 Upper St., N1 0NU | 020-7359-3399
Bayswater | 75 Bishop's Bridge Rd., W2 6BG | 020-7221-0055
Earls Court | 147 Earl's Court Rd., SW5 9RQ | 020-7373-0220
www.masalazone.com

One way to sample the "fragrant", "interesting" "potpourri" of subcontinental flavours at this "buzzy" Indian street-food purveyor, ranked as London's Most Popular chain, is to order the "huge" grand thali, which is "enough for two people" and "decently priced"; the "contemporary" decor "changes depending on location", but the service, which is "prompt" and "professional", is "consistent throughout".

NEW MASH ● *American/Steak*   ▽ 25 | 29 | 27 | £78

Soho | 77 Brewer St., W1F 9ZN | 020-7734-2608 |
www.mashsteak.dk

An "original" art deco interior provides the "opulent" backdrop for this high-end Soho venue whose name is an acronym for Modern American Steak House (though it's an import from Denmark); start your evening with a cocktail in the "stunning" bar area, then dig into "generous" portions of "delicious" meats, all delivered by "friendly", "competent" staff.

Massimo ⊠ *Italian/Mediterranean*   21 | 24 | 19 | £74

Westminster | Corinthia Hotel London | 10 Northumberland Ave., WC2N 5AE | 020-7998-0555 | www.massimo-restaurant.co.uk

The "wow factor" comes from the "stunning" decor of this upscale Italian in the Corinthia Hotel near Trafalgar Square, with "high ceilings", grand pillars and spherical brass-and-glass chandeliers; but diners are divided over every other aspect – some praise the "superb" fish-centric Med dishes and the "caring" service, while others baulk at "steep prices" for "fashionista portions" and "attitude" from some staff; P.S. there's also a "fantastic champagne selection".

Matsuri *Japanese*   23 | 19 | 22 | £65

St. James's | 15 Bury St., SW1Y 6AL | 020-7839-1101 |
www.matsuri-restaurant.com

For a "high-end Tokyo" experience in St. James's, try this Japanese with a bar and table grills where chefs "put on a show" as they prepare a "delectable selection of sushi and teppanyaki"; the "decor is a bit dated, but ok" for what it is, while the "pricey" costs are lower at lunch, thanks to "great-value bento boxes".

Maxwell's ● *American*   19 | 20 | 19 | £30

Covent Garden | 8 James St., WC2E 8BH | 020-7836-0303 |
www.maxwells.co.uk

If you "need a quick bite in Covent Garden" before "heading off to the theatre" and don't mind somewhere "manic" and "touristy", this "diner-style" venue is "well worth the money" for "safe" hamburgers and other American treats plus "great cocktails"; what's more, service usually remains "polite" and "attentive", even though "it gets so crowded", particularly during the daily happy hour.

Maze *French*   24 | 23 | 23 | £74

Mayfair | Marriott Grosvenor Sq. | 10-13 Grosvenor Sq., W1K 6JP | 020-7107-0000 | www.gordonramsay.com

"Buzzing all the time", this "modern" Gordon Ramsay French venue in the Marriott Grosvenor Square specialises in "creative" "little bites" that "blend" in "Asian influences" to "wonderful" effect; "polite" service and a "big", "interesting wine list" (on an iPad) are more reasons why it's "worthwhile", but beware, as the cost "increases dramatically" if "you need a lot" of food.

Maze Grill *Steak*   23 | 21 | 22 | £58

Mayfair | Marriott Grosvenor Sq. | 10-13 Grosvenor Sq., W1K 6JP | 020-7495-2211 | www.gordonramsay.com

"If Maze is too high for your budget or you're not dressed for the occasion", then head for this "lively" all-day steakhouse sibling next door in the Marriott Grosvenor Square, where the decor is "more casual", it's easier to "grab a table" and prices are "cheaper" (though still "rather expensive"); thankfully, Gordon Ramsay's menu, highlighting "premium cuts of meat" and "sides big enough to share", is equally "excellent", just like "well-trained staff".

MEATliquor ● *Burgers*   23 | 20 | 14 | £23

Marylebone | 74 Welbeck St., W1G 0BA | 020-7224-4239 | www.meatliquor.com

"Filling" burgers that leave "juices and sauce dripping down to your elbows" plus "tasty" sides (the chilli fries are a "highlight") and "interesting" cocktails keep customers queuing at this "loud", "edgy", no-reservations Marylebone joint with graffiti-decked walls; service from the "hipster" staff can be "brusque" at times, but prices are moderate – and it is, after all, thought by some to be at the "forefront" of the "burger revolution".

MEATmarket *Burgers*   ∇ 23 | 16 | 18 | £20

Covent Garden | Covent Garden Mkt. | Tavistock St., WC2E 8BE | 020-7240-4852 | www.themeatmarket.co.uk

"Hedonistic" burgers and "boozy" milkshakes "do nothing for the waistline but wonders for the taste buds" at this "hip", inexpensive, takeaway-focused offshoot of U.S.-style burger joint MEATliquor; set in a "quirky" location above Covent Garden market, the place is festooned with "funny signs and slogans" that are "worth a read" while you wait for the "friendly" staff to fetch your food.

NEW MEATmission ● *Burgers*   - | - | - | M

Hoxton | 14-15 Hoxton Mkt., N1 6HG | 020-7739-8212 | www.meatmission.com

The burger evangelists from MEATliquor and MEATmarket have moved east with this trendy Hoxton incarnation, housed in a former Christian mission, complete with stained glass ceiling; expect the usual rough 'n' ready surroundings (e.g. tables made from salvaged boards) and new additions to the menu including 'monkey fingers' (battered, marinated chicken fillets); P.S. unusually, bookings are taken.

Medcalf *British*
▽ | 22 | 21 | 21 | £40

Clerkenwell | 40 Exmouth Mkt., EC1R 4QE | 020-7833-3533 | www.medcalfbar.co.uk

"Casually trendy", as "befits" its Exmouth Market location, this "gorgeously decorated" former butcher's shop (dating back to the early 1900s) presents a "simple, well-done" Modern British menu; "friendly service" is another aspect that makes it "a lovely treat" – but good luck "trying to get in without booking".

Mediterraneo ● *Italian*
23 | 16 | 20 | £43

Notting Hill | 37 Kensington Park Rd., W11 2EU | 020-7792-3131 | www.mediterraneo-restaurant.co.uk

"If you're in Notting Hill, don't miss" this cousin of Osteria Basilico "up the street", doling out "amazing pastas" and other "notable" Italian treats that are "great value"; the "warm", rustic setting is always "vibrant" with "noisy" "hordes" "jostling" to get a "cramped" table, so "make sure you book" and try to forgive service if it feels "rushed".

Medlar *European/French*
25 | 17 | 23 | £59

Chelsea | 438 King's Rd., SW10 0LJ | 020-7349-1900 | www.medlarrestaurant.co.uk

"Eat like nobility" at this "brilliant" Chelsea spot from two Chez Bruce protégés whose "inventive" New French menu of "fragrant creations" (with influences from all over Europe) "fully deserves the hype"; while some take issue with the "austere" setting, "top-notch service", an "attractive wine selection" and "a cheese board to rival restaurants in France" make amends, as does the "fantastic value"; P.S. "plead for a window table".

Mela ● *Indian*
22 | 17 | 20 | £31

Covent Garden | 152-156 Shaftesbury Ave., WC2H 8HL | 020-7836-8635 | www.melarestaurant.co.uk

"Delightful staff" "make you feel like you're a regular" at this "convivial" Covent Garden Indian where the "variety of creative dishes" on a "terrific", "ever-changing" menu satisfies "those wanting something a bit classier than Brick Lane"; what's more, it's "incredible value", especially for pre-theatre dining, when you can be "in and out in less than an hour".

Mele e Pere *Italian*
▽ | 20 | 15 | 21 | £36

Soho | 46 Brewer St., W1F 9TF | 020-7096-2096 | www.meleepere.co.uk

A "keen", "friendly" crew front this retro-styled Soho basement Italian serving "skillfully prepared", "quality" food alongside "well-sourced" wines "for every taste", "superb" cocktails and "remarkable" house-brewed vermouth; although it's moderately priced overall, the set lunch and dinner menus are a "steal", and the "chilled, relaxed" ambience was made for "casual" dining.

	FOOD	DECOR	SERVICE	COST

Mem & Laz *Mediterranean*   ∇ **27** | **23** | **24** | **£22**

Islington | 8 Theberton St., N1 0QX | 020-7704-9089

Islington locals head to this "vibrant", "often-packed" brasserie to eat "delicious", "great-value" Mediterranean fare in a "friendly", "cosy" environment bedecked with colourful, hanging lamps and handmade, mosaic glass chandeliers.

Memories of China *Chinese*   **23** | **20** | **20** | **£59**

Belgravia | 65-69 Ebury St., SW1W 0NZ | 020-7730-7734
Kensington | 353 Kensington High St., W8 6NW | 020-7603-6951
www.memories-of-china.co.uk

Long-time regulars and a "just-as-enthusiastic younger following" call this "fancy" Belgravia Chinese and its lower-profile Kensington offshoot a "reliable choice" for "ample portions" of "high-quality" Cantonese and Mandarin dishes; although the bill can be "pricey", the eatery is "recommended" for its "accessible" menu as well as its generally "competent service".

The Mercer ⧉ *British*   ∇ **22** | **21** | **23** | **£50**

City | 34 Threadneedle St., EC2R 8AY | 020-7628-0001 |
www.themercer.co.uk

"Worth trying" for its Traditional British "food to savour" – not to mention "helpful service" and "tasteful, elegant surroundings" – this "well-kept secret" in a former Threadneedle Street banking hall is a "great place" for a weekday "business" breakfast, lunch or dinner (it's closed at weekends); what's more, it's "reasonably priced given the location".

Meson Don Felipe ⧉ *Spanish*   ∇ **23** | **15** | **16** | **£29**

Waterloo | 53 The Cut, SE1 8LF | 020-7928-3237 |
www.mesondonfelipe.com

Now that this "tightly packed" Waterloo haunt is "better known", you should "book a table or be prepared to queue" for its "excellent" Spanish tapas and mains, backed up by an "extensive wine list"; even though the "staff could smile a bit more", the "decor's cheery" and the location "great for before the Old or Young Vic".

Mestizo *Mexican*   **21** | **19** | **21** | **£30**

Euston | 103 Hampstead Rd., NW1 3EL | 020-7387-4064 |
www.mestizomx.com

"You'll feel like you're walking into Mexico" at this "lively little haven" in Euston with a "mind-boggling array of tequilas" and an "extensive" "bargain" menu (check out the all-you-can-eat options) that "doesn't conform to stereotypical offerings", all delivered by way of "helpful" service; just remember that "booking in the evening is essential", as it gets rather "busy", especially at the "heaving bar downstairs".

Mews of Mayfair *British*   **19** | **19** | **17** | **£48**

Mayfair | 10-11 Lancashire Ct., New Bond St., W1S 1EY |
020-7518-9388 | www.mewsofmayfair.com

"A good spot to hide away", this discreet Modern Brit down a cobbled Mayfair street serves "expensive", "sophisticated" cuisine ("could be more generous with portions") and an "extensive wine list" via service that's at times "slow" though usually "well meaning"; additionally, there's a glossy lounge, a bar, a "quirky private dining room" and a patio.

Michael Nadra *European*   ▽ 25 | 18 | 24 | £57

Chiswick | 6-8 Elliott Rd., W4 1PE | 020-8742-0766 | www.restaurant-michaelnadra.co.uk

Chef-owner Michael Nadra's namesake Chiswick eatery teams a "fantastic", frequently changing Modern Euro menu with an "extensive, expensive" international wine list; "welcoming service" and "cool" minimalist confines put it "high on the list" for seekers of an "intimate", "grown-up" dining experience.

Mien Tay *Vietnamese*   24 | 9 | 16 | £20

Hoxton | 122 Kingsland Rd., E2 8DP | 020-7729-3074
Battersea | 180 Lavender Hill, SW11 5TQ | 020-7350-0721
www.mientay.co.uk

"Superb" Vietnamese "street food" keeps this duo in Battersea and Hoxton "always packed", despite what critics call "basic", somewhat "uncomfortable" settings and service that can be "less than friendly"; indeed, it boasts "hordes" of admirers who laud the "phenomenal value".

Min Jiang *Chinese*   25 | 25 | 22 | £57

Kensington | Royal Garden Hotel | 2-24 Kensington High St., 10th fl., W8 4PT | 020-7937-8000 | www.minjiang.co.uk

Along with "breathtaking" views across Kensington Gardens, the Royal Garden Hotel's "well-kept" 10th-floor dining room offers a "delicious" Chinese menu headlined by "exceptional" Beijing duck and "excellent dim sum"; it may be "expensive", but for "special occasions like birthdays and anniversaries", it "delights".

Mint Leaf *Indian*   22 | 22 | 21 | £49

City | 12 Angel Ct., EC2R 7HB | 020-7600-0992 | www.mintleaflounge.com 🗷
St. James's | Suffolk Pl., SW1Y 4HX | 020-7930-9020 | www.mintleafrestaurant.com ◑

"Modern", "fancy", often "stunning" Indian dishes are the speciality of this pair where "bit-high" prices also get you access to "polished service" and "delicious", "unusual cocktails"; the "dark", "loud" St. James's basement is a "slick", "disco"-like setting with DJ-driven "dancing in the bar" at weekends, while the lighter, loungey City off-shoot offers an "upmarket", "relaxing atmosphere" plus a champagne bar on the mezzanine.

Mishkin's ◑ *Jewish*   20 | 20 | 19 | £25

Covent Garden | 25 Catherine St., WC2B 5JS | 020-7240-2078 | www.mishkins.co.uk

"Tasty" non-kosher, "NY-style" Jewish deli "favourites" make this midpriced "great addition" from the team behind Polpo et al. something "different" for Covent Garden; service can often seem "distracted", but the "brilliant atmosphere" and "dangerously good" cocktail list ("a shrine to gin") are boons to what fans dub a "gutsy" endeavor.

Miyama ⊠ *Japanese*   23 | 13 | 20 | £46

City | 17 Godliman St., EC4V 5BD | 020-7489-1937
Mayfair | 38 Clarges St., W1 7EN | 020-7493-3807
www.miyamarestaurant.co.uk

"Look beyond the dated decor" of this "unpretentious" Japanese duo in Mayfair and the City and you'll find an "amazingly broad range" of "superb" sushi and noodles; what's more, it all comes with "attentive service" and "without costing an arm and a leg", especially if you choose the "fantastic-value set menus", offered at both lunch and dinner.

The Modern Pantry *International*   25 | 21 | 23 | £40

Clerkenwell | 47-48 St. John's Sq., EC1V 4JJ | 020-7553-9210 | www.themodernpantry.co.uk

The "clever", "inventive" International cuisine "draws on all corners of the globe" to create "amazing flavours" with "just enough quirk" at this "stylishly minimal" converted Clerkenwell townhouse with a "bright" all-day cafe ("great" for alfresco meals) and "elegant" upstairs dining room (for a "grown-up treat"); wholly "lovely" service and an "excellent wine list" further "enchant the locals", as does the "lovely brunch".

Momo ◑ *Moroccan*   21 | 25 | 19 | £48

Mayfair | 25 Heddon St., W1B 4BH | 020-7434-4040 | www.momoresto.com

"Exotic", "buzzy" and "unique", this Mayfair hangout presents "well-executed" Moroccan eats backed by "great North African wines", all at "high-end" prices; "so-so service" can be a letdown, but it's "great for group eating", especially in the "lush outside space", "a home away from home in the summer".

Mon Plaisir ◑⊠ *French*   21 | 17 | 19 | £37

Covent Garden | 21 Monmouth St., WC2H 9DD | 020-7836-7243 | www.monplaisir.co.uk

"*Toujours un plaisir*" rave Francophiles of this over-70-year-old Covent Garden "institution" where a "rabbit warren" of "charming", "cheek-by-jowl" rooms plays host to "dependable" French bistro staples, plus an "excellent cheese trolley" and "reasonably priced wines"; service can be "a little offhand", but it's often "fine", helping to make the place perpetually "useful for pre- and post-theatre suppers".

Morgan M ⊠ *French*   28 | 18 | 24 | £62

Farringdon | 50 Long Ln., EC1A 9EJ | 020-7609-3560 | www.morganm.com

"Stupendous" New French cuisine comes from "a craftsman who cares" about "careful, complex assemblies of flavours" at this vegetarian-friendly venue opposite Smithfield Market (relocated from Islington); indeed, the pricey fare "more than makes up for the lack of visual excitement" in the "quiet", green-hued environment, as does the "spot-on" service.

	FOOD	DECOR	SERVICE	COST

Morito *African/Spanish* — 26 | 17 | 19 | £25

Clerkenwell | 32 Exmouth Mkt., EC1R 4QE | 020-7278-7007 | www.morito.co.uk

For "delicious", "perfectly seasoned" tapas that share the Spanish–North African "flavours of its illustrious neighbour" in Exmouth Market, this "buzzing" "younger sibling" of Moro is "worth a visit of its own", despite the "tiny", "spartan" space where other diners "are all but sharing your seat"; "smiling service" is part of the deal, as are the "well-chosen" wines and "stonking" "good value".

Moro *African/Spanish* — 26 | 20 | 24 | £44

Clerkenwell | 34-36 Exmouth Mkt., EC1R 4QE | 020-7833-8336 | www.moro.co.uk

"Gutsy flavours" deliver "constant surprises" at this Exmouth Market North African-Spanish hotspot where an "ever-changing" menu of "rustic" yet "inventive" "delights" (along with an "extensive" wine and sherry list) is served from an open kitchen; "service with a smile" helps foster a "palpable energy", while the decor is "simple, vibrant and welcoming".

Morton's ⊠ *Mediterranean* — 22 | 22 | 22 | £66

Mayfair | private club | 28 Berkeley Sq., W1J 6EN | 020-7499-0363 | www.mortonsclub.com

There's "no sign of a recession" at this private club comprising a "beautiful", "top-end" Mediterranean restaurant with "attractive modern art" and a "stunning view over Berkeley Square", a "relaxed, vibrant" ground-floor bar and an "energetic" basement "nightclub that's one of the 'in' spots in modern London"; "first-class service all round" and a "private living room for meetings or parties" are boons to its rarified clientele and their guests.

Mosimann's ⊠ *International* — 26 | 27 | 27 | £83

Belgravia | private club | The Belfry | 11 W. Halkin St., SW1X 8JL | 020-7235-9625 | www.mosimann.com

"Luxurious without being over the top" and with a "private membership to keep it discreet", this "sophisticated" venue in a former Belgravia church offers chef Anton Mosimann's "refined" International dishes and "top-class" service; it's "understandably expensive", but for a "special treat", it's "doesn't get much better" – if you can get in.

Motcombs *International* — 21 | 17 | 21 | £49

Belgravia | 26 Motcomb St., SW1X 8JU | 020-7235-6382 | www.motcombs.co.uk

A "lively crowd" of "locals and visiting Europeans" create the "noisy", "convivial" atmosphere at this "comfy, casual" "hangout" in Belgravia, comprising an "old-fashioned" (some say "scruffy") ground-floor brasserie, cosy basement and "fantastic" "outdoor scene" on the pavement; "charming, efficient" staff serve somewhat "predictable" International dishes that, while "not cheap", are "well prepared".

	FOOD	DECOR	SERVICE	COST

Moti Mahal ☒ *Indian* | 25 | 21 | 22 | £45 |

Covent Garden | 45 Great Queen St., WC2B 5AA | 020-7240-9329 |
www.motimahal-uk.com

"Respecting the diversity and richness of Indian food", this "busy,
buzzy" Covent Garden eatery "rewards" diners with a "thoughtful"
menu laced with "succulent, fragrant" dishes; tables are on the
"crammed" side and it's a "tad expensive, but there are deals to be
had", and the "friendly service" keeps things ticking, making it a
handy "pre/post-theatre location".

Mr. Chow ◑ *Chinese* | 22 | 20 | 20 | £62 |

Knightsbridge | 151 Knightsbridge, SW1X 7PA | 020-7589-7347 |
www.mrchow.com

"The original low-key power restaurant", this Knightsbridge pillar of an
international Chinese mini-chain has been "always packed" and pep-
pered with "celebrities" since the 1960s, thanks in large part to staff
who "know the meaning of good service"; even if the "novelty has
faded" for some, many supporters still stop by for the "well-prepared"
"traditional" Mandarin dishes, for which it's wise to be armed with
"an expense account" ("lunch is the better bet").

Mr. Kong ◑ *Chinese* | 21 | 11 | 18 | £24 |

Chinatown | 21 Lisle St., WC2H 7BA | 020-7437-7341 |
www.mrkongrestaurant.com

"Quality and reliability" characterise the "generous plates" of "delightful" Cantonese fare at this Chinatown "staple" whose menu
stars "amazing duck" and a "tremendous variety" of vegetarian options; sure, there's "no atmosphere", but with "nice service" thrown
into the mix, it's a "great place to spend a little for a feast" – very little; P.S. it's open until the early hours every day.

Murano ☒ *European/Italian* | 26 | 22 | 24 | £81 |

Mayfair | 20 Queen St., W1J 5PR | 020-7495-1127 |
www.muranolondon.com

One of the "most sophisticated and splendid ladies' lunch spots", proclaim fans "in awe and admiration" of chef Angela Hartnett's "imaginative" Italian-influenced cooking at this "upscale"Modern European
in Mayfair offering two- or five-course prix fixes; furthermore, a "welcoming" vibe from the "non-stuffy service" and the "stunning", "modern" decor means for some, just "one visit is not enough".

NEW Naamyaa Café ◑ *Thai* | – | – | – | M |

Islington | 407 St. John St., EC1V 4AB | 020-3600-3600 |
www.naamyaa.com

From Alan Yau (Busaba Eathai, Hakkasan), this spacious new all-day
Bangkok-inspired cafe in Islington serves midpriced traditional and
Western-style Thai fare; slick lighting, rustic brick work and ornate ce-
ramic tiling are some of the modern space's fetching accoutrements.

Nando's *Portuguese* | 18 | 15 | 14 | £17 |

Fitzrovia | 57-59 Goodge St., W1 1TH | 020-7637-0708

(continued)

(continued)

Nando's

Covent Garden | 66-68 Chandos Pl., WC2N 4HG | 020-7836-4719
Marylebone | 113 Baker St., W1U 6RS | 020-3075-1044 ●
Bethnal Green | 366 Bethnal Green Rd., E2 0AH |
020-7729-5783
Chalk Farm | 57-58 Chalk Farm Rd., NW1 8AN | 020-7424-9040 ●
Hampstead | 252-254 West End Ln., NW6 1LU | 020-7794-1331
Islington | 324 Upper St., N1 2XQ | 020-7288-0254
Lewisham | 16 Lee High Rd., SE13 5LQ | 020-8463-0119
Clapham | 59-63 Clapham High St., SW4 7TG | 020-7622-1475
Bayswater | 63 Westbourne Grove, W2 4UA | 020-7313-9506 ●
www.nandos.co.uk
Additional locations throughout London

"You always know what you're getting" at this Portuguese chain that doles out "endless portions" of "decent, tasty", flame-grilled peri-peri chicken with a variety of sauces, including some that are "ferociously hot"; although the decor is nothing special and service can be "robotic", it's "super affordable" and a "great option for a quick meal".

National Dining Rooms *British*   ∇ 20 | 20 | 16 | £37

Charing Cross | National Gallery, Sainsbury Wing | Trafalgar Sq., WC2N 5DN | 020-7747-2525 | www.thenationaldiningrooms.co.uk

"Lovely views" of Trafalgar Square are afforded from this "oasis" in the National Gallery whose "quality" Modern British menu is "reasonably priced considering the location"; some "communal tables" make it an "easy way to dine alone", either for late-morning "grazing", lunch and, on Fridays when it's open until 8.30 PM, dinner.

Nautilus Fish ⊠⇄ *Seafood*   26 | 12 | 22 | £16

Hampstead | 27-29 Fortune Green Rd., NW6 1DU | 020-7435-2532

Perhaps the "best fish 'n' chips in North London" is found at this stalwart, making it "worth the walk from West Hampstead tube"; affordable prices and "family-friendly service" are further incentives, and if "basic decor" is a deterrent, the "takeaway quality" is equally "high".

New Culture Revolution *Chinese*   20 | 12 | 17 | £19

Islington | 42 Duncan St., N1 8BW | 020-7833-9083
Chelsea | 305 King's Rd., SW3 5EP | 020-7352-9281
www.newculturerevolution.co.uk

"Purify your soul" with "big bowls of comforting warm noodles" and other "healthy", "heartwarming" Mandarin dishes at this "reliable" duo in Chelsea and Islington; the "bland", "basic setting" and so so service means many "don't want to linger", but the "amazing value" keeps most coming back for more.

NEW Newman Street Tavern *British*   - | - | - | M

Fitzrovia | 48 Newman St., W1T 1QQ | 020-3667-1445 |
www.newmanstreettavern.co.uk

There's a gutsy, gamey focus at this midpriced Traditional Brit in Fitzrovia, where the seasonal menu changes daily; set on two high-ceilinged levels, the space includes a ground-floor bar and an upstairs dining room decorated with antique tables and vintage chairs.

	FOOD	DECOR	SERVICE	COST

New Mayflower ⚫ *Chinese*
24 | 13 | 17 | £25

Soho | 68-70 Shaftesbury Ave., W1D 6LY | 020-7734-9207
Despite a "lack of space" and "dated" look, this Soho Chinese is "worth going to again and again" to sample its complete selection of dishes, particularly the seafood; if occasionally "abrupt service" grates, all is forgiven when the affordable bill is presented.

NEW New Street Grill *British*
- | - | - | E

City | The Old Bengal Warehouse | 16A New St., EC2M 4TR | 020-3503-0785 | www.newstreetgrill.com
Big cuts of meat for sharing distinguish the upscale Traditional British dishes served at this plush, pricey City dining room in the Old Bengal Warehouse; the interior has a dark, evocative look with leather banquettes, while a walled courtyard bar boasts an expansive wine list majoring on Bordeaux, Burgundy and New World varietals.

New World ⚫ *Chinese*
20 | 13 | 16 | £24

Chinatown | 1 Gerrard Pl., W1D 5PA | 020-7434-2508
Expect "a never-ending stream" of "traditional dim sum delivered on trolleys" at this "cavernous" Chinatown venue where all of the Cantonese eats, including the more "exotic dishes", are a "safe bet", and "well priced" too; "speedy service" makes it "a good choice even at busy times", such as the "exciting Sunday lunch".

1901 *British*
23 | 22 | 21 | £46

City | Andaz Liverpool St. | 40 Liverpool St., EC2M 7QN | 020-7618-7000 | www.andazdining.com
At this "buzzing, huge hall of a place" set in the City's Andaz Liverpool Street Hotel, the "excellent", sometimes "inspired" Modern British fare competes with "beautiful" decor flourishes such as a stained-glass dome; service gets mixed reports ("attentive" vs. "needs to improve"), but most agree it's a "proper" choice for everything from a "quick" "work lunch" to a "special occasion".

Nobu Berkeley St. ⚫ *Japanese/Peruvian*
26 | 22 | 22 | £79

Mayfair | 15 Berkeley St., W1J 8DY | 020-7290-9222 | www.noburestaurants.com
With a "buzzing atmosphere", a "celeb" following, "excellent" Japanese-Peruvian creations and "marvellous bar scene", this "trendy" Berkeley Square sibling of the Park Lane flagship "fully deserves" its reputation as a hot spot; if a few haulk at the "expensive" prices, most agree "eating here is as exciting as ever".

Nobu London *Japanese/Peruvian*
27 | 21 | 21 | £82

Mayfair | Metropolitan Hotel | 19 Old Park Ln., W1K 1LB | 020-7447-4747 | www.noburestaurants.com
The "stunning" selection of "pricey" Japanese-Peruvian dishes – "blackened cod is the signature for good reason" – "cannot be faulted for consistency" at this iconic venue in the Metropolitan Hotel; even though there are views of Green Park, some feel that the decor "lacks that wow factor" – however, the atmosphere is "lively", not least because it's a "place to spot celebrities".

	FOOD	DECOR	SERVICE	COST

NEW No. 11 Pimlico ❶ *European* | - | - | - | M |

Pimlico | 11 Pimlico Rd., SW1W 8NA | 020-7730-6784 |
www.no11pimlicoroad.co.uk

A mélange of mismatched chairs and soft grey hues lends an eccentric
look to this airy Pimlico gastropub, offering weekday breakfast, weekend brunch and a midpriced Modern European lunch and dinner menu
covering everything from light salads to hearty roasts; there's also an
on-site wine shop and an upstairs space for private parties.

Noor Jahan *Indian* | 23 | 13 | 19 | £33 |

Paddington | 26 Sussex Pl., W2 2TH | 020-7402-2332 |
www.noorjahan2.com
South Kensington | 2 Bina Gdns., SW5 0LA | 020-7373-6522 |
www.noorjahanrestaurants.co.uk

"When you're in an Indian food mood" in Paddington or South Ken and
don't mind "simple decor", check out this "trusted" duo "for your favourite curry"; "courteous staff" and "great value" ("for the areas")
are other pluses, so no surprise "it's often full" ("better book").

NOPI *Asian/Mideastern* | 25 | 23 | 22 | £53 |

Soho | 21-22 Warwick St., W1B 5NE | 020-7494-9584 |
www.nopi-restaurant.com

A "rainbow of colours and tastes" dominates the "delicious" menu
of small plates at this moderately expensive, all-day Soho Pan-Asian–
Middle Eastern from Yotam Ottolenghi; the "functional" yet "beautiful", "comfortable" interior and "casual, friendly" service makes
for an all-round "happy atmosphere".

North Sea ⊠ *Seafood* | 24 | 13 | 21 | £23 |

Bloomsbury | 7-8 Leigh St., WC1H 9EW | 020-7387-5892 |
www.northseafishrestaurant.co.uk

The "freshest fish, lovingly prepared" and served with chunky chips –
that's the "famed" formula of this inexpensive Bloomsbury chippy;
the setting is "reminiscent of a classic British joint" (in other words
"old-fashioned"), with "friendly" service and the option to take away;
P.S. reservations recommended at weekends.

Noura *Lebanese* | 22 | 17 | 20 | £42 |

Mayfair | 16 Curzon St., W1J 5HP | 020-7495-1050 ❶
Belgravia | 12 William St., SW1X 9HL | 020-7235-5900
Belgravia | 16 Hobart Pl., SW1W 0HH | 020-7235-9444 ❶
www.noura.co.uk

"Large" portions of "delicious Lebanese" cuisine with "all the
trimmings" – "fit for vegans or carnivores" – come via "friendly, fast"
service at this "welcoming" chainlet; prices are "a bit expensive" for
the genre, but they also get you "smart" decor and an "out-of-this-
world" wine selection.

Novikov ❶ *Asian/Italian* | 21 | 22 | 21 | £76 |

Mayfair | 50 Berkeley St., W1J 8HA | 020-7399-4330 |
www.novikovrestaurant.co.uk

There's a "terrific buzz" at this "lively" Mayfair venue from prolific
Russian restaurateur Arkady Novikov, comprising a ground floor

"Far East fusion section" with granite walls and a spacious, sky-lit Italian eatery below; the consensus on the expensive food is that it's "decent but unexciting", however, that doesn't seem to deter its "elegant" clientele.

NEW Oblix ● American — | — | — | E

Tower Bridge | The Shard | 31 St. Thomas St., 32nd fl., SE1 9RY | 020-7268-6700 | www.oblixrestaurant.com

Dark, lava stone-clad corridors on the 32nd floor of The Shard lead to this glass-wrapped space serving New York-style rotisserie and grilled food; on one side is a relaxed lounge with sofas and live evening entertainment, while on the other is a sleeker dining room with an open kitchen, wood-fired oven and a sommelier's station where you can sample wines before buying.

Odette's European 25 | 23 | 25 | £60

Primrose Hill | 130 Regent's Park Rd., NW1 8XL | 020-7586-8569 | www.odettesprimrosehill.com

Achieving a "balance between creative and conventional", this "consistent" Primrose Hill Modern European delivers "delicious", "well-put-together" meals in an intimate setting that includes a dining garden; staff are "attentive and friendly", and even though it's "not cheap", it's still considered "good value for money", especially the lunch and early-bird set menus.

Old Brewery British 17 | 21 | 18 | £29

Greenwich | Pepys Bldg. | Old Royal Naval College, SE10 9LW | 020-3327-1280 | www.oldbrewerygreenwich.com

"Your table will be within touching distance of dramatic copper vats" used to make Meantime beers at this brick-walled Greenwich microbrewery in the Old Royal Naval College's grounds; during the day, separate cafe and pub-style menus are available, and for dinner, a "small", "nicely cooked" Modern British menu is proffered by the "smiling" staff inside and in the garden if the "weather is warm enough".

Old Bull & Bush European 18 | 19 | 18 | £31

Hampstead | North End Rd., NW3 7HE | 020-8905-5456 | www.thebullandbush.co.uk

With its "great location just off the Heath" and "pleasant" service, this midpriced Modern Euro is "always full" with Hampstead locals enjoying "tasty victuals", especially the "famous Sunday roast"; combining a "cosy" bar and "more formal" restaurant, the "family venue" also boasts "log fires" in winter and an outdoor terrace in summer.

Oliveto Italian 24 | 14 | 17 | £34

Belgravia | 49 Elizabeth St., SW1W 9PP | 020-7730-0074 | www.olivorestaurants.com

"Fabulous" thin-crust pizza and Sardinian pastas, all "value for money", have made this "small" Belgravia Italian (offshoot of Olivo) a "popular local" haunt; service that varies from "charming" to "slow when it's busy" deters some, but if you can "ignore that" and the "bland" decor, it's "well worth it".

	FOOD	DECOR	SERVICE	COST

Olivo *Italian* — **22** | **16** | **21** | **£39**

Belgravia | 21 Eccleston St., SW1W 9LX | 020-7730-2505 |
www.olivorestaurants.com

"Deservedly popular and not that pricey", this "cosy" Belgravia Italian
pairs pastas to "dream about" and other "superb", seafood-centric
Sardinian cuisine with "excellent service"; loyalists who "make a
point of going there" assess that its "down-to-earth", "adult" vibe is
"a bit of a refuge in comparison" with its younger sister, Oliveto,
though "not less busy".

NEW Olivocarne *Italian* — **-** | **-** | **-** | **E**

Belgravia | 61 Elizabeth St., SW1W 9PP | 020-7730-7997 |
www.olivorestaurants.com

Adding to Belgravia's collection of popular Olivo eateries, this latest
entry focuses on pricey, meat-centric Sardinian dishes; running over
two floors, the setting is at once contemporary and folksy.

Olivomare *Italian/Seafood* — **24** | **17** | **21** | **£51**

Belgravia | 10 Lower Belgrave St., SW1W 0LJ | 020-7730-9022 |
www.olivorestaurants.com

"Belgravia cognoscenti" feast on "imaginative", "wonderful seafood" with "Sardinian flavour" at this "modern" "cousin to Olivo and
Oliveto", where service is a "balance of friendly and professional"
and the bill is "pricey without being expensive"; if it's "too bad about
the incredible noise levels" – and what some find "bizarre" surroundings, with its all-white "modern" decor broken up by a fish
mural – most usually welcome "an excuse for a return visit".

One Blenheim Terrace Ⓜ *British* — **24** | **22** | **23** | **£54**

St. John's Wood | 1 Blenheim Terr., NW8 0EH | 020-7372-1722 |
www.oneblenheimterrace.co.uk

"A credit to St. John's Wood", this "elegant neighbourhood gem"
presents a "cleverly thought-out", somewhat pricey Modern British
menu with "an artistic twist"; a "modern setting" (sleek leather chairs,
white tablecloths), "warm, inviting atmosphere" and "friendly service" add to its credentials.

NEW One Leicester Street *European* — **-** | **-** | **-** | **M**

Leicester Square | One Leicester Street Hotel | 1 Leicester St.,
WC2H 7BL | 020-3301-8020 | www.oneleicesterstreet.com

Located in an upscale, revamped Georgian hotel close to Leicester
Square, this grey-hued, copper-tinged Modern European with a
kitchen headed by acclaimed chef Tom Harris serves an all-day mix
of moderately priced sharing plates and mains; alfresco tables allow
for people-watching, while upstairs resides a discreet, parquet-floored
bar that doubles as a private function room.

1 Lombard Street Ⓩ *French* — **23** | **22** | **22** | **£57**

City | 1 Lombard St., EC3V 9AA | 020-7929-6611 |
www.1lombardstreet.com

"Delicious" New French cuisine presented by "discreet", "efficient"
staff, a "lovely", "formal setting" in a former banking hall and ex-

pense-account prices make this City dining room "perfect for business"; an "extensive" wine list presented on an iPad is another reason admirers call it "definitely worth the experience".

1 Lombard Street Brasserie 🗷 *European* | 21 | 21 | 20 | £44 |

City | 1 Lombard St., EC3V 9AA | 020-7929-6611 |
www.1lombardstreet.com

Sharing the same "interesting architecture" as its swankier, same-named sister, this "busy, buzzy" Modern European in a former City banking hall is "the more affordable option", with a "better-than-average" menu that "has everything you want"; whether you come for breakfast, lunch or dinner, expect "fast service" and a crowd "awash" with "bankers, brokers and financiers".

One-O-One *French/Seafood* | 22 | 17 | 22 | £67 |

Belgravia | Sheraton Park Tower | 101 Knightsbridge, SW1X 7RN |
020-7290-7101 | www.oneoonerestaurant.com

A "haven of calm" inside Belgravia's Sheraton Park Tower, this expensive New French seafood spot always has "something you'll want to try"; some find the setting "bland", but that's made up for by the "great service".

108 Marylebone Lane *British* | 21 | 20 | 21 | £42 |

Marylebone | Marylebone Hotel | 108 Marylebone Ln., W1U 2QE |
020-7969-3900 | www.one08.co.uk

With "prompt" service from "attentive" staff and a "safe" Traditional British menu, this "tastefully decorated" bi-level bistro inside a Marylebone hotel is a "decent-value" "standby" if you're in the area; it's "a convenient place for after-work" "cocktails and nibbles" too.

101 Thai Kitchen *Thai* | 24 | 20 | 22 | £37 |

Hammersmith | 352 King St., W6 0RX | 020-8746-6888 |
www.101thaikitchen.com

"Thai me down here anytime" declare devotees of this Hammersmith "hole-in-the-wall" serving "curries made with care" and other "excellent" dishes for "reasonable" prices; though some wish they could "keep it secret", it's "always packed with locals" enjoying the "fab" service and "simple", "stylish" surrounds.

Opera Tavern ◑ *Italian/Spanish* | 25 | 20 | 22 | £42 |

Covent Garden | 23 Catherine St., WC2B 5JS | 020-7836-3680 |
www.operatavern.co.uk

A seasonally changing menu of "flavourful" Spanish-Italian tapas, including "melt-in-the-mouth" Iberico pork, "hits the spot" at this "casual", "tucked away" bi-level Covent Garden kitchen (sibling of Dehesa and Salt Yard); some warn that it's "pricey" and "easy to run up a large bill", but "friendly" staff and a "buzzy" atmosphere are pluses.

Orange Restaurant ◑ *European* | 22 | 22 | 20 | £48 |

Belgravia | The Orange | 37-39 Pimlico Rd., SW1W 8NE | 020-7881-9844 |
www.theorange.co.uk

This "bustling" Belgravia sibling of Thomas Cubitt offers "something for everyone" on its Modern European "comfort-food" menu, including "good pizza"; both the ground-floor pub and "beautifully deco-rated", fireplace-equipped upstairs room boast "country home-style decor" and a "friendly" ambience, and though prices aren't cheap, fans deem them "good value for London"; P.S. it's part of a small hotel.

Original Lahore ● *Pakistani*   ▽ 23 | 14 | 18 | £22

Hendon | 148-150 Brent St., NW4 2DR | 020-8203-6904
St. John's Wood | 2-4 Gateforth St., NW8 8EH | 020-723-0808
www.originallahore.com

"Amazing kebabs and naan" are just some of the "tasty" dishes sold for "excellent prices" at this "friendly" pair of Pakistani eateries in Hendon and St. John's Wood; the decor may be "getting tired", but that doesn't deter devotees who could "go here every day".

Orrery *French*   23 | 22 | 23 | £63

Marylebone | 55 Marylebone High St., W1U 5RB | 020-7616-8000 |
www.orreryrestaurant.co.uk

"Good-humoured" staff are "committed to making you feel at home" at this "discreetly located" Marylebone New French where "exquisite", "beautifully presented" dishes (including an "excep-tional" cheese board) and "serious" wines are "worth the price" for a "special night out" or "fabulous" Sunday lunch; "large, lovely win-dows" overlooking St. Marylebone Church plus a rooftop terrace en-hance the "chic", "comfortable" atmosphere.

Orso ● *Italian*   21 | 17 | 20 | £45

Covent Garden | 27 Wellington St., WC2E 7DB | 020-7240-5269 |
www.orsorestaurant.co.uk

"Understated" and "underground", this "quirky" Italian "hideaway on the edge of Covent Garden" is "reliable" for "decent-value" fare (including "terrific" pizzas and pastas) served by "agreeable staff"; though "perhaps it needs some redecorating", late hours make it a "great post-theatre spot", where diners are often "rewarded" with "glimpses of celebrities".

Oslo Court ☒ *French*   26 | 18 | 27 | £54

St. John's Wood | Charlbert St., off Prince Albert Rd., NW8 7EN |
020-7722-8795

"Resistance is useless" when it comes to the "enormous" portions of "excellent" "old-school" French fare (served as part of a prix fixe menu), at this somewhat pricey eatery in St. John's Wood, where "ef-fusive" staff ensure everything "runs like a superbly oiled machine"; it may be a bit of a "time warp" to the "'70s", but most find it a "highly entertaining experience"; P.S. try to "save space for dessert".

Osteria Antica Bologna *Italian*   ▽ 22 | 18 | 19 | £39

Clapham | 23 Northcote Rd., SW11 1NG | 020-7978-4771 |
www.osteria.co.uk

Day-trippers returning to London "ease back in with great plea-sure" at this trattoria a stone's throw from Clapham Junction station, where a Boot-based wine list complements "generous portions" of "classic pasta dishes" and other "reliable", moderately priced

Italian fare; solid service and charming decor, make it an "ideal" local pit stop.

Osteria Basilico ❷ *Italian*   24 | 17 | 20 | £40

Notting Hill | 29 Kensington Park Rd., W11 2EU | 020-7727-9957 | www.osteriabasilico.co.uk

Those who crave "hearty" Italian food (e.g. "generous" antipasti, "gigantic" calamari) enjoy this "reliably good", moderately priced Notting Hill trattoria; although it's "small and always packed", the setting can seem "romantic".

Osteria dell'Arancio *Italian*   22 | 19 | 24 | £48

Chelsea | 383 King's Rd., SW10 0LP | 020-7349-8111 | www.osteriadellarancio.co.uk

"Attentive, friendly hosts" with a "helpful attitude" serve "comforting" dishes at this "cosy", "inviting" King's Road trattoria, which some say "feels like a proper New York Italian"; prices that are "not cheap" make it a "special-occasion" spot for some, while others say it also suits a "quiet weekday dinner" for "couples or groups of friends".

Ottolenghi *Bakery/Mediterranean*   26 | 19 | 20 | £32

Islington | 287 Upper St., N1 2TZ | 020-7288-1454
Belgravia | 13 Motcomb St., SW1X 8LB | 020-7823-2707
Kensington | 1 Holland St., W8 4NA | 020-7937-0003
Notting Hill | 63 Ledbury Rd., W11 2AD | 020-7727-1121
www.ottolenghi.co.uk

"Yotam Ottolenghi can do no wrong" cheer fans of this Mediterranean (particularly North African–Middle Eastern) cafe/deli/bakery chainlet where the "healthy", "creative" and often vegetarian dishes include "amazing" salads and "a mouth-watering display of desserts"; the communal tables lead some to brand it "somewhere to drop-in rather than linger" (only the Islington branch is full-service), but it's "fab" for a "quick", "reasonably priced" breakfast, lunch or dinner.

NEW Outlaw's at the Capital ☒ *Seafood*   - | - | - | E

Knightsbridge | The Capital | 22-24 Basil St., SW3 1AT | 020-7589-5171 | www.capitalhotel.co.uk

Acclaimed Cornish chef Nathan Outlaw brings his piscatorial flair to Knightsbridge's Capital Hotel, offering an expensive menu of sustainable seafood in an understated Nina Campbell–designed dining room; extra lures include tasting menus (including one for vegetarians), and more affordable set lunch and dinner options.

Oxo Tower *European*   22 | 25 | 22 | £69

South Bank | Oxo Tower Wharf | Barge House St., 8th fl., SE1 9PH | 020-7803-3888 | www.harveynichols.com

With such "spectacular" river views, "it almost doesn't matter" what you eat, but fortunately, the "pricey" Modern European menu of this eighth-floor South Bank eyrie is judged to be both "innovative and delicious"; couple that with "excellent" service and an "extensive" wine list, and it's clear why those who "want something a bit special" and "memorable" say they're "not disappointed" here.

	FOOD	DECOR	SERVICE	COST

Oxo Tower Brasserie *Asian/Mediterranean*   23 | 23 | 21 | £52

South Bank | Oxo Tower Wharf | Barge House St., 8th fl., SE1 9PH | 020-7803-3888 | www.harveynichols.com

You get the same "amazing" eighth-floor views as its neighbour (Oxo Tower), but for slightly lower prices at this "lively" South Bank brasserie offering "excellent" Med and Pan-Asian plates and "value" set menus, all via "attentive" service; and with a setting that's "not overly formal", it's "a must for tourists", even if only for a drink at the bar.

Özer Restaurant & Bar *Turkish*   21 | 20 | 19 | £34

Marylebone | 5 Langham Pl., W1B 3DG | 020-7323-0505 | www.ozerrestaurant.com

"Amazing" lamb tagine and other "upmarket" Turkish dishes are a "steal for the money" at this "friendly" Marylebone "gem" where there's "loads of choice" (including an extensive wine list); "off the beaten path but well worth it", the "cosy", "modern" space is supplemented by a patio suitable for "watching the world go by".

Painted Heron *Indian*   24 | 18 | 20 | £45

Chelsea | 112 Cheyne Walk, SW10 0DJ | 020-7351-5232 | www.thepaintedheron.com

"One of Chelsea's best-kept secrets", this Indian "hideout" along the Thames serves "traditional curries with a modern twist", using "unique ingredients like venison and pheasant" for a "satisfying" if "pricey" meal; what's more, "charming" service and sophisticated, modern decor make it "a good date spot".

The Palm *American/Steak*   22 | 20 | 21 | £65

Knightsbridge | 1 Pont St., SW1X 9EJ | 020-7201-0710 | www.thepalm.com

"Proper porterhouses" and other "juicy" cuts are "cooked to perfection" and teamed with "enormous sides" at this Knightsbridge link of the "quintessential American steakhouse" chain, where "efficient" staff "give good recommendations on both food and wine"; "wonderful murals of favoured patrons" jazz up the decor, and while some scorn the "lofty prices", most "would go again".

The Palmerston *British*   ∇ 23 | 19 | 21 | £36

Dulwich | 91 Lordship Ln., SE22 8EP | 020-8693-1629 | www.thepalmerston.net

"Whether you want a quiet dinner with a loved one, a laugh with friends or to impress the in-laws", this "gorgeous" Dulwich gastropub is a "reliable" option, with Modern British fare that's "superbly cooked" and "fantastic value" to boot; other enticements include "friendly" staff, two fireplaces and works by "local artists" on the walls.

**The Pantechnicon Public House
and Dining Room** *European*   21 | 20 | 22 | £44

Belgravia | 10 Motcomb St., SW1X 8LA | 020-7730-6074 | www.thepantechnicon.com

The "owners have the formula just right" at this "swanky" Cubitt House outpost in Belgravia, where "tasty", "reasonably priced"

Modern European dishes and "friendly" service make it a "big family hit", especially for a "fantastic Sunday lunch"; from casual snacks in the "noisy" ground-floor pub and leisurely patio dining to a "more formal" meal in the "charming" upstairs dining room (complete with a "blazing fireplace"), it's an all-around "delightful experience".

Paradise ● *Indian* ▽ 26 | 19 | 27 | £33

Hampstead | 49 South End Rd., NW3 2QB | 020-7794-6314 | www.paradisehampstead.co.uk

"High-quality, old-style curry" and tandoor-cooked dishes whose execution some respondents deem "second-to-none" come via solid service at this low-key, reasonably priced Hampstead Indian, "still going strong after 40-plus years"; in warmer weather, there are a few tables available outside.

Paradise by way of Kensal Green ● *British* 23 | 24 | 21 | £39

Kensal Green | 19 Kilburn Ln., W10 4AE | 020-8969-0098 | www.theparadise.co.uk

The "playful name" hints at the "laid-back vibe" and "cool crowd" of "fashionistas" at this "gorgeous" Kensal Green hangout, "one of the pillars of the gastro revolution", with a "fairly priced", "wholesome" Modern British menu and "warm, welcoming" staff; what's more, there's a "beautiful" roof terrace and it doubles as a "party venue" that's "open late" for "boozing", dancing and karaoke, plus live music at weekends.

Paramount ● *European* 21 | 23 | 19 | £70

Soho | Centre Point | 101-103 New Oxford St., 32nd fl., WC1A 1DD | 020-7420-2900 | www.paramount.uk.net

"You feel you're in an exclusive place when they whisk you up in the lift" to this "wow destination" on the 32nd floor of Soho's Centre Point, where the "contemporary" setting boasts "amazing 360-degree views of London"; while prices are "expensive", the Modern Euro fare is "delicious", and though sometimes "slow" service is a "turnoff", the "superb wine list" and "cool bar" make amends.

Pasha *Turkish* 22 | 18 | 23 | £30

Islington | 301 Upper St., N1 2TU | 020-7226-1454 | www.pashaislington.co.uk

"Tasty, high-class Turkish" cuisine proves quite "popular" in Islington at this "comfortable" eatery decked out in "contemporary, sophisti-cated decor"; what's more, "prices are low for what you get", namely "generous portions" and "helpful" service.

Patara *Thai* 24 | 20 | 21 | £41

Mayfair | 3-7 Maddox St., W1S 2QB | 020-7499-6008
Soho | 15 Greek St., W1D 4DP | 020-7437-1071
Knightsbridge | 9 Beauchamp Pl., SW3 1NQ | 020-7581-8820
South Kensington | 181 Fulham Rd., SW3 6JN | 020-7351-5692
www.patarauk.com

"If you're looking for a different take on Thai food" and a menu with "plenty of variety", including some "unusual dishes not found else-

where", this "upscale" chainlet with "a lively clientele" is a "reliable"
option; while "not cheap", "efficient", "friendly" service and "stylish" environs help make it "worth every penny".

Paternoster Chop House *Steak*   `22` `19` `20` `£48`
City | Warwick Ct., Paternoster Sq., EC4M 7DX | 020-7029-9400 |
www.paternosterchophouse.co.uk

The 'beast of the day' on the menu means it's "always an interesting experience for meat lovers" at this "friendly", rustic City
steakhouse where all of the dishes are "enjoyable"; the "pleasant
setup" features an open kitchen where "you can see the food as
it's cooked" plus an alfresco terrace in the "beautiful surrounds"
near St. Paul's Cathedral.

NEW Patty & Bun Ⓜ *Burgers*   ▽ `21` `13` `20` `£18`
Marylebone | 54 James St., W1U 1EU | 020-7487-3188 |
www.pattyandbun.co.uk

"Juicy" burgers plus "mighty fine" sides served by "welcoming" staff is
the "simple but effective" formula at this permanent Marylebone
home of a former pop-up eatery; with only 30 seats and no reservations accepted, expect "long waiting lines" at busy times, but it's
such "good value", many reckon it's "worth queuing for".

Pearl Liang *Chinese*   `25` `19` `17` `£35`
Paddington | 8 Sheldon Sq., W2 6EZ | 020-7289-7000 |
www.pearlliang.co.uk

"Despite being in the middle of nowhere" ("bring your GPS"), this
Paddington Chinese is "always packed" thanks to its "lip-smackingly
good" Peking duck, "fantastic selection" of dim sum and other "delicious", "diverse" dishes offered alongside an "interesting cocktail
menu"; "prices are on the high side" considering sometimes "spotty"
service, but they match the "fancy ambience" bedecked with "grand"
bright-pink furnishings.

The Pepper Tree *Thai*   `27` `17` `22` `£17`
Clapham | 19 Clapham Common S., SW4 7AB | 020-7622-1758 |
www.thepeppertree.co.uk

Enthusiasts opine that this "reliable" Clapham canteen "could charge
double" for its "reasonably priced", "high-quality" Thai plates and they
"would still come here"; although the "efficient" staff can seem "eager
to get you in and out as fast as possible", the communal benches
may be "uncomfortable for a long meal" anyway.

Pescatori Ⓩ *Italian/Seafood*   `22` `19` `22` `£43`
Fitzrovia | 57 Charlotte St., W1T 4PD | 020-7580-3289
Mayfair | 11 Dover St., W1S 4LH | 020-7493-2652
www.pescatori.co.uk

"You can be sure of a warm welcome" at this "quiet" Italian seafood
duo in Fitzrovia and Mayfair, whose "enjoyable" fare "fits the bill" for
something "not too stuffy or formal", whether a "business lunch" or
an "after-work meal"; though cost-calculators suspect the "pricing
is high for what you get", they're mollified by the "great-value set
menus"; P.S. "go alfresco" via the summertime terrace seating.

	FOOD	DECOR	SERVICE	COST

The Petersham *European* | 23 | 22 | 23 | £58 |

Richmond | Petersham Hotel | Nightingale Ln., TW10 6UZ | 020-8940-7471 | www.petershamhotel.co.uk

There's a "fabulous vista down the Thames" from this "dignified" dining room in a "historic hotel" "on the slopes of Richmond Hill", where the kitchen turns out "well-prepared" Modern European cuisine; although "high prices" deter some, "friendly, nonintrusive service", an "extensive" wine list and "ample parking" encourage revisits.

Petersham Nurseries Café Ⓜ *European* | 24 | 21 | 20 | £49 |

Richmond | Petersham Nurseries | Church Ln., TW10 7AG | 020-8940-5230 | www.petershamnurseries.com

In a "picturesque" position overlooking meadows where "cows graze happily", this "stylish" eatery in a Richmond greenhouse presents a fairly "expensive", "delicious" Modern European menu with an Italian bias and "reasonably priced" wines to accompany; the "floral" setting is as suited to a "special occasion" as it is for a "light lunch".

Petrus Ⓢ *French* | 28 | 26 | 27 | £100 |

Belgravia | 1 Kinnerton St., SW1X 8EA | 020-7592-1609 | www.gordonramsay.com

"The real deal for high-end dining", this "sophisticated" Belgravia "jewel" in the Gordon Ramsay empire is "one for a special occasion", with "sensational", "richly flavoured" New French cuisine and "impeccable" service; although it's "expensive", most deem the prices "completely worth it" for such a "magical, unforgettable" experience; P.S. the set lunch menu is "excellent value".

Pho *Vietnamese* | 22 | 16 | 18 | £18 |

Fitzrovia | 3 Great Titchfield St., W1W 8AX | 020-7436-0111 Ⓢ
Farringdon | 86 St. John St., EC1M 4EH | 020-7253-7624 Ⓢ
Soho | 163-165 Wardour St., W1F 8WN | 020-7434-3938
NEW **Spitalfields** | 48 Brushfield St., E1 6AG | 020-7377-6436
Stratford | Westfield Stratford City | 2 Stratford Pl., balcony, E20 1ES | 020-8555-5737
Shepherd's Bush | Westfield Shopping Ctr. | Ariel Way, balcony, W12 7GE | 07824-662320
www.phocafe.co.uk

"Cheap and cheerful", this "no-frills" Vietnamese cafe chain is "always crazy-busy" with the "masses" tucking into "flavourful" bowls of "satisfying" noodle soup or salads boosted with "lots of fresh herbs"; "friendly", "speedy" staff keep everything flowing.

Phoenix Palace ◗ *Chinese* | 23 | 18 | 17 | £30 |

Marylebone | 5-9 Glentworth St., NW1 5PG | 020-7486-3515 | www.phoenixpalace.co.uk

"Good-value" dim sum and Cantonese dishes with "interesting" flavours (in portions large "enough to share") fill the "extensive" menu at this "family-friendly" Marylebone Chinese; the "kitschy" gold interior and "lively yet not too loud" atmosphere lend it an "exotic buzz".

	FOOD	DECOR	SERVICE	COST

Pied à Terre ⓩ *French* | 28 | 23 | 27 | £93

Fitzrovia | 34 Charlotte St., W1T 2NH | 020-7636-1178 |
www.pied-a-terre.co.uk

"Innovative", "immaculately prepared" haute New French cuisine
is "beautifully presented" at this "elegant", "cosy" "boutique
space" in Fitzrovia; what's more, it's "outstandingly well run",
typified by an "excellent" sommelier and generally "charming"
service, and while it "may not be cheap", that's all the more reason it's a "must for special occasions".

Pig's Ear *British/French* | 21 | 18 | 16 | £37

Chelsea | 35 Old Church St., SW3 5BS | 020-7352-2908 |
www.thepigsear.info

There's "lots of quaint local flavour" to soak up at this "buzzing gastropub" on a "charming Chelsea backstreet", where "interesting"
traditional British and French brasserie fare comes at moderate
prices; service varies "depending on the night and the staff" say regulars who prefer to dodge the "cramped", "noisy" downstairs bar
and "book a table upstairs" in the "rustic" dining room.

Ping Pong *Chinese* | 17 | 17 | 16 | £29

Fitzrovia | 48 Eastcastle St., W1W 8DX | 020-7079-0550
City | Bow Bells Hse. | 1 Bread St., EC4M 9BE | 020-7651-0880 ⓩ
Marylebone | 10 Paddington St., W1U 5QL | 020-7009-9600
Marylebone | 29 James St., W1U 1DZ | 020-7034-3100
Soho | 45 Great Marlborough St., W1F 7JL | 020-7851-6969 ◑
Tower Bridge | St. Katherine Docks | St. Katharine's Way, E1W 1BA |
020-7680-7850
South Bank | Royal Festival Hall | Festival Terr., SEI 8XX |
020-7960-4160 ◑
Notting Hill | 74-76 Westbourne Grove, W2 5SH |
020-7313-9832
www.pingpongdimsum.com

The "lively" atmosphere and "loud" music may make this "trendy",
"workplace canteen"–style chain seem like a "club", but it's
mainly known for "tasty" Chinese dim sum at "no-frills prices";
and with "prompt" service, it suits a "quick bite at lunch" or "low-
key evening out".

Pitt Cue Co. ⓩ *BBQ* | 28 | 17 | 24 | £23

Soho | 1 Newburgh St., W1F 7RB | 020-7287-5578 |
www.pittcue.co.uk

"A fancified European vision of American BBQ", this "decently
priced" Soho haunt (London's No. 1 Best Buy) is armed with a team
of "brilliant, obsessive chefs", who prepare a "mind-blowing" menu
of pulled pork, ribs and such, served alongside an "amazing bourbon
selection" and "stunning" cocktails; it's "always busy", so "expect to
wait" for what some deem the "comically microscopic" downstairs
dining room – nevertheless, the consensus is that "every visit
proves a delight".

Pix Pintxos ◑ *Spanish* | ▽ 17 | 17 | 14 | £28

Covent Garden | 63 Neal St., WC2H 9PJ | 020-7836-9779

(continued)

Pix Pintxos

Soho | 16 Bateman St., W1D 3AH | 020-7437-0377

NEW **Islington** | 330 Upper St., N1 2XQ | 020-7359-1569
www.pix-bar.com

"Numerous" Spanish tapas are "nicely presented" at this Covent Garden and Soho duo (and it's Islington offshoot) where prices are indicated by the length of the skewer (the shorter ones are cheaper, but prices are generally moderate); it can feel "quite cramped" when full, but that doesn't hurt its reputation as a "great little place."

Pizarro   *Spanish*   26 | 22 | 23 | £43

Tower Bridge | 194 Bermondsey St., SE1 3TQ | 020-7378-9455 |
www.pizarrorestaurant.com

"Scrumptious" "stand-outs" abound on chef Jose Pizarro's daily changing Spanish menu at this Bermondsey Street venue; service may be "wonderful" and the modern setting may be large, but no reservations are accepted in the evenings or at weekends, so be prepared to "wait around for a table".

Pizza East   *Pizza*   21 | 22 | 18 | £28

Shoreditch | Tea Bldg. | 56 Shoreditch High St., E1 6JJ | 020-7729-1888 |
www.pizzaeast.com ●

NEW **Kentish Town** | Highgate Studios | 79 Highgate Rd., NW5 1TL |
020-3310-2000 | www.pizzaeastkentishtown.com ●

Ladbroke Grove | 310 Portobello Rd., W10 5TA | 020-8969-4500 |
www.pizzaeastportobello.com

It's "always jam-packed" at these "trendy", midpriced joints where diners break out of their "pepperoni comfort zone" via "posh", "inventive" thin-crust pizzas with "meaty" toppings that "satisfy Italian taste buds"; "service can be slow", but that just leaves more time to engage in the "wonderful people-watching"; P.S. it's quite "kid-friendly" too.

Pizza Express   *Italian/Pizza*   16 | 14 | 15 | £20

Soho | 10 Dean St., W1D 3RW | 020-7437-9595

Highgate | 30 High St., N6 5JG | 020-8341-3434

Muswell Hill | 290 Muswell Hill Broadway, N10 2QR |
020-8883 -5845

Dulwich | 94 The Village, SE21 7AQ | 020-8883-5845

Blackheath | 64 Tranquil Vale, SE3 0BN | 020-8318-2595

Greenwich | 4 Church St., SE10 9BG | 020-8853-2770

Balham | 47 Bedford Hill, SW12 9EY | 020-8772-3232

Streatham | 34 Streatham High Rd., SW16 1DB |
020-8769-0202

Wandsworth | 539 Old York Rd., SW18 1TG | 020-8877-9812

Chelsea | 363 Fulham Rd., SW10 9TN | 020-7352-5300
www.pizzaexpress.com

Additional locations throughout London

As "dependable" as they come, this omnipresent chain is a "great all-round place" for "spending time with family and friends" over "good" (if "not fab") pizza and other Italian standards; it's "noisy when busy", but "loyal repeat customers" feel that, with "prompt service", it's "good value for money".

Plateau 🎇 *French* `21` `23` `20` `£47`

Canary Wharf | Canada Pl. | Canada Sq., 4th fl., E14 5ER | 020-7715-7100 | www.plateaurestaurant.co.uk

"Mingle" with a "loud and successful crowd" of "traders and bankers" while taking in a "neat view" of "one of the green spots of Canary Wharf" at this "light", "modern" venue, which provides "delicious" New French cuisine and "overall good" service; as it's priced for "a big spender", some people "like the bar better", but whichever section you settle into, it's sure "to make a great first impression".

NEW Plum + Spilt Milk ● *British* `-` `-` `-` `M`

King's Cross | Great Northern Hotel | King's Cross, N1C 4TB | 020-3388-0818 | www.plumandspiltmilk.com

Huge windows overlook King's Cross Square at this all-day hotel restaurant where jeans-clad staff in Doc Martens serve up Mark Sargeant's moderately priced Modern British food; there's also a clubby bar, jammed with a mishmash of wall art; P.S. the name comes from the colour scheme of the original dining carriage on the historic Great Northern Railway.

Plum Valley ● *Chinese* ▽ `23` `20` `19` `£28`

Chinatown | 20 Gerrard St., W1D 6JQ | 020-7494-4366

"An oasis of calm" amid "the hustle and bustle of Chinatown", this "upscale, modern" venue provides an "incredible selection" of Chinese cuisine "for the hard-core food lover", including "excellent dim sum" and "innovative vegetarian dishes"; such a "serious" culinary focus commands costs that some feel are "a bit pricey" for the genre, but it's "worth trying" nonetheless – just prepare for service that can be either "sweet" or "surly".

Poissonnerie de l'Avenue ● *French/Seafood* `24` `19` `23` `£63`

Chelsea | 82 Sloane Ave., SW3 3DZ | 020-7589-2457 | www.poissonneriedelavenue.com

"Right out of the 1960s", this "elegant" Chelsea institution "never fails to impress" with the "superb seafood" on its "classic", "pricey" French menu and "great service"; sure, younger diners may find the experience "a bit staid", but it's "unlikely to upset" the "old-money crowd" that frequents it.

Pollen Street Social 🎇 *British* `25` `22` `23` `£73`

Mayfair | 8-10 Pollen St., W1S 1NQ | 020-7290-7600 | www.pollenstreetsocial.com

Jason Atherton "skillfully merges his love for travel" with "genuinely exciting" Modern British fare – featuring "Asian twists" and "inventive" combinations of flavours and textures – at this "snazzy", "not inexpensive" Mayfair haunt, comprising a tapas bar, "modern dining room" and dessert counter; a "great vibe" born of "movers, shakers" and "bright young things" permeates throughout, while "engaging, creative bar staff" and a "surprising wine list" also earn plaudits.

Polpo *Italian*

| 22 | 19 | 19 | £35 |

Farringdon | 2-3 Cowcross St., EC1M 6DR | 020-7250-0034
Covent Garden | 6 Maiden Ln., WC2E 7NA | 020-7836-8448 ◑
Soho | 41 Beak St., W1F 9SB | 020-7734-4479
www.polpo.co.uk

"Delicious" tapas-style dishes are complemented by "excellent" Aperol spritzes at this "good-value" chainlet of Venetian-style bacaros; the "simple", "cosy" environs are always "busy", but staff remain "friendly"; P.S. bookings are taken only for lunch, so expect to "queue for a table" at night.

Popeseye ☒⇗ *Steak*

| ▽ 24 | 13 | 23 | £38 |

Putney | 277 Upper Richmond Rd., SW15 6SP | 020-8788-7733
Olympia | 108 Blythe Rd., W14 0HD | 020-7610-4578
www.popeseye.com

"Don't expect a large menu", as this "old-style" steakhouse duo "off the beaten track" in Putney and Olympia "stick to what they're good at" – "various cuts of wonderful red meat, chips and a good selection of sauces"; the atmosphere is strictly "no-frills", but it's boosted by "friendly" service and a bill that's "not too pricey"; P.S. cash only.

Poppies Fish & Chips *Seafood*

| ▽ 22 | 20 | 20 | £17 |

Spitalfields | 6-8 Hanbury St., E1 6QR | 020-7247-0892
NEW Camden Town | 30 Hawley Crescent, NW1 8NP |
020-7267-0440 ◑
www.poppiesfishandchips.co.uk

"Competently delivered", sustainably caught fish, chips and mushy peas are piled into fake newspaper at this Spitalfield fryer and its Camden sibling; a "nostalgic" atmosphere and reasonable prices add to its appeal; P.S. "try the sticky toffee pudding".

Portal ☒ *Portuguese*

| ▽ 27 | 24 | 22 | £52 |

Farringdon | 88 St. John St., EC1M 4EH | 020-7253-6950 |
www.portalrestaurant.com

"Fantastic Portuguese food" with a "modern" slant is served in "satisfying portions" at this "welcoming" Farringdon space, which also boasts an "excellent selection" of Iberian wines and a bar serving tapas; and with its "enthusiastic service" and "airy" brick-walled conservatory setting, no wonder admirers deem it a "lovely" "option for business and visitors alike".

Porters English Restaurant *British*

| 19 | 16 | 18 | £29 |

Covent Garden | 17 Henrietta St., WC2E 8QH | 020-7836-6466 |
www.porters-restaurant.com

With "bubble and squeak", "meat pies and puddings" on its "hearty" menu, this "perennial" "standby" in Covent Garden offers a "good-value" introduction to Traditional British cuisine in cheerful, wood-panelled dining rooms; unsurprisingly, it's a magnet for "tourists", with a menu that's "excellent for all ages" and "efficient service" that can handle any "loud and lively group".

Portobello Ristorante
Pizzeria ● *Italian/Pizza*

23 | 17 | 19 | £30

Notting Hill | 7 Ladbroke Rd., W11 3PA | 020-7221-1373 | www.portobellolondon.co.uk

Pizza is served "by the metre or half-metre" at this "casual" Notting Hill Italian also offering "gorgeous" starters and "top-quality" mains to please even "fussy" palates; "value prices" ensure it's "loud" with "tons of kids during the day", but the atmosphere is also "delightfully romantic" at night and, on the "sunny" terrace, "almost like being in Italy" in summer.

Portrait *British*

22 | 25 | 22 | £40

Soho | National Portrait Gallery | 2 St. Martin's Pl., 3rd fl., WC2H 0HE | 020-7312-2490 | www.searcys.co.uk

"Wonderful views" of landmarks (e.g. Nelson's Column, Big Ben, the London Eye) and "pleasing" decor are the highlights of this "upbeat" Modern Brit above the National Portrait Gallery; as for the food, it's "tasty", relatively reasonably priced and delivered via "good service".

Prezzo *Italian*

20 | 18 | 20 | £26

Charing Cross | 31-32 Northumberland Ave., WC2N 5BW | 020-7930-4288

Marylebone | 7-9 Great Cumberland Pl., W1H 7LU | 020-7723-7172

Mayfair | 15 N. Audley St., W1K 6WZ | 020-7493-4990

Mayfair | 17 Hertford St., W1J 7RS | 020-7499-4690

Leicester Square | 8 Haymarket, SW1Y 4BP | 020-7839-1129

Victoria | 22 Terminus Pl., SW1V 1JR | 020-7233-9099

King's Cross | King's Cross Station, N1C 4AL | 020-7833-4458

NEW **Wandsworth** | Southside Shopping Ctr., SW18 4TF | 020-8874-9559

Kensington | 35 Kensington High St., W8 5EB | 020-7937-2800 www.prezzorestaurants.co.uk

Additional locations throughout London

Regulars are "happy to visit" this "busy" contemporary Italian chain with numerous locations for its "large, tasty pizzas" and other "no-frills", "red-sauce" fare; while there are "no surprises" on the menu, "affordable" costs and "helpful staff" make it "good for a neighbourhood meal out with friends".

Princess Garden ● *Chinese*

24 | 19 | 22 | £45

Mayfair | 8-10 N. Audley St., W1K 6ZD | 020-7493-3223 | www.princessgardenofmayfair.com

"Palates that appreciate superior Chinese dishes" will revel in the "fabulous" food at this "high-end" Mayfair dining room where the "diverse menu" includes "incredible dim sum"; furthermore, "knowledgeable staff" and a "lively but not overly noisy" ambience help make it suited for "that special occasion".

The Princess of Shoreditch *British*

∇ 20 | 16 | 21 | £37

Shoreditch | 76-78 Paul St., EC2A 4NE | 020-7729-9270 | www.theprincessofshoreditch.com

A "comfortable", "candlelit" first-floor dining room serves "well-prepared", moderately priced Modern British cuisine at this

Shoreditch gastropub; meanwhile, the bar offers "great draft and bottled beers" and the same "personal", "efficient" service as can be found upstairs.

Princess Victoria *British*

▽ 25 | 24 | 24 | £33

Shepherd's Bush | 217 Uxbridge Rd., W12 9DH | 020-8749-5886 | www.princessvictoria.co.uk

"Don't be fooled by the fact it's a pub" – the affordable British menu includes some "spectacular dishes" (not to mention "delicious bar snacks") at this "large, airy" Shepherd's Bush "landmark"; the "delightful surroundings" include a "pretty" garden, "charming staff" and, rumour has it, "even the odd celebrity".

Princi London ● *Bakery/Italian*

24 | 22 | 16 | £17

Soho | 135 Wardour St., W1F 0UT | 020-7478-8888 | www.princi.co.uk

"Full of energy" (read: "loud"), this "modern" canteen-style bakery import from Milan is an "oasis of quality" in Soho, serving "generous cold-cut platters", pizzas and sweet "indulgences", all a "feast for the eyes and the taste buds"; indeed, "it's not a well-kept secret anymore", so a "fight for a table" is possible, but at least prices are reasonable and service "fairly quick and friendly".

Prism 🅂 *British*

▽ 19 | 21 | 19 | £56

City | 147 Leadenhall St., EC3V 4QT | 020-7256-3888 | www.harveynichols.com

This bank hall–turned–"reliable" British eatery is a "serviceable" spot for "a business lunch" in the City with its "vast ceiling height, classic columns" and expense-account pricing; after work "can get noisy when the bar is full", but some who've stayed for dinner feel that the "atmosphere leaves something to be desired" the later it gets; P.S. oenophiles say the wine list includes "some good things at reasonable prices".

The Providores *International*

25 | 17 | 19 | £39

Marylebone | 109 Marylebone High St., W1U 4RX | 020-7935-6175 | www.theprovidores.co.uk

"Be prepared to go where the chef wants to take you" at Peter Gordon's no-reservations International in Marylebone, where the moderately priced menu of "consistently imaginative", "tasty" tapas-sized dishes is paired with a New Zealand-focused wine list; while the "cramped" setting and "so-so" service don't impress everyone, most deem it, overall, a "memorable" experience.

Punjab ● *Indian*

23 | 17 | 20 | £26

Covent Garden | 80 Neal St., WC2H 9PA | 020-7836-9787 | www.punjab.co.uk

With a "well-deserved reputation" stretching back to the 1940s, this "informal" Covent Garden Indian proffers a "classic" menu that "never disappoints", especially "for the price you're paying"; the place is "a bit cramped" with "missable decor", but thanks in part to the "friendly" service, fans vow to "return again and again".

	FOOD	DECOR	SERVICE	COST

Quadrato *Italian* ∇ 19 | 18 | 18 | £62
Canary Wharf | Four Seasons Canary Wharf | 46 Westferry Circus,
E14 8RS | 020-7510-1857 | www.fourseasons.com
"What a beautiful setting" sigh admirers of this airy Canary Wharf
hotel dining room on the Thames, where the "fine" northern Italian
offerings include a "fantastic" Sunday brunch buffet; sure, it's "pricey",
but that's to be expected given that it's in the Four Seasons.

Quaglino's ⊠ *European* 21 | 22 | 19 | £58
St. James's | 16 Bury St., SW1Y 6AJ | 020-7930-6767 |
www.quaglinos.co.uk
Accessed down a "grand staircase", this venerable St. James's "gastro-
dome" boasts an all-around "impressive dining room", with "sumptuous decor", a "see-and-be-seen" scene and "quality", "upper-crust"
European fare; modernists say it "needs a few new tricks" (first for
the "patchy" service), but there's praise for its live entertainment on
Friday and Saturday and a "dangerously good cocktail bar".

NEW The Quality Chop House ⊠ *British* - | - | - | M
Farringdon | 92-94 Farringdon Rd., EC1R 3EA | 020-7278-1452 |
www.thequalitychophouse.com
After a brief detour as a dedicated meatball purveyor, this historic
Farringdon site with roots as a 19th-century working man's 'eating
house' revamped itself by upholstering the wooden bench seating
and introducing a short, moderately priced Modern British menu;
next to the dining room is a wine shop-cum-bar where you can partake in your purchases after paying a corkage charge.

Quilon *Indian* - | - | - | E
Victoria | Crowne Plaza St. James Hotel | 41 Buckingham Gate, SW1E 6AF |
020-7821-1899 | www.quilon.co.uk
Long appreciated for its upscale, refined Southwest coastal Indian
cooking that mixes the traditional with the experimental, this pricey
venue attached to a Victoria hotel is furnished in elegant hues, with
comfy banquettes and a cosy entrance bar.

Quirinale ⊠ *Italian* 25 | 17 | 22 | £49
Westminster | 1 Great Peter St., SW1P 3LL | 020-7222-7080 |
www.quirinale.co.uk
People who "work in Whitehall" plan "discreet" "chats with MPs" at
this spot where the Italian menu is "fantastic" and the basement
setting is either one of "understated luxury" or "depressing" depending on who you ask; there's always "buzz" during the day, and
while the evenings are "more relaxed", bargain-hunters come by for
the early-bird set dinner menu that's an "absolute steal" (similar to
the prix fixe lunch).

Quo Vadis ⊠ *British* 23 | 23 | 22 | £64
Soho | 26-29 Dean St., W1D 3LL | 020-7437-9585 |
www.quovadissoho.co.uk
Chef Jeremy Lee's "new take on old English" cuisine results in "well-
prepared and -presented" dishes that change daily at this "lively",

pricey Soho dining room; the "superb art deco surroundings" and "attentive" staff keep the place "just the right side of formal".

Racine French
24 | 19 | 21 | £52

Knightsbridge | 239 Brompton Rd., SW3 2EP | 020-7584-4477 | www.racine-restaurant.com

For a "taste of France in Knightsbridge", "upscale" diners head for this "casual, crowded" brasserie, serving "satisfying" "soul food for the Francophile" and a "comprehensive" wine list at "fair prices"; the kitchen is supported by "charming" staff, and the "cosy setting" also adds appeal, shoring up its standing as a "perennial fave".

Randall & Aubin British/Seafood
25 | 22 | 23 | £42

Soho | 14-16 Brewer St., W1F 0SQ | 020-7287-4447 | www.randallandaubin.com

"Don't be fooled" by the "campy", disco-balled setting and "blatant flirting from the staff" – this "buzzy, no-bookings" Soho "stalwart" serves an "excellent", "reasonably priced" Modern Brit menu highlighted by "some of the best seafood around"; "loud music" and a "hectic atmosphere" complete the "fun" picture.

Rasa Indian/Vegetarian
24 | 14 | 20 | £25

Farringdon | Holiday Inn King's Cross | 1 King's Cross Rd., WC1X 9HX | 020-7833-9787 🅢
Mayfair | 6 Dering St., W1S 1AD | 020-7629-1346
Stoke Newington | 55 Stoke Newington Church St., N16 0AR | 020-7249-0344
www.rasarestaurants.com

It might seem like "one of the best kept secrets" around, but this "wonderful" South Indian chainlet has "many fans" who are impressed by the "beautifully prepared" dishes listed on a mostly vegetarian menu; the "bare-bones" decor "won't attract romantics", but "knockdown prices" keep most happy.

Rasoi Vineet Bhatia Indian
28 | 23 | 26 | £87

Chelsea | 10 Lincoln St., SW3 2TS | 020-7225-1881 | www.rasoi-uk.com
Expect "an explosion of flavour" from an "incredible" Indian menu rife with "eloquent twists" and "imaginative" tasting dishes at chef-owner Vineet Bhatia's Chelsea townhouse; the "intimate" setting and "great" service further make it "well worth the visit for a special occasion", and despite the high prices, it's "highly recommended for everyone".

The Real Greek Greek
20 | 18 | 19 | £25

Covent Garden | 60-62 Long Acre, WC2E 9JE | 020-7240-2292
Marylebone | 56 Paddington St., W1U 4HY | 020-7486-0466
Spitalfields | Old Spitalfields Mkt. | 6 Horner Sq., E1 6EW | 020-7375-1364
South Bank | Riverside Hse. | 2 Southwark Bridge Rd., SE1 9HA | 020-7620-0162
Shepherd's Bush | Westfield Shopping Ctr. | Ariel Way & Southern Terr., W12 7GB | 020-8743-9168
www.therealgreek.com

"Tapas-style" Greek dishes made for "sharing" are the speciality of this "reliable" chain with "friendly" staff, and "you won't need a bailout to pay for it"; some find the food "not very inspiring" and deem the decor "nothing special", but communal tables and live music at some locations make it a natural for "good times with friends".

	FOOD	DECOR	SERVICE	COST

The Red Fort ● *Indian* | 23 | 21 | 21 | £50 |

Soho | 77 Dean St., W1D 3SH | 020-7437-2525 | www.redfort.co.uk
"Modern", "sophisticated" Indian cuisine comes via "knowledgeable" service at this "reliable", "lovely" spot in Dean Street; prices are "high", and while some say it's "well worth paying a bit extra", others just stick to the "good-value" prix fixe lunch and pre-theatre menus.

Red Pepper *Italian/Pizza* | 21 | 13 | 18 | £30 |

St. John's Wood | 8 Formosa St., W9 1EE | 020-7266-2708 |
www.theredpepper.net
Locals pack into this "popular" St. John's Wood Italian for "good-quality" wood-fired pizza and pasta, overlooking the fact that the setting is "small, cramped and noisy" ("waiters must be slim in order to weave between the tables"); service is "friendly", but its best aspect may be "value" pricing.

Regency Café ⊄ *British* | ∇ 23 | 19 | 20 | £11 |

Westminster | 17-19 Regency St., SW1P 4BY | 020-7821-6596
"One of the last strongholds of the old English working man's cafe", this "no-fuss, low-price" corner spot in Westminster serves "reliable" British "greasy spoon" classics with "all the tasty trimmings"; despite "long queues" at the counter, "the food comes quickly" enough – and is "worth the wait" anyhow.

Restaurant Gordon Ramsay ☒ *French* | 28 | 25 | 28 | £123 |

Chelsea | 68 Royal Hospital Rd., SW3 4HP | 020-7352-4441 |
www.gordonramsay.com
Gordon Ramsay's Chelsea flagship has devotees "gushing" about "one of the most charming, indulgent experiences you can have", praising chef Clare Smyth's "technically perfect" New French dishes; what's more, "attentive" staff ensure diners "feel welcome and comfortable" in a setting that's "beautiful in its simplicity"; P.S. the more "affordable lunch menu" is one way to beat the high-end prices.

Reubens *Deli/Jewish/Kosher* | 20 | 12 | 13 | £33 |

Marylebone | 79 Baker St., W1U 6RG | 020-7486-0035 |
www.reubensrestaurant.co.uk
"All the traditional favourites" can be found at this "reliable kosher eatery" whose "excellent location" in Marylebone comprises a "packed" upstairs deli "for takeaway and quick meals" and a "more formal" downstairs dining area; although "service can be off-hand", at least the place offers "good value for a West End restaurant".

Rhodes Twenty Four ☒ *British* | 25 | 24 | 25 | £74 |

City | Tower 42 | 25 Old Broad St., 24th fl., EC2N 1HQ | 020-7877-7703 |
www.rhodes24.co.uk
"Superlative" views ("can't be beat for a sunset") are afforded from the 24th-floor perch of this "very grown up" City dining room, which serves chef Gary Rhodes' "top-class" Traditional British menu and

"excellent" wines to "business groups at lunch and a mixed clientele in the evenings"; it's "expensive", but "worth it" assure respondents who also appreciate the "impeccable" "professional" service.

The Rib Room Steak   24 | 21 | 24 | £74

Knightsbridge | Jumeirah Carlton Tower Hotel | Cadogan Pl., SW1X 9PY | 020-7858-7250 | www.theribroom.co.uk

"After all these years", this Knightsbridge hotel "classic" remains an "excellent" choice for a meat-centric meal thanks to "high-quality" steakhouse food enhanced by "exceptional" service and an "old-school gentleman's club" ambience; happily, lunch and dinner prix fixes can ease the pain of prices that seem aimed at those who "don't look at the bill".

The Riding House Café European   21 | 24 | 21 | £37

Fitzrovia | 43-51 Great Titchfield St., W1W 7PQ | 020-7927-0840 | www.ridinghousecafe.co.uk

"Whatever you're in the mood for" - be it "large, hangover-worthy English breakfasts", "sharing plates" fit for a "classy date" or just "tea and cake" - the midpriced Modern Euro "comfort-food classics" at this "popular", "laid-back" Fitzrovia brasserie/bar are "great all day"; indeed, the "attention to detail is evident" in everything, from the "quirky" decor ("blue velvet chairs, dark wood and squirrel lamps") to the "swift service" from "friendly" staff.

The Ritz British/French   24 | 28 | 26 | £77

Piccadilly | The Ritz | 150 Piccadilly, W1J 9BR | 020-7300-2370 | www.theritzlondon.com

"Comfort and calm rule" at this "luxurious" Louis XVI–style dining room at the famed hotel in Piccadilly, where "superlative service" and "splurge"-worthy, "beautifully prepared" Traditional British–French dishes heighten the "over-the-top opulence"; there's "old-fashioned dancing" with a live band on Fridays (in summer) and Saturdays (yearround), while the adjacent Palm Court offers "a step back in time" with afternoon tea; P.S. gentlemen, "don't forget to wear a tie" and jacket.

The River Café Italian   27 | 23 | 24 | £71

Hammersmith | Thames Wharf Studio | Rainville Rd., W6 9HA | 020-7386-4200 | www.rivercafe.co.uk

"Children are as welcome as high fliers" at this "convivial" Hammersmith institution with "a lot of culinary history" behind its "accomplished", daily-changing Italian menu of "creatively delicious", "expensive-but-worth-it" dishes; the "modern aesthetics" of its former warehouse setting, which includes a riverside terrace, are complemented by a "relaxed, casual atmosphere" and "friendly" service.

Rivington Grill British   23 | 21 | 21 | £37

Shoreditch | 28-30 Rivington St., EC2A 3DZ | 020-7729-7053
Greenwich | 178 Greenwich High Rd., SE10 8NN | 020-8293-9270
www.rivingtongrill.co.uk

"Simple" white-walled environs and "chirpy staff" set a "relaxing" tone at the "trendy" Shoreditch branch of this Traditional British brasserie where the all-day menu may be "a bit pricey" "for what you get", but at least is "high-quality", with burgers that alone make it "worth visiting"; located by the Greenwich Picturehouse, the younger sibling (with more limited hours) is "one of the more elegant local options".

Roast British   25 | 24 | 21 | £52

Borough | Borough Mkt. | Floral Hall, Stoney St., SE1 1TL | 0845-034-7300 | www.roast-restaurant.com

"A little tour" of Borough Market "prepares your stomach" for the "consistently high-quality" British fare served at this "beautiful" glass-walled, all-day venue perched "above the hustle and bustle" of the traders; the "impressive wine list" includes many English varieties, and while some say the overall experience is "too expensive" for everyday dining, many find it "worth the occasional splurge".

Rocca Italian   24 | 24 | 26 | £26

Dulwich | 75-79 Dulwich Vill., SE21 7BJ | 020-8299-6333
South Kensington | 73 Old Brompton Rd., SW7 3JS | 020-7225-3413 ◗
www.roccarestaurants.com

This "friendly", "relaxed" Italian duo in South Kensington and Dulwich Village boast a "pleasant buzz" and "attractive surroundings"; the Italian menu of "delicious pizzas" and daily specials benefit from "fair pricing", which extends to "good-value" wines.

Rock & Sole Plaice Seafood   24 | 9 | 16 | £17

Covent Garden | 47 Endell St., WC2H 9AJ | 020-7836-3785
A "lovely variety" of "firm, well-cooked" fish fried in "crispy" batter is available with "large" portions of "chunky" chips at this "classic" Covent Garden seafood spot; "don't go for the decor", instead join the tourists and locals in the takeaway queue (even though it can be "daunting"), then "snag an outside table" – it's a "great way to pass" some time, and "a bargain" given the area.

Rodizio Rico ◗ Brazilian   20 | 14 | 18 | £32

Islington | 77-78 Upper St., N1 0NU | 020-7354-1076
Greenwich | O2 Arena | Greenwich Peninsula, SE10 0DX | 020-8858-6333
Bayswater | 111 Westbourne Grove, W2 4UW | 020-7792-4035
Fulham | 11 Jerdan Pl., SW6 1BE | 020-7183-6085
www.rodiziorico.com

"When you're in the mood to pig out", this "taste-bud-tingling" Brazilian churrascaria chainlet delivers "never-ending rounds" of "every kind of meat imaginable", all served as part of a set-price feast (prices differ from weekday to weekend); "service is a little slow at times" and the "basic" dining rooms are "not for the faint hearted" (read: "loud"), but "groups" usually find it "great fun", and "wonderful value" too.

Roka Japanese   26 | 23 | 22 | £65

Fitzrovia | 37 Charlotte St., W1T 1RR | 020-7580-6464 ◗
Canary Wharf | Park Pavilion | 40 Canada Sq., E14 5FW | 020-7636-5228
www.rokarestaurant.com

"Delicious, elaborate and beautifully presented" dishes and sushi plates are complemented by "innovative cocktails" at this "fantas-

	FOOD	DECOR	SERVICE	COST

tic", "pricey", robatayaki-style Japanese duo in Fitzrovia and Canary Wharf; the natural-wood decor, "great" atmosphere and "young, knowledgeable" staff all further contribute to its overall "hip" factor.

Rosa's *Thai* 　　　　　　　　　　| 22 | 15 | 17 | £22 |

Soho | 48 Dean St., W1D 5BF | 020-7494-1638
Spitalfields | 12 Hanbury St., E1 6QR | 020-7247-1093
Stratford | Westfield Stratford City | 2 Stratford Pl., E20 1EJ | 020-8519-1302
www.rosaslondon.com

"Well-prepared, standard" Thai "street food" comes for "reasonable prices" at this chainlet; though the service is "hit-and-miss", it's usually "fast", making it "a great spot for a quick eat" – that is, "if you can get a seat" in the "cramped", "basic" digs.

NEW Rosita & The Sherry Bar *Spanish* 　| – | – | – | M |

Battersea | 124 Northcote Rd., SW11 6QU | 020-7998-9093 | www.rositasherry.net

At this Battersea Spaniard, midpriced tapas and some larger dishes are accompanied by about two dozen sherries plus plenty of wine and cava; the unpretentious environs are heavy on polished wood, with a handsome marble counter at the bar.

Rossopomodoro *Pizza* 　　　　　　| 23 | 17 | 17 | £25 |

Covent Garden | 50-52 Monmouth St., WC2H 9EP | 020-7240-9095
Hoxton | 1 Rufus St., N1 6PE | 020-7739-1899
Camden Town | 10 Jamestown Rd., NW1 7BY | 020-7424-9900
Chelsea | 214 Fulham Rd., SW10 9NB | 020 7352-7677
Notting Hill | 184A Kensington Park Rd., W11 2ES | 020-7229-9007
www.rossopomodoro.co.uk

"Hard-core delicious" pizzas with "perfectly charred" crusts and a "well-priced" wine list make this "casual" Neapolitan chain a "decent", "good-value" option; it can get "crowded" and "a little bit too loud" for some, but at least service is generally "quick, fast and friendly".

Roti Chai *Indian* 　　　　　　　| 24 | 21 | 20 | £29 |

Marylebone | 3 Portman Mews S., W1H 6HS | 020-7408-0101 | www.rotichai.com

At this bi-level Marylebone Indian, the ground floor cafe serves an "amazing array" of "well-spiced", tapaslike street food, and the downstairs dining room offers regional dishes; the "quirky", "modern" decor, "reasonable" prices and "knowledgeable" staff all help keep it "bustling" with "a mixed crowd"; P.S. a retail counter offers iconic imports like Parle-G biscuits and Rooh Afza syrup to go.

Rotunda *British* 　　　　　　| ∇ 19 | 18 | 16 | £72 |

King's Cross | Kings Pl. | 90 York Way, N1 9AG | 020-7014-2840 | www.rotundabarandrestaurant.co.uk

With "stunning views of the Battlebridge Basin" and "alfresco seating in season", this "laid-back" venue within the Kings Place arts centre offers "simple" and "delicious" British food (made using produce from "its own farm" in Northumberland), and an "interesting wine list"; though perhaps "a bit out of the way for a stand-alone journey", it's "perfect before a concert", as long as you can afford the extra expense.

Roux at Parliament Square 🅱 *European* ∇ 24 | 24 | 24 | £58

Westminster | Royal Institution of Chartered Surveyors | 11 Great George St., SW1P 3AD | 020-7334-3737 | www.rouxatparliamentsquare.co.uk

"MP spot" while dining on "fabulous" Modern European fare at this "lovely" Parliament Square option, a Michel Roux Jr. venue in a grand listed building that "deserves to be better known"; the "efficient service" and "elegant upstairs bar" also earn admirers, and while prices are high, the set lunch is "great value".

Roux at The Landau *European* 26 | 25 | 27 | £81

Marylebone | The Langham Hotel | 1 Portland Pl., W1 1JA | 020-7965-0165 | www.thelandau.com

A "fancy" Modern European menu boasting "high-quality execution" is matched by "excellent unobtrusive service" and a "warm", "formal" setting filled with "interesting art" and "beautiful lighting" at this Langham Hotel collaboration between Albert and Michel Roux Jr.; "well-spaced tables" make it "good for business" as well as more "intimate dining", and while it's "very expensive", "you get what you pay for"; P.S. the set lunch is more "affordable".

Rowley's *British* 23 | 20 | 21 | £51

St. James's | 113 Jermyn St., SW1Y 6HJ | 020-7930-2707 | www.rowleys.co.uk

A mix of "well-heeled" locals, "business associates" and "tourists" fill this "clubby" St. James's dining room exhibiting "old London flair" to match its "consistent", "hearty" Traditional British menu that majors on "melt-in-the-mouth" steaks with "unlimited chips", accompanied by "pleasant service"; some feel it's "reasonably priced" while others deem it "expensive", but most concede it's "worth every penny", especially for a special occasion like "a birthday treat".

Royal China *Chinese* 23 | 17 | 16 | £35

Marylebone | 24-26 Baker St., W1U 7AB | 020-7487-4688
Canary Wharf | 30 Westferry Circus, E14 8RR | 020-7719-0888
Bayswater | 13 Queensway, W2 4QJ | 020-7221-2535
Fulham | 805 Fulham Rd., SW6 5HE | 020-7731-0081
www.royalchinagroup.co.uk

Dim sum is the "bee's knees" – and the "meal of choice" – at this "Hong Kong–style" chainlet whose "reasonably priced" Chinese food is "always up to a good standard"; while the decor is just "ok", and service ranges from "friendly" to "nonexistent", queues can be seen "half way down the road" at some branches, especially at the weekend lunchtime (they only take bookings for dinner).

Royal China Club *Chinese* 25 | 17 | 17 | £51

Marylebone | 40-42 Baker St., W1U 7AJ | 020-7486-3898 | www.royalchinagroup.co.uk

Specialising in "high-quality dim sum" and "fish and lobster fresh from tanks", this Baker Street Cantonese, the compatriot of nearby

Royal China, is playing "in the premier league of fine Chinese dining" – and charging "relatively high" prices to match; that it accepts reservations is an "added bonus", as are mostly "helpful" staff and the "comprehensive wine list".

NEW The Royal Quarter Café *European* | - | - | - | M

Victoria | Wellington House, 72-73 Buckingham Gate, SW1E 6BE | 020-7799-4999 | www.royalquartercafe.com

Not far from Buckingham Palace, this bright, elongated corner cafe with banquette seating and chunky oak tables serves midpriced Modern European comfort food including light salads and a decadent afternoon tea; takeaway is also available from the counter.

R.S.J. ☒ *British* | 22 | 15 | 21 | £40

Waterloo | 33 Coin St., SE1 9NR | 020-7928-4554 | www.rsj.uk.com

"Dine before or after the National Theatre" at this "relaxed" "oasis in a foodie desert" near Waterloo, where patrons praise the "interesting" Modern British menu, "good-value" prix fixe and "unique" Loire Valley wine list; a few find it's "nothing special", but "friendly" staff "lift it a grade", lending a "warm welcome" and "getting you out in time for the curtain".

Rules *British* | 24 | 26 | 24 | £62

Covent Garden | 35 Maiden Ln., WC2E 7LB | 020-7836-5314 | www.rules.co.uk

You "can't get more traditional" than this "right, rigorous and reliable" Covent Garden "institution" that's been serving "hearty" British "classics" – like "roast beef on the trolley" and game raised on its Scottish farm – in "striking surroundings" since 1798; it's "pricey" and "a bit touristy", but for many it provides a "warm and welcoming step back into the past".

Saf *International/Vegan* | ▽ 23 | 19 | 19 | £28

Kensington | Whole Foods Mkt. | 63-97 Kensington High St., W8 5SE | 020-7368-4555 | www.safrestaurant.co.uk

"Innovative without sacrificing taste" is the word on the International vegan fare whipped up at this "simple, airy" Kensington option whose eco-friendliness extends to "awesome botanical drinks", "cool organic cocktails" and biodynamic wines; "healthy" eaters appreciate that you leave "far from stuffed", but others baulk that the "small portions" command such relatively "hefty prices".

Sagar *Indian/Vegetarian* | 21 | 14 | 21 | £21

Fitzrovia | 17A Percy St., W1T 1DU | 020-7631-3319
Covent Garden | 31 Catherine St., WC2B 5JS | 020-7836-6377
Hammersmith | 157 King St., W6 9JT | 020-8741-8563
www.sagarveg.co.uk

This "excellent" South Indian vegetarian chainlet's "flavoursome, healthy" eats represent "outstanding value" (most notably the "ridiculously cheap lunchtime deals"); if the settings are "not the most inviting" ("cramped", "uncomfortable"), "pleasant staff" make up for it.

	FOOD	DECOR	SERVICE	COST

Sake No Hana ⧈ *Japanese* — 25 | 24 | 21 | £62

St. James's | The Economist | 23 St. James's St., SW1A 1HA |
020-7925-8988 | www.sakenohana.com
The "beautiful" bamboo-clad setting of this "impressive" St.
James's eatery (reached via an escalator from street level) sets
the tone for "excellent" sushi and other Japanese cuisine; though
some say the prices are "astronomical", "fantastic people-watching"
is a bonus.

Sakura *Japanese* — 22 | 17 | 18 | £35

Mayfair | 23 Conduit St., W1S 2XS | 020-7629-2961
"Scrumptious" sushi and shabu-shabu are offered at this "busy"
Mayfair Japanese fronted by "friendly" and "knowledgeable" staff,
although its best feature may be that it's "excellent value" (for the
neighbourhood, that is).

Sale e Pepe ❶ *Italian* — 24 | 19 | 23 | £49

Knightsbridge | 9-15 Pavilion Rd., SW1X 0HD | 020-7235-0098 |
www.saleepepe.co.uk
This "gem tucked behind Harrods" serves "well-prepared", "tasty"
Italian food – including "feather-light pasta" with "to-die-for fillings" –
in a "fun" but "loud" atmosphere; a "friendly welcome" from the "excellent" staff enhances the "joyous experience".

Salloos ⧈ *Pakistani* — 24 | 16 | 20 | £56

Belgravia | 62-64 Kinnerton St., SW1X 8ER | 020-7235-4444 |
www.salloosrestaurant.co.uk
"Fine spices" "tantalise" in "high-quality Pakistani" dishes, especially "magnificent" tandoori lamb chops, which are "professionally
served" at this stalwart Belgravia "hidden gem"; it's "on the expensive side", but "worth it" for the "fantastic" flavours – if not the
"somewhat tired decor".

NEW Salon ⧈Ⓜ *British* — - | - | - | M

Brixton | Brixton Mkt. | 18 Market Row, SW9 8LD | 020-7501-9152 |
www.salonbrixton.co.uk
Sitting above a deli in Brixton's increasingly gourmet market, this
moderately priced, intimate dining room focuses on inventive, seasonal British dishes using ingredients that come, in part, from the
shop downstairs; a two-to-three course set menu is offered at lunch,
a four-course at dinner, while organic and biodynamic wines are
available at all times; P.S. open Thursday–Saturday only.

Salt Yard ⧈ *Italian/Spanish* — 24 | 18 | 20 | £42

Fitzrovia | 54 Goodge St., W1T 4NA | 020-7637-0657 | www.saltyard.co.uk
Belying it's "humble" Fitzrovia location, this "noisy, bohemian"
venue offers "top-class" Italian-Spanish tapas, often with "brilliant,
avant-garde twists" (the signature courgette flowers with goat
cheese and honey are "a dream"); though it's often "full of media
types", it's also a "perfect date spot" thanks to mostly "congenial
service" and a "broad, well-priced wine list" (the food menu can be
"a little pricey in places").

	FOOD	DECOR	SERVICE	COST

Sam's Brasserie & Bar *European* | 24 | 23 | 22 | £37 |

Chiswick | Barley Mow Ctr. | 11 Barley Mow Passage, W4 4PH |
020-8987-0555 | www.samsbrasserie.co.uk

Chiswick locals say it's "a joy" to come to this "informal neighbour-hood brasserie" delivering Modern European dishes that are "well executed and served with style" in a "spacious", "comfortable" restaurant and "laid-back bar"; "lovely staff" further make it a "worthy place" that's especially "good for families" since it's affordable.

Sands End ● *British* | ▽ 22 | 23 | 24 | £36 |

Fulham | 135-137 Stephendale Rd., SW6 2PR | 020-7731-7823 |
www.thesandsend.co.uk

"Off the beaten track" in Fulham, this "boozer" "shines" with an "in-viting", "upscale" atmosphere, "fantastic" British gastropub fare, "well-chosen wine list" and "accommodating" staff; if you're looking for a quiet dinner, best to come early, because word is the bar be-comes "loud as the evening wears on".

San Lorenzo ⊠ *Italian* | 21 | 20 | 20 | £70 |

Knightsbridge | 22 Beauchamp Pl., SW3 1NH | 020-7584-1074 |
www.sanlorenzolondon.co.uk

Though "not as hot as it used to be" in the '90s, there's still "people-watching for sure" at this "vibrant" Knightsbridge venue where an "elite crowd" pays "eyebrow raising prices" for "pleasantly cooked Italian food"; though the decor feels "dated" to some, "competent service" keeps it a "civilised" option.

Santa Maria del Sur ● *Argentinean/Steak* | 26 | 18 | 21 | £46 |

Battersea | 129 Queenstown Rd., SW8 3RH | 020-7622-2088 |
www.santamariadelsur.co.uk

"Expertly cooked, high-quality steaks" flown in from Argentina and served with "interesting sides and a strong wine list" – that's the rec-ipe at this "local-feel" Battersea steakhouse; the bill may be "expen-sive", but the "great atmosphere" and decent service add to its appeal, making it "heartily recommended" for meat lovers.

Santini *Italian* | 20 | 18 | 19 | £63 |

Belgravia | 29 Ebury St., SW1W 0NZ | 020-7730-4094 |
www.santini-restaurant.com

"If you're feeling flush and like being surrounded by Belgravia aris-tocracy, it's worth trying" this "expensive", "elegant" eatery where "tasty" Italian cuisine, including "some imaginative items", is deliv-ered by "proficient" staff; "nicely spaced tables" keep the interior "comfortable and quiet", and there's also a patio, set on an olive-tree-bedecked corner.

Sardo ⊠ *Italian* | 21 | 18 | 20 | £42 |

Fitzrovia | 45 Grafton Way, W1T 5DQ | 020-7387-2521 |
www.sardo-restaurant.com

"Owner-managed with pride", this "no-fuss" Fitzrovia Italian "near Warren Street tube" is a "real find" for "genuine Sardinian cuisine", including "outstanding" bread; "amicable service", "great wines" and relatively "reasonable" prices make it sometimes "difficult to get a table", so it's "best to book".

Sartoria ⒵ *Italian*   23 | 22 | 23 | £55

Mayfair | 20 Savile Row, W1S 3PR | 020-7534-7000 | www.sartoriabar.co.uk

"Perfect for Savile Row and the local art-loving crowd", this "comfortable" and "professional" "Mayfair gem" offers "elegant Italian" cuisine accompanied by wine served by a "helpful sommelier"; although some find it "pricey", the "sophisticated atmosphere" and "stylish" sartorial displays are a reminder of the "high quality" it presents.

Satay House *Malaysian*   26 | 19 | 20 | £24

Paddington | 13 Sale Pl., W2 1PX | 020-7723-6763 | www.satay-house.co.uk

It's "a little off the beaten track" in a Paddington backstreet, but this "low-key" and long-standing Malaysian (est. 1973), prepares "superb", "value-for-money" (at least "for London") dishes; "simple but nice decor" and "pleasant, attentive" staff complete the picture.

Satsuma *Japanese*   20 | 18 | 18 | £25

Soho | 56 Wardour St., W1D 4JG | 020-7437-8338 | www.osatsuma.com

This "canteen-style" Soho Japanese serves a "fab" menu of moderately priced, "well-presented" sashimi and katsu curries to diners sat on "big benches" at "long tables", or at "quirky", cocoon-like orange pods.

Savoy Grill *British/French*   24 | 25 | 24 | £71

Covent Garden | Savoy Hotel | 101 The Strand, WC2 0EU | 020-7592-1600 | www.gordonramsay.com

A "delightful throwback" to an era of "old-school splendour", this grill in the Savoy Hotel impresses with a "heavenly" art deco setting and "fantastic" French-British cuisine; while it may "fall a little short" when it comes to "value for money", the "superb" service lives up to many supporters' suggestion that it's "one of the world's great experiences in luxury hotel dining".

Scalini *Italian*   24 | 18 | 23 | £67

Chelsea | 1-3 Walton St., SW3 2JD | 020-7225-2301

"Don't expect a quiet, romantic dinner" or privacy (the "tables are very close to one another") at this "homey" Chelsea trattoria, but do count on a "bustling", "jolly atmosphere", a "to-die-for" Italian menu and a possible "neck ache from looking at all the celebs"; true, it's "not cheap", but "amazing, friendly service" is part of the package.

Scott's *Seafood*   26 | 24 | 25 | £80

Mayfair | 20 Mount St., W1K 2HE | 020-7495-7309 | www.scotts-restaurant.com

Expect to be "surrounded by oligarchs and tycoons" at this "sophisticated" Mayfair "institution" where the "classic" fish menu and "quality" raw bar appeals to the "serious seafood eater"; decent service and a "fun, lively" feel add to its appeal, and if some grumble about "expensive" prices, most agree it's "worth the pounds – both financial and calorific!"

Season at the Fifth Floor
Restaurant *European*

21 | 19 | 20 | £49

Knightsbridge | Harvey Nichols | 109-125 Knightsbridge, 5th fl., SW1X 7RJ | 020-7235-5250 | www.harveynichols.com
There's an "adventurous", even "mysterious air" to this light-filled dining room atop Harvey Nichols, where an "interesting, attractively presented", expensive Modern European menu means you can "shop, then drop in for refreshment"; at the very least, it makes for "a fall-back place", as it's often "not crowded", although the adjacent bar usually heaves.

Sedap *Malaysian*

∇ 26 | 12 | 22 | £23

Shoreditch | 102 Old St., EC1V 9AY | 020-7490-0200 | www.sedap.co.uk
The name means 'delicious' in Malay, and this "small, family-run" "standby" on Old Street lives up to its billing with "amazing" fare (which includes some Chinese influences); "don't expect fine dining or beautiful surroundings", but do count on a "cheap" bill.

Seven Park Place ⊠Ⓜ *British/French*

∇ 24 | 23 | 27 | £88

St. James's | St. James's Hotel & Club | 7-8 Park Pl., SW1A 1LS | 020-7316-1600 | www.stjameshotelandclub.com
"Polished", "friendly" staff deliver Chef William Drabble's "complex", "fantastic" British-New French fare (served as two- or three-course set menus) to "spacious" booths at this "elegant, stylish" St. James's hotel venue; foodies call it a "fine-dining experience" that's "probably still a little below the radar", so take their advice: "enjoy it before it becomes trendy".

NEW Shake Shack *Burgers*

- | - | - | ⏐

Covent Garden | 24 Market Bldg., WC2E 8RD | 020-3598-1360 | www.shakeshack.com
U.S.-style burgers, hot dogs and shakes are given a British twist at this inexpensive Covent Garden outpost of restaurateur Danny Meyer's iconic chain through creations such as the Cumberland sausage dog and the blending of St. John bakery biscuits into its signature 'concretes' (dense frozen custards); many do takeaway, but simple wooden seats are available inside and out; P.S. bring your pooch – the menu also has 'treats for those with four feet'.

Shanghai Blues ● *Chinese*

24 | 24 | 18 | £45

Holborn | 193-197 High Holborn, WC1V 7BD | 020-7404-1668 | www.shanghaiblues.co.uk
Devotees praise "innovative, classy dim sum", "spot-on" specials and other "high-quality dishes" at this "stylish", "dark" Holborn Chinese; those who "mainly go for the atmosphere" overlook the "sometimes surly service" and prices "on the high side" since it's "just the place for intimate gatherings" and "big parties" alike; P.S. weekend nights bring live jazz.

NEW The Shed 🗷Ⓜ *British* — | — | — | M

Notting Hill | 122 Palace Gardens Terr., W8 4RT | 020-7229-4024 | www.theshed-restaurant.com

Brothers Oliver and Richard Gladwin serve small plates of seasonal British food (some of it foraged) from a modestly priced menu that's broken into whimsical sections labelled 'mouthfuls', 'slow' and 'fast'; despite the Notting Hill location, the duo have re-created rural West Sussex in the rustic environs, complete with a ramshackle collection of furniture and lumberjack-shirted staff.

NEW The Shiori 🗷Ⓜ *Japanese* — | — | — | E

Bayswater | 45 Moscow Rd., W2 4AH | 020-7221-9790 | www.theshiori.com

Making a jump across town from its basic seven-seater Euston digs to a 16-seater lair in Bayswater gives Londoners more access to Japanese chef-patron Takashi Takagi's upscale, precise and cultured kaiseki dining experience; there are three set lunches and a choice of nine or 12-course dinners, plus a sake list designed to titillate the connoisseur.

Shrimpy's *Californian/Mexican* — | — | — | M

King's Cross | King's Cross Filling Station | Good's Way, N1C 4UR | 020-8880-6111 | www.shrimpys.co.uk

The people behind popular Bethnal Green hangout Bistrotheque took over an old petrol station in King's Cross to house this moderately priced diner whipping up Californian and Mexican inspired food; the simple space sports white walls adorned with drawings by artist Donal Urquhart, a small terrace for when the sun shines and counter seating for walk ins; P.S. bring a card, they don't take cash.

Signor Sassi ● *Italian* 23 | 19 | 21 | £53

Knightsbridge | 14 Knightsbridge Green, SW1X 7QL | 020-7584-2277 | www.signorsassi.co.uk

"Warm welcomes" from "jovial staff" "brandishing oversized peppermills" set the stage for "ample portions" of "solid, traditional Italian" dishes ("lots of fish") at this long-standing "hideaway near Harrods and Hyde Park" in Knightsbridge; although it's "expensive", advocates assure that it's "worth the price", especially considering the "fun" vibe and all of those "famous patrons".

Simpson's-in-the-Strand *British* 21 | 23 | 23 | £60

Covent Garden | Savoy Hotel | 102 The Strand, WC2R 0EW | 020-7836-9112 | www.simpsonsinthestrand.co.uk

"Immerse yourself in the ambience of a time gone by" at this "elegant" oak-panelled dining room in the Savoy Hotel, where an "old-school", "quintessentially British" menu – led by "roast beef on the trolley" – proves the art of "carving is not dead"; although it's pricey and geared "somewhat for the tourist trade", the consensus is it's "wonderful for what it is", with the bonus of "fantastic" service.

Singapore Garden *Malaysian/Singaporean* 22 | 17 | 20 | £35

Chiswick | 474 Chiswick High Rd., W4 5TT | 020-8994-2222

(continued)

Singapore Garden

Swiss Cottage | 83 Fairfax Rd., NW6 4DY | 020-7328-5314
www.singaporegarden.co.uk

"Popular" on account of its "homely" Singaporean-Malay cooking,
this "smart" Swiss Cottage venue is "great for after work" – and even
if "small portions" make it seem "pricey", it "remains a good resource" with "friendly service"; meanwhile, the Chiswick sibling is
a "small, busy" takeaway/delivery service "of a higher standard
than the norm".

Sketch – The Gallery *European*   21 | 27 | 22 | £69

Mayfair | Sketch | 9 Conduit St., W1S 2XG | 020-7659-4500 |
www.sketch.uk.com

"Make sure you dress the part" to "see and be seen" amid "weird
and wonderful" "contemporary decor" – think "exotically lit stair-
cases", "cocoon egg toilets" – at this "over-the-top" Modern European
dinner spot inside a "fab" Mayfair townhouse; the food is just as
"original" as the setting, and "delicious" to boot, while the service is
mostly "friendly" – but "you certainly pay for the privilege".

Sketch – The Lecture Room &   22 | 28 | 23 | £92
Library ⓈⓂ *European*

Mayfair | Sketch | 9 Conduit St., W1S 2XG | 020-7659-4500 |
www.sketch.uk.com

A "wild place to hang out", this Mayfair destination delivers "an as-
sault on the senses" via an "enchanting", maroon-and gold-hued environment that's earned the No. 1 Decor score in London; the "inventive"
Modern European menu is complemented by "some lovely wines",
while "friendly" service with a "sense of humour" and "expensive"
pricing further ensure that "every visit becomes an occasion".

Sketch – The Parlour ❶ *British*   21 | 28 | 19 | £47

Mayfair | Sketch | 9 Conduit St., W1S 2XG | 020-7659-4500 |
www.sketch.uk.com

"Warm, dreamy" and "magical", this morning and afternoon
tearoom in a "stunning" Mayfair townhouse employs "friendly"
staff to ferry its "fantastic pastries" and "creative" British light savouries; there's a plea to "reduce prices", but that aside, it's an
"amusing" option for a "quaint" repast; P.S. after 9 PM, it's a cocktail-
fuelled private club.

Skylon *European*   20 | 24 | 21 | £47

South Bank | Royal Festival Hall | Belvedere Rd., SE1 8XX | 020-7654-7800 |
www.skylonrestaurant.co.uk

"Dramatic views" of the Thames "through floor-to-ceiling glass"
add to the "delightful experience" at this "huge", "atmospheric"
Modern European in the Royal Festival Hall that combines a casual, "reasonable" grill with a "pricey" "fine-dining" destination
boasting "slick" service and "a wine list that must be envied";
some say the "trendy bar" is "the best part", especially "if cocktails
are your thing".

	FOOD	DECOR	SERVICE	COST

Smiths of Smithfield – Dining Room 🅩 *British*

21 | 20 | 19 | £51

Farringdon | 67-77 Charterhouse St., 2nd fl., EC1M 6HJ | 020-7251-7950

Smiths of Smithfield – Top Floor *British*

Farringdon | 67-77 Charterhouse St., 3rd fl., EC1M 6HJ | 020-7251-7950
www.smithsofsmithfield.co.uk

Right on Smithfield market is John Torode's meaty Modern Brit empire, a "giant warehouse" that includes a "casual" midpriced bar and grill serving "juicy", "crave-worthy" burgers and a "smart", more expensive top floor, steak-focused fine-dining eyrie with a terrace overlooking St Paul's; while some complain that none of it is "cheap", the "lovely atmosphere" throughout compensates.

Smollensky's *American/Steak*

18 | 19 | 18 | £40

Covent Garden | 105 The Strand, WC2R 0AA | 020-7497-2101
Canary Wharf | 1 Reuters Plaza, E14 5AJ | 020-7719-0101 🅩
www.smollenskys.com

"Ribs, ribs and more ribs" are some of the highlights of this "dependable", moderately priced American-style steakhouse duo with modern decor; Canary Wharf is geared to "business meetings", while Covent Garden is a "noisy" "party place" that's "ideal for a pre-theatre meal", not least because "pleasant" staff ensure you "finish in time to see the start of the show".

NEW The Social Eating House 🅩 *British/International*

- | - | - | M

Soho | 58 Poland St., W1F 7NR | 020-7993-3251 |
www.socialeatinghouse.com

Jason Atherton (of Pollen Street Social) takes on Soho with this moderately priced, informal contemporary bistro that blends the best of British cuisine with a few International influences; the look is exposed-brick walls, weathered leather banquettes and restored furniture, both in the ground-floor dining room and the first-floor bar, called The Blind Pig.

Sofra *Turkish*

21 | 16 | 18 | £30

Covent Garden | 36 Tavistock St., WC2E 7PB | 020-7240-3773
Marylebone | 1 St. Christophers Pl., W1U 1LT | 020-7224-4080
Mayfair | 18 Shepherd St., W1J 7JG | 020-7493-3320
www.sofra.co.uk

"Tasty", "dependable" Turkish fare that's "great value" draws "pre-theatre"-goers and "after-shopping" crowds to this moderately priced chainlet; "the decor is not the attraction here" (in some areas "you get squeezed like sardines"), so many prefer to come on a "balmy summer evening" when, depending on locale, you can sit alfresco or under a "retracted roof".

Soho House 🌓🅩 *British*

20 | 23 | 23 | £52

Soho | private club | 40 Greek St., W1D 5JJ | 020-7734-5188 |
www.sohohouselondon.com

Those who can get in regularly rub shoulders with "well-known entertainment" figures at this "energetic" private members' club in a

	FOOD	DECOR	SERVICE	COST

"cosy" Soho townhouse; "friendly" staff whom you "cannot fault" convey Modern British meals that are "reliably good" if "not exciting" – but that may not matter, as this is more a "place to be seen" than to dine.

Solly's Kosher/Mideastern
20 | 14 | 16 | £30

Golders Green | 146-150 Golders Green Rd., NW11 8HE | 020-8455-2121
Many diners have "lots of happy memories" of this "busy", basic Golders Green kosher eatery offering "reliable" Middle Eastern dishes alongside "friendly" service; however, others say the "customer attention could be improved", so they just stick to the "small takeaway section".

Song Que Café Vietnamese
25 | 9 | 13 | £19

Hoxton | 134 Kingsland Rd., E2 8DY | 020-7613-3222
"Arrive early to avoid the crowds" for what acolytes assure is the "best Vietnamese food outside of Vietnam" at this Hoxton "mainstay" whose pho and other "tasty, comforting" fare comes at "cheap" prices; what's more, fans "don't mind" that the "street-kitchen" setting is "no-frills" (to say the least) and staff "don't mess about being polite" as they provide "quick" service.

Sophie's ● American/Steak
22 | 21 | 21 | £40

Covent Garden | 29-31 Wellington St., WC2E 7DB | 020-7836-8836
Chelsea | 311-313 Fulham Rd., SW10 9QH | 020-7352-0088
www.sophiessteakhouse.co.uk
Everyone "knows it's going to be a long wait" at these "no-booking" American steakhouses in Chelsea and Covent Garden, yet diners continue to turn up for the "cool vibe" and "hearty food at a fair price", including "quality steaks" and "great ribs (nothing spare about them)"; thankfully, there are "chatty", "attentive" staff and "potent cocktails" to help pass the time; P.S. they're "child-friendly" too.

Souk Bazaar ● African
21 | 25 | 21 | £29

Covent Garden | 27 Litchfield St., WC2H 9NJ | 020-7240-1796
Souk Medina ● African
Covent Garden | 1a Short's Gdns., WC2H 9AT | 020-7240-1796
www.soukrestaurant.net
Boasting "quirky" Moroccan furnishings and the "feel of a real souk", it's "like stepping into a genie's lamp" at this "dark" Covent Garden duo; many find the staff "lovely" and the North African eats "delicious" – plus the "big" portions make them "good value" – but the real draw may be the "entertaining" "belly dancer later in the evening".

Spice Market SE Asian
22 | 24 | 20 | £53

Leicester Square | W London Leicester Square Hotel | 10 Wardour St., W1 6QF | 020-7758-1080 | www.spicemarketlondon.co.uk
There's "plenty of 'wow'" in the "sexy decor", "eye-candy" crowd and "great-looking" staff at chef Jean-Georges Vongerichten's off-shoot of his New York hotspot, spread over two floors of Leicester Square's W Hotel, a "hip, trendy backdrop" for feasting on "upscale" Southeast Asian treats; although a few think it's more "for the see-

and-be-seen crowd than food enthusiasts", the majority proclaim "this place has legs".

Spice Village *Indian*

27 | 20 | 23 | £20

Tooting | 32 Upper Tooting Rd., SW17 7PD | 020-8672-0710 ◑
Southall | 185-189 The Broadway, UB1 1LX |
020-8574-4475 ⊠
www.spicevillageltd.com

With large Asian communities in both Southall and Tooting, many reckon they're "the places to eat the best curries", and this pair of minimalist, modern Indian eateries producing "excellent" halal tandoori dishes come "highly recommended"; to top things off, staff are "friendly" and prices are "reasonable"; P.S. no alcohol.

Spuntino ◐ *American/Italian*

23 | 24 | 21 | £32

Soho | 61 Rupert St., W1D 7PW | no phone |
www.spuntino.co.uk

Past the "queue out of the door", the "calculatedly scruffy setting" – "a fabulous cross between a deserted subway station and burnt-out diner" – adds to the "novelty factor" of this "achingly cool" Polpo sibling in Soho; befitting its translated name ('snack'), the menu features "hearty" American-Italian small plates, all "reasonably priced" and offered by "edgy" staff alongside "deadly cocktails"; P.S. with no reservations and not a lot of space, it's "hard to come with a group".

The Square *French*

28 | 24 | 26 | £113

Mayfair | 6-10 Bruton St., W1J 6PU | 020-7495-7100 |
www.squarerestaurant.com

Chef Philip Howard demonstrates "real flair" at this "stylish, chic", art-filled Mayfair venue where the "exceptional" New French dishes (served within prix fixe and à la carte menus) are a "delight to the eyes as well as the palate" and are "priced accordingly"; furthermore, the "superb" service and "expensive but fair"-priced wines – "dispensed by a very knowledgeable sommelier" – ensure it's "spectacular in every respect".

Sri Nam ⊠ *Thai*

21 | 19 | 20 | £31

Canary Wharf | 10 Cabot Sq., E14 4EY | 020-7715-9515 |
www.orientalrestaurantgroup.co.uk

"Conducive to a quiet dinner" or a "group" lunch in Canary Wharf, this silk-swathed, bi-level dining room produces "yum" Thai cuisine; there's "good service" too, but its best feature may be that it's "quite affordable given the location".

Star of India ◐ *Indian*

26 | 19 | 21 | £39

South Kensington | 154 Old Brompton Rd., SW5 0BE | 020-7373-2901 |
www.starofindia.eu

As "gourmet Indians" go, "there are newer but none better" – or so say fans of this 60-year-old South Ken institution crafting "consistent", "wonderful" "dishes with flair"; indeed, not many mind that the "space is small" and "packed tight" and the decor's a little "frumpy" in light of the mostly "excellent service" and relative value.

	FOOD	DECOR	SERVICE	COST

Stingray Café *Italian* ▽ 23 | 16 | 20 | £19
Kentish Town | 135 Fortress Rd., NW5 2HR | 020-7482-4855
Stringray Café *Italian*
Highbury | 36 Highbury Park, N5 2AA | 020-7354-9309
Shoreditch | 109 Columbia Rd., E2 7RL | 020-7613-1141
www.stringraycafe.co.uk
"Cheap" and "cheery", this "down-to-earth" Italian chainlet specialises in "great" pizza, pastas and other mains, all available with "a
good glass of wine"; and with such "value for money", no surprise
that it's "always busy"; P.S. takeaway also available.

St. John *British* 26 | 19 | 23 | £55
Farringdon | 26 St. John St., EC1M 4AY | 020-3301-8069 |
www.stjohnrestaurant.com
A "mythical place" for "hard-core carnivores", chef Fergus Henderson's "bit pricey" Farringdon temple to "nose-to-tail" cooking beck-
ons with "excellent" Modern British dishes, often fashioned from
the "bits that are usually thrown away", always served by "friendly"
staff; the "cavernous", "industrial-chic" dining room with an open
kitchen is augmented by an "informal, no-reservations needed" bar
area suits that after-work bites and a glass of wine.

St. John Bread & Wine *British* 25 | 19 | 23 | £43
Spitalfields | 94-96 Commercial St., E1 6LZ | 020-3301-8069 |
www.stjohnbreadandwine.com
Chef Fergus Henderson's Spitalfields spin-off offers a "chopped
down" (in price and range) version of the "rustic" Modern Brit
menu at the original, St. John, dishing out everything from "legendary" Old Spot bacon sandwiches to "hot-from-the-oven"
madeleines; "friendly, informal" service matches the "laid-
back", basic setting, and although it can be "noisy at peak times",
it's "always an enjoyable experience".

NEW STK ● *Steak* - | - | - | E
Covent Garden | Me London Hotel | 336-337 The Strand, WC2R 1HA |
020-7395-3450 | www.stkhouse.com
This pricey U.S. import, housed on the ground floor of the Me
London Hotel on the Strand, is as much about style (think
loungelike surroundings, purple lighting, white leather booths)
as it is about steaks, which come in a variety of cuts; highlights
of the sides selection include the likes of parmesan truffle fries and
shrimp 'rice krispies'.

NEW Story 🅂🄼 *British* - | - | - | E
Tower Bridge | 201 Tooley St., SE1 2UE | 020-7183-2117 |
www.restaurantstory.co.uk
At this spot just shy of Tower Bridge, chef Tom Sellers takes an
innovative approach to Modern British cuisine in his pricey six-
or ten-course set menus featuring novel takes on classics; the
simple, library-themed, wood-heavy setting features views into
the glass-walled kitchen and out to Tooley Street through floor-
to-ceiling windows.

	FOOD	DECOR	SERVICE	COST

Strada *Italian*
17 | 16 | 17 | £26

Marylebone | 31 Marylebone High St., W1M 4PY | 020-7935-1004
Spitalfields | 88 Commercial St., E1 6LY | 020-7247-4117
Camden Town | 40-42 Parkway, NW1 7AH | 020-7428-9653
Islington | 105-106 Upper St., N1 1QN | 020-7226-9742
Highgate | 4 S. Grove, N6 6BS | 020-8347-8686
Clapham | 11-13 Battersea Rise, SW11 1HG | 020-7801-0794
Barnes | 375 Lonsdale Rd., SW13 9PY | 020-8392-9216
Putney | 147 Upper Richmond Rd., SW15 2TX | 020-8789-6996
Fulham | 175 New King's Rd., SW6 4SW | 020-7731-6404
Kensington | 29 High St. Kensington, W8 SNP | 020-7938-4648
www.strada.co.uk
Additional locations throughout London

If you crave "well-made pizza" and other "decent Italian" options at "cheap" prices, this chain is "never a letdown" – as long as you "don't go expecting culinary creativity"; "many wines by the glass" and service that generally comes "with a smile" make it an altogether "lovely", "local" choice, either "with the kids or without".

Suda *Thai*
▽ 23 | 22 | 19 | £25

Covent Garden | 23 Slingsby Pl., WC2E 9AB | 020-7240-8010 | www.suda-thai.com

"Well-presented" Thai dishes with "complex" flavours are the draw at this "attractive" spot spread across two "spacious" floors in Covent Garden, with tables spilling onto "a small pedestrian square"; service is "quick", and prices are "moderate", making it "good for groups"; P.S. there's also a lineup of exotic cocktails and healthy shakes.

Sumosan ● *Japanese*
22 | 20 | 18 | £63

Mayfair | 26 Albemarle St., W1S 4HY | 020-7495-5999 | www.sumosan.com

"For those more interested in food than the whole 'who's who'" of more "flamboyant" Mayfair restaurants, this modern, minimalist Japanese with a six-seat sushi bar offers a "wonderful menu" of "artistically presented" dishes that "never disappoint" (unlike the service, which is occasionally "slow"); "yes, you pay for it", but fans assure "it's worth every penny".

NEW SushiSamba ● *Brazilian/Japanese*
21 | 27 | 20 | £58

City | Heron Tower | 110 Bishopsgate, 38th fl., EC2N 4AY | 020-3640-7330 | www.sushisamba.com

"Spectacular views" contribute to the "breathtaking experience" at this 38th-floor Japanese-Brazilian in the Heron Tower skyscraper, which attracts "tourists and City types" with its "stylish" decor; the servings may be "on the smaller side", but the "morsels do taste pretty good", and while the bill can be "high", some suggest it's "worth it for the lift ride alone".

Sushi-Say Ⓜ *Japanese*
▽ 29 | 20 | 23 | £47

Willesden | 33 Walm Ln., NW2 5SH | 020-8459-2971
It "might seem unassuming from the outside", but inside this "cosy" Willesden Green venue, an "amazing" "husband-and-wife team" produce "fabulous sushi" and other Japanese dishes of the "highest

quality", backed by a "great sake list"; despite expensive prices, it's "always full", so try to "book well in advance".

Sushi Tetsu ☒Ⓜ *Japanese*   `-  -  -  M`

Clerkenwell | 12 Jerusalem Passage, EC1V 4JP | 020-3217-0090 | www.sushitetsu.co.uk

This tiny, low-key Clerkenwell Japanese focuses on high-quality, moderately priced sushi and sashimi, served à la carte or in an omakase (chef's choice) menu; there are just seven seats at the blond-wood bar, and bookings, which are taken two months in advance, go quickly.

Sweetings ☒ *Seafood*   `23  15  21  £49`

City | 39 Queen Victoria St., EC4N 4SA | 020-7248-3062 | www.sweetingsrestaurant.com

Looking like something out of "olde England" with its Victorian decor, this "venerable" City "time capsule" (est. 1889) serves "superb", "straight-forward" seafood via "friendly" staff who cater for "the business set"; it's "expensive, but a real treat" for visitors – "just get there early", before the queue forms, as reservations aren't accepted.

Tamarind *Indian*   `25  21  24  £56`

Mayfair | 20 Queen St., W1J 5PR | 020-7629-3561 | www.tamarindrestaurant.com

"Exquisite" Indian recipes with "subtle spicing" and a touch of "continental flair" are the highlights of this "intimate" Mayfair basement; a few feel the bill is "way too much to spend", but "attentive service" and a "lovely wine list" help make it "pure pleasure" for many.

Taqueria *Mexican*   `24  13  17  £28`

Notting Hill | 139-143 Westbourne Grove, W11 2RS | 020-7229-4734 | www.taqueria.co.uk

"If only it had more locations" sigh devotees of this Notting Hill "Mexican food mecca" where the "sense-tingling" small plates are "great for sharing" (though the "prices are a little large"); "refreshing" margaritas are another "highlight", as are "friendly" staff who encourage a "laid-back" vibe that "puts a smile on your face"; P.S. at weekends be "prepared to wait, since it doesn't take reservations".

Taro *Japanese*   `24  15  21  £16`

Soho | 10 Old Compton St., W1D 4TF | 020 7439-2275
Soho | 61 Brewer St., W1F 9UW | 020-7734-5826
www.tarorestaurants.co.uk

"Melt-in-the-mouth-delicious" sushi and other "excellent" Japanese dishes are the draws at this "no-frills" duo in Soho, which "hit all the right notes" for a "quick bite to eat", especially if you don't mind "sharing a table or bench"; with "competitive" prices and solid service to ensure a "friendly" atmosphere, no wonder it's "bustling".

🆕 Tartufo ☒Ⓜ *European*   `-  -  -  E`

Chelsea | No. 11 Cadogan Gdns. | 11 Cadogan Gdns., SW3 2RJ | 020-7730-6383 | www.tartufolondon.co.uk

On the lower ground floor of a discreet boutique hotel in Chelsea, this high-end dining room delivers Modern European dishes with a strong Northern Italian bias; along with idiosyncratic design touches in the decor (e.g. period tea sets, eclectic monochrome prints), there's a cosy private room and open interior courtyard.

Tas ● *Turkish*   22 | 18 | 21 | £25

Bloomsbury | 22 Bloomsbury St., WC1B 3QJ | 020-7637-4555
Farringdon | 37 Farringdon Rd., EC1M 3JB | 020-7430-9721
Borough | 72 Borough High St., SE1 1XF | 020-7403-7200
Waterloo | 33 The Cut, SE1 8LF | 020-7928-1444

Tas Pide ● *Turkish*

South Bank | 20-22 New Globe Walk, SE1 9DR | 020-7928-3300
www.tasrestaurants.co.uk

"Ideal for meeting friends after work" or when "on a tight budget", this "swift, reliable" "standby" promises "generous" portions of "satisfying", "tasty" Turkish fare with "lots of vegetarian choices"; they "can get loud at times", but "courteous" staff help keep them as "cheerful" as they are "welcoming"; P.S. they're open late too.

Tate Modern Restaurant *British*   19 | 23 | 19 | £36

South Bank | Tate Modern | Bankside, 6th fl., SE1 9PG | 020-7887-8888 | www.tate.org.uk

"After museum overload", this "dependable" Modern Brit on the sixth floor of Tate Modern is a "great" spot to drink in "excellent views" of the Thames and St. Paul's while sampling "dependable" food and wine; "fast, friendly" service adds to its appeal.

Tayyabs ● *Pakistani*   25 | 15 | 14 | £21

Whitechapel | 83-89 Fieldgate St., E1 1JU | 020-7247-6400 | www.tayyabs.co.uk

"Sumptuous" mains accompanied by "standout" naan and lassis are dished out at this Whitechapel Pakistani with a BYO policy; it's "quite cramped", "noisy" and you might "queue for an hour, often more" ("ever so slightly" less if you have a reservation), but prices are "reasonable", so "patience" pays off.

10 Cases ⓈＺ *European*   23 | 21 | 22 | £38

Covent Garden | 16 Endell St., WC2H 9BD | 020-7836-6801 | www.the10cases.co.uk

Overflowing with "character and charm", this Covent Garden spot takes an "original idea" – spotlighting 10 cases each of 10 "delicious" red and white wines, all served by the glass, carafe and bottle – and pairs it with "appealing" European eats; even if the choices are "limited" and the "few tables" sometimes full, fans toast the "cool" "bistro atmosphere" and staff who ensure you're "well looked after".

Tendido Cero *Spanish*   21 | 17 | 18 | £43

South Kensington | 174 Old Brompton Rd., SW5 0BA | 020-7370-3685 | www.cambiodetercio.co.uk

"Tantalising tapas served with style" are the specialities of this "always busy" (hence "noisy"), hip South Kensington Spanish "landmark" from the same people as Cambio de Tercio; a "reasonable bill" and "excellent wine choices" bolster the "feel-good factor", not to mention the "efficient, friendly" staff.

	FOOD	DECOR	SERVICE	COST

Tendido Cuatro *Spanish*   ▽ 19 | 18 | 20 | £37

Fulham | 108-110 New King's Rd., SW6 4LY | 020-7371-5147 |
www.cambiodetercio.co.uk

"Traditional tapas", paella and other Spanish fare are "done to a high
standard" and "wonderfully presented" by "polite" staff at this "stylish, modern" Fulham offshoot of Cambio de Tercio; reasonable
prices help it attract its fair share of "noisy groups" in the evening,
while it's also "recommended" for a "decent" weekend brunch.

10 Greek Street ⑤ *European*   23 | 17 | 20 | £41

Soho | 10 Greek St., W1D 4DH | 020-7734-4677 | www.10greekstreet.com
"Innovative combinations" of "sunshine-filled" ingredients are found
in the "great-value", daily-changing Modern European menu at this
slightly "cramped" Soho bistro; in the evenings the no-reservations
policy makes a queue "inevitable", but the "cutting-edge" wine list,
served by glass, carafe or bottle, and "lovely" service help make it
"worth" waiting for.

Tentazioni ⑤ *Italian*   ▽ 24 | 18 | 22 | £45

Tower Bridge | Lloyd's Wharf | 2 Mill St., SE1 2BD | 020-7237-1100 |
www.tentazioni.co.uk

"Gorgeous" "homemade Italian food" "served with flair" makes it
"worth the trek" to this venue "hidden in a side street" near Tower
Bridge; although some find the decor a bit of "a letdown" ("too red"),
it's trumped by the "leisurely" atmosphere, informed by "lovely
staff" who "cope with big groups quite well"; P.S. it's pricey, save for
the "excellent inexpensive lunch".

Ten Ten Tei ⑤ *Japanese*   ▽ 25 | 14 | 21 | £25

Soho | 56 Brewer St., W1 9TJ | 020-7287-1738
A "fantastic array" of "well-executed" Japanese "classics", including
"tasty sushi" and tempura, and "dependable" staff are "the stars" at
this "unpretentious" Soho venue with "basic decor (especially
downstairs)"; factor in "incredible value for money", and no wonder
it's often "very busy", with "a queue out the door".

Terroirs ⑤ *Mediterranean*   22 | 18 | 19 | £37

Covent Garden | 5 William IV St., WC2N 4DW | 020-7036-0660 |
www.terroirswinebar.com

The "rustic" Mediterranean menus of "ingredient-driven small
plates" and "top-quality charcuterie" are "worth seeking out" as
much as the "bewildering yet genuinely exciting" wine list (including biodynamic varieties) at this "lively", Covent Garden "hangout"; although service gets mixed marks, "reasonable" prices and a
"buzzy", "French-bistro" vibe make it a "great place to meet friends" –
and "perfect post-theatre".

Texture ●⑤Ⓜ *European/Scandinavian*   26 | 23 | 26 | £69

Marylebone | 34 Portman St., W1H 7BY | 020-7224-0028 |
www.texture-restaurant.co.uk

"Grown-ups" appreciate this "elegant", "warm" Marylebone dining
room's "wonderful", "clever" European food with Scandinavian in-

fluences, which is presented by "excellent" staff in "nicely judged portions" alongside an "interesting" list of champagnes and sparkling wines; everything's expensive, but if you're on a budget, try the set lunch menu – given the "quality and care" that goes into it, it's "a bargain".

Thai Square *Thai*
19 | 17 | 16 | £28

City | 136-138 Minories, EC3N 1NT | 020-7680-1111 🗷
City | 1-7 Great St. Thomas Apostle, EC4V 2BH | 020-7329-0001 🗷
Covent Garden | 148 The Strand, WC2R 1JA |
020-7497-0904 🗷
Mayfair | 5 Princes St., W1B 2LF | 020-7499-3333 🗷
St. James's | 21-24 Cockspur St., SW1Y 5BL | 020-7839-4000 ◗
Soho | 27-28 St. Anne's Ct., W1F 0BN | 020-7287-2000 🗷
Islington | 347-349 Upper St., N1 0PD | 020-7704-2000
Putney | 2-4 Lower Richmond Rd., SW15 1LB | 020-8780-1811
Richmond | 29 Kew Rd., TW9 2NQ | 020-8940-5253
South Kensington | 19 Exhibition Rd., SW7 2HE |
020-7584-8359
www.thaisq.com
Additional locations throughout London

Somewhere "between your local Thai" and "really upscale ones" sits this midpriced chain offering "reliable" Siamese eats accompanied by beers that "wash it down nicely"; also on offer are "relaxing" environs and "helpful" staff who ensure that you "shouldn't be waiting long".

Thai Thai *Thai*
▽ 21 | 22 | 19 | £29

Shoreditch | 110 Old St., EC1V 9BD | 020-7490-5230 |
www.thaithaieast.co.uk

"Nicely laid out", with modern decor, this spacious Shoreditch standby hits the spot for reasonably priced, "expertly cooked" Thai cuisine; it "tends to get busy", but "efficient" service keeps things moving.

Theo Randall at The InterContinental 🗷 *Italian*
25 | 20 | 23 | £56

Mayfair | InterContinental Park Ln. | 1 Hamilton Pl., W1J 7QY | 020-7318-8747 | www.theorandall.com

"Superb" pastas, "well-executed meats and fish" and other "earthy" Italian cooking, plus "gracious service" and a "serene ambience", add up to a "special treat" at chef Theo Randall's InterContinental Park Lane venue; although a few find the low-ceilinged dining room "dreary" and warn that "the price can rack up", most "can't fault the experience"; P.S. the set menu is "superlative".

34 *Steak*
23 | 24 | 23 | £61

Mayfair | 34 Grosvenor Sq., W1K 2HD | 020-3350-3434 |
www.34-restaurant.co.uk

"All the glamour you'd expect" from an establishment overseen by the Caprice group comes via "splendid", "elegant" Edwardian and art deco–inspired adornments at this "buzzy" Mayfair steakhouse offering "a fabulous selection" of "succulent" mains and "divine" desserts; what's more, it's all presented with the sort of "spot-on"

| | FOOD | DECOR | SERVICE | COST |

service "London oligarchs" demand – at the kind of "expensive" prices they have no trouble paying.

The Thomas Cubitt   *British*   **21** | **20** | **19** | **£41**

Belgravia | 44 Elizabeth St., SW1W 9PA | 020-7730-6060 | www.thethomascubitt.co.uk

With a "solid" Traditional British menu downstairs, "fantastic" Modern British upstairs and a "thoughtful wine list", this Belgravia venue "defines all that's good about gastropubs"; "popular with the beautiful people", "the pub section is more packed than a London tube at rush hour", while the "tranquil" dining room resembles "the posh townhouse you can't afford"; whichever area you choose, expect "competent" service and "make a reservation – otherwise, you'll salivate as an onlooker".

Timo ☒ *Italian*   ▽ **24** | **18** | **25** | **£51**

Kensington | 343 Kensington High St., W8 6NW | 020-7603-3888 | www.timorestaurant.net

"Smartly dressed" regulars promise that they "will go back forever" to this "understated", cream-and-green-hued Kensington spot offering a "simple" yet "top-quality" Italian menu and "wonderful" service; it's a bit "expensive", but the prices probably "won't kill you", especially if you "choose the lunchtime menu".

Tinello ☒ *Italian*   **25** | **21** | **22** | **£49**

Belgravia | 87 Pimlico Rd., SW1W 8PH | 020-7730-3663 | www.tinello.co.uk

What was once an "excellent find" by Belgravia cognoscenti is "now emerging as a go-to Italian", where "fabulous, thoughtful Tuscan cooking", a "lovely wine list" and "attentive service" ensure the place gets "jammed"; the "low-key, but stylish space" with "exposed brick and subdued lighting" attracts a "chic, business-casual clientele" who venture "upstairs for atmosphere, downstairs to hold a conversation" and pay "slightly pricey" costs throughout.

Tokyo Diner ● *Japanese*   **22** | **14** | **19** | **£18**

Chinatown | 2 Newport Pl., WC2H 7JJ | 020-7287-8777 | www.tokyodiner.com

Resembling a "typical workingman's place" in Tokyo, this "crowded", "no-frills" Chinatown Japanese "does a good line in noodles, sushi" and other "tasty" dishes – all served "fast", with a "no-tip rule", making it "great value"; what's more, there's "extra rice if you want it", "Japanese newspapers at hand" and "unlimited complimentary green tea".

Tom Aikens ☒ *French*   **25** | **22** | **23** | **£84**

Chelsea | 43 Elystan St., SW3 3NT | 020-7584-2003 | www.tomaikens.co.uk

The eponymous celeb chef's "cutting-edge" style is "clearly visible" in the "innovative", "fabulous" dishes at his Chelsea New French, an "expense-account" affair blessed with a "sensational" wine list; add "knowledgeable" and "relaxed" staff plus earthy, rustic decor, and the result is a "thrilling gastro experience".

	FOOD	DECOR	SERVICE	COST

Tom's Deli *Deli/International*   24 | 17 | 21 | £23

Notting Hill | 226 Westbourne Grove, W11 2RH | 020-7221-8818 | www.tomsdelilondon.co.uk

"You'll want to linger all day" over the "awesome" International menu at Tom Conran's Notting Hill venue comprising a ground-floor deli "crammed" with "treats", and an art-filled upstairs cafe; although it "looks tired" to some eyes, don't be surprised if it's "crowded" right up until closing time, 6.30 PM daily.

Tom's Kitchen *British*   23 | 19 | 20 | £46

Covent Garden | Somerset Hse. | The Strand, WC2R 1LA | 020-7845-4646
NEW Canary Wharf | 11 Westferry Circus, E14 4HD | 020-3011-1555
Chelsea | 27 Cale St., SW3 3QP | 020-7349-0202
www.tomskitchen.co.uk

"There's always a reason to pop by" this "relaxed" chainlet, as chef Tom Aikens' "inventive", upscale Modern British food is a "safe bet for weekend brunch" (try the "delicious" eggs Benedict), weekday lunch or "proper dinner"; and feel free to "take the kids", because "friendly", "attentive" staff ensure they're "well-looked-after".

Tonkotsu *Japanese*   - | - | - | M

Soho | 63 Dean St., W1D 4QG | 020-7437-0071 | www.tonkotsu.co.uk
Taking inspiration from classic Japanese noodle bars, this no-reservations Soho spot (from the people behind Tsuru), offers sensibly priced ramen dishes, gyoza and sides, served in stripped back, industrial chic surrounds; covers are split over two floors, but for solo diners the plum spot is perched at the bar overlooking the open kitchen and its huge pots of bubbling stock.

Tortilla *Mexican*   22 | 18 | 22 | £10

Bloomsbury | 6 Market Pl., W1W 8AH | 020-7637-2800
City | 28 Leadenhall Mkt., EC3V 1LR | 020-7929-7837 Ⓢ
NEW Covent Garden | 460 The Strand, WC2R 0RG | 020-7930-0269
Canary Wharf | 18 N. Colonnade, E14 4EU | 020-7719-9160
Stratford | Westfield Stratford City | 213 The Balcony, E20 1ES | 020-8555-3663
Islington | 13 Islington High St., N1 9LQ | 020-7833-3130
Wimbledon | 22 The Broadway, SW19 1RE | 020-8947-3589
South Bank | 106 Southwark St., SE1 0TA | 020-7620-0285 Ⓢ
Hammersmith | 6 King St., W6 0QA | 020-8741-7959
www.tortilla.co.uk

Soft tortillas are stuffed with "tasty" fillings such as "smoky" grilled chicken and "zingy" guacamole at this Mexican burrito chain, a "regular indulgence" for those in need of a "quick", "affordable" meal; although eat-in is available, most take away, which can result in a "snaking queue out the door at lunchtime" – but don't be put off, because "fast" service ensures the line "moves at a rapid pace".

Tramshed *Chicken/Steak*   20 | 24 | 18 | £37

Shoreditch | 32 Rivington St., EC2A 3EQ | 020-7749-0478 | www.chickenandsteak.co.uk
It's the "giant" Damien Hirst installation (a formaldehyde-encased cow and cock set on a pedestal) and works by other artists that draw

a "young", "hip" crowd to this Shoreditch Modern Brit; the minimalist, moderately priced menu – consisting of seasonal sharing starters followed by "upmarket chicken and chips" or "tasty" steak – "lacks the wow factor" of the "amazing space", but it's "perfectly acceptable", just like the "friendly", "efficient" service.

Trinity *European*   26 | 23 | 25 | £56

Clapham | 4 The Polygon, SW4 0JG | 020-7622-1199 | www.trinityrestaurant.co.uk

"Adventurous tastes" ("bone marrow, pig's trotters") abound on Adam Byatt's "fantastic-value" Modern Euro menu at this "laid-back" "gem" on the "edge of Clapham Common" – sibling to the nearby Bistro Union; "slick service" and "cool decor" complete the "memorable" picture, one that's "smart without being stuffy, and indulgent without being excessive".

Trishna *Indian*   26 | 19 | 22 | £47

Marylebone | 15-17 Blandford St., W1U 3DG | 020-7935-5624 | www.trishnalondon.com

The "exquisitely seasoned", "inventive" cuisine at this "high-class" Marylebone dining room offers an "original" take on Indian fare (try the fish tikka, it "will blow your mind"); service is "friendly and attentive", while the marble-and-oak decor "brings a touch of modernity"; P.S. the tasting menus (with "well-chosen" paired wines) are a "great bargain".

The Troubadour *International*   20 | 23 | 20 | £23

Earls Court | 265 Old Brompton Rd., SW5 9JA | 020-7370-1434 | www.troubadour.co.uk

There's "something addictive" about the "arty", "bohemian feel" of this "quirky" Earl's Court cultural "haunt" from 1954, a "chilled-out place to relax" all day over a "quality" International menu, "awesome coffee" and "great cocktails"; additional features include a "lovely" garden and a downstairs club that usually has "decent singer/songwriters on the bill", following in the footsteps of famous past headliners.

Truc Vert *French*   ∇ 19 | 15 | 16 | £33

Mayfair | 42 N. Audley St., W1K 6ZR | 020-7491-9988 | www.trucvert.co.uk

When you'd like a "respite from the Oxford Street crowds", this Mayfair cafe is a "soothing" "place to hang your hat for a while" and tuck into "nicely prepared", daily changing French bistro fare with "creative undertones", and all "for less money than you'd expect"; the "comprehensive wine list" is a plus, especially if you snag a table outside in summer.

Trullo *Italian*   24 | 20 | 22 | £43

Islington | 300-302 St. Paul's Rd., N1 2LH | 020-7226-2733 | www.trullorestaurant.com

"Vibrant" Italian dishes are crafted with "skilful hands" and served by "cheery" staff at this Islington local where the "paper-topped tables" are "crowded" with the local "intelligentsia celebrating birthdays or their latest book deals"; and not only is it a "bargain for the quality", but there's also a "cosy" cellar offering an alternative setting to the main dining room.

Tsunami ❶ *Japanese* | 23 | 20 | 21 | £40 |

Fitzrovia | 93 Charlotte St., W1T 4PY | 020-7637-0050 🗷
Clapham | 5-7 Voltaire Rd., SW4 6DQ | 020-7978-1610
www.tsunamirestaurant.co.uk

Expect a "chilled vibe" at this "dark", "intimate" Japanese duo in Clapham and Charlotte Street, but it's the "brilliant", "beautifully presented" sushi and such, "superb service" and "fantastic cocktails" that make it a "perfect date" venue; while "not super-expensive or super-cheap", it's a "reliable" backup for "trendy" dining in "lovely" surroundings; P.S. the "takeaway option is a lifesaver for lazy nights in".

Tsuru 🗷 *Japanese* | ∇ 22 | 16 | 18 | £19 |

City | 10 Queen St., EC4N 1TX | 020-7248-1525
City | 201 Bishopsgate, EC2M 3UG | 020-7377-1166
South Bank | 4 Canvey St., SE1 9AN | 020-7928-2228
www.tsuru-sushi.co.uk

They're "concerned with the provenance of the ingredients" at this "minimalist" Japanese chainlet which becomes like a "fast-food restaurant during lunchtime" (when most take the "super-fresh", "sustainably sourced sushi" to go); the "good-value" menu expands with "mouth-watering katsu curries" and teriyaki in the evening, when you should "expect to be finished by 9 PM", because that's when it closes.

Tuttons ❶ *British* | 20 | 19 | 19 | £34 |

Covent Garden | 11-12 Russell St., WC2B 5HZ | 020-7836-4141 |
www.tuttons.com

"Whether you're looking for a pre-meeting breakfast or post-opera supper, the location is hard to beat" at this "lively" stalwart at the edge of the Covent Garden piazza, which serves a "reliable", midpriced menu focusing on Traditional British dishes; the "charming service" is perhaps at its best "when not busy" – a rare occurrence, especially in summer when the "delightful" outdoor terrace is mobbed.

28-50 Wine Workshop & Kitchen *French* | 21 | 20 | 23 | £43 |

Holborn | 140 Fetter Ln., EC4A 1BT | 020-7242-8877 🗷
Marylebone | 15-17 Marylebone Ln., W1U 2NE | 020-7486-7922
www.2850.co.uk

Benefiting from "professional, friendly" staff and an atmosphere that's "equally good for couples or groups", this "casual" bar-cum-French dining room with locations in Marylebone and nearby Fleet Street is "a must for any wine lover", thanks to its "extensive" selection of "interesting" glasses, carafes and bottles; as for the "straightforward", bistro-style food, some find it "secondary, really" to the *vin*.

202 *European* | 19 | 20 | 17 | £33 |

Notting Hill | 202 Westbourne Grove, W11 2RH | 020-7727-2722 |
www.202london.com

"Food and fashion mix" at this Modern European set inside a "stylishly casual" Notting Hill "concept store" where "cool, funky locals" "shop, be seen" and have a "delicious" "quick" meal ferried to them by "friendly" staff; at weekends, "expect a wait", as seemingly all the local "mummies" stop in for a "girlie brunch".

222 Veggie Vegan *Vegan*　　24 | 19 | 23 | £31

Earls Court | 222 North End Rd., W14 9NU | 020-7381-2322 | www.222veggievegan.com

The "varied selection" of "tasty", "nutritious" vegan dishes on offer at this "friendly" Earls Court cafe "might even persuade carnivores" to "take the plunge", and it all comes "without any trace" of "pretentiousness"; prices are "competitive for the quality", particularly a lunchtime buffet that's "really good value for money".

2 Veneti ⊠ *Italian*　　23 | 21 | 21 | £39

Marylebone | 10 Wigmore St., W1U 2RD | 020-7637-0789 | www.2veneti.com

"Medics" from nearby Harley Street rub shoulders with "concert performers from Wigmore Hall" next door at this "cosy" brick-walled Marylebone Venetian, where "unique dishes" offer "a genuine taste of the region", and the "fresh pasta is a dream"; "cheerful" staff are on hand to "discuss the ingredients and make useful suggestions", and best of all, it's "affordable".

Umu ⊠ *Japanese*　　27 | 25 | 24 | £95

Mayfair | 14-16 Bruton Pl., W1J 6LX | 020-7499-8881 | www.umurestaurant.com

"Sheer delight" is found at this "romantic" Mayfair Japanese, offering "sophisticated" Kyoto-style kaiseki meals with "clever fusion twists" plus sushi and sashimi; it's expensive but "worth every penny" according to admirers who also applaud the "superior" sake selection, tended by a sommelier with "infectious" enthusiasm.

Union Café ● *British/Mediterranean*　　21 | 16 | 20 | £41

Marylebone | 96 Marylebone Ln., W1U 2QA | 020-7486-4860 | www.brinkleys.com

For a "chat with friends" or an "informal business lunch", this "buzzy" Marylebone local is "reliable but never boring", thanks to an "interesting" menu of Modern British–Mediterranean comfort dishes; the setting may be "bland", and the usually "friendly" staff "a bit off-hand" when it's full, but an "outstanding-value wine list" keeps the "repeat" trade brisk.

Union Jacks *British/Pizza*　　18 | 17 | 20 | £25

Covent Garden | 5 North Hall, Covent Garden Piazza, WC2E 8RA | 020-3640-7086

Holborn | 4 Central St. Giles Piazza, WC2H 8AB | 020-3597-7888

Chiswick | 217-221 Chiswick High Rd., W4 2DW | 020-3617-9988

www.unionjacksrestaurants.com

Jamie Oliver is behind this chainlet distributing a midpriced selection of "fancy" flatbreads ("essentially pizza"), whose "innovative combinations" of toppings recall "traditional" British recipes (some deem the concept "slightly strange", others assure that it "really works"); "old-school decor, cool background tunes" and "zippy service" ensure a "fun", "relaxed" time.

NEW Upstairs at the Ten Bells 🅼 *British*   – | – | – | M

Spitalfields | 84 Commercial St., E1 6LY | 075-3049-2986 |
www.tenbells.com

Originally just a short term pop-up, this Modern Brit proved so popular that it's now a permanent fixture in the Georgian-style dining room above a Spitalfields pub; the reasonably priced, weekly changing menu incorporates unusual ingredients like pigs' ears and veal tongue, and there's a cut-down, fixed-price version available at lunchtimes.

Vanilla Black 🅂 *Vegetarian*   24 | 19 | 24 | £47

Holborn | 17-18 Tooks Ct., EC4A 1LB | 020-7242-2622 |
www.vanillablack.co.uk

"Surprising and delighting even the most devout carnivores", this "out-of-the-way wonder" in Holborn creates "exciting", "original", "gourmet vegetarian" treats, which arrive via "polite", "attentive service"; it comes "highly recommended" for a "fancy date night", despite a "plain", "sparsely furnished" setting – and perhaps because it's "not an everyday" kind of place pricewise.

Vapiano ● *Italian*   23 | 20 | 18 | £17

Marylebone | 19-21 Great Portland St., W1W 8QB | 020-7268-0080
Southwark | 90B Southwark St., SE1 0FD | 020-7593-2010
www.vapiano.co.uk

"Tasty, inexpensive" pizza, pasta and salads are "tailored to your request" by "friendly" counter staff at the Marylebone and Southwark outposts of this casual international Italian chain; it's "nicely decorated" with large windows, but it "can get busy, so queue up early".

Vasco & Piero's Pavilion 🅂 *Italian*   23 | 18 | 23 | £41

Soho | 15 Poland St., W1F 8QE | 020-7437-8774 | www.vascosfood.com
Open since 1971, this "sophisticated" Italian "cocoon" "shelters you from the drunken wave" of Soho with "abundant" plates of "delicious" dishes from a daily changing, Umbrian-influenced menu; "friendly" hosts and prices that are a relative "steal" add appeal.

Veeraswamy *Indian*   24 | 23 | 24 | £51

Mayfair | Victory Hse. | 99 Regent St., W1B 4RS | 020-7734-1401 |
www.veeraswamy.com

Dating back to the 1920s, this "landmark for Indian food" overlooking Regent Street lures spice lovers with "classic" dishes "bursting with flavours" as well as "irresistible" desserts; service is "friendly" and "quick" (handy for "good-value" pre-theatre dinners), while the "lavish" "Maharajas-style decor" and "colourful ambience" adds to its appeal.

Verru 🅂 *E European/Scandinavian*   ▽ 22 | 19 | 22 | £43

Marylebone | 69 Marylebone Ln., W1U 2PH | 020-7935-0858 |
www.verru.co.uk

A "highly original" Scandinavian-Baltic fusion menu on which "traditional fare" gets "gourmet, artistic twists" is delivered by "friendly, attentive" staff at this bare-brick-walled Marylebone haunt with a "romantic, cosy atmosphere"; lunchtime and pre-theatre set menus are a "bargain", but "the à la carte is not far off", and "the wine list is varied enough for all palates and budgets".

Viajante ●Ⓜ️ *International*   26 | 22 | 26 | £101

Bethnal Green | Town Hall Hotel | Patriot Sq., E2 9NF | 020-7871-0461 | www.viajante.co.uk
Chef Nuno Mendes "trained at El Bulli, and it shows", as evidenced in his "fascinating", "at times surprising" "flavour sensations", which are "beautifully presented" (sometimes by the man himself) in nearly unadorned surroundings at this Bethnal Green International; while the tasting-menu-only format commands a very pricey bill, especially if you opt for the "recommended" wine pairings, many believe it's "amazing value" considering the "outstanding quality".

Viet Ⓢ *Vietnamese*   ▽ 23 | 14 | 18 | £20

Soho | 34 Greek St., W1D 5DJ | 020-7494-9888
It's "worth the wait" for "a quick fix of the real thing" at this Soho Vietnamese, where the "cafeteria decor" doesn't deter customers from queuing for a meal that is inexpensive and "full of flavour"; and though alcohol is not served, you're welcome to bring your own.

Viet Hoa ● *Vietnamese*   22 | 16 | 18 | £20

Hoxton | 70-72 Kingsland Rd., E2 8DP | 020-7729-8293 | www.viethoarestaurant.co.uk
"Jostle with East London types" seeking "pre-clubbing noodles" at this Hoxton standard for "ridiculously reasonably priced" Vietnamese eats like a "cure-all hot-and-sour soup"; service is often "attentive", while the "cavernous" space is decked out with "plenty of wood and unadorned walls"; P.S. downstairs is the Mess, a "cook-your-own-BBQ affair".

Village East ● *British*   23 | 24 | 20 | £40

Tower Bridge | 171-173 Bermondsey St., SE1 3UW | 020-7357-6082 | www.villageeast.co.uk
"New York City" in style, this "lively", "trendy Bermondsey Street haunt" is "worth seeking out" for "quality" Modern British eats; there's a "big bar to just drop in for a drink" – ask "helpful" staff what's recommended from the "strong, affordable wine list" or "amazing cocktails".

Villandry *Deli/European*   18 | 17 | 17 | £39

Marylebone | 170 Great Portland St., W1W 5QB | 020-7631 3131 | www.villandry.com
Whether for a "business breakfast, lunch or glass of wine after work", this "upmarket" Great Portland Street venue covers all the bases, with a "relaxed" cafe and a "white-tablecloth" restaurant serving "simple" Modern European fare, along with a "gourmet deli" selling "fresh foods and unusual gifts"; though critics find the setting "plain" and the tariffs "pricey", "friendly" staff who are always "willing to help" redeem.

Vinoteca *European*   23 | 20 | 22 | £35
Farringdon | 7 St. John St., EC1M 4AA | 020-7253-8786 🗷
Marylebone | 15 Seymour Pl., W1H 5BD | 020-7724-7288
Soho | 53-55 Beak St., W1F 9SH | 020-3544-7411
www.vinoteca.co.uk
An "interesting" vino selection (including a "terrific range by the glass") makes these "super-casual" wine bars oenophile magnets, while an "artful" Modern European menu of "frequently changing" dishes delights diners; "fantastic" sommeliers, "convivial" compatriots and prices that are "reasonable for the quality" support the view that it's "worth a try".

Vivat Bacchus 🗷 *European*   20 | 16 | 19 | £39
Farringdon | 47 Farringdon St., EC4A 4LL | 020-7353-2648
Tower Bridge | 4 Hays Ln., SE1 2HB | 020-7234-0891
www.vivatbacchus.co.uk
An "amazing" cheese cave and a wine list as thick as a "novel" are the draws at this South African–owned duo in Farringdon and near Tower Bridge, which also turn out an "interesting", midpriced Modern European menu (including a few "off-*piste*" dishes); "friendly", "knowledgeable" service and a "bright, lively" atmosphere further enhance the "thoroughly enjoyable experience".

Wagamama *Japanese*   17 | 13 | 16 | £21
Covent Garden | 1 Tavistock St., WC2E 7PG | 020-7836-3330
Spitalfields | Old Spitalfields Mkt. | 9 Horner Sq., E1 6EW | 020-7539-3580
NEW Finchley | Great North Leisure Park | Chaplin Sq., N12 0GL | 020-8446-9084 🗷
Hampstead | 58-62 Heath St., NW3 1EN | 020-7433-0366 🗷
Islington | N1 Ctr. | 40 Parkfield St., N1 0PS | 020-7226-2664
Greenwich | Greenwich Peninsula, SE10 0ES | 020-8269-1214
Tower Bridge | 2B Tower Pl., EC3 N4EB | 020-7283-5897
Putney | 50-54 High St., SW15 1SQ | 020-8785-3636
Ealing | 12 High St., W5 5DB | 020-8567-7352
NEW Fulham | Fulham Broadway Shopping Ctr. | Fulham Rd., SW6 1BW | 020-7386-8017
www.wagamama.com
Additional locations throughout London
"Warming" noodle soups, other "filling" Japanese eats and free green tea are served with "speed" by "cheerful" staff at this "casual", child-friendly chain; although the general "noise and bustle" and cafeteria-style communal tables prove "too much" for some, the "inexpensive" prices appeal to "those on a tight budget".

Wahaca *Mexican*   22 | 19 | 20 | £24
NEW Fitzrovia | 19-23 Charlotte St., W1T 1RL | 020-7323-2342
Covent Garden | 66 Chandos Pl., WC2N 4HG | 020-7240-1883
Soho | 80 Wardour St., W1F OTF | 020-7734-0195
Canary Wharf | Park Pavilion | 40 Canada Sq., E14 5FW | 020-7516-9145
Stratford | Westfield Stratford City | 6 Chestnut Plaza, E20 1GL | 020-3288-1025
NEW Islington | 68-69 Upper St., N1 0NY | 020-3697-7990

(continued)

Wahaca

South Bank | Queen Elizabeth Hall | Belvedere Rd., SE1 8XX |
020-7928-1876
NEW Waterloo | 119 Waterloo Rd., SE1 8UL | 020-3697-4140
Shepherd's Bush | Westfield Shopping Ctr. | Ariel Way, W12 7GB |
020-8749-4517
www.wahaca.co.uk

Inspired by the "colourful, vibrant" street food of Mexico, this "clever
concept" chain presents "small", "fun and flavour-packed" plates
for "reasonable prices"; while some complain about the "chaotic"
atmosphere and "invariable wait" for a table (no reservations), others are happy to pass the time with an "eye-watering margarita" at
the bar, whipped up by "friendly" staff.

Wapping Food *European* | 19 | 26 | 18 | £45 |

Wapping | Wapping Hydraulic Power Station | Wapping Wall, E1W 3ST |
020-7680-2080 | www.thewappingproject.com

"Set in the cool confines of an old power station", this "engaging"
Wapping venue features "Victorian industrial machinery inter-
spersed with the tables", "ever-changing" art exhibitions and an
"accomplished" Modern European menu with "reasonable" prices;
"quirky" staff and an "interesting Australian wine list" bolster its
reputation as a "unique gem", "especially for weekend brunch".

The Warrington *British* | ∇ 19 | 19 | 18 | £34 |

St. John's Wood | 93 Warrington Crescent, W9 1EH | 020-7286-8282 |
www.laucelinn.com

"Fantastic pub downstairs, light and airy dining room upstairs" is the
makeup of this "wonderfully restored" Victorian landmark in St.
John's Wood – a "relaxing", "family-friendly" venue with a "quality"
British menu covering "everything from pub grub to fine dining";
most feel service is "ok", while the "selection of properly stored ales
and beers" is "fine" indeed.

The Waterside Inn Restaurant Ⓜ *French* | 29 | 27 | 28 | £126 |

Bray | Waterside Inn | Ferry Rd., Berkshire, SL6 2AT | 01628-620 691 |
www.waterside-inn.co.uk

It's "worth *le voyage*" outside London to the Roux family's "idyllic"
Bray venue for Classic French cooking so "exquisite" and staff so "attentive" (yet "surprisingly relaxed"), they've been voted No. 1 for
Food and Service in this year's survey; perks to mitigate the bank-
account-bashing prices are a "top-drawer" sommelier and the
"peacefulness" of its "romantic" setting overlooking the Thames.

The Wells *European* | 22 | 22 | 21 | £45 |

Hampstead | 30 Well Walk, NW3 1BX | 020-7794-3785 |
www.thewellshampstead.co.uk

"Wonderfully welcoming (especially to dogs)" and "pleasantly decorated", this Modern European gastropub "not far from the heath"
in Hampstead is more than just "a neighbourhood joint", it's a "destination", thanks to "imaginative", "tasty" cooking served in a

ground-floor pub and an upstairs dining room (where the menu is "a little expensive"); a "good wine selection", "places for backgammon and chess" and a "great Sunday roast" are some more reasons it's "worth the trek".

Wheeler's of St. James's Ⓢ *Seafood*   21 | 18 | 21 | £54
St. James's | 72-73 St. James's St., SW1A 1PH | 020-7408-1440 | www.wheelersrestaurant.org

"Casual diners mix with suits" at Marco Pierre White's spacious, "traditional" St. James's dining rooms, "the place to go" for an "excellent selection" of "top-dollar, top-quality" seafood; the "prix fixe menus can be a real bargain", especially for "this neck of the woods", and it's a "lovely place for a group" too, with "delightful" service that adds to its "classic London" appeal.

Whitechapel Gallery Dining Room Ⓜ *European*   ▽ 18 | 17 | 18 | £39
Whitechapel | Whitechapel Gallery | 77-82 Whitechapel High St., E1 7QX | 020-7522-7888 | www.whitechapelgallery.org

A "great resource" for Whitechapel, this "cosy" oak-panelled "oasis" in a "significant" art gallery boasts the talents of chef Angela Hartnett, who consults on the "limited, but quite good" European menu; what's more, the "relatively quiet" atmosphere benefits from "warm" service from staff who ensure customers feel "well looked after".

Wild Honey *British*   23 | 19 | 21 | £51
Mayfair | 12 St. George St., W1S 2FB | 020-7758-9160 | www.wildhoneyrestaurant.co.uk

"Far from the madding crowd", this "relaxing" Modern Brit (sibling of Arbutus) off Bond Street shows an element of "inventiveness" across its "refined" menu, which includes a "top-notch" cheese selection and "great" wines by the carafe; wood-panelled walls decked with contemporary photography and "attentive" service all add to the "lovely, intimate" ambience.

Wilton's Ⓢ *British/Seafood*   26 | 24 | 26 | £82
St. James's | 55 Jermyn St., SW1Y 6LX | 020-7629-9955 | www.wiltons.co.uk

Exuding the "traditional elegance" and "posh" ambience of a "gentleman's club", this "typically British" St. James's stalwart (operating on its site since 1742), serves "impeccably presented" dishes including "simply prepared" seafood and "great" game; "raising one small finger brings immediate attention" from the "charming staff", and "although it's expensive", most agree the overall "experience is worth every penny".

NEW Wishbone Ⓜ *Chicken*   - | - | - | I
Brixton | Brixton Mkt. | Market Row, SW9 8PR | 020-7274-0939 | www.wishbonebrixton.co.uk

Aiming to transform fried chicken in the same way they did with burgers, the team behind MEATliquor set up shop in Brixton Market, turning out a concise, wallet-friendly menu of deep-fried, free-range birds and a small selection of sides; the retro-leaning, brightly decorated bi-level digs decked out with Formica tables also include a bar serving cocktails and craft beers.

The Wolseley ❶ *European*

FOOD	DECOR	SERVICE	COST
23	26	23	£54

Piccadilly | 160 Piccadilly, W1J 9EB | 020-7499-6996 | www.thewolseley.com

"There's a wonderful sense of occasion" to this "luxurious", "bustling" Viennese-style Modern Euro Piccadilly brasserie, voted London's Most Popular restaurant for being full of "charm and character" and a "smattering of celebs" (ensuring "lots of head turning"); a "wide variety" of "reliable" eats fills the slightly pricey menu, and "nothing is too much trouble" for the "sparkling" service; P.S. while reservations are recommended, it also holds some tables for walk-ins during the day.

Wong Kei ❶ ⌷ *Chinese*

FOOD	DECOR	SERVICE	COST
19	7	9	£16

Chinatown | 41-43 Wardour St., W1D 6PY | 020-7437-8408

"Huge portions" of "divine" noodles and other "reliable", "student-priced" Cantonese eats come at "a rapid pace" at this "multifloor" Chinatown "legend"; "you won't want to linger" due to "service with a growl" (considered "part of its great charm") and the "atmosphere of a bus station", but still, loyalists "can't resist", it being such a "quintessential London experience".

Woodlands *Indian/Vegetarian*

FOOD	DECOR	SERVICE	COST
23	15	20	£26

Marylebone | 77 Marylebone Ln., W1U 2PS | 020-7486-3862
Leicester Square | 37 Panton St., SW1Y 4EA | 020-7839-7258
Hampstead | 102 Heath St., NW3 1DR | 020-7794-3080
www.woodlandsrestaurant.co.uk

This "steady", "reliable", "good-value" chainlet specialises in South Indian vegetarian dishes, with "a few interesting twists" thrown into the mix; service from the "warm, friendly" staff engenders a "relaxing ambience", making it "well worth a visit".

Wright Brothers Oyster & Porter House *Seafood*

FOOD	DECOR	SERVICE	COST
24	22	22	£42

Borough | Borough Mkt. | 11 Stoney St., SE1 9AD | 020-7403-9554
Wright Brothers Soho Oyster House ❶ *Seafood*
Soho | 13 Kingly St., W1 5PW | 020-7434-3611
www.thewrightbrothers.co.uk

"Jostle at the bar for a plate of oysters" and other "seafood delights" at this "fish-lover's paradise" next to Borough Market, a "buzzing", "casual" place with "plain wood tables", "reasonable prices" and "knowledgeable staff who remember your face"; likewise, the "unpretentious", equally "crowded" Soho offshoot (a three-floor endeavour combining a restaurant and raw bar) is "well worth a trip" for "when you want to splurge".

XO *Asian*

FOOD	DECOR	SERVICE	COST
20	19	19	£39

Belsize Park | 29 Belsize Ln., NW3 5AS | 020-7433-0888 | www.rickerrestaurants.com

"A touch of glamour" in Belsize Park, this spot from Ricker Restaurants (E&O, Great Eastern Dining Room, et al.) hits the mark for a "girls' night out or post-movie date" with its "smart", "modern" look, "notable wine list" and "variety"-packed Pan-Asian menu that's only "a bit expensive"; a few think the "great formula is now dating gently", but it's "reliable", "fast" and "friendly" too.

Yalla Yalla *Lebanese*   24 | 18 | 19 | £21

Fitzrovia | 12 Winsley St., W1 8HQ | 020-7637-4748 ▣
Soho | 1 Greens Ct., W1F 0HA | 020-7287-7663
www.yalla-yalla.co.uk

"Generous portions" of "healthy" Mideastern eats are "perfect for sharing with a group of friends" and "priced reasonably" at this "popular" Lebanese chainlet; "enthusiastic" staff "aim for a high turnover", but since there's "limited seating" in the "slightly spartan" environs, you can expect a "long wait" – though "delicious takeaway" is another option.

Yashin Sushi *Japanese*   28 | 21 | 23 | £63

Kensington | 1A Argyll Rd., W8 7DB | 020-7938-1536 | www.yashinsushi.com

"Put yourself in the chef's hands" and savour "amazing fare that feels authentic and innovative at the same time" at this "tiny" bilevel Kensington Japanese, "pitched perfectly to its neighbourhood"; service earns a respectable rating, but be aware that "prices are as eye-watering as the food is mouth-watering".

Yauatcha ◗ *Chinese*   27 | 24 | 21 | £52

Soho | 15 Broadwick St., W1F 0DL | 020-7494-8888 | www.yauatcha.com

Along with "inventive, exciting" dim sum and "to-die-for" cocktails, this "buzzing", "ultra-chic" Soho Chinese also encompasses an " unusual" patisserie serving a "huge selection" of teas and "incredible-looking" desserts; service is "efficient", and although some suspect it's "double the price" of competitors in nearby Chinatown, most deem it "reasonably priced considering the quality".

Yming ◗▣ *Chinese*   23 | 16 | 22 | £37

Soho | 35-36 Greek St., W1D 5DL | 020-7734-2721 | www.yminglondon.com

It's "nothing much to look at", but this spot in a "little corner of Soho" is "not your average" Chinese thanks to "courteous" staff who "make everyone feel special", "fantastic", "reliable" northern-influenced dishes and "reasonable prices"; as "casual" and "relaxed" as it is, it's still quite "popular", so it's advisable to book at weekends.

York & Albany *British*   20 | 19 | 18 | £42

Camden Town | 127-129 Parkway, NW1 7PS | 020-7388-3344 | www.gordonramsay.com

Set in a John Nash–designed former coach inn near Regent's Park, this Gordon Ramsay gastropub boasts a "plush" setting and an "enjoyable", "sensibly priced" Modern British menu, which is delivered by mostly "commendable" staff; admirers say it's "best for breakfast" or a "leisurely lunch" in the "cosy" red-hued dining room, while others stick to the "fabulous" street-level bar or the "rustic deli".

	FOOD	DECOR	SERVICE	COST

Yoshino ⊠ *Japanese*
24 | 14 | 21 | £29

Piccadilly | 3 Piccadilly Pl., W1J 0DB | 020-7287-6622 | www.yoshino.net
"Charming", "friendly staff" "greet customers with smiles and advice" at this "well-hidden secret off Piccadilly", where the "excellent" sushi complements a "wide variety" of "traditional", "beautifully presented" Japanese offerings; what's more, it's "great value" (especially the bento boxes), and there's also a "packed deli counter" for "delicious" takeaway lunches.

Yum Yum *Thai*
23 | 23 | 21 | £27

Stoke Newington | 187 Stoke Newington High St., N16 0LH | 020-7254-6751 | www.yumyum.co.uk
"It's all in the name" according to admirers of the "brilliant" Thai treats sold at this "calm" Stoke Newington haunt; though some deem it "slightly on the expensive side" if you don't catch the "excellent-value" lunch menu, it's "popular with locals" and "large parties" at all times, due to "warm" service and "charming" indoor/outdoor seating.

Zafferano *Italian*
24 | 21 | 23 | £67

Belgravia | 15 Lowndes St., SW1X 9EY | 020-7235-5800 | www.zafferanorestaurant.com
"Put the glad rags on" for a visit to this "wonderful" Belgravia haunt with a "pricey" yet "sublime" Italian menu, "great service" and "lovely" setting; "busy with lots of people who want to be seen" as well as those celebrating "special occasions", it's no surprise there's a "great buzz" in the air.

Zaika *Indian*
25 | 23 | 22 | £51

Kensington | 1 Kensington High St., W8 5NP | 020-7795-6533 | www.zaika-restaurant.co.uk
"Surprising taste combinations" abound on the "amazing", "innovative" modern Indian menu offered at this "upscale" "treat", a "dark", "exotic setting" in a former Kensington bank, with a "wonderful bar" and "superb" staff who "treat you like royalty"; yes, "it comes at a price", but since it's "not your typical" "special-occasion" destination, most find it "worth every penny".

Zayna *Indian/Pakistani*
▽ 28 | 22 | 21 | £44

Marylebone | 25 New Quebec St., W1H 7SF | 020-7723-2229 | www.zaynarestaurant.co.uk
"Extraordinary", "beautiful" North Indian–Pakistani cuisine "always pleases", as do the "reasonable prices" at this Marylebone "neighbourhood gem" near Marble Arch; the "intimate" setting features wood carvings, a basement seating area (if you're "claustrophobic", "try to avoid") and staff who provide "service with a smile" even when it gets "crowded".

Ziani ● *Italian*
24 | 18 | 22 | £53

Chelsea | 45 Radnor Walk, SW3 4BP | 020-7351-5297 | www.ziani.co.uk
"Bring the kids, they're honoured guests" as far as "bantering", "energetic staff" are concerned at this "fast and furious" Chelsea Italian dispensing "excellent" Venetian victuals; on the downside, it's

somewhat "pricey", and the "cramped", "noisy" digs "fill up quickly", but otherwise "everything works" here, solidifying its status as a "dependable neighbourhood favourite".

Zizzi *Italian*

FOOD	DECOR	SERVICE	COST
18	16	18	£26

Fitzrovia | 33-41 Charlotte St., W1T 1RX | 020-7436-9440
Holborn | 8 Central St. Giles Plaza, WC2H 8LA | 020-7240-8447
Marylebone | 35-38 Paddington St., W1 4HQ | 020-7224-1450
Finchley | 202-208 Regent's Park Rd., N3 3HP | 020-8371-6777
Highgate | 1 Hampstead Ln., N6 4RS | 020-8347-0090
Greenwich | Greenwich Promenade | Cutty Sark Gardens, SE10 9HT | 020-8269-0808
Tower Bridge | 31 Shad Thames, SE1 2YR | 020-7367-6100
Tower Bridge | Plaza Level West | Tower Pl., EC3R 5BU | 020-7283-6918
Paddington | 17 Sheldon Sq., W2 6EP | 020-7286-4770
Notting Hill | 2 Notting Hill Gate, W11 3JE | 020-7243-2888
www.zizzi.co.uk
Additional locations throughout London

"Definitely family-friendly", this "relaxed" Italian chain is a "moderately priced" and "reliable" neighbourhood option with "decent" pizza, pastas and classics; "pleasant" service is another reason it's so "popular".

NEW Zoilo *Argentinean*

FOOD	DECOR	SERVICE	COST
-	-	-	M

Marylebone | 9 Duke St., W1U 3EG | 020-7486-9699 | www.zoilo.co.uk
This bare-brick Marylebone venture vends Argentinean cuisine that goes beyond steak on a moderately priced menu that changes monthly; on the ground floor there's a bar, while the lower floor features tables surrounding an open kitchen.

Zucca Ⓜ *Italian*

FOOD	DECOR	SERVICE	COST
27	19	23	£42

Tower Bridge | 184 Bermondsey St., SE1 3TQ | 020-7378-6809 | www.zuccalondon.com

"Superb ingredients" are transformed into "imaginative" Italian food, including "remarkable" antipasti, at this "culinary beacon in Bermondsey"; with "attentive" staff, "simple, elegant" surrounds and "reasonable prices", it's not hard to see why the "buzzing crowd" reserve "weeks in advance" to secure a spot here.

Zuma *Japanese*

FOOD	DECOR	SERVICE	COST
27	24	21	£76

Knightsbridge | 5 Raphael St., SW7 1DL | 020-7584-1010 | www.zumarestaurant.com

"Fantastic sushi" and other "excellent" dishes are presented with "understated flair" by mostly "attentive" staff at this "cool, trendy" Knightsbridge Japanese with a "busy vibe"; despite the "oh-so-expensive" bill, supporters say that it's a "must-try", even if only for the "excellent" cocktails at the "lively" bar.

INDEXES

LOCATION MAPS

Special Features

Listings cover the best in each category and include names, locations and Food ratings. Multi-location restaurants' features may vary by branch.

BREAKFAST

(See also Hotel Dining)

Aubaine | **multi.**	18
Automat | **W1S**	19
Baker & Spice | **multi.**	21
Balans | **multi.**	19
Botanist | **SW1W**	18
Breakfast Club | **multi.**	21
NEW Brompton Asian | **SW3**	-
Butlers Wharf | **SE1**	23
Café Boheme | **W1D**	18
Carluccio's | **multi.**	16
Cecconi's | **W1S**	23
Chiswell St. Dining | **EC1**	22
Cinnamon Club | **SW1P**	26
Coq d'Argent | **EC2R**	23
Delaunay | **WC2B**	21
NEW Dirty Burger | **NW5**	-
Dishoom | **multi.**	23
Empress | **E9**	23
Fifteen | **N1**	-
Fortnum's Fountain | **W1A**	20
Franco's | **SW1Y**	22
NEW Great British | **W1K**	-
Julie's | **W11**	18
La Brasserie | **SW3**	20
Ladurée | **SW1X**	24
La Fromagerie | **W1U**	24
Lantana | **W1T**	24
Lucky 7 | **W2**	18
Lutyens | **EC4**	23
Mercer | **EC2R**	22
NEW No. 11 Pimlico | **SW1W**	-
NOPI | **W1B**	25
1 Lombard Brass. | **EC3V**	21
Ottolenghi | **multi.**	26
Oxo Tower | **SE1**	22
Oxo Tower Brass. | **SE1**	23
Portrait | **WC2H**	22
Providores | **W1U**	25
Riding House | **W1W**	21

Rivington Grill | **EC2A**	23
Roast | **SE1**	25
Simpson's/Strand | **WC2R**	21
St. John Bread | **E1**	25
Tom's Deli | **W11**	24
Tom's Kitchen | **SW3**	23
Troubadour | **SW5**	20
202 | **W11**	19
Villandry | **W1W**	18
Wolseley | **W1J**	23
York/Albany | **NW1**	20

BRUNCH

Angelus | **W2**	25
Annie's | **multi.**	23
Aubaine | **multi.**	18
Automat | **W1S**	19
NEW Balthazar | **WC2B**	19
NEW Bistro Union | **SW4**	-
Blue Elephant | **SW6**	24
Bombay Brass. | **SW7**	23
Breakfast Club | **multi.**	21
Camino | **multi.**	22
Caravan | **EC1R**	24
Cecconi's | **W1S**	23
Christopher's | **WC2E**	-
NEW Colbert | **SW1W**	17
Delaunay | **WC2B**	21
NEW Duck & Waffle | **EC2N**	20
NEW Grain Store | **N1C**	-
Hélène Darroze | **W1K**	25
Hoxton Grill | **EC2A**	22
Indigo | **WC2B**	23
Joe Allen | **WC2E**	19
La Brasserie | **SW3**	20
Le Caprice | **SW1A**	24
L'Etranger | **SW7**	25
Lucky 7 | **W2**	18
Modern Pantry | **EC1V**	25
Motcombs | **SW1X**	21
NEW Naamyaa | **EC1V**	-

Pizarro	**SE1**	26	Brasserie Zédel	**W1F**	17
NEW Plum + Spilt Milk	**N1C**	–	**NEW** Buddha-Bar	**SW1X**	–
Portrait	**WC2H**	22	Caldesi	**W1U**	18
Providores	**W1U**	25	Cassis Bistro	**SW3**	22
Quadrato	**E14**	19	Cecconi's	**W1S**	23
Riding House	**W1W**	21	Chez Gérard	**EC2N**	–
NEW Royal Quarter	**SW1E**	–	China Tang	**W1K**	21
Sam's Brass.	**W4**	24	Christopher's	**WC2E**	–
Sophie's	**SW10**	22	Cigalon	**WC2A**	22
Tendido Cuatro	**SW6**	19	Cinnamon Club	**SW1P**	26
Tom's Deli	**W11**	24	Cinnamon Kitchen	**EC2M**	24
Tom's Kitchen	**SW3**	23	Clarke's	**W8**	25
202	**W11**	19	C London	**W1K**	23
Villandry	**W1W**	18	Club Gascon	**EC1A**	27
Wapping Food	**E1W**	19	Corrigan's Mayfair	**W1K**	25

BUSINESS DINING

			NEW Coya	**W1J**	24
Alain Ducasse	**W1K**	27	Criterion	**W1J**	21
Alba	**EC1Y**	22	Cut/45 Park Ln.	**W1K**	25
Al Duca	**SW1Y**	22	Dabbous	**W1T**	26
Alloro	**W1S**	22	Dean St.	**W1D**	22
Almeida	**N1**	22	Delaunay	**WC2B**	21
Alyn Williams	**W1S**	23	Dinner/Heston	**SW1X**	26
Amaranto	**W1J**	24	Dock Kitchen	**W10**	24
Amaya	**SW1X**	27	Dorchester	**W1K**	25
Angelus	**W2**	25	Downtown Mayfair	**W1S**	21
Apsleys	**SW1X**	26	**NEW** Duck & Waffle	**EC2N**	20
Arbutus	**W1D**	24	Elena's L'Etoile	**W1T**	20
Assaggi	**W2**	25	Espelette	**W1K**	25
Aurelia	**W1S**	22	Fino	**W1T**	26
Automat	**W1S**	19	**NEW** Fish Market	**EC2M**	–
Avenue	**SW1A**	20	French Table	**KT6**	28
Babbo	**W1S**	21	Galvin at Windows	**W1K**	25
Bank Westminster	**SW1E**	20	Galvin Bistrot	**W1U**	25
Bar Boulud	**SW1X**	24	Galvin Chapelle/Café	**E1**	26
Bellamy's	**W1J**	24	Gaucho	**multi.**	22
Belvedere	**W8**	21	Gauthier	**W1D**	28
Benares	**W1J**	25	Gilbert Scott	**NW1**	19
Bentley's	**W1B**	25	Gilgamesh	**NW1**	19
Bibendum	**SW3**	23	Glasshouse	**TW9**	26
Bistrot Bruno	**EC1M**	25	Goodman	**multi.**	27
Blakes	**SW7**	20	Goring Dining Room	**SW1**	25
Bonds	**EC2R**	22	Greenhouse	**W1J**	27
Boundary	**E2**	23	**NEW** Green Man	**WC2N**	21
Brasserie Blanc	**multi.**	18	Green's	**multi.**	21
NEW Brasserie Chavot	**W1S**	–	Hakkasan	**multi.**	26
			Hélène Darroze	**W1K**	25

Hereford Rd. | **W2**	24
Hibiscus | **W1S**	25
High Road Brass. | **W4**	22
Hix | **W1F**	22
Hix Mayfair | **W1S**	25
Hix Oyster | **EC1M**	24
NEW HKK | **EC2A**	-
Il Convivio | **SW1W**	23
Imperial City | **EC3V**	22
Ishbilia | **SW1X**	24
Ivy | **WC2H**	24
J. Sheekey | **WC2N**	26
J. Sheekey Oyster | **WC2N**	25
JW Steak | **W1K**	23
Kai Mayfair | **W1K**	25
Kazan | **SW1V**	24
Kenza | **EC2M**	24
Kitchen W8 | **W8**	25
Koffmann's | **SW1X**	27
La Bodega Negra | **W1D**	17
La Genova | **W1K**	23
Langan's Brass. | **W1J**	21
L'Anima | **EC2A**	25
La Petite Maison | **W1K**	26
L'Atelier/Robuchon | **WC2H**	28
La Trompette | **W4**	27
Launceston Pl. | **W8**	25
L'Autre Pied | **W1U**	25
Le Café Anglais | **W2**	22
Le Café/Marché | **EC1M**	25
Le Caprice | **SW1A**	24
Le Cercle | **SW1X**	24
Ledbury | **W11**	28
Le Gavroche | **W1K**	28
Le Manoir/Quat | **OX44**	27
Le Pont/Tour | **SE1**	23
L'Escargot | **W1D**	25
Les Deux | **WC2N**	19
L'Etranger | **SW7**	25
Lima | **W1T**	23
Locanda Locatelli | **W1H**	25
Lutyens | **EC4**	23
Marco Pierre White | **E1**	23
Marcus Wareing | **SW1X**	27
Massimo | **WC2N**	21
Matsuri | **SW1Y**	23

Maze | **W1K**	24
Maze Grill | **W1K**	23
Medlar | **SW10**	25
Memories/China | **multi.**	23
Mercer | **EC2R**	22
Mews/Mayfair | **W1S**	19
Michael Nadra | **W4**	25
Min Jiang | **W8**	25
Miyama | **W1**	23
Morgan M | **EC1A**	28
Mr. Chow | **SW1X**	22
Murano | **W1J**	26
NEW Naamyaa | **EC1V**	-
NEW New St. Grill | **EC2M**	-
1901 | **EC2M**	23
Nobu Berkeley | **W1J**	26
Nobu London | **W1K**	27
NOPI | **W1B**	25
Novikov | **W1J**	21
NEW Olivocarne | **SW1W**	-
Olivomare | **SW1W**	24
1 Lombard Brass. | **EC3V**	21
One-O-One | **SW1X**	22
Orrery | **W1U**	23
Oxo Tower | **SE1**	22
Palm | **SW1X**	22
Pantechnicon/Dining | **SW1X**	21
Paramount | **WC1A**	21
Paternoster Chop | **EC4M**	22
Petrus | **SW1X**	28
Pied à Terre | **W1T**	28
Plateau | **E14**	21
NEW Plum + Spilt Milk | **N1C**	-
Poissonnerie/l'Avenue | **SW3**	24
Pollen St. Social | **EC1V**	25
Polpo | **WC2E**	22
Portobello | **W11**	23
Princess Garden | **W1K**	24
Prism | **EC3V**	19
Providores | **W1U**	25
Quadrato | **E14**	19
Quaglino's | **SW1Y**	21
NEW Quality Chop | **EC1R**	-
Quilon | **SW1E**	-
Quirinale | **SW1P**	25
Quo Vadis | **W1D**	23

Rasoi Vineet | **SW3**	28		Zaika | **W8**	25
Red Fort | **W1D**	23		Zuma | **SW7**	27
Rest. Gordon Ramsay | **SW3**	28			

SPECIAL FEATURES

NEW Chooks | **N10**	—
Christopher's | **WC2E**	—
Chuen Cheng Ku | **W1D**	20
Churchill Arms | **W8**	21
Ciao Bella | **WC1N**	23
Cigala | **WC1N**	20
Cinnamon Club | **SW1P**	26
Citrus | **W1J**	21
Cocomaya | **multi.**	24
Cottons | **multi.**	22
Daphne's | **SW3**	22
Daylesford | **multi.**	21
Delaunay | **WC2B**	21
Duke of Sussex | **W4**	22
Eagle | **EC1R**	24
E&O | **W11**	23
Ed's Easy Diner | **W1D**	19
Elistano | **SW3**	21
Fifteen | **N1**	—
Fino | **W1T**	26
Fish | **SE1**	23
NEW Fish & Chip Shop | **N1**	—
Fortnum's Fountain | **W1A**	20
Frankie's | **SW3**	17
Frederick's | **N1**	23
Gaucho | **multi.**	22
Gay Hussar | **W1D**	21
Glasshouse | **TW9**	26
Gourmet Burger | **multi.**	18
Harwood Arms | **SW6**	27
Hawksmoor | **multi.**	26
Il Baretto | **W1U**	23
Il Portico | **W8**	19
Indigo | **WC2B**	23
Joe Allen | **WC2E**	19
Julie's | **W11**	18
Kensington Pl. | **W8**	20
Kettner's | **W1D**	22
La Brasserie | **SW3**	20
Ladurée | **multi.**	24
La Famiglia | **SW10**	20
La Fromagerie | **W1U**	24
La Porchetta | **multi.**	22
Le Café Anglais | **W2**	22
L'Etranger | **SW7**	25
Locanda Locatelli | **W1H**	25

Locanda Ottoemezzo | **W8**	25
Lucio | **SW3**	20
Lucky 7 | **W2**	18
Mango Tree | **SW1X**	20
Manicomio | **SW3**	18
Maroush | **multi.**	23
Masala Zone | **multi.**	22
Mediterraneo | **W11**	23
Mela | **WC2H**	22
Min Jiang | **W8**	25
Mishkin's | **WC2B**	20
Nautilus Fish | **NW6**	26
Noura | **multi.**	22
Oliveto | **SW1W**	24
Opera Tavern | **WC2B**	25
Orso | **WC2E**	21
Ottolenghi | **multi.**	26
Oxo Tower | **SE1**	22
Oxo Tower Brass. | **SE1**	23
Patara | **multi.**	24
Petersham | **TW10**	23
Phoenix Palace | **NW1**	23
Pitt Cue Co. | **W1F**	28
Pizza East | **multi.**	21
Pizza Express | **SW10**	16
Plateau | **E14**	21
Popeseye | **multi.**	24
Porters English | **WC2E**	19
Portobello | **W11**	23
Princi London | **W1F**	24
Quadrato | **E14**	19
Quaglino's | **SW1Y**	21
Randall/Aubin | **W1F**	25
Rasa | **multi.**	24
Real Greek | **SE1**	20
Red Pepper | **W9**	21
Reubens | **W1U**	20
Ritz | **W1J**	24
River Café | **W6**	27
Royal China | **multi.**	23
Royal China Club | **W1U**	25
Rules | **WC2E**	24
Sale e Pepe | **SW1X**	24
Sam's Brass. | **W4**	24
San Lorenzo | **SW3**	21
Santini | **SW1W**	20

Smollensky's | **WC2R**	18
Sofra | **multi.**	21
Sophie's | **SW10**	22
Strada | **multi.**	17
Tas | **multi.**	22
Tom's Deli | **W11**	24
Tom's Kitchen | **SW3**	23
Truc Vert | **W1K**	19
202 | **W11**	19
Villandry | **W1W**	18
Wagamama | **multi.**	17
Wahaca | **multi.**	22
Warrington | **W9**	19
Wolseley | **W1J**	23
Yoshino | **W1J**	24
Zafferano | **SW1X**	24
Ziani | **SW3**	24
Zizzi | **multi.**	18
Zuma | **SW7**	27

COCKTAIL SPECIALISTS

Bob Bob Ricard | **W1F**	22
Brumus | **SW1Y**	22
Ceviche | **W1D**	27
Dabbous | **W1T**	26
Hakkasan | **multi.**	26
Hawksmoor | **multi.**	26
La Bodega Negra | **W1D**	17
Las Iguanas | **multi.**	21
MEATliquor | **W1G**	23
Mint Leaf | **multi.**	22
Mishkin's | **WC2B**	20
Ping Pong | **multi.**	17
Pitt Cue Co. | **W1F**	28
Portal | **EC1M**	27
Quo Vadis | **W1D**	23
Ritz | **W1J**	24
Roka | **multi.**	26
Rules | **WC2E**	24
Skylon | **SE1**	20
Spuntino | **W1D**	23
NEW SushiSamba | **EC2N**	21
Tsunami | **multi.**	23
Village East | **SE1**	23
Zuma | **SW7**	27

DELIVERY/ TAKEAWAY

(D=delivery, T=takeaway)

Alounak | D, T | **multi.**	23
Al Waha | D | **W2**	22
Baker & Spice | T | **multi.**	21
Beirut Express | T | **multi.**	23
Beiteddine | D, T | **SW1X**	26
Bento | T | **NW1**	23
Big Easy | T | **SW3**	21
Blue Elephant | D, T | **SW6**	24
Café Spice | D, T | **E1**	25
Cantina Laredo | T | **WC2H**	23
Carluccio's | T | **multi.**	16
Chilango | T | **multi.**	21
Chor Bizarre | T | **W1S**	25
Chuen Cheng Ku | T | **W1D**	20
Churchill Arms | T | **W8**	21
Crazy Homies | T | **W2**	18
Daylesford | T | **multi.**	21
Defune | T | **W1U**	25
Delaunay | T | **WC2B**	21
Delfino | T | **W1K**	20
Ed's Easy Diner | T | **W1D**	19
Esarn Kheaw | T | **W12**	23
Fairuz | D, T | **W1U**	22
Feng Sushi | D, T | **multi.**	19
Fish | T | **SE1**	23
NEW Fish & Chip Shop | T | **N1**	–
French/Grace | T | **SW9**	–
Gaucho | T | **multi.**	22
Golden Dragon | T | **W1D**	23
Good Earth | D | **multi.**	25
Gopal's | T | **W1D**	19
Halepi | T | **W2**	24
Harbour City | T | **W1D**	19
Honey & Co | T | **W1T**	–
Ikeda | T | **W1K**	26
Imperial City | T | **EC3V**	22
Ishbilia | D, T | **SW1X**	24
Jin Kichi | T | **NW3**	27
José | T | **SE1**	28
Khan's | T | **W2**	20
Kiku | T | **W1J**	24
Koi | D, T | **W8**	21
Kulu Kulu | T | **multi.**	22

La Fromagerie | D, T | **W1U**	24
Lahore Kebab | T | **E1**	25
La Porchetta | T | **multi.**	22
La Porte/Indes | T | **W1H**	22
Leon | T | **multi.**	20
Lucky 7 | T | **W2**	18
Ma Goa | T | **SW15**	22
Mandalay | T | **W2**	24
Mango Tree | T | **SW1X**	20
Manicomio | T | **multi.**	18
Mao Tai | T | **SW6**	25
Masala Zone | T | **multi.**	22
Matsuri | T | **SW1Y**	23
MEATmarket | T | **WC2E**	23
Mela | T | **WC2H**	22
Memories/China | T | **multi.**	23
Nautilus Fish | T | **NW6**	26
Noor Jahan | T | **multi.**	23
North Sea | T | **WC1H**	24
Noura | D, T | **multi.**	22
Original Lahore | T | **NW4**	23
Ottolenghi | T | **multi.**	26
Özer | T | **W1B**	21
Patara | T | **multi.**	24
Pizarro | T | **SE1**	26
Pizza Express | T | **SW10**	16
Princi London | T | **W1F**	24
Rasa | T | **multi.**	24
Red Pepper | T | **W9**	21
Reubens | T | **W1U**	20
Rock & Sole | T | **WC2H**	24
Royal China | T | **multi.**	23
Royal China Club | T | **W1U**	25
NEW Royal Quarter | T | **SW1E**	-
Salloos | T | **SW1X**	24
Singapore Gdn. | D, T | **NW6**	22
Solly's | T | **NW11**	20
Star of India | T | **SW5**	26
Stingray/Stringray | T | **multi.**	23
Tamarind | D, T | **W1J**	25
Tas | D, T | **multi.**	22
Thai Sq. | T | **multi.**	19
Tom's Deli | T | **W11**	24
Truc Vert | D, T | **W1K**	19
Tsunami | T | **multi.**	23
Villandry | T | **W1W**	18

Yalla Yalla | T | **multi.**	24
Yoshino | T | **W1J**	24

DINING ALONE

(Other than hotels and places with counter service)

Amaya | **SW1X**	27
Aubaine | **multi.**	18
Baker & Spice | **multi.**	21
NEW Barsito | **SW4**	-
NEW Bar Tozino | **SE1**	-
NEW Bo London | **W1S**	-
NEW Bone Daddies | **W1F**	21
Books/Cooks | **W11**	25
NEW BRGR.CO | **W1F**	-
NEW Bubbledogs | **W1T**	18
Busaba Eathai | **multi.**	23
Carluccio's | **multi.**	16
Chuen Cheng Ku | **W1D**	20
Comptoir Gascon | **EC1M**	25
Comptoir Libanais | **multi.**	20
Daylesford | **multi.**	21
NEW Dirty Burger | **NW5**	-
Ed's Easy Diner | **multi.**	19
Fino | **W1T**	26
NEW Five Guys | **WC2E**	-
Fortnum's Fountain | **W1A**	20
Gail's | **multi.**	22
NEW Green Man | **WC2N**	21
Hakkasan | **multi.**	26
NEW Kitchen Table | **W1T**	-
Ladurée | **multi.**	24
La Fromagerie | **W1U**	24
Le Colombier | **SW3**	23
Leon | **multi.**	20
Manicomio | **SW3**	18
Matsuri | **SW1Y**	23
NEW MEATmission | **N1**	-
Mon Plaisir | **WC2H**	21
New Culture Rev. | **multi.**	20
NEW New St. Grill | **EC2M**	-
Noura | **multi.**	22
Ottolenghi | **multi.**	26
NEW Patty & Bun | **W1U**	21
Ping Pong | **multi.**	17
Polpo | **W1F**	22
Porters English | **WC2E**	19

SPECIAL FEATURES

William Drabble
Seven Park | **SW1A** 24

Alain Ducasse
Alain Ducasse | **W1K** 27

Nobu Matsuhisa & Mark Edwards
Nobu Berkeley | **W1J** 26
Nobu London | **W1K** 27

Pierre Gagnaire
Sketch/Lecture | **W1S** 22

Chris & Jeff Galvin
Galvin at Windows | **W1K** 25
Galvin Bistrot | **W1U** 25
Galvin Chapelle/Café | **E1** 26

Alexis Gauthier
Gauthier | **W1D** 28

Peter Gordon
Providores | **W1U** 25

Bill Granger
Granger & Co. | **W11** 19

Angela Hartnett
Murano | **W1J** 26
Whitechapel | **E1** 18

Fergus Henderson
St. John | **EC1M** 26
St. John Bread | **E1** 25

Mark Hix
Hix | **W1F** 22
Hix Mayfair | **W1S** 25
Hix Oyster | **EC1M** 24
Tramshed | **EC2A** 20

Philip Howard
Kitchen W8 | **W8** 25
Square | **W1J** 28

Atul Kochhar
Benares | **W1J** 25

Pierre Koffmann
Koffmann's | **SW1X** 27

Rowley Leigh
Le Café Anglais | **W2** 22

Alvin Leung
NEW Bo London | **W1S** -

Giorgio Locatelli
Locanda Locatelli | **W1H** 25

Bruno Loubet
Bistrot Bruno | **EC1M** 25
NEW Grain Store | **N1C** -

Thomasina Miers
Wahaca | **multi.** 22

Jamie Oliver
Barbecoa | **EC4M** 23
Fifteen | **N1** -
Jamie's Italian | **multi.** 20
Union Jacks | **multi.** 18

Yotam Ottolenghi
NOPI | **W1B** 25
Ottolenghi | **multi.** 26

Nathan Outlaw
NEW Outlaw's | **SW3** -

Bruce Poole
Chez Bruce | **SW17** 28

Wolfgang Puck
Cut/45 Park Ln. | **W1K** 25

Gordon Ramsay
Bread St. Kitchen | **EC4M** 20
Foxtrot Oscar | **SW3** 19
Maze | **W1K** 24
Maze Grill | **W1K** 23
Petrus | **SW1X** 28
Rest. Gordon Ramsay | **SW3** 28
Savoy Grill | **WC2** 24
York/Albany | **NW1** 20

Theo Randall
Theo Randall | **W1J** 25

Gary Rhodes
Rhodes 24 | **EC2N** 25

Joël Robuchon
L'Atelier/Robuchon | **WC2H** 28

Ruth Rogers
River Café | **W6** 27

Albert Roux
Waterside Inn | **SL6** 29

Michel Roux Jr
Le Gavroche | **W1K** 28
Roux/Parliament | **SW1P** 24
Roux/Landau | **W1** 26

Vivek Singh
Cinnamon Club | **SW1P** 26
Cinnamon Kitchen | **EC2M** 24

Cyrus Todiwala
  Café Spice | **E1**   25

John Torode
  Smiths/Smithfield | **EC1M**   21

Jean-Georges Vongerichten
  Spice Mkt. | **W1**   22

Marcus Wareing
  Gilbert Scott | **NW1**   19
  Marcus Wareing | **SW1X**   27

Marco Pierre White
  Frankie's | **multi.**   17
  Marco Pierre White | **E1**   23
  Wheeler's | **SW1A**   21

FIREPLACES

Abbeville | **SW4**   23
Admiral Codrington | **SW3**   19
Al Hamra | **W1J**   23
Amaranto | **W1J**   24
Anglesea Arms | **W6**   21
Babylon | **W8**   22
Bam-Bou | **W1T**   22
NEW Bird/Smithfield | **EC1A**   -
Café Med | **NW8**   19
Cambio/Tercio | **SW5**   24
Cheyne Walk | **SW3**   20
Churchill Arms | **W8**   21
Clos Maggiore | **WC2E**   25
Cottons | **NW1**   22
Criterion | **W1J**   21
Daphne's | **SW3**   22
Espelette | **W1K**   25
Gazette | **SW12**   20
Gopal's | **W1D**   19
Goring Dining Room | **SW1**   25
Grazing Goat | **W1**   20
Greig's | **W1J**   21
Gun | **E14**   23
Harwood Arms | **SW6**   27
Hix Mayfair | **W1S**   25
Hoxton Grill | **EC2A**   22
Il Baretto | **W1U**   23
Julie's | **W11**   18
Le Cercle | **SW1X**   24
Lemonia | **NW1**   21
L'Escargot | **W1D**   25
NEW Oblix | **SE1**   -

Old Bull/Bush | **NW3**   18
Palmerston | **SE22**   23
Pantechnicon/Dining | **SW1X**   21
Pig's Ear | **SW3**   21
Princess Victoria | **W12**   25
Rules | **WC2E**   24
Sands End | **SW6**   22
Thomas Cubitt | **SW1W**   21
Vapiano | **W1W**   23
Waterside Inn | **SL6**   29
Wells | **NW3**   22

GROUP DINING

Aqua Nueva | **W1B**   21
Babylon | **W8**   22
Baltic | **SE1**   23
Belgo | **multi.**   21
Blue Elephant | **SW6**   24
Bumpkin | **multi.**   19
Eight Over Eight | **SW3**   23
Il Bordello | **E1W**   25
Joe Allen | **WC2E**   19
Kenza | **EC2M**   24
Las Iguanas | **multi.**   21
Le Mercury | **N1**   20
Lemonia | **NW1**   21
Les Deux | **WC2N**   19
Little Bay | **multi.**   21
Lutyens | **EC4**   23
Made in Italy | **multi.**   19
Mao Tai | **SW6**   25
Masala Zone | **multi.**   22
Oxo Tower Brass. | **SE1**   23
Ping Pong | **multi.**   17
Pizza East | **multi.**   21
Rodizio Rico | **multi.**   20
Sale e Pepe | **SW1X**   24
Sofra | **multi.**   21
Tas | **multi.**   22

HISTORIC PLACES

(Year opened; * building)
1550 | Fat Duck* | **SL6**   28
1677 | Green's* | **SW1Y**   21
1690 | Giovanni's* | **WC2N**   23
1690 | Wells* | **NW3**   22
1700 | Bellamy's* | **W1J**   24

1721	Old Bull/Bush	**NW3**	18
1740	Bingham*	**TW10**	24
1741	L'Escargot*	**W1D**	25
1742	Princess of Shoreditch*	**EC2A**	20
1742	Wilton's	**SW1Y**	26
1746	Bleeding Heart*	**EC1N**	23
1750	Food/Thought*	**WC2H**	24
1750	Gauthier*	**W1D**	28
1750	Gun*	**E14**	23
1755	Randall/Aubin*	**W1F**	25
1762	Bull & Last*	**NW5**	24
1776	Tom's Kitchen*	**WC2R**	23
1779	Sketch/Gallery*	**W1S**	21
1779	Sketch/Lecture*	**W1S**	22
1780	Andrew Edmunds*	**W1F**	24
1790	Carluccio's*	**EC1A**	16
1790	Rowley's*	**SW1Y**	23
1798	Don*	**EC4N**	23
1798	Rules*	**WC2E**	24
1800	Anglesea Arms*	**W6**	21
1800	Belvedere*	**W8**	21
1800	Churchill Arms*	**W8**	21
1800	Tokyo Diner*	**WC2H**	22
1810	Angelus*	**W2**	25
1810	Pig's Ear*	**SW3**	21
1820	York/Albany*	**NW1**	20
1828	Simpson's/Strand*	**WC2R**	21
1830	Mosimann's*	**SW1X**	26
1834	Albion*	**N1**	22
1837	Hix Mayfair*	**W1S**	25
1846	Les Trois Garçons*	**E1**	23
1850	Brumus*	**SW1Y**	22
1851	Flemings Grill*	**W1J**	21
1851	Scott's	**W1K**	26
1855	Baltic*	**SE1**	23
1855	Bonds*	**EC2R**	22
1857	Warrington*	**W9**	19
1865	Petersham*	**TW10**	23
1867	Kettner's*	**W1D**	22
1867	Pantechnicon/Dining*	**SW1X**	21
1871	Rock & Sole	**WC2H**	24
1873	Gilbert Scott*	**NW1**	19
1874	Criterion	**W1J**	21

1879	Opera Tavern*	**WC2B**	25
1880	Bombay Brass.*	**SW7**	23
1881	Duke of Cambridge*	**N1**	22
1886	Tuttons*	**WC2B**	20
1889	Savoy Grill	**WC2**	24
1889	Sweetings	**EC4N**	23
1890	Bradley's*	**NW3**	22
1890	La Fromagerie*	**W1U**	24
1890	Maggie Jones's*	**W8**	21
1890	R.S.J.*	**SE1**	22
1890	Wapping Food*	**E1W**	19
1896	Elena's L'Etoile*	**W1T**	20
1896	J. Sheekey*	**WC2N**	26
1897	Espelette*	**W1K**	25
1897	Hélène Darroze*	**W1K**	25
1898	Duke of Sussex*	**W4**	22
1900	Annie's*	**W4**	23
1900	Artigiano*	**NW3**	22
1900	Balans*	**SW5**	19
1900	Frontline*	**W2**	23
1900	Goodman*	**W1S**	27
1900	Julie's*	**W11**	18
1900	La Famiglia*	**SW10**	20
1900	Langan's Brass.*	**W1J**	21
1900	St. John Bread*	**E1**	25
1905	Almeida*	**N1**	22
1906	Ritz*	**W1J**	24
1910	Bocca/Gelupo*	**W1D**	25
1910	Goring Dining Room*	**SW1**	25
1910	Viajante*	**E2**	26
1911	Bibendum*	**SW3**	23
1911	Bibendum Oyster*	**SW3**	23
1914	Golden Hind	**W1U**	24
1920	Orso*	**WC2E**	21
1920	Tamarind*	**W1J**	25
1921	Delaunay*	**WC2B**	21
1921	Wolseley*	**W1J**	23
1923	Bluebird*	**SW3**	20
1924	Prism*	**EC3V**	19
1926	Quo Vadis	**W1D**	23
1926	Veeraswamy	**W1B**	24
1929	Quaglino's	**SW1Y**	21
1930	Bistrotheque*	**E2**	21
1930	Haché*	**NW1**	23
1930	Sale e Pepe*	**SW1X**	24
1931	Dorchester	**W1K**	25

1933 | Babylon* | **W8**	22
1939 | Geales | **W8**	20
1939 | Lutyens* | **EC4**	23
1942 | Mon Plaisir | **WC2H**	21
1946 | Le Caprice | **SW1A**	24
1946 | Regency Café | **SW1P**	23
1947 | Punjab | **WC2H**	23
1950 | Fortnum's Fountain | **W1A**	20
1950 | Greig's | **W1J**	21
1952 | Star of India | **SW5**	26
1953 | Gay Hussar | **W1D**	21
1953 | Guinea Grill | **W1J**	24
1954 | Troubadour | **SW5**	20
1955 | Brompton B&G* | **SW3**	20
1956 | Pescatori | **W1T**	22
1960 | Archipelago* | **W1T**	22
1961 | Rib Room | **SW1X**	24
1962 | La Poule au Pot | **SW1W**	22

HOTEL DINING

Andaz Liverpool St.	
1901 | **EC2M**	23
Berkeley	
Koffmann's | **SW1X**	27
Marcus Wareing | **SW1X**	27
Bingham Hotel	
Bingham | **TW10**	24
Blakes Hotel	
Blakes | **SW7**	20
Brown's Hotel	
Hix Mayfair | **W1S**	25
Church Street Hotel	
Angels/Gypsies | **SE5**	25
Connaught	
Espelette | **W1K**	25
Hélène Darroze | **W1K**	25
Corinthia Hotel London	
Massimo | **WC2N**	21
Crowne Plaza St. James Hotel	
Quilon | **SW1E**	–
Dean Street Townhse.	
Dean St. | **W1D**	22
Dorchester	
Alain Ducasse | **W1K**	27
China Tang | **W1K**	21
Dorchester | **W1K**	25

Flemings Hotel	
Flemings Grill | **W1J**	21
45 Park Ln.	
Cut/45 Park Ln. | **W1K**	25
Four Seasons Canary Wharf	
Quadrato | **E14**	19
Four Seasons/Park Ln.	
Amaranto | **W1J**	24
Goring Hotel	
Goring Dining Room | **SW1**	25
Grange Hotel St. Paul	
Benihana | **EC4V**	20
Great Northern Hotel	
NEW Plum + Spilt Milk | **N1C**	–
Grosvenor Hse.	
Corrigan's Mayfair | **W1K**	25
JW Steak | **W1K**	23
Haymarket Hotel	
Brumus | **SW1Y**	22
Holiday Inn King's Cross	
Rasa | **WC1X**	24
Hoxton Hotel	
Hoxton Grill | **EC2A**	22
Hyatt Regency - The Churchill	
Locanda Locatelli | **W1H**	25
InterContinental Park Ln.	
Theo Randall | **W1J**	25
Jumeirah Carlton Tower Hotel	
Rib Room | **SW1X**	24
Lanesborough	
Apsleys | **SW1X**	26
Langham Hotel	
Roux/Landau | **W1**	26
Le Manoir aux Quat'Saisons Hotel	
Le Manoir/Quat | **OX44**	27
London Hilton on Park Ln.	
Galvin at Windows | **W1K**	25
Mandarin Oriental Hyde Park	
Bar Boulud | **SW1X**	24
Dinner/Heston | **SW1X**	26
Marriott Grosvenor Sq.	
Maze | **W1K**	24
Maze Grill | **W1K**	23
Marylebone Hotel	
108 Marylebone | **W1U**	21

Me London Hotel
   NEW STK | **WC2R** ⌐|

Metropolitan Hotel
   Nobu London | **W1K** 27⌐

Myhotel Bloomsbury
   NEW Gail's Kitchen | **WC1B** ⌐|

No. 11 Cadogan Gdns.
   NEW Tartufo | **SW3** ⌐|

One Aldwych Hotel
   Indigo | **WC2B** 23⌐

One Leicester Street Hotel
   NEW 1 Leicester St. | **WC2H** ⌐|

Orange
   Orange | **SW1W** 22⌐

Park Lane Hotel
   Citrus | **W1J** 21⌐

Petersham Hotel
   Petersham | **TW10** 23⌐

Public House & Hotel
   Grazing Goat | **W1** 20⌐

Ritz
   Ritz | **W1J** 24⌐

Royal Garden Hotel
   Min Jiang | **W8** 25⌐

Savoy Hotel
   NEW Kaspar's | **WC2R** ⌐|
   Savoy Grill | **WC2** 24⌐

Sheraton Park Tower
   One-O-One | **SW1X** 22⌐

Sofitel St. James
   Balcon | **SW1Y** 23⌐

South Place Hotel
   NEW Angler | **EC2M** ⌐|

St. James's Hotel
   Seven Park | **SW1A** 24⌐

St. Martins Lane Hotel
   Asia de Cuba | **WC2N** 23⌐

St. Pancras Renaissance Hotel
   Gilbert Scott | **NW1** 19⌐

Threadneedles Hotel
   Bonds | **EC2R** 22⌐

Town Hall Hotel
   Corner Room | **E2** 29⌐
   Viajante | **E2** 26⌐

Waterside Inn
   Waterside Inn | **SL6** 29⌐

Westbury Hotel
   Alyn Williams | **W1S** 23⌐

W London Leicester Sq.
   Spice Mkt. | **W1** 22⌐

Zetter
   Bistrot Bruno | **EC1M** 25⌐

LATE DINING

(Weekday closing hour)

Al Hamra | 12 AM | **W1J** 23⌐

Alounak | varies | **multi.** 23⌐

Asia de Cuba | varies | **WC2N** 23⌐

Automat | 1 AM | **W1S** 19⌐

Avenue | 1 AM | **SW1A** 20⌐

Balans | varies | **multi.** 19⌐

Bam-Bou | 1 AM | **W1T** 22⌐

Beirut Express | 12 AM, 2 AM | **multi.** 23⌐

Beiteddine | 12 AM | **SW1X** 26⌐

Belgo | 11:30 PM | **SW4** 21⌐

NEW Bird/Smithfield | varies | **EC1A** ⌐|

Blakes | 12 AM | **SW7** 20⌐

Boisdale | 12 AM | **E14** 22⌐

Brasserie Blanc | 12 AM | **SE1** 18⌐

Brasserie Zédel | 12 AM | **W1F** 17⌐

NEW Buddha-Bar | varies | **SW1X** ⌐|

Bumpkin | 12 AM | **multi.** 19⌐

Buona Sera | 12 AM | **multi.** 20⌐

Café Boheme | 2:30 AM | **W1D** 18⌐

Cafe Pacifico | 12 AM | **WC2H** 20⌐

NEW Casa Negra | varies | **EC2A** ⌐|

Cecconi's | 1 AM | **W1S** 23⌐

Ceviche | 12 AM | **W1D** 27⌐

Charlotte's | 12 AM | **multi.** 25⌐

NEW Chicken Shop | 12 AM | **NW5** ⌐|

Chiswell St. Dining | varies | **EC1** 22⌐

Chuen Cheng Ku | 12 AM | **W1D** 20⌐

Cinnamon Kitchen | 12 AM | **EC2M** 24⌐

Circus | varies | **WC2H** 18⌐

NEW Colbert | 1 AM | **SW1W** 17⌐

NEW Coya | 1 AM | **W1J** 24⌐

Diner | 12 AM | **multi.** 18⌐

NEW Dirty Burger | varies | **NW5** ⌐|

NEW Duck & Waffle | 24 hrs. | EC2N	20
Efes | 12 AM | W1W	22
805 | varies | SE15	24
NEW Electric Diner | varies | W11	—
Fino | 12 AM | W1T	26
Four Seasons | varies | W1D	23
Frederick's | 12 AM | N1	23
Fulham/Kensington Wine | 12 AM | SW6	18
Gaby's | 12 AM | WC2H	23
Gaucho | 12 AM | W1B	22
Gilgamesh | varies | NW1	19
Greig's | 12 AM | W1J	21
Hakkasan | varies | W1J	26
Halepi | 12 AM | W2	24
Hawksmoor | varies | W1J	26
Haz | 12 AM | E1	23
Hoxton Grill | 12 AM | EC2A	22
Hoxton Sq. | varies | N1	16
Imperial China | 12 AM | WC2H	21
Inamo | 12 AM | SW1Y	19
Ishbilia | 12 AM | SW1X	24
Ishtar | 12 AM | W1U	20
Ivy | 12 AM | WC2H	24
Jamie's Italian | varies | E20	20
Joe Allen | 12:45 AM | WC2E	19
J. Sheekey | 12 AM | WC2N	26
J. Sheekey Oyster | 12 AM | WC2N	25
La Bodega Negra | 1 AM | W1D	17
Lahore Kebab | varies | E1	25
La Porchetta | 12 AM | N10	22
Le Caprice | 12 AM | SW1A	24
Le Deuxième | 12 AM | WC2E	22
Le Mercury | 1 AM | N1	20
Little Bay | 12 AM | multi.	21
Little Italy | 4 AM | W1D	21
Malabar | 12 AM | W8	20
Mangal Ocakbasi | 12 AM | E8	—
Maroush | varies | multi.	23
NEW MASH | 1 AM | W1F	25
Maxwell's | 12 AM | WC2E	19
MEATliquor | varies | W1G	23
NEW MEATmission | 12 AM | N1	—
Mint Leaf | varies | SW1Y	22

Mr. Chow | 12 AM | SW1X	22
Mr. Kong | 2:45 AM | WC2H	21
New Mayflower | 4 AM | W1D	24
New World | 12 AM | W1D	20
Nobu Berkeley | varies | W1J	26
NEW No. 11 Pimlico | 12 AM | SW1W	—
NEW Oblix | 12 AM | SE1	—
Opera Tavern | 12 AM | WC2B	25
Original Lahore | varies | multi.	23
Orso | 12 AM | WC2E	21
Paradise/Kensal | varies | W10	23
Paramount | varies | WC1A	21
Ping Pong | varies | multi.	17
Pix Pintxos | 12 AM | WC2H	17
Pizza East | varies | multi.	21
NEW Plum + Spilt Milk | 12 AM | N1C	—
Poppies Fish | 12 AM | NW1	22
Princi London | 12 AM | W1F	24
Rodizio Rico | 12 AM | multi.	20
Santa Maria | 12 AM | SW8	26
Sketch/Parlour | 2 AM | W1S	21
Sophie's | 12 AM | WC2E	22
Souk | 12 AM | WC2H	21
Spuntino | 12 AM | W1D	23
NEW STK | 1 AM | WC2R	—
Sumosan | 12 AM | W1S	22
NEW SushiSamba | varies | EC2N	21
Texture | 12 AM | W1H	26
Tokyo Diner | 12 AM | WC2H	22
Tsunami | varies | SW4	23
Union Café | 12 AM | W1U	21
Vapiano | varies | multi.	23
Viajante | 1 AM | E2	26
Wolseley | 12 AM | W1J	23
Wright Brothers | 12 AM | W1	24
Yauatcha | 12 AM | W1F	27

NEWCOMERS

Acciuga | W8	—
Ametsa | SW1X	—
Angler | EC2M	—
Aqua Shard | SE1	—
A Wong | SW1V	—
Balthazar | WC2B	19
Barsito | SW4	—

Bar Tozino | **SE1**	_-_
Beagle | **E2**	_-_
Beard To Tail | **EC2A**	_-_
Bird/Smithfield | **EC1A**	_-_
Bistro Union | **SW4**	_-_
Bo London | **W1S**	_-_
Bone Daddies | **W1F**	_21_
Brasserie Chavot | **W1S**	_-_
BRGR.CO | **W1F**	_-_
Brompton Asian | **SW3**	_-_
Bubbledogs | **W1T**	_18_
Buddha-Bar | **SW1X**	_-_
Casa Negra | **EC2A**	_-_
Chabrot Bistrot | **EC1A**	_-_
Chicken Shop | **NW5**	_-_
Chooks | **N10**	_-_
Clockjack Oven | **W1D**	_-_
Clove Club | **EC2A**	_-_
Colbert | **SW1W**	_17_
Coya | **W1J**	_24_
Dirty Burger | **NW5**	_-_
Duck & Waffle | **EC2N**	_20_
Electric Diner | **W11**	_-_
Fish & Chip Shop | **N1**	_-_
Fish Market | **EC2M**	_-_
Five Guys | **WC2E**	_-_
Flat Iron | **W1**	_-_
Gail's Kitchen | **WC1B**	_-_
Grain Store | **N1C**	_-_
Great British | **W1K**	_-_
Greenberry Café | **NW1**	_-_
Green Man | **WC2N**	_21_
Happenstance | **EC4M**	_-_
HKK | **EC2A**	_-_
Hutong | **SE1**	_-_
Joe's Southern | **WC2E**	_-_
Kaspar's | **WC2R**	_-_
Kitchen Table | **W1T**	_-_
Lardo | **E8**	_-_
Little Social | **W1S**	_-_
Lockhart | **W1H**	_-_
MASH | **W1F**	_25_
MEATmission | **N1**	_-_
Naamyaa | **EC1V**	_-_
Newman St. | **W1T**	_-_
New St. Grill | **EC2M**	_-_
No. 11 Pimlico | **SW1W**	_-_
Oblix | **SE1**	_-_
Olivocarne | **SW1W**	_-_
1 Leicester St. | **WC2H**	_-_
Outlaw's | **SW3**	_-_
Patty & Bun | **W1U**	_21_
Plum + Spilt Milk | **N1C**	_-_
Quality Chop | **EC1R**	_-_
Rosita/Sherry Bar | **SW11**	_-_
Royal Quarter | **SW1E**	_-_
Salon | **SW9**	_-_
Shake Shack | **WC2E**	_-_
Shed | **W8**	_-_
Shiori | **W2**	_-_
Social Eating Hse. | **W1F**	_-_
STK | **WC2R**	_-_
Story | **SE1**	_-_
SushiSamba | **EC2N**	_21_
Tartufo | **SW3**	_-_
Upstairs/Ten Bells | **E1**	_-_
Wishbone | **SW9**	_-_
Zoilo | **W1U**	_-_

NOTABLE WINE LISTS

Alain Ducasse | **W1K**	_27_
Alloro | **W1S**	_22_
Alyn Williams | **W1S**	_23_
Amaranto | **W1J**	_24_
Andrew Edmunds | **W1F**	_24_
Angelus | **W2**	_25_
NEW Angler | **EC2M**	_-_
Apsleys | **SW1X**	_26_
Arbutus | **W1D**	_24_
Aurelia | **W1S**	_22_
Babbo | **W1S**	_21_
Bar Boulud | **SW1X**	_24_
Bellamy's | **W1J**	_24_
Belvedere | **W8**	_21_
Bibendum | **SW3**	_23_
Cambio/Tercio | **SW5**	_24_
Cantina Vino. | **SE1**	_19_
Cassis Bistro | **SW3**	_22_
Chez Bruce | **SW17**	_28_
Christopher's | **WC2E**	_-_
Chutney Mary | **SW10**	_25_
Cigalon | **WC2A**	_22_

Cinnamon Club | **SW1P**	26
Clarke's | **W8**	25
C London | **W1K**	23
Club Gascon | **EC1A**	27
Coq d'Argent | **EC2R**	23
Cut/45 Park Ln. | **W1K**	25
Dinner/Heston | **SW1X**	26
Don | **EC4N**	23
Dorchester | **W1K**	25
Enoteca Turi | **SW15**	25
Fat Duck | **SL6**	28
Fino | **W1T**	26
French Table | **KT6**	28
Fulham/Kensington Wine | **multi.**	18
Galvin Chapelle/Café | **E1**	26
Gaucho | **multi.**	22
Gauthier | **W1D**	28
Glasshouse | **TW9**	26
Greenhouse | **W1J**	27
NEW Green Man | **WC2N**	21
Hakkasan | **multi.**	26
Hélène Darroze | **W1K**	25
Hibiscus | **W1S**	25
NEW HKK | **EC2A**	-
Il Baretto | **W1U**	23
Il Convivio | **SW1W**	23
Koffmann's | **SW1X**	27
Latium | **W1T**	25
La Trompette | **W4**	27
Le Cercle | **SW1X**	24
Ledbury | **W11**	28
Le Gavroche | **W1K**	28
Le Manoir/Quat | **OX44**	27
Le Pont/Tour | **SE1**	23
L'Escargot | **W1D**	25
L'Etranger | **SW7**	25
Locanda Locatelli | **W1H**	25
Lutyens | **EC4**	23
Magdalen | **SE1**	25
Ma Goa | **SW15**	22
Marcus Wareing | **SW1X**	27
NEW MASH | **W1F**	25
Maze | **W1K**	24
Michael Nadra | **W4**	25
Morgan M | **EC1A**	28
Murano | **W1J**	26
NEW New St. Grill | **EC2M**	-
Novikov | **W1J**	21
NEW Oblix | **SE1**	-
Odette's | **NW1**	25
1 Lombard St. | **EC3V**	23
Orrery | **W1U**	23
Petrus | **SW1X**	28
Pied à Terre | **W1T**	28
Plateau | **E14**	21
Providores | **W1U**	25
Quo Vadis | **W1D**	23
Rest. Gordon Ramsay | **SW3**	28
Rib Room | **SW1X**	24
Ritz | **W1J**	24
Roux/Landau | **W1**	26
R.S.J. | **SE1**	22
Sartoria | **W1S**	23
Savoy Grill | **WC2**	24
Scott's | **W1K**	26
Sketch/Lecture | **W1S**	22
Square | **W1J**	28
NEW SushiSamba | **EC2N**	21
Tate Modern | **SE1**	19
10 Cases | **WC2H**	23
Terroirs | **WC2N**	22
Texture | **W1H**	26
Theo Randall | **W1J**	25
34 | **W1K**	23
Tom Aikens | **SW3**	25
Trishna | **W1U**	26
28-50 Wine | **EC4A**	21
Umu | **W1J**	27
Vinoteca | **multi.**	23
Vivat Bacchus | **multi.**	20
Waterside Inn | **SL6**	29
Wild Honey | **W1S**	23
Wilton's | **SW1Y**	26
Zafferano | **SW1X**	24
Zucca | **SE1**	27
Zuma | **SW7**	27

OUTDOOR DINING

Abbeville | **SW4**	23
Abingdon | **W8**	21
Admiral Codrington | **SW3**	19
Albion | **N1**	22

Al Hamra | **W1J**	23
Almeida | **N1**	22
Amaranto | **W1J**	24
NEW Angler | **EC2M**	-
Anglesea Arms | **W6**	21
Aqua Nueva | **W1B**	21
Archipelago | **W1T**	22
Artigiano | **NW3**	22
Aubaine | **SW3**	18
Babylon | **W8**	22
Bam-Bou | **W1T**	22
Bank Westminster | **SW1E**	20
Barrafina | **W1D**	28
NEW Beagle | **E2**	-
Belvedere | **W8**	21
Bistrot Bruno | **EC1M**	25
Blueprint | **SE1**	22
Boundary | **E2**	23
Butlers Wharf | **SE1**	23
Café Spice | **E1**	25
Cantina/Ponte | **SE1**	19
Caraffini | **SW1**	22
Cinnamon Kitchen | **EC2M**	24
NEW Colbert | **SW1W**	17
Coq d'Argent | **EC2R**	23
Daylesford | **multi.**	21
Dean St. | **W1D**	22
NEW Duck & Waffle | **EC2N**	20
Eagle | **EC1R**	24
E&O | **W11**	23
El Gaucho | **SW3**	23
Elistano | **SW3**	21
Fish | **SE1**	23
NEW Grain Store | **N1C**	-
Hush | **W1S**	19
Ishbilia | **SW1X**	24
Julie's | **W11**	18
La Famiglia | **SW10**	20
La Poule au Pot | **SW1W**	22
La Trompette | **W4**	27
L'Aventure | **NW8**	25
Le Colombier | **SW3**	23
Ledbury | **W11**	28
Le Pont/Tour | **SE1**	23
Manicomio | **SW3**	18
Mediterraneo | **W11**	23

Modern Pantry | **EC1V**	25
Momo | **W1B**	21
Moro | **EC1R**	26
Motcombs | **SW1X**	21
NEW New St. Grill | **EC2M**	-
Old Brewery | **SE10**	17
Olivomare | **SW1W**	24
Orrery | **W1U**	23
Osteria Antica | **SW11**	22
Osteria Basilico | **W11**	24
Oxo Tower | **SE1**	22
Oxo Tower Brass. | **SE1**	23
Özer | **W1B**	21
Paradise/Kensal | **W10**	23
Plateau | **E14**	21
Porters English | **WC2E**	19
Quadrato | **E14**	19
Quo Vadis | **W1D**	23
Ritz | **W1J**	24
River Café | **W6**	27
Roka | **multi.**	26
Rotunda | **N1**	19
Santini | **SW1W**	20
Scott's | **W1K**	26
Smiths/Smithfield | **EC1M**	21
Strada | **E1**	17
NEW SushiSamba | **EC2N**	21
Tom's Deli | **W11**	24
202 | **W11**	19
Villandry | **W1W**	18
Wapping Food | **E1W**	19

PEOPLE-WATCHING

Admiral Codrington | **SW3**	19
Amaya | **SW1X**	27
Aqua Kyoto | **W1B**	22
Asia de Cuba | **WC2N**	23
Aubaine | **multi.**	18
Avenue | **SW1A**	20
Balans | **multi.**	19
NEW Balthazar | **WC2B**	19
Bam-Bou | **W1T**	22
Bar Boulud | **SW1X**	24
Bellamy's | **W1J**	24
Boundary | **E2**	23
Brasserie Zédel | **W1F**	17

SPECIAL FEATURES

Savoy Grill	**WC2**	24
Scalini	**SW3**	24
Scott's	**W1K**	26
Signor Sassi	**SW1X**	23
Sketch/Gallery	**W1S**	21
Sketch/Lecture	**W1S**	22
Sophie's	**SW10**	22
Spice Mkt.	**W1**	22
Spuntino	**W1D**	23
Suda	**WC2E**	23
Sumosan	**W1S**	22
NEW SushiSamba	**EC2N**	21
Tendido Cero	**SW5**	21
Tendido Cuatro	**SW6**	19
34	**W1K**	23
Tinello	**SW1W**	25
Tom Aikens	**SW3**	25
Tom's Deli	**W11**	24
Tom's Kitchen	**SW3**	23
Tramshed	**EC2A**	20
Tsuru	**multi.**	22
202	**W11**	19
Wahaca	**multi.**	22
Waterside Inn	**SL6**	29
Whitechapel	**E1**	18
Wild Honey	**W1S**	23
Wilton's	**SW1Y**	26
Wolseley	**W1J**	23
Yauatcha	**W1F**	27
York/Albany	**NW1**	20
Zafferano	**SW1X**	24
Zuma	**SW7**	27

POWER SCENES

Alain Ducasse	**W1K**	27
Avenue	**SW1A**	20
Babbo	**W1S**	21
NEW Balthazar	**WC2B**	19
Bar Boulud	**SW1X**	24
Bentley's	**W1B**	25
Bibendum	**SW3**	23
Bonds	**EC2R**	22
Boundary	**E2**	23
Caravaggio	**EC3A**	19
Cigalon	**WC2A**	22
Cinnamon Club	**SW1P**	26

Cinnamon Kitchen	**EC2M**	24
C London	**W1K**	23
Club Gascon	**EC1A**	27
Corrigan's Mayfair	**W1K**	25
Cut/45 Park Ln.	**W1K**	25
Daphne's	**SW3**	22
Dean St.	**W1D**	22
Delaunay	**WC2B**	21
Galvin Chapelle/Café	**E1**	26
Gilbert Scott	**NW1**	19
Goring Dining Room	**SW1**	25
Greenhouse	**W1J**	27
Green's	**multi.**	21
Hélène Darroze	**W1K**	25
Hix Mayfair	**W1S**	25
NEW HKK	**EC2A**	-
Ivy	**WC2H**	24
J. Sheekey	**WC2N**	26
Koffmann's	**SW1X**	27
Langan's Brass.	**W1J**	21
L'Anima	**EC2A**	25
La Petite Maison	**W1K**	26
L'Atelier/Robuchon	**WC2H**	28
Launceston Pl.	**W8**	25
Le Caprice	**SW1A**	24
Ledbury	**W11**	28
Le Gavroche	**W1K**	28
Le Manoir/Quat	**OX44**	27
Locanda Locatelli	**W1H**	25
Lutyens	**EC4**	23
Marcus Wareing	**SW1X**	27
Maze	**W1K**	24
Mr. Chow	**SW1X**	22
Murano	**W1J**	26
NEW New St. Grill	**EC2M**	-
Nobu Berkeley	**W1J**	26
Nobu London	**W1K**	27
Novikov	**W1J**	21
NEW Oblix	**SE1**	-
1 Lombard St.	**EC3V**	23
NEW Outlaw's	**SW3**	-
Palm	**SW1X**	22
Petrus	**SW1X**	28
Plateau	**E14**	21
Prism	**EC3V**	19
Quirinale	**SW1P**	25

Quo Vadis	**W1D**	23
Rest. Gordon Ramsay	**SW3**	28
Rhodes 24	**EC2N**	25
Ritz	**W1J**	24
Sake No Hana	**SW1A**	25
Savoy Grill	**WC2**	24
Scott's	**W1K**	26
Sketch/Lecture	**W1S**	22
Square	**W1J**	28
NEW SushiSamba	**EC2N**	21
34	**W1K**	23
Tinello	**SW1W**	25
Tom Aikens	**SW3**	25
Umu	**W1J**	27
Waterside Inn	**SL6**	29
Wild Honey	**W1S**	23
Wilton's	**SW1Y**	26
Wolseley	**W1J**	23
Zafferano	**SW1X**	24
Zuma	**SW7**	27

PRIVATE ROOMS

(Restaurants charge less at off
times; call for capacity)

NEW Acciuga	**W8**	-
Admiral Codrington	**SW3**	19
Alain Ducasse	**W1K**	27
Albannach	**WC2N**	20
Alloro	**W1S**	22
Almeida	**N1**	22
Amaya	**SW1X**	27
NEW Angler	**EC2M**	-
NEW Aqua Shard	**SE1**	-
Babylon	**W8**	22
Baltic	**SE1**	23
Bam-Bou	**W1T**	22
Benares	**W1J**	25
Benihana	**multi.**	20
Bentley's	**W1B**	25
Bistrotheque	**E2**	21
Bob Bob Ricard	**W1F**	22
Boundary	**E2**	23
Cambio/Tercio	**SW5**	24
Chez Bruce	**SW17**	28
China Tang	**W1K**	21
Christopher's	**WC2E**	-
Chuen Cheng Ku	**W1D**	20

Chutney Mary	**SW10**	25
Cigalon	**WC2A**	22
Cinnamon Club	**SW1P**	26
C London	**W1K**	23
Corrigan's Mayfair	**W1K**	25
Daphne's	**SW3**	22
Dehesa	**W1F**	25
Dinner/Heston	**SW1X**	26
NEW Duck & Waffle	**EC2N**	20
E&O	**W11**	23
Eight Over Eight	**SW3**	23
Fairuz	**W1U**	22
Franco's	**SW1Y**	22
Gilgamesh	**NW1**	19
Greenhouse	**W1J**	27
Green's	**multi.**	21
Greig's	**W1J**	21
Guinea Grill	**W1J**	24
Hakkasan	**W1T**	26
Hawksmoor	**E1**	26
Hibiscus	**W1S**	25
NEW HKK	**EC2A**	-
Hush	**W1S**	19
NEW Hutong	**SE1**	-
Il Convivio	**SW1W**	23
Ishbilia	**SW1X**	24
Ivy	**WC2H**	24
Julie's	**W11**	18
Kai Mayfair	**W1K**	25
Kensington Pl.	**W8**	20
Koffmann's	**SW1X**	27
L'Anima	**EC2A**	25
La Porte/Indes	**W1H**	22
La Poule au Pot	**SW1W**	22
Launceston Pl.	**W8**	25
Le Café Anglais	**W2**	22
Le Cercle	**SW1X**	24
Le Colombier	**SW3**	23
Le Manoir/Quat	**OX44**	27
Le Pont/Tour	**SE1**	23
L'Escargot	**W1D**	25
Les Trois Garçons	**E1**	23
Lutyens	**EC4**	23
Manicomio	**multi.**	18
Mao Tai	**SW6**	25
Marcus Wareing	**SW1X**	27

Masala Zone | **multi.** 22
Massimo | **WC2N** 21
Matsuri | **SW1Y** 23
Maze | **W1K** 24
Memories/China | **SW1W** 23
Min Jiang | **W8** 25
Mint Leaf | **SW1Y** 22
Mon Plaisir | **WC2H** 21
Motcombs | **SW1X** 21
Mr. Chow | **SW1X** 22
Murano | **W1J** 26
NEW New St. Grill | **EC2M** –
Nobu London | **W1K** 27
Noura | **W1J** 22
1 Lombard St. | **EC3V** 23
1 Lombard Brass. | **EC3V** 21
One-O-One | **SW1X** 22
Palm | **SW1X** 22
Paradise/Kensal | **W10** 23
Patara | **SW3** 24
Pied à Terre | **W1T** 28
Plateau | **E14** 21
Poissonnerie/l'Avenue | **SW3** 24
Prism | **EC3V** 19
Quaglino's | **SW1Y** 21
Quo Vadis | **W1D** 23
Rasa | **multi.** 24
Rasoi Vineet | **SW3** 28
Rib Room | **SW1X** 24
Rivington Grill | **EC2A** 23
Royal China | **multi.** 23
Rules | **WC2E** 24
Santini | **SW1W** 20
Sartoria | **W1S** 23
Savoy Grill | **WC2** 24
Scott's | **W1K** 26
Sketch/Lecture | **W1S** 22
Smiths/Smithfield | **EC1M** 21
Spice Mkt. | **W1** 22
Square | **W1J** 28
St. John | **EC1M** 26
Sumosan | **W1S** 22
Tentazioni | **SE1** 24
Thai Sq. | **multi.** 19
Thomas Cubitt | **SW1W** 21
Timo | **W8** 24

Tom Aikens | **SW3** 25
Tom's Kitchen | **SW3** 23
NEW Upstairs/Ten Bells | **E1** –
Vasco & Piero's | **W1F** 23
Veeraswamy | **W1B** 24
Villandry | **W1W** 18
Vivat Bacchus | **EC4A** 20
Warrington | **W9** 19
Waterside Inn | **SL6** 29
Wells | **NW3** 22
Wilton's | **SW1Y** 26
York/Albany | **NW1** 20
Zafferano | **SW1X** 24
Zuma | **SW7** 27

PUDDING SPECIALISTS

Alain Ducasse | **W1K** 27
Almeida | **N1** 22
Amaya | **SW1X** 27
Asia de Cuba | **WC2N** 23
Aubaine | **W1S** 18
Baker & Spice | **multi.** 21
NEW Balthazar | **WC2B** 19
Bar Boulud | **SW1X** 24
Belvedere | **W8** 21
Bibendum | **SW3** 23
Bistrot Bruno | **EC1M** 25
Blakes | **SW7** 20
Bocca/Gelupo | **W1D** 25
Cassis Bistro | **SW3** 22
Chez Bruce | **SW17** 28
C London | **W1K** 23
Club Gascon | **EC1A** 27
NEW Colbert | **SW1W** 17
Cut/45 Park Ln. | **W1K** 25
Delaunay | **WC2B** 21
Dinner/Heston | **SW1X** 26
Fat Duck | **SL6** 28
Fifteen | **N1** –
Fortnum's Fountain | **W1A** 20
Galvin at Windows | **W1K** 25
Galvin Bistrot | **W1U** 25
Galvin Chapelle/Café | **E1** 26
Gauthier | **W1D** 28
Gilbert Scott | **NW1** 19

QUICK BITES

SPECIAL FEATURES

Gaby's | **WC2H**	23
NEW Gail's Kitchen | **WC1B**	-
Giaconda/Dining | **WC2H**	23
Gilbert Scott | **NW1**	19
Granger & Co. | **W11**	19
NEW Great British | **W1K**	-
NEW Green Man | **WC2N**	21
Green's | **multi.**	21
Herman ze German | **WC2N**	23
High Road Brass. | **W4**	22
Honest Burgers | **SW9**	27
Honey & Co | **W1T**	-
Hush | **multi.**	19
Imli Street | **W1F**	22
Inamo | **W1F**	19
Khan's | **W2**	20
Koya | **W1D**	24
Ladurée | **multi.**	24
La Petite Maison | **W1K**	26
Le Café Anglais | **W2**	22
Lutyens | **EC4**	23
MEATmarket | **WC2E**	23
Mien Tay | **multi.**	24
NEW Naamyaa | **EC1V**	-
Nando's | **multi.**	18
National Dining Rms. | **WC2N**	20
NEW Newman St. | **W1T**	-
1901 | **EC2M**	23
North Sea | **WC1H**	24
Novikov | **W1J**	21
Olivomare | **SW1W**	24
Pepper Tree | **SW4**	27
Petersham Nurseries | **TW10**	24
Pho | **multi.**	22
Princi London | **W1F**	24
Roti Chai | **W1H**	24
Royal China Club | **W1U**	25
Sketch/Parlour | **W1S**	21
Taqueria | **W11**	24
Tendido Cuatro | **SW6**	19
Terroirs | **WC2N**	22
Theo Randall | **W1J**	25
Tom's Kitchen | **multi.**	23
Tonkotsu | **W1D**	-
Tortilla | **multi.**	22
Tsuru | **multi.**	22

28-50 Wine | **EC4A**	21
Wagamama | **multi.**	17
Wahaca | **WC2N**	22
Warrington | **W9**	19
NEW Wishbone | **SW9**	-

QUIET CONVERSATION

Alain Ducasse | **W1K**	27
Al Sultan | **W1J**	22
Alyn Williams | **W1S**	23
Amaranto | **W1J**	24
Apsleys | **SW1X**	26
Babbo | **W1S**	21
Bank Westminster | **SW1E**	20
Benares | **W1J**	25
Bengal Clipper | **SE1**	21
Bentley's | **W1B**	25
Bibendum | **SW3**	23
Bingham | **TW10**	24
Blakes | **SW7**	20
Bonds | **EC2R**	22
Cigalon | **WC2A**	22
Clarke's | **W8**	25
Clos Maggiore | **WC2E**	25
Corrigan's Mayfair | **W1K**	25
Cut/45 Park Ln. | **W1K**	25
Dinner/Heston | **SW1X**	26
Dorchester | **W1K**	25
Espelette | **W1K**	25
French Table | **KT6**	28
NEW Gail's Kitchen | **WC1B**	-
Gilbert Scott | **NW1**	19
Goring Dining Room | **SW1**	25
Green's | **multi.**	21
Hélène Darroze | **W1K**	25
Hibiscus | **W1S**	25
NEW HKK | **EC2A**	-
Il Convivio | **SW1W**	23
Indigo | **WC2B**	23
JW Steak | **W1K**	23
Kitchen W8 | **W8**	25
Koffmann's | **SW1X**	27
Koi | **W8**	21
La Genova | **W1K**	23
Launceston Pl. | **W8**	25

L'Autre Pied	**W1U**	25	Bar Boulud	**SW1X**	24
Le Gavroche	**W1K**	28	Belvedere	**W8**	21
Le Manoir/Quat	**OX44**	27	Bibendum	**SW3**	23
Lutyens	**EC4**	23	Bingham	**TW10**	24
Magdalen	**SE1**	25	Bleeding Heart	**EC1N**	23
Massimo	**WC2N**	21	Blue Elephant	**SW6**	24
Mediterraneo	**W11**	23	NEW Buddha-Bar	**SW1X**	-
Medlar	**SW10**	25	Cassis Bistro	**SW3**	22
Mews/Mayfair	**W1S**	19	Cheyne Walk	**SW3**	20
Min Jiang	**W8**	25	China Tang	**W1K**	21
Morgan M	**EC1A**	28	Chutney Mary	**SW10**	25
Murano	**W1J**	26	Cigalon	**WC2A**	22
NEW New St. Grill	**EC2M**	-	Clarke's	**W8**	25
One-O-One	**SW1X**	22	C London	**W1K**	23
Orrery	**W1U**	23	Clos Maggiore	**WC2E**	25
Petrus	**SW1X**	28	Club Gascon	**EC1A**	27
Pied à Terre	**W1T**	28	Cut/45 Park Ln.	**W1K**	25
Quadrato	**E14**	19	Daphne's	**SW3**	22
NEW Quality Chop	**EC1R**	-	Dinner/Heston	**SW1X**	26
Quirinale	**SW1P**	25	Dock Kitchen	**W10**	24
Rasoi Vineet	**SW3**	28	Elena's L'Etoile	**W1T**	20
Rib Room	**SW1X**	24	Ffiona's	**W8**	23
Ritz	**W1J**	24	Frederick's	**N1**	23
Roux/Parliament	**SW1P**	24	Galvin at Windows	**W1K**	25
Salloos	**SW1X**	24	Gilbert Scott	**NW1**	19
Sketch/Lecture	**W1S**	22	Greenhouse	**W1J**	27
Square	**W1J**	28	NEW Green Man	**WC2N**	21
Texture	**W1H**	26	Hakkasan	**W1T**	26
Theo Randall	**W1J**	25	Hélène Darroze	**W1K**	25
Tinello	**SW1W**	25	NEW HKK	**EC2A**	-
28-50 Wine	**EC4A**	21	Julie's	**W11**	18
Waterside Inn	**SL6**	29	NEW Kaspar's	**WC2R**	-
Wilton's	**SW1Y**	26	Kazan	**SW1V**	24
		Koffmann's	**SW1X**	27

ROMANTIC PLACES

		La Famiglia	**SW10**	20
Alain Ducasse	**W1K**	27	La Petite Maison	**W1K**	26
Albion	**N1**	22	La Poule au Pot	**SW1W**	22
Alyn Williams	**W1S**	23	L'Atelier/Robuchon	**WC2H**	28
Amaranto	**W1J**	24	La Trompette	**W4**	27
Amaya	**SW1X**	27	Launceston Pl.	**W8**	25
Andrew Edmunds	**W1F**	24	L'Aventure	**NW8**	25
Angelus	**W2**	25	Le Café/Marché	**EC1M**	25
Apsleys	**SW1X**	26	Le Caprice	**SW1A**	24
Archipelago	**W1T**	22	Le Cercle	**SW1X**	24
Aurora	**W1F**	24	Ledbury	**W11**	28
Babylon	**W8**	22	Le Gavroche	**W1K**	28

Le Manoir/Quat | **OX44**	27
Le Pont/Tour | **SE1**	23
Les Trois Garçons | **E1**	23
Locanda Locatelli | **W1H**	25
Locanda Ottoemezzo | **W8**	25
Maggie Jones's | **W8**	21
Marcus Wareing | **SW1X**	27
Massimo | **WC2N**	21
Min Jiang | **W8**	25
Momo | **W1B**	21
Murano | **W1J**	26
1901 | **EC2M**	23
Nobu London | **W1K**	27
Novikov | **W1J**	21
NEW Oblix | **SE1**	-
Odette's | **NW1**	25
Old Brewery | **SE10**	17
Orrery | **W1U**	23
Osteria Antica | **SW11**	22
Paramount | **WC1A**	21
Petrus | **SW1X**	28
Quaglino's | **SW1Y**	21
Rasoi Vineet | **SW3**	28
Rest. Gordon Ramsay | **SW3**	28
Ritz | **W1J**	24
River Café | **W6**	27
San Lorenzo | **SW3**	21
Sketch/Lecture | **W1S**	22
Spice Mkt. | **W1**	22
Square | **W1J**	28
NEW SushiSamba | **EC2N**	21
34 | **W1K**	23
Tinello | **SW1W**	25
Tom Aikens | **SW3**	25
Veeraswamy | **W1B**	24
Viajante | **E2**	26
Waterside Inn | **SL6**	29
Zafferano | **SW1X**	24
Zuma | **SW7**	27

SET-PRICE MENUS

(Call for prices and times)

Abingdon | **W8**	21
Alain Ducasse | **W1K**	27
Al Duca | **SW1Y**	22
Alloro | **W1S**	22
Almeida | **N1**	22

Alyn Williams | **W1S**	23
Amaya | **SW1X**	27
Angelus | **W2**	25
Apsleys | **SW1X**	26
Arbutus | **W1D**	24
Baltic | **SE1**	23
Bar Boulud | **SW1X**	24
Bellamy's | **W1J**	24
Belvedere | **W8**	21
Benares | **W1J**	25
Bengal Clipper | **SE1**	21
Bibendum | **SW3**	23
NEW Bo London | **W1S**	-
Butlers Wharf | **SE1**	23
Café des Amis | **WC2E**	18
Café Japan | **NW11**	26
Café Spice | **E1**	25
Caravaggio | **EC3A**	19
Chancery | **EC4A**	24
Charlotte's | **multi.**	25
Chez Bruce | **SW17**	28
Chor Bizarre | **W1S**	25
Christopher's | **WC2E**	-
Chutney Mary | **SW10**	25
Cigala | **WC1N**	20
Cinnamon Club | **SW1P**	26
Clos Maggiore | **WC2E**	25
NEW Clove Club | **EC2A**	-
Club Gascon | **EC1A**	27
Coq d'Argent | **EC2R**	23
Criterion | **W1J**	21
Defune | **W1U**	25
El Pirata | **W1J**	22
Enoteca Turi | **SW15**	25
Fat Duck | **SL6**	28
Fifteen | **N1**	-
Galvin Bistrot | **W1U**	25
Gauthier | **W1D**	28
Glasshouse | **TW9**	26
Goring Dining Room | **SW1**	25
Greenhouse | **W1J**	27
Hélène Darroze | **W1K**	25
Hibiscus | **W1S**	25
High Road Brass. | **W4**	22
Hunan | **SW1W**	27
Il Convivio | **SW1W**	23

Indigo	**WC2B**	23	Quilon	**SW1E**	-
J. Sheekey	**WC2N**	26	Racine	**SW3**	24
Kai Mayfair	**W1K**	25	Rasa	**multi.**	24
Kensington Pl.	**W8**	20	Rasoi Vineet	**SW3**	28
Kiku	**W1J**	24	Red Fort	**W1D**	23
La Poule au Pot	**SW1W**	22	Rest. Gordon Ramsay	**SW3**	28
L'Atelier/Robuchon	**WC2H**	28	Rib Room	**SW1X**	24
Latium	**W1T**	25	Ritz	**W1J**	24
La Trompette	**W4**	27	Roux/Parliament	**SW1P**	24
Launceston Pl.	**W8**	25	Royal China	**W2**	23
L'Autre Pied	**W1U**	25	Sartoria	**W1S**	23
L'Aventure	**NW8**	25	Savoy Grill	**WC2**	24
Le Café/Marché	**EC1M**	25	NEW Shiori	**W2**	-
Le Cercle	**SW1X**	24	Sketch/Lecture	**W1S**	22
Le Colombier	**SW3**	23	Sofra	**multi.**	21
Ledbury	**W11**	28	Sophie's	**multi.**	22
Le Gavroche	**W1K**	28	Square	**W1J**	28
Le Manoir/Quat	**OX44**	27	Tamarind	**W1J**	25
L'Escargot	**W1D**	25	Tentazioni	**SE1**	24
Les Trois Garçons	**E1**	23	Theo Randall	**W1J**	25
L'Etranger	**SW7**	25	Tom Aikens	**SW3**	25
Le Vacherin	**W4**	24	Trishna	**W1U**	26
Lucio	**SW3**	20	Umu	**W1J**	27
Marcus Wareing	**SW1X**	27	Vasco & Piero's	**W1F**	23
Maze	**W1K**	24	Veeraswamy	**W1B**	24
Maze Grill	**W1K**	23	Waterside Inn	**SL6**	29
Mela	**WC2H**	22	Wheeler's	**SW1A**	21
Memories/China	**W8**	23	Yoshino	**W1J**	24
Murano	**W1J**	26	Zaika	**W8**	25
Nobu Berkeley	**W1J**	26	Ziani	**SW3**	24
Nobu London	**W1K**	27		
Noura	**multi.**	22	**SINGLES SCENES**	
Odette's	**NW1**	25	Admiral Codrington	**SW3**	19
Olivo	**SW1W**	22	Albannach	**WC2N**	20
One-O-One	**SW1X**	22	Aqua Kyoto	**W1B**	22
Orrery	**W1U**	23	Asia de Cuba	**WC2N**	23
Oslo Court	**NW8**	26	Avenue	**SW1A**	20
NEW Outlaw's	**SW3**	-	Balans	**multi.**	19
Oxo Tower	**SE1**	22	Bank Westminster	**SW1E**	20
Özer	**W1B**	21	Big Easy	**SW3**	21
Patara	**multi.**	24	Bluebird	**SW3**	20
Pied à Terre	**W1T**	28	Botanist	**SW1W**	18
Plateau	**E14**	21	Bountiful Cow	**WC1R**	22
Poissonnerie/l'Avenue	**SW3**	24	Cecconi's	**W1S**	23
Porters English	**WC2E**	19	China Tang	**W1K**	21
Princess Garden	**W1K**	24	Christopher's	**WC2E**	-

Circus | **WC2H**	18	Chancery | **EC4A**	24
Coq d'Argent | **EC2R**	23	Cocomaya | **multi.**	24
E&O | **W11**	23	Constancia | **SE1**	25
Eight Over Eight | **SW3**	23	Copita | **W1F**	24
Enterprise | **SW3**	21	Corner Room | **E2**	29
Fifteen | **N1**	–	Donostia | **W1H**	24
Fino | **W1T**	26	El Parador | **NW1**	25
Gilgamesh | **NW1**	19	Espelette | **W1K**	25
Hakkasan | **W1T**	26	Ganapati | **SE15**	26
Hush | **W1S**	19	Goldmine | **W2**	25
Inamo | **W1F**	19	Green Cottage | **NW3**	25
Kenza | **EC2M**	24	Hot Stuff | **SW8**	25
Kettner's | **W1D**	22	Ikeda | **W1K**	26
La Bodega Negra | **W1D**	17	Juniper Dining | **N5**	28
Las Iguanas | **multi.**	21	Kenza | **EC2M**	24
Le Cercle | **SW1X**	24	Lamberts | **SW12**	28
Maze | **W1K**	24	L'Aventure | **NW8**	25
Mews/Mayfair | **W1S**	19	Locanda Ottoemezzo | **W8**	25
Mint Leaf | **multi.**	22	Made/Camden | **NW1**	24
Momo | **W1B**	21	Mandalay | **W2**	24
Moro | **EC1R**	26	Mao Tai | **SW6**	25
Motcombs | **SW1X**	21	Mem & Laz | **N1**	27
NEW Newman St. | **W1T**	–	Michael Nadra | **W4**	25
Nobu Berkeley | **W1J**	26	New Mayflower | **W1D**	24
Nobu London | **W1K**	27	Paradise | **NW3**	26
Novikov | **W1J**	21	Popeseye | **multi.**	24
Oxo Tower | **SE1**	22	Portal | **EC1M**	27
Oxo Tower Brass. | **SE1**	23	Princess Victoria | **W12**	25
NEW Plum + Spilt Milk | **N1C**	–	Quirinale | **SW1P**	25
Quaglino's | **SW1Y**	21	Sedap | **EC1V**	26
Randall/Aubin | **W1F**	25	Seven Park | **SW1A**	24
Roka | **W1T**	26	Sushi-Say | **NW2**	29
Sketch/Gallery | **W1S**	21	Tentazioni | **SE1**	24
Smiths/Smithfield | **EC1M**	21	Ten Ten Tei | **W1**	25
Sophie's | **multi.**	22	Timo | **W8**	24
Spice Mkt. | **W1**	22	Zayna | **W1H**	28
Sumosan | **W1S**	22		
NEW SushiSamba | **EC2N**	21		

SPECIAL OCCASIONS

Wahaca | **W1F**	22	Alain Ducasse | **W1K**	27
Zuma | **SW7**	27	Almeida | **N1**	22
		Alyn Williams | **W1S**	23

SLEEPERS

(Good food, but little known)

Alloro | **W1S**	22	Amaranto | **W1J**	24
Aurora | **W1F**	24	Amaya | **SW1X**	27
Beiteddine | **SW1X**	26	Angelus | **W2**	25
Books/Cooks | **W11**	25	Apsleys | **SW1X**	26
		Asia de Cuba | **WC2N**	23

Babbo | **W1S**	21
Belvedere | **W8**	21
Bentley's | **W1B**	25
Bibendum | **SW3**	23
Blakes | **SW7**	20
NEW Buddha-Bar | **SW1X**	-
Cassis Bistro | **SW3**	22
Cecconi's | **W1S**	23
Chez Bruce | **SW17**	28
China Tang | **W1K**	21
Chutney Mary | **SW10**	25
Cigalon | **WC2A**	22
Cinnamon Club | **SW1P**	26
C London | **W1K**	23
Club Gascon | **EC1A**	27
Corrigan's Mayfair | **W1K**	25
NEW Coya | **W1J**	24
Criterion | **W1J**	21
Cut/45 Park Ln. | **W1K**	25
Dabbous | **W1T**	26
Daphne's | **SW3**	22
Dean St. | **W1D**	22
Delaunay | **WC2B**	21
Dinner/Heston | **SW1X**	26
Dorchester | **W1K**	25
Fat Duck | **SL6**	28
Fifteen | **N1**	-
French Table | **KT6**	28
Galvin at Windows | **W1K**	25
Galvin Bistrot | **W1U**	25
Galvin Chapelle/Café | **E1**	26
Gauthier | **W1D**	28
Gilbert Scott | **NW1**	19
Glasshouse | **TW9**	26
Goring Dining Room | **SW1**	25
Greenhouse | **W1J**	27
Hakkasan | **multi.**	26
Harwood Arms | **SW6**	27
Hélène Darroze | **W1K**	25
Hibiscus | **W1S**	25
Hix Mayfair | **W1S**	25
NEW HKK | **EC2A**	-
Ivy | **WC2H**	24
J. Sheekey | **WC2N**	26
Kai Mayfair | **W1K**	25
Koffmann's | **SW1X**	27

L'Anima | **EC2A**	25
La Petite Maison | **W1K**	26
La Poule au Pot | **SW1W**	22
L'Atelier/Robuchon | **WC2H**	28
La Trompette | **W4**	27
Launceston Pl. | **W8**	25
Le Caprice | **SW1A**	24
Le Cercle | **SW1X**	24
Ledbury | **W11**	28
Le Gavroche | **W1K**	28
Le Manoir/Quat | **OX44**	27
Le Pont/Tour | **SE1**	23
Locanda Locatelli | **W1H**	25
Lutyens | **EC4**	23
Mao Tai | **SW6**	25
Marcus Wareing | **SW1X**	27
Massimo | **WC2N**	21
Maze | **W1K**	24
Medlar | **SW10**	25
Min Jiang | **W8**	25
Momo | **W1B**	21
Morgan M | **EC1A**	28
Murano | **W1J**	26
NEW New St. Grill | **EC2M**	-
1901 | **EC2M**	23
Nobu Berkeley | **W1J**	26
Nobu London | **W1K**	27
Novikov | **W1J**	21
Orrery | **W1U**	23
NEW Outlaw's | **SW3**	-
Palm | **SW1X**	22
Paramount | **WC1A**	21
Petersham | **TW10**	23
Petrus | **SW1X**	28
Pied à Terre | **W1T**	28
Plateau | **E14**	21
Pollen St. Social | **EC1V**	25
Providores | **W1U**	25
Quaglino's | **SW1Y**	21
Quo Vadis | **W1D**	23
Racine | **SW3**	24
Rasoi Vineet | **SW3**	28
Rest. Gordon Ramsay | **SW3**	28
Rib Room | **SW1X**	24
Ritz | **W1J**	24
River Café | **W6**	27

Roux/Parliament | **SW1P** 24
Roux/Landau | **W1** 26
Rules | **WC2E** 24
Santini | **SW1W** 20
Savoy Grill | **WC2** 24
Scott's | **W1K** 26
Seven Park | **SW1A** 24
Simpson's/Strand | **WC2R** 21
Sketch/Lecture | **W1S** 22
Skylon | **SE1** 20
Smiths/Smithfield | **EC1M** 21
Spice Mkt. | **W1** 22
Square | **W1J** 28
NEW SushiSamba | **EC2N** 21
Texture | **W1H** 26
Theo Randall | **W1J** 25
34 | **W1K** 23
Tinello | **SW1W** 25
Tom Aikens | **SW3** 25
Trinity | **SW4** 26
Umu | **W1J** 27
Waterside Inn | **SL6** 29
Wilton's | **SW1Y** 26
Wolseley | **W1J** 23
Zafferano | **SW1X** 24
Zaika | **W8** 25
Zuma | **SW7** 27

TRENDY

Angels/Gypsies | **SE5** 25
NEW Angler | **EC2M** -
Aqua Kyoto | **W1B** 22
Asia de Cuba | **WC2N** 23
Bar Boulud | **SW1X** 24
Bob Bob Ricard | **W1F** 22
Bocca/Gelupo | **W1D** 25
NEW Bone Daddies | **W1F** 21
Brawn | **E2** 26
NEW Brompton Asian | **SW3** -
NEW Bubbledogs | **W1T** 18
NEW Buddha-Bar | **SW1X** -
Burger & Lobster | **multi.** 23
Circus | **WC2H** 18
C London | **W1K** 23
NEW Colbert | **SW1W** 17
Copita | **W1F** 24

NEW Coya | **W1J** 24
Crazy Homies | **W2** 18
Dabbous | **W1T** 26
Dean St. | **W1D** 22
Downtown Mayfair | **W1S** 21
NEW Duck & Waffle | **EC2N** 20
E&O | **W11** 23
Eight Over Eight | **SW3** 23
El Pirata | **W2** 22
Enterprise | **SW3** 21
Franco Manca | **multi.** 26
NEW Gail's Kitchen | **WC1B** -
Galvin Chapelle/Café | **E1** 26
Hakkasan | **multi.** 26
Hawksmoor | **multi.** 26
Hix | **W1F** 22
NEW HKK | **EC2A** -
Hoxton Grill | **EC2A** 22
Hush | **W1S** 19
Kenza | **EC2M** 24
La Bodega Negra | **W1D** 17
Le Caprice | **SW1A** 24
Les Trois Garçons | **E1** 23
Lima | **W1T** 23
Lucio | **SW3** 20
Lucky 7 | **W2** 18
Maze | **W1K** 24
MEATliquor | **W1G** 23
MEATmarket | **WC2E** 23
NEW MEATmission | **N1** -
Mishkin's | **WC2B** 20
Moro | **EC1R** 26
NEW Naamyaa | **EC1V** -
NEW Newman St. | **W1T** -
Nobu Berkeley | **W1J** 26
Nobu London | **W1K** 27
NOPI | **W1B** 25
Novikov | **W1J** 21
NEW Oblix | **SE1** -
Olivo | **SW1W** 22
Opera Tavern | **WC2B** 25
Pitt Cue Co. | **W1F** 28
Pizarro | **SE1** 26
Pizza East | **E1** 21
NEW Plum + Spilt Milk | **N1C** -
Pollen St. Social | **EC1V** 25

Polpo	**multi.**	22
Roka	**multi.**	26
Sake No Hana	**SW1A**	25
Salt Yard	**W1T**	24
Scott's	**W1K**	26
Sketch/Gallery	**W1S**	21
Sketch/Parlour	**W1S**	21
Spice Mkt.	**W1**	22
Spuntino	**W1D**	23
NEW STK	**WC2R**	-
NEW SushiSamba	**EC2N**	21
Taqueria	**W11**	24
Tendido Cuatro	**SW6**	19
Tramshed	**EC2A**	20
Tsunami	**multi.**	23
202	**W11**	19
Umu	**W1J**	27
Viajante	**E2**	26
Wapping Food	**E1W**	19
Whitechapel	**E1**	18
Wolseley	**W1J**	23
Yauatcha	**W1F**	27
Zatterano	**SW1X**	24
Zucca	**SE1**	27
Zuma	**SW7**	27

VIEWS

NEW Angler	**EC2M**	-
Aqua Kyoto	**W1B**	22
Aqua Nueva	**W1B**	21
NEW Aqua Shard	**SE1**	-
Babylon	**W8**	22
Bank Westminster	**SW1E**	20
Barbecoa	**EC4M**	23
Belvedere	**W8**	21
Bingham	**TW10**	24
Bistrot Bruno	**EC1M**	25
Blueprint	**SE1**	22
Boundary	**E2**	23
Butcher & Grill	**SW11**	20
Butlers Wharf	**SE1**	23
Cantina/Ponte	**SE1**	19
Cheyne Walk	**SW3**	20
Coq d'Argent	**EC2R**	23
Dinner/Heston	**SW1X**	26
NEW Duck & Waffle	**EC2N**	20

Fernandez & Wells	**WC2R**	21
Fish	**SE1**	23
Galvin at Windows	**W1K**	25
Gaucho	**multi.**	22
Gilbert Scott	**NW1**	19
Greenhouse	**W1J**	27
Gun	**E14**	23
NEW Hutong	**SE1**	-
NEW Kaspar's	**WC2R**	-
Kettner's	**W1D**	22
Le Manoir/Quat	**OX44**	27
Le Pont/Tour	**SE1**	23
Maze	**W1K**	24
Maze Grill	**W1K**	23
Min Jiang	**W8**	25
National Dining Rms.	**WC2N**	20
Nobu London	**W1K**	27
NEW Oblix	**SE1**	-
Orrery	**W1U**	23
Oslo Court	**NW8**	26
Oxo Tower	**SE1**	22
Oxo Tower Brass.	**SE1**	23
Paramount	**WC1A**	21
Petersham	**TW10**	23
Pho	**E20**	22
Plateau	**E14**	21
Portrait	**WC2H**	22
Quadrato	**E14**	19
Real Greek	**SE1**	20
Rhodes 24	**EC2N**	25
River Café	**W6**	27
Roast	**SE1**	25
Roka	**E14**	26
Rotunda	**N1**	19
Royal China	**E14**	23
Simpson's/Strand	**WC2R**	21
Skylon	**SE1**	20
Smiths/Smithfield	**EC1M**	21
Tate Modern	**SE1**	19
Thai Sq.	**SW15**	19
Tom's Kitchen	**WC2R**	23
Tuttons	**WC2B**	20
Union Jacks	**WC2H**	18
Wahaca	**SE1**	22
Waterside Inn	**SL6**	29

Alain Ducasse | **W1K**	27
Alloro | **W1S**	22
Almeida | **N1**	22
Alyn Williams | **W1S**	23
Amaranto | **W1J**	24
Amaya | **SW1X**	27
NEW Angler | **EC2M**	-
Apsleys | **SW1X**	26
Asia de Cuba | **WC2N**	23
Assaggi | **W2**	25
Aurelia | **W1S**	22
Babbo | **W1S**	21
Bank Westminster | **SW1E**	20
Bar Boulud | **SW1X**	24
Belvedere | **W8**	21
Benares | **W1J**	25
Bentley's | **W1B**	25
Bibendum | **SW3**	23
Bistrot Bruno | **EC1M**	25
Blakes | **SW7**	20
Brasserie Blanc | **multi.**	18
Brasserie Zédel | **W1F**	17
NEW Buddha-Bar | **SW1X**	-
Caravaggio | **EC3A**	19
Cassis Bistro | **SW3**	22
Cecconi's | **W1S**	23
Chez Bruce | **SW17**	28
Chez Gérard | **EC2N**	-
China Tang | **W1K**	21
Chiswell St. Dining | **EC1**	22
Christopher's | **WC2E**	-
Chutney Mary | **SW10**	25
Cigalon | **WC2A**	22
Cinnamon Club | **SW1P**	26
Cinnamon Kitchen | **EC2M**	24
Clarke's | **W8**	25
C London | **W1K**	23
Club Gascon | **EC1A**	27
NEW Colbert | **SW1W**	17
Coq d'Argent | **EC2R**	23
Corrigan's Mayfair | **W1K**	25
NEW Coya | **W1J**	24
Criterion | **W1J**	21
Cut/45 Park Ln. | **W1K**	25
Dabbous | **W1T**	26
Daphne's | **SW3**	22
Delaunay | **WC2B**	21
Dinings | **W1H**	28
Dinner/Heston | **SW1X**	26
Dock Kitchen | **W10**	24
Don | **EC4N**	23
Dorchester | **W1K**	25
Downtown Mayfair | **W1S**	21
Fat Duck | **SL6**	28
Fino | **W1T**	26
Galvin at Windows | **W1K**	25
Galvin Bistrot | **W1U**	25
Galvin Chapelle/Café | **E1**	26
Gaucho | **multi.**	22
Gilbert Scott | **NW1**	19
Glasshouse | **TW9**	26
Goodman | **multi.**	27
Goring Dining Room | **SW1**	25
Greenhouse | **W1J**	27
Green's | **multi.**	21
Hakkasan | **multi.**	26
Hawksmoor | **multi.**	26
Hélène Darroze | **W1K**	25
Hibiscus | **W1S**	25
Hix | **W1F**	22
Hix Mayfair | **W1S**	25
NEW HKK | **EC2A**	-
Hush | **W1S**	19
Il Convivio | **SW1W**	23
Ivy | **WC2H**	24
J. Sheekey | **WC2N**	26
J. Sheekey Oyster | **WC2N**	25
JW Steak | **W1K**	23
Kai Mayfair | **W1K**	25
Kazan | **SW1V**	24
Kitchen W8 | **W8**	25
Koffmann's | **SW1X**	27
Langan's Brass. | **W1J**	21
L'Anima | **EC2A**	25
La Petite Maison | **W1K**	26
L'Atelier/Robuchon | **WC2H**	28
Launceston Pl. | **W8**	25
L'Autre Pied | **W1U**	25
Le Café Anglais | **W2**	22
Le Caprice | **SW1A**	24

Le Cercle	**SW1X**	24	Quirinale	**SW1P**	25
Ledbury	**W11**	28	Quo Vadis	**W1D**	23
Le Gavroche	**W1K**	28	Rasoi Vineet	**SW3**	28
Le Manoir/Quat	**OX44**	27	Rest. Gordon Ramsay	**SW3**	28
Le Pont/Tour	**SE1**	23	Rhodes 24	**EC2N**	25
Les Deux	**WC2N**	19	Ritz	**W1J**	24
Locanda Locatelli	**W1H**	25	River Café	**W6**	27
Lutyens	**EC4**	23	Roast	**SE1**	25
Marco Pierre White	**E1**	23	Roka	**W1T**	26
Marcus Wareing	**SW1X**	27	Roux/Parliament	**SW1P**	24
Massimo	**WC2N**	21	Roux/Landau	**W1**	26
Matsuri	**SW1Y**	23	Sake No Hana	**SW1A**	25
Maze	**W1K**	24	San Lorenzo	**SW3**	21
Maze Grill	**W1K**	23	Santini	**SW1W**	20
Medlar	**SW10**	25	Sartoria	**W1S**	23
Memories/China	**SW1W**	23	Savoy Grill	**WC2**	24
Min Jiang	**W8**	25	Scott's	**W1K**	26
Morgan M	**EC1A**	28	Season/Fifth Fl.	**SW1X**	21
Mr. Chow	**SW1X**	22	Seven Park	**SW1A**	24
Murano	**W1J**	26	Shanghai Blues	**WC1V**	24
NEW Naamyaa	**EC1V**	–	Sketch/Lecture	**W1S**	22
NEW New St. Grill	**EC2M**	–	Skylon	**SE1**	20
1901	**EC2M**	23	Smiths/Smithfield	**EC1M**	21
Nobu Berkeley	**W1J**	26	Spice Mkt.	**W1**	22
Nobu London	**W1K**	27	Square	**W1J**	28
NOPI	**W1B**	25	Sumosan	**W1S**	22
Novikov	**W1J**	21	NEW SushiSamba	**EC2N**	21
NEW Oblix	**SE1**	–	Tamarind	**W1J**	25
1 Lombard St.	**EC3V**	23	Texture	**W1H**	26
One-O-One	**SW1X**	22	Theo Randall	**W1J**	25
Orrery	**W1U**	23	34	**W1K**	23
NEW Outlaw's	**SW3**	–	Tinello	**SW1W**	25
Oxo Tower	**SE1**	22	Tom Aikens	**SW3**	25
Palm	**SW1X**	22	Trinity	**SW4**	26
Paramount	**WC1A**	21	28-50 Wine	**EC4A**	21
Paternoster Chop	**EC4M**	22	Umu	**W1J**	27
Petrus	**SW1X**	28	Veeraswamy	**W1B**	24
Pied à Terre	**W1T**	28	Viajante	**E2**	26
Plateau	**E14**	21	Waterside Inn	**SL6**	29
NEW Plum + Spilt Milk	**N1C**	–	Wheeler's	**SW1A**	21
Poissonnerie/l'Avenue	**SW3**	24	Wild Honey	**W1S**	23
Pollen St. Social	**EC1V**	25	Wilton's	**SW1Y**	26
Princess Garden	**W1K**	24	Wolseley	**W1J**	23
Quadrato	**E14**	19	Zafferano	**SW1X**	24
NEW Quality Chop	**EC1R**	–	Zaika	**W8**	25
Quilon	**SW1E**	–	Zuma	**SW7**	27

Cuisines

Includes names, locations and Food ratings.

AFGHAN

Afghan Kitchen | **N1**   24

AMERICAN

Automat | **W1S**   19
Big Easy | **SW3**   21
Bodeans | **multi.**   22
Breakfast Club | **multi.**   21
Burger & Lobster | **multi.**   23
Christopher's | **WC2E**   –
Cut/45 Park Ln. | **W1K**   25
Diner | **multi.**   18
Ed's Easy Diner | **multi.**   19
🆕 Electric Diner | **W11**   –
Hoxton Grill | **EC2A**   22
Joe Allen | **WC2E**   19
🆕 Joe's Southern | **WC2E**   –
JW Steak | **W1K**   23
🆕 Lockhart | **W1H**   –
Lucky 7 | **W2**   18
🆕 MASH | **W1F**   25
Maxwell's | **WC2E**   19
🆕 Oblix | **SE1**   –
Palm | **SW1X**   22
Shrimpy's | **N1C**   –
Smollensky's | **multi.**   18
Sophie's | **multi.**   22
Spuntino | **W1D**   23

ARGENTINEAN

Buen Ayre | **E8**   25
Constancia | **SE1**   25
El Gaucho | **multi.**   23
Garufa/Garufin | **multi.**   26
Gaucho | **multi.**   22
Santa Maria | **SW8**   26
🆕 Zoilo | **W1U**   –

ASIAN

Asia de Cuba | **WC2N**   23
Bam-Bou | **W1T**   22
Banana Tree | **multi.**   21
🆕 Brompton Asian | **SW3**   –
🆕 Buddha-Bar | **SW1X**   –

Circus | **WC2H**   18
E&O | **W11**   23
Eight Over Eight | **SW3**   23
Gilgamesh | **NW1**   19
Inamo | **multi.**   19
NOPI | **W1B**   25
Novikov | **W1J**   21
Oxo Tower Brass. | **SE1**   23
Spice Mkt. | **W1**   22
XO | **NW3**   20

AUSTRALIAN

Flat White | **W1F**   24
Granger & Co. | **W11**   19
Kaffeine | **W1W**   25
Lantana | **W1T**   24

BAKERIES

Baker & Spice | **multi.**   21
Cocomaya | **multi.**   24
Gail's | **multi.**   22
Ladurée | **multi.**   24
Ottolenghi | **multi.**   26
Princi London | **W1F**   24

BARBECUE

Barbecoa | **EC4M**   23
Bodeans | **multi.**   22
Pitt Cue Co. | **W1F**   28

BELGIAN

Belgo | **multi.**   21
Leon De Bruxelles | **WC2H**   19

BRAZILIAN

Cabana | **multi.**   21
Canela | **WC2H**   21
Rodizio Rico | **multi.**   20
🆕 SushiSamba | **EC2N**   21

BRITISH (MODERN)

Adam St. | **WC2N**   23
Admiral Codrington | **SW3**   19
Anchor/Hope | **SE1**   25

NEW Angler | **EC2M**	–|
Anglesea Arms | **W6**	21|
Annie's | **multi.**	23|
Avenue | **SW1A**	20|
Babylon | **W8**	22|
Balans | **multi.**	19|
Balcon | **SW1Y**	23|
NEW Beagle | **E2**	–|
NEW Beard To Tail | **EC2A**	–|
Belvedere | **W8**	21|
Bingham | **TW10**	24|
NEW Bird/Smithfield | **EC1A**	–|
Bluebird | **SW3**	20|
Botanist | **SW1W**	18|
Bradley's | **NW3**	22|
Brompton B&G | **SW3**	20|
Bumpkin | **multi.**	19|
Chez Bruce | **SW17**	28|
Chiswell St. Dining | **EC1**	22|
Clarke's | **W8**	25|
NEW Clove Club | **EC2A**	–|
Corrigan's Mayfair | **W1K**	25|
Cow | **W2**	22|
Dinner/Heston | **SW1X**	26|
Dorchester | **W1K**	25|
Duke of Cambridge | **N1**	22|
Empress | **E9**	23|
English Pig | **SW1P**	20|
Enterprise | **SW3**	21|
Fat Duck | **SL6**	28|
Fifteen | **N1**	–|
Fox/Grapes | **SW19**	20|
Frederick's | **N1**	23|
French/Grace | **SW9**	–|
Great Queen St. | **WC2B**	24|
Groucho Club | **W1D**	18|
Gun | **E14**	23|
Harwood Arms | **SW6**	27|
Hereford Rd. | **W2**	24|
Ivy | **WC2H**	24|
Julie's | **W11**	18|
Kensington Pl. | **W8**	20|
Lamberts | **SW12**	28|
Launceston Pl. | **W8**	25|
Le Caprice | **SW1A**	24|
Medcalf | **EC1R**	22|

Mews/Mayfair | **W1S**	19|
National Dining Rms. | **WC2N**	20|
1901 | **EC2M**	23|
NEW No. 11 Pimlico | **SW1W**	–|
Old Brewery | **SE10**	17|
1 Blenheim Terrace | **NW8**	24|
Palmerston | **SE22**	23|
Paradise/Kensal | **W10**	23|
NEW Plum + Spilt Milk | **N1C**	–|
Pollen St. Social | **EC1V**	25|
Portrait | **WC2H**	22|
Princess of Shoreditch | **EC2A**	20|
Prism | **EC3V**	19|
Randall/Aubin | **W1F**	25|
R.S.J. | **SE1**	22|
Seven Park | **SW1A**	24|
NEW Shed | **W8**	–|
Smiths/Smithfield | **EC1M**	21|
NEW Social Eating Hse. | **W1F**	–|
Soho Hse. | **W1D**	20|
St. John | **EC1M**	26|
St. John Bread | **E1**	25|
NEW Story | **SE1**	–|
Tate Modern | **SE1**	19|
Tom's Kitchen | **multi.**	23|
Tramshed | **EC2A**	20|
Union Café | **W1U**	21|
Wild Honey | **W1S**	23|
York/Albany | **NW1**	20|

BRITISH (TRADITIONAL)

Abbeville | **SW4**	23|
Albion | **N1**	22|
Annabel's | **W1J**	21|
Bentley's | **W1B**	25|
Bleeding Heart | **EC1N**	23|
Boisdale | **multi.**	22|
Bonds | **EC2R**	22|
Browns | **multi.**	19|
Bull & Last | **NW5**	24|
Butcher & Grill | **multi.**	20|
Canteen | **multi.**	18|
Dean St. | **W1D**	22|
Ffiona's | **W8**	23|
Fortnum's Fountain | **W1A**	20|

CUISINES

Foxtrot Oscar | **SW3**	19
Frontline | **W2**	23
Gilbert Scott | **NW1**	19
Goring Dining Room | **SW1**	25
Grazing Goat | **W1**	20
Green's | **multi.**	21
Grumbles | **SW1V**	19
Hix | **W1F**	22
Hix Mayfair | **W1S**	25
Hix Oyster | **EC1M**	24
Langan's Brass. | **W1J**	21
Maggie Jones's | **W8**	21
Mark's Club | **W1J**	21
Mercer | **EC2R**	22
108 Marylebone | **W1U**	21
Pig's Ear | **SW3**	21
Porters English | **WC2E**	19
Princess Victoria | **W12**	25
Quo Vadis | **W1D**	23
Rhodes 24 | **EC2N**	25
Ritz | **W1J**	24
Rivington Grill | **multi.**	23
Roast | **SE1**	25
Rotunda | **N1**	19
Rowley's | **SW1Y**	23
Sands End | **SW6**	22
Savoy Grill | **WC2**	24
Simpson's/Strand | **WC2R**	21
Sketch/Parlour | **W1S**	21
Thomas Cubitt | **SW1W**	21
Tuttons | **WC2B**	20
Warrington | **W9**	19
Wilton's | **SW1Y**	26

BURGERS

Automat | **W1S**	19
NEW BRGR.CO | **W1F**	-
Burger & Lobster | **multi.**	23
Byron | **multi.**	19
Diner | **multi.**	18
NEW Dirty Burger | **NW5**	-
NEW Five Guys | **WC2E**	-
Gourmet Burger | **multi.**	18
Haché | **multi.**	23
Honest Burgers | **multi.**	27
Lucky 7 | **W2**	18

Maxwell's | **WC2E**	19
MEATliquor | **W1G**	23
MEATmarket | **WC2E**	23
NEW MEATmission | **N1**	-
NEW Patty & Bun | **W1U**	21
NEW Shake Shack | **WC2E**	-

BURMESE

Mandalay | **W2**	24

CARIBBEAN

Asia de Cuba | **WC2N**	23
Cottons | **multi.**	22

CHICKEN

NEW Chicken Shop | **NW5**	-
NEW Chooks | **N10**	-
NEW Clockjack Oven | **W1D**	-
Tramshed | **EC2A**	20
NEW Wishbone | **SW9**	-

CHINESE

(* dim sum specialist)

NEW A Wong* | **SW1V**	-
Barshu | **W1D**	23
Ba Shan | **W1S**	24
NEW Bo London* | **W1S**	-
Cha Cha Moon | **W1F**	18
China Tang* | **W1K**	21
Chuen Cheng Ku* | **W1D**	20
Dragon Castle | **SE17**	22
Empress/Sichuan | **WC2H**	21
Four Seasons | **multi.**	23
Golden Dragon* | **W1D**	23
Goldmine | **W2**	25
Good Earth | **multi.**	25
Green Cottage | **NW3**	25
Hakkasan* | **multi.**	26
Haozhan | **W1D**	24
Harbour City* | **W1D**	19
NEW HKK | **EC2A**	-
Hunan | **SW1W**	27
NEW Hutong | **SE1**	-
Imperial China* | **WC2H**	21
Imperial City | **EC3V**	22
Joy King Lau* | **WC2H**	21
Kai Mayfair | **W1K**	25
Lotus Floating | **E14**	22

Mama Lan | **multi.**	⏤
Mandarin Kitchen | **W2**	25
Mao Tai* | **SW6**	25
Memories/China | **multi.**	23
Min Jiang* | **W8**	25
Mr. Chow | **SW1X**	22
Mr. Kong | **WC2H**	21
New Culture Rev. | **multi.**	20
New Mayflower | **W1D**	24
New World* | **W1D**	20
Pearl Liang* | **W2**	25
Phoenix Palace* | **NW1**	23
Ping Pong* | **multi.**	17
Plum Valley | **W1D**	23
Princess Garden | **W1K**	24
Royal China | **multi.**	23
Royal China Club* | **W1U**	25
Shanghai Blues* | **WC1V**	24
Wong Kei | **W1D**	19
Yauatcha* | **W1F**	27
Yming | **W1D**	23

COFFEEHOUSES

Flat White | **W1F**	24
Kaffeine | **W1W**	25
Lantana | **W1T**	24
Regency Café | **SW1P**	23

DELIS

(See also sandwiches)
Bill's Produce | **multi.**	19
Daylesford | **multi.**	21
Gaby's | **WC2H**	23
La Fromagerie | **multi.**	24
Mishkin's | **WC2B**	20
Ottolenghi | **multi.**	26
Reubens | **W1U**	20
Tom's Deli | **W11**	24
Villandry | **W1W**	18

EASTERN EUROPEAN

Baltic | **SE1**	23
Bob Bob Ricard | **W1F**	22
Verru | **W1U**	22

EUROPEAN (MODERN)

Abingdon | **W8**	21
About Thyme | **SW1V**	24
Admiral Codrington | **SW3**	19

Alyn Williams | **W1S**	23
Andrew Edmunds | **W1F**	24
Arbutus | **W1D**	24
Arts Club | **W1S**	22
Aurora | **W1F**	24
Bank Westminster | **SW1E**	20
Bingham | **TW10**	24
Blueprint | **SE1**	22
Bread St. Kitchen | **EC4M**	20
NEW Brompton Asian | **SW3**	⏤
Brompton B&G | **SW3**	20
Brumus | **SW1Y**	22
Camden Brass. | **NW1**	23
Chancery | **EC4A**	24
Chapters All Day | **SE3**	24
Charlotte's | **multi.**	25
Corner Room | **E2**	29
Criterion | **W1J**	21
Dabbous | **W1T**	26
Delaunay | **WC2B**	21
Dock Kitchen | **W10**	24
Don | **EC4N**	23
Ducksoup | **W1D**	21
Flemings Grill | **W1J**	21
Frederick's | **N1**	23
Fulham/Kensington Wine | **multi.**	18
NEW Gail's Kitchen | **WC1B**	⏤
George | **W1K**	23
Giaconda/Dining | **WC2H**	23
Glasshouse | **TW9**	26
NEW Happenstance | **EC4M**	⏤
Hedone | **W4**	23
High Road Brass. | **W4**	22
Hix | **W1F**	22
Hush | **multi.**	19
Indigo | **WC2B**	23
Ivy | **WC2H**	24
NEW Kaspar's | **WC2R**	⏤
Kettner's | **W1D**	22
NEW Kitchen Table | **W1T**	⏤
Kitchen W8 | **W8**	25
La Trompette | **W4**	27
L'Autre Pied | **W1U**	25
Le Caprice | **SW1A**	24
Le Deuxième | **WC2E**	22
Little Bay | **multi.**	21

CUISINES

Lutyens | **EC4**	23
Made/Camden | **NW1**	24
Magdalen | **SE1**	25
Michael Nadra | **W4**	25
Murano | **W1J**	26
Odette's | **NW1**	25
Old Bull/Bush | **NW3**	18
NEW 1 Leicester St. | **WC2H**	-
1 Lombard Brass. | **EC3V**	21
Orange | **SW1W**	22
Oxo Tower | **SE1**	22
Pantechnicon/Dining | **SW1X**	21
Paramount | **WC1A**	21
Petersham | **TW10**	23
Petersham Nurseries | **TW10**	24
Quaglino's | **SW1Y**	21
Riding House | **W1W**	21
Roux/Parliament | **SW1P**	24
Roux/Landau | **W1**	26
NEW Royal Quarter | **SW1E**	-
Saf | **W8**	23
Sam's Brass. | **W4**	24
Season/Fifth Fl. | **SW1X**	21
Sketch/Gallery | **W1S**	21
Sketch/Lecture | **W1S**	22
Skylon | **SE1**	20
NEW Tartufo | **SW3**	-
10 Cases | **WC2H**	23
10 Greek St. | **W1D**	23
Texture | **W1H**	26
Trinity | **SW4**	26
202 | **W11**	19
Villandry | **W1W**	18
Vinoteca | **multi.**	23
Vivat Bacchus | **multi.**	20
Wapping Food | **E1W**	19
Wells | **NW3**	22
Whitechapel | **E1**	18
Wolseley | **W1J**	23

FISH 'N' CHIPS

NEW Fish & Chip Shop | **N1**	-
Geales | **multi.**	20
Golden Hind | **W1U**	24
Nautilus Fish | **NW6**	26
North Sea | **WC1H**	24

Poppies Fish | **multi.**	22
Rock & Sole | **WC2H**	24

FRENCH

Alain Ducasse | **W1K**	27
Almeida | **N1**	22
Annabel's | **W1J**	21
Belvedere | **W8**	21
Bibendum | **SW3**	23
Bleeding Heart | **EC1N**	23
Boundary | **E2**	23
Bradley's | **NW3**	22
Café des Amis | **WC2E**	18
Cellar Gascon | **EC1A**	23
Chez Gérard | **EC2N**	-
Cigalon | **WC2A**	22
Clos Maggiore | **WC2E**	25
Club Gascon | **EC1A**	27
Coq d'Argent | **EC2R**	23
NEW Electric Diner | **W11**	-
Elena's L'Etoile | **W1T**	20
Espelette | **W1K**	25
French Table | **KT6**	28
Galvin at Windows | **W1K**	25
Galvin Chapelle/Café | **E1**	26
Gauthier | **W1D**	28
Greenhouse | **W1J**	27
Hélène Darroze | **W1K**	25
Hibiscus | **W1S**	25
Koffmann's | **SW1X**	27
L'Atelier/Robuchon | **WC2H**	28
La Trompette | **W4**	27
L'Aventure | **NW8**	25
Le Cercle | **SW1X**	24
Ledbury | **W11**	28
Le Gavroche | **W1K**	28
Le Manoir/Quat | **OX44**	27
Le Mercury | **N1**	20
Le Pont/Tour | **SE1**	23
Le Relais | **multi.**	24
L'Escargot | **W1D**	25
Les Deux | **WC2N**	19
Les Trois Garçons | **E1**	23
L'Etranger | **SW7**	25
Marcus Wareing | **SW1X**	27
Mark's Club | **W1J**	21

Maze	**W1K**	24
Medlar	**SW10**	25
Morgan M	**EC1A**	28
1 Lombard St.	**EC3V**	23
One-O-One	**SW1X**	22
Orrery	**W1U**	23
Oslo Court	**NW8**	26
Petrus	**SW1X**	28
Pied à Terre	**W1T**	28
Plateau	**E14**	21
Poissonnerie/l'Avenue	**SW3**	24
Rest. Gordon Ramsay	**SW3**	28
Ritz	**W1J**	24
Savoy Grill	**WC2**	24
Seven Park	**SW1A**	24
Square	**W1J**	28
Tom Aikens	**SW3**	25
Waterside Inn	**SL6**	29

FRENCH (BISTRO)

Aubaine	**multi.**	18
Bar Boulud	**SW1X**	24
Bibendum Oyster	**SW3**	23
Bistrot Bruno	**EC1M**	25
Bistrotheque	**E2**	21
Café Boheme	**W1D**	18
Cassis Bistro	**SW3**	22
Chabrot Bistro des Amis	**SW1X**	20
NEW Chabrot Bistrot	**EC1A**	–
Comptoir Gascon	**EC1M**	25
Galvin Bistrot	**W1U**	25
NEW Green Man	**WC2N**	21
Grumbles	**SW1V**	19
La Bouchée	**SW7**	24
L'Absinthe	**NW1**	23
La Poule au Pot	**SW1W**	22
Le Boudin Blanc	**W1J**	24
Le Café/Marché	**EC1M**	25
Le Vacherin	**W4**	24
NEW Little Social	**W1S**	–
Mon Plaisir	**WC2H**	21
Truc Vert	**W1K**	19
28-50 Wine	**multi.**	21

FRENCH (BRASSERIE)

Angelus	**W2**	25
Balcon	**SW1Y**	23

NEW Balthazar	**WC2B**	19
Bellamy's	**W1J**	24
Brasserie Blanc	**multi.**	18
NEW Brasserie Chavot	**W1S**	–
Brasserie Zédel	**W1F**	17
Cheyne Walk	**SW3**	20
NEW Colbert	**SW1W**	17
Côte	**multi.**	18
Gazette	**multi.**	20
La Brasserie	**SW3**	20
Langan's Brass.	**W1J**	21
Le Café Anglais	**W2**	22
Le Colombier	**SW3**	23
Pig's Ear	**SW3**	21
Racine	**SW3**	24

GASTROPUB

Abbeville	British/Euro.	**SW4**	23
Abingdon	Euro.	**W8**	21
Admiral Codrington	British/Euro.	**SW3**	19
Albion	British	**N1**	22
Anchor/Hope	British	**SE1**	25
Anglesea Arms	British	**W6**	21
Bull & Last	British	**NW5**	24
Cow	British	**W2**	22
Draft House	Eclectic	**multi.**	20
Duke of Cambridge	British	**N1**	22
Duke of Sussex	British/Spanish	**W4**	22
Eagle	Med.	**EC1R**	24
Empress	British	**E9**	23
Enterprise	Eclectic	**SW3**	21
Fox/Grapes	British	**SW19**	20
Great Queen St.	British	**WC2B**	24
Gun	British	**E14**	23
Harwood Arms	British	**SW6**	27
Orange	Euro.	**SW1W**	22
Palmerston	British	**SE22**	23
Paradise/Kensal	British	**W10**	23
Pig's Ear	British/French	**SW3**	21
Princess of Shoreditch	British	**EC2A**	20
Princess Victoria	British	**W12**	25
Sands End	British/Irish	**SW6**	22
Thomas Cubitt	British	**SW1W**	21
Warrington	British	**W9**	19

Wells | Euro. | **NW3**	22
York/Albany | Euro. | **NW1**	20

GERMAN

Herman ze German | **WC2N**	23

GREEK

Carob Tree | **NW5**	23
Halepi | **W2**	24
Lemonia | **NW1**	21
Real Greek | **multi.**	20

HOT DOGS

NEW Bubbledogs | **W1T**	18
Herman ze German | **WC2N**	23

HUNGARIAN

Gay Hussar | **W1D**	21

INDIAN

Amaya | **SW1X**	27
Babur | **SE23**	27
Benares | **W1J**	25
Bengal Clipper | **SE1**	21
Bombay Brass. | **SW7**	23
Bombay Palace | **W2**	24
Café Spice | **E1**	25
Chakra | **W11**	23
Chor Bizarre | **W1S**	25
Chutney Mary | **SW10**	25
Chutneys | **NW1**	23
Cinnamon Club | **SW1P**	26
Cinnamon Kitchen | **EC2M**	24
Dishoom | **multi.**	23
Dockmaster's | **E14**	22
Ganapati | **SE15**	26
Gaylord | **W1W**	21
Gopal's | **W1D**	19
Haandi | **multi.**	21
Hot Stuff | **SW8**	25
Imli Street | **W1F**	22
Indian Zing | **W6**	23
Khan's | **W2**	20
La Porte/Indes | **W1H**	22
Ma Goa | **SW15**	22
Malabar | **W8**	20
Malabar Junction | **WC1B**	19
Masala Zone | **multi.**	22

Mela | **WC2H**	22
Mint Leaf | **multi.**	22
Moti Mahal | **WC2B**	25
Noor Jahan | **multi.**	23
Painted Heron | **SW10**	24
Paradise | **NW3**	26
Punjab | **WC2H**	23
Quilon | **SW1E**	-
Rasa | **multi.**	24
Rasoi Vineet | **SW3**	28
Red Fort | **W1D**	23
Roti Chai | **W1H**	24
Sagar | **multi.**	21
Spice Village | **multi.**	27
Star of India | **SW5**	26
Tamarind | **W1J**	25
Trishna | **W1U**	26
Veeraswamy | **W1B**	24
Woodlands | **multi.**	23
Zaika | **W8**	25
Zayna | **W1H**	28

INDONESIAN

Bali Bali | **WC2H**	20

INTERNATIONAL

Archipelago | **W1T**	22
Bevis Marks | **E1**	23
Blakes | **SW7**	20
Bob Bob Ricard | **W1F**	22
Books/Cooks | **W11**	25
Cantina Vino. | **SE1**	19
Cape Town Fish | **W1F**	23
Caravan | **multi.**	24
Daylesford | **multi.**	21
Draft House | **multi.**	20
Elk/Woods | **N1**	21
NEW Grain Store | **N1C**	-
Granger & Co. | **W11**	19
NEW Greenberry Café | **NW1**	-
Juniper Dining | **N5**	28
Kentish Canteen | **NW5**	22
Kopapa | **WC2H**	22
Light House | **SW19**	24
Modern Pantry | **EC1V**	25
Mosimann's | **SW1X**	26
Motcombs | **SW1X**	21

Providores | **W1U**	25
Saf | **W8**	23
NEW Social Eating Hse. | **W1F**	-
Tom's Deli | **W11**	24
Troubadour | **SW5**	20
Viajante | **E2**	26

ITALIAN

NEW Acciuga | **W8**	-
A Cena | **TW1**	25
Aglio e Olio | **SW10**	22
Alba | **EC1Y**	22
Al Duca | **SW1Y**	22
Alloro | **W1S**	22
Amaranto | **W1J**	24
Amerigo Vespucci | **E14**	23
Amico Bio | **multi.**	22
Antonio's | **N1**	23
Apsleys | **SW1X**	26
Artigiano | **NW3**	22
Assaggi | **W2**	25
Babbo | **W1S**	21
Bocca/Gelupo | **W1D**	25
Buona Sera | **multi.**	20
Caldesi | **W1U**	18
Cantina/Ponte | **SE1**	19
Caraffini | **SW1**	22
Caravaggio | **EC3A**	19
Carluccio's | **multi.**	16
Cecconi's | **W1S**	23
Citrus | **W1**	21
C London | **W1K**	23
Como Lario | **SW1W**	21
Daphne's | **SW3**	22
Dehesa | **W1F**	25
Delfino | **W1K**	20
Downtown Mayfair | **W1S**	21
Elena's L'Etoile | **W1T**	20
Elistano | **SW3**	21
Enoteca Turi | **SW15**	25
500 | **N19**	25
Franco's | **SW1Y**	22
Frankie's | **multi.**	17
Giovanni's | **WC2N**	23
Harry's Bar | **W1K**	25
Il Baretto | **W1U**	23

Il Bordello | **E1W**	25
Il Convivio | **SW1W**	23
Il Portico | **W8**	19
Jamie's Italian | **multi.**	20
La Famiglia | **SW10**	20
La Genova | **W1K**	23
L'Anima | **EC2A**	25
La Porchetta | **multi.**	22
NEW Lardo | **E8**	-
Latium | **W1T**	25
Little Italy | **W1D**	21
Locanda Locatelli | **W1H**	25
Locanda Ottoemezzo | **W8**	25
Lucio | **SW3**	20
Made in Italy | **multi.**	19
Manicomio | **multi.**	18
Massimo | **WC2N**	21
Mediterraneo | **W11**	23
Mele e Pere | **W1F**	20
Murano | **W1J**	26
Novikov | **W1J**	21
Oliveto | **SW1W**	24
Olivo | **SW1W**	22
NEW Olivocarne | **SW1W**	-
Olivomare | **SW1W**	24
Opera Tavern | **WC2B**	25
Orso | **WC2E**	21
Osteria Antica | **SW11**	22
Osteria Basilico | **W11**	24
Osteria dell'Arancio | **SW10**	22
Pescatori | **multi.**	22
Pizza Express | **multi.**	16
Polpo | **multi.**	22
Portobello | **W11**	23
Prezzo | **multi.**	20
Princi London | **W1F**	24
Quadrato | **E14**	19
Quirinale | **SW1P**	25
Red Pepper | **W9**	21
River Café | **W6**	27
Rocca | **multi.**	24
Rossopomodoro | **multi.**	23
Sale e Pepe | **SW1X**	24
Salt Yard | **W1T**	24
San Lorenzo | **SW3**	21
Santini | **SW1W**	20

CUISINES

Sardo | **W1T**	21
Sartoria | **W1S**	23
Scalini | **SW3**	24
Signor Sassi | **SW1X**	23
Spuntino | **W1D**	23
Stingray/Stringray | **multi.**	23
Strada | **multi.**	17
Tentazioni | **SE1**	24
Theo Randall | **W1J**	25
Timo | **W8**	24
Tinello | **SW1W**	25
Trullo | **N1**	24
2 Veneti | **W1U**	23
Vapiano | **multi.**	23
Vasco & Piero's | **W1F**	23
Zafferano | **SW1X**	24
Ziani | **SW3**	24
Zizzi | **multi.**	18
Zucca | **SE1**	27

JAPANESE

(* sushi specialist)

Abeno | **multi.**	24
Akari | **N1**	24
Aqua Kyoto* | **W1B**	22
Atari-Ya* | **multi.**	26
Benihana | **multi.**	20
Bento* | **NW1**	23
Bincho | **W1D**	23
NEW Bone Daddies | **W1F**	21
Café Japan* | **NW11**	26
Chisou* | **multi.**	23
Defune* | **W1U**	25
Dinings* | **W1H**	28
Feng Sushi* | **multi.**	19
Hare & Tortoise* | **multi.**	22
Hi Sushi* | **multi.**	22
Ikeda* | **W1K**	26
Jin Kichi* | **NW3**	27
Kiku* | **W1J**	24
Koi* | **W8**	21
Koya | **W1D**	24
K10 | **EC2R**	22
Kulu Kulu* | **multi.**	22
L'Etranger | **SW7**	25
Matsuri* | **SW1Y**	23
Miyama* | **multi.**	23

Nobu Berkeley* | **W1J**	26
Nobu London* | **W1K**	27
Roka* | **multi.**	26
Sake No Hana* | **SW1A**	25
Sakura* | **W1S**	22
Satsuma* | **W1D**	20
NEW Shiori | **W2**	-
Sumosan* | **W1S**	22
NEW SushiSamba | **EC2N**	21
Sushi-Say* | **NW2**	29
Sushi Tetsu* | **EC1V**	-
Taro* | **multi.**	24
Ten Ten Tei* | **W1**	25
Tokyo Diner* | **WC2H**	22
Tonkotsu | **W1D**	-
Tsunami* | **multi.**	23
Tsuru* | **multi.**	22
Umu* | **W1J**	27
Wagamama | **multi.**	17
Yashin Sushi* | **W8**	28
Yoshino* | **W1J**	24
Zuma* | **SW7**	27

JEWISH

Gaby's | **WC2H**	23
Mishkin's | **WC2B**	20
Reubens | **W1U**	20
Solly's | **NW11**	20

KOREAN

Asadal* | **WC1V**	23

KOSHER/ KOSHER-STYLE

Bevis Marks | **E1**	23
Reubens | **W1U**	20
Solly's | **NW11**	20

LEBANESE

Al Hamra | **W1J**	23
Al Sultan | **W1J**	22
Al Waha | **W2**	22
Beirut Express | **multi.**	23
Beiteddine | **SW1X**	26
Comptoir Libanais | **multi.**	20
Fairuz | **W1U**	22
Ishbilia | **SW1X**	24

Kenza | **EC2M** 24
Maroush | **multi.** 23
Noura | **multi.** 22
Yalla Yalla | **multi.** 24

MALAYSIAN

Champor | **SE1** 22
Satay House | **W2** 26
Sedap | **EC1V** 26
Singapore Gdn. | **multi.** 22

MEDITERRANEAN

Aurelia | **W1S** 22
Baker & Spice | **multi.** 21
Blue Legume | **multi.** 22
Brawn | **E2** 26
Café Med | **NW8** 19
Cantina Vino. | **SE1** 19
Carob Tree | **NW5** 23
Cassis Bistro | **SW3** 22
Chez Bruce | **SW17** 28
Ciao Bella | **WC1N** 23
Del'Aziz | **multi.** 20
Eagle | **EC1R** 24
Franco's | **SW1Y** 22
French Table | **KT6** 28
La Petite Maison | **W1K** 26
Leon | **multi.** 20
Massimo | **WC2N** 21
Mem & Laz | **N1** 27
Morton's | **W1J** 22
Ottolenghi | **multi.** 26
Oxo Tower Brass. | **SE1** 23
Terroirs | **WC2N** 22
Union Café | **W1U** 21

MEXICAN

Cafe Pacifico | **WC2H** 20
Cantina Laredo | **WC2H** 23
NEW Casa Negra | **EC2A** -
Chilango | **multi.** 21
Crazy Homies | **W2** 18
La Bodega Negra | **W1D** 17
Lupita | **multi.** 25
Mestizo | **NW1** 21
Shrimpy's | **N1C** -
Taqueria | **W11** 24

Tortilla | **multi.** 22
Wahaca | **multi.** 22

MIDDLE EASTERN

Baker & Spice | **multi.** 21
French/Grace | **SW9** -
Gaby's | **WC2H** 23
Honey & Co | **W1T** -
NOPI | **W1B** 25
Ottolenghi | **multi.** 26
Solly's | **NW11** 20

MOROCCAN

Adams Cafe | **W12** 21
Kenza | **EC2M** 24
Momo | **W1B** 21

NOODLE SHOPS

NEW Bone Daddies | **W1F** 21
Koya | **W1D** 24
New Culture Rev. | **multi.** 20
Tonkotsu | **W1D** -
Wagamama | **multi.** 17

NORTH AFRICAN

Adams Cafe | **W12** 21
Del'Aziz | **multi.** 20
Morito | **EC1R** 26
Moro | **EC1R** 26
Ottolenghi | **multi.** 26
Souk | **WC2H** 21

PAKISTANI

Lahore Kebab | **multi.** 25
Original Lahore | **multi.** 23
Salloos | **SW1X** 24
Tayyabs | **E1** 25
Zayna | **W1H** 28

PAN-LATIN

Las Iguanas | **multi.** 21

PERSIAN

Alounak | **multi.** 23

PERUVIAN

Ceviche | **W1D** 27
NEW Coya | **W1J** 24
Lima | **W1T** 23

Nobu Berkeley	**W1J**	26	Cape Town Fish	**W1F**	23
Nobu London	**W1K**	27	Caviar House	**W1J**	23

PIZZA

Buona Sera	**multi.**	20	Fish	**SE1**	23
Delfino	**W1K**	20	**NEW** Fish & Chip Shop	**N1**	-
Franco Manca	**multi.**	26	**NEW** Fish Market	**EC2M**	-
La Porchetta	**multi.**	22	FishWorks	**multi.**	20
NEW Lardo	**E8**	-	Geales	**multi.**	20
Made in Italy	**multi.**	19	Golden Hind	**W1U**	24
Oliveto	**SW1W**	24	Green's	**multi.**	21
Osteria Basilico	**W11**	24	Hawksmoor	**W1J**	26
Pizza East	**multi.**	21	J. Sheekey	**WC2N**	26
Pizza Express	**multi.**	16	J. Sheekey Oyster	**WC2N**	25
Portobello	**W11**	23	**NEW** Kaspar's	**WC2R**	-
Princi London	**W1F**	24	Le Pont/Tour	**SE1**	23
Red Pepper	**W9**	21	Loch Fyne	**multi.**	22
Rossopomodoro	**multi.**	23	Lutyens	**EC4**	23
Stingray/Stringray	**multi.**	23	Mandarin Kitchen	**W2**	25
Union Jacks	**multi.**	18	Nautilus Fish	**NW6**	26

PORTUGUESE

Canela	**WC2H**	21	North Sea	**WC1H**	24
Eyre Brothers	**EC2A**	25	Olivomare	**SW1W**	24
Nando's	**multi.**	18	One-O-One	**SW1X**	22
Portal	**EC1M**	27	**NEW** Outlaw's	**SW3**	-

SANDWICHES

(See also Delis)

Fernandez & Wells	**multi.**	21	Pescatori	**multi.**	22
Ladurée	**multi.**	24	Poissonnerie/l'Avenue	**SW3**	24
La Fromagerie	**multi.**	24	Randall/Aubin	**W1F**	25
NEW Royal Quarter	**SW1E**	-	Rock & Sole	**WC2H**	24
			Scott's	**W1K**	26

SCANDINAVIAN

Lutyens	**EC4**	23	Sweetings	**EC4N**	23
Texture	**W1H**	26	Wheeler's	**SW1A**	21
Verru	**W1U**	22	Wilton's	**SW1Y**	26
			Wright Brothers	**multi.**	24

SCOTTISH

SINGAPOREAN

Albannach	**WC2N**	20	Singapore Gdn.	**multi.**	22
Boisdale	**multi.**	22			

SMALL PLATES

(See also Spanish tapas specialist)

SEAFOOD

NEW Angler	**EC2M**	-	Akari	Japanese	**N1**	24
Bentley's	**W1B**	25	Amaya	Indian	**SW1X**	27
Bibendum Oyster	**SW3**	23	Bocca/Gelupo	Italian	**W1D**	25
Burger & Lobster	**multi.**	23	Brawn	British	**E2**	26
			Caravan	Euro.	**multi.**	24
			Cellar Gascon	French	**EC1A**	23
			Club Gascon	French	**EC1A**	27
			NEW Coya	Peruvian	**W1J**	24
			Dinings	Japanese	**W1H**	28
			Dishoom	Indian	**multi.**	23

Ducksoup | Euro. | **W1D**	21
Fulham/Kensington Wine | Euro. | **multi.**	18
Hunan | Chinese | **SW1W**	27
Imli Street | Indian | **W1F**	22
L'Atelier/Robuchon | French | **WC2H**	28
Le Cercle | French | **SW1X**	24
Maze | French | **W1K**	24
Polpo | Italian | **multi.**	22
Providores | Eclectic | **W1U**	25
Real Greek | Greek | **multi.**	20
Riding House | Euro. | **W1W**	21
NEW Shed | British | **W8**	-
Spuntino | Amer./Italian | **W1D**	23
Terroirs | Med. | **WC2N**	22

SPANISH

(* tapas specialist)

NEW Ametsa | **SW1X**	-
Angels/Gypsies* | **SE5**	25
Aqua Nueva* | **W1B**	21
Barcelona Tapas* | **multi.**	22
Darrafina* | **W1D**	28
Barrica* | **W1T**	25
Boqueria* | **SW2**	-
Brindisa* | **multi.**	23
Cambio/Tercio | **SW5**	24
Camino* | **multi.**	22
Cigala* | **WC1N**	20
Copita' | **W1F**	24
Dehesa* | **W1F**	25
Donostia* | **W1H**	24
El Parador* | **NW1**	25
El Pirata* | **multi.**	22
Eyre Brothers | **EC2A**	25
Fernandez & Wells* | **multi.**	21
Fino* | **W1T**	26
NEW Gail's Kitchen | **WC1B**	-
Iberica* | **multi.**	23
José* | **SE1**	28
Meson Don Felipe* | **SE1**	23
Morito* | **EC1R**	26
Moro* | **EC1R**	26
Opera Tavern* | **WC2B**	25
Pix Pintxos* | **multi.**	17
Pizarro* | **SE1**	26

NEW Rosita/Sherry Bar | **SW11**	-
Salt Yard* | **W1T**	24
Tendido Cero* | **SW5**	21
Tendido Cuatro* | **SW6**	19

STEAKHOUSES

NEW Beard To Tail | **EC2A**	-
Black & Blue | **multi.**	19
Bountiful Cow | **WC1R**	22
Butlers Wharf | **SE1**	23
Christopher's | **WC2E**	-
Constancia | **SE1**	25
Cut/45 Park Ln. | **W1K**	25
El Gaucho | **multi.**	23
NEW Flat Iron | **W1**	-
Garufa/Garufin | **multi.**	26
Gaucho | **multi.**	22
Goodman | **multi.**	27
Greig's | **W1J**	21
Guinea Grill | **W1J**	24
Hawksmoor | **multi.**	26
Hix Oyster | **EC1M**	24
JW Steak | **W1K**	23
Le Relais | **multi.**	24
Marco Pierre White | **E1**	23
NEW MASH | **W1F**	25
Maze Grill | **W1K**	23
NEW Oblix | **SE1**	-
Palm | **SW1X**	22
Paternoster Chop | **EC4M**	22
Rib Room | **SW1X**	24
Santa Maria | **SW8**	26
Smollensky's | **multi.**	18
Sophie's | **multi.**	22
NEW STK | **WC2R**	-
34 | **W1K**	23

TAIWANESE

Hunan | **SW1W**	27
Loong's Legend | **multi.**	21

TEX-MEX

Hoxton Sq. | **N1**	16

THAI

Blue Elephant | **SW6**	24
Busaba Eathai | **multi.**	23

CUISINES

Churchill Arms	**W8**	21	Sofra	**multi.**	21
Crazy Bear	**multi.**	20	Tas	**multi.**	22
Esarn Kheaw	**W12**	23		

VEGETARIAN

Esarn Kheaw | **W12** — 23

KaoSarn | **multi.** — -

Mango Tree | **SW1X** — 20

NEW Naamyaa | **EC1V** — -

101 Thai | **W6** — 24

Patara | **multi.** — 24

Pepper Tree | **SW4** — 27

Rosa's | **multi.** — 22

Sri Nam | **E14** — 21

Suda | **WC2E** — 23

Thai Sq. | **multi.** — 19

Thai Thai | **EC1V** — 21

Yum Yum | **N16** — 23

VEGETARIAN

(* vegan)

Amico Bio | **multi.** — 22

Chutneys | **NW1** — 23

Food/Thought | **WC2H** — 24

Gate* | **multi.** — 23

Morgan M | **EC1A** — 28

Rasa | **multi.** — 24

Saf* | **W8** — 23

Sagar | **multi.** — 21

222 Veggie* | **W14** — 24

Vanilla Black | **EC4A** — 24

Woodlands | **multi.** — 23

TUNISIAN

Adams Cafe | **W12** — 21

VIETNAMESE

Banh Mi Bay | **multi.** — 24

Cafe East | **SE16** — 24

Cây Tre | **multi.** — 22

Mien Tay | **multi.** — 24

Pho | **multi.** — 22

Song Que | **E2** — 25

Viet | **W1D** — 23

Viet Hoa | **E2** — 22

TURKISH

Antepliler | **N1** — 26

Efes | **W1W** — 22

Gallipoli | **N1** — 21

Haz | **multi.** — 23

Ishtar | **W1U** — 20

Kazan | **SW1V** — 24

Mangal Ocakbasi | **E8** — -

Özer | **W1B** — 21

Pasha | **N1** — 22

WEST AFRICAN

805 | **SE15** — 24

Locations

Includes names, cuisines and Food ratings.

Central London

BLOOMSBURY/ FITZROVIA

Abeno	*Japanese*	24
Archipelago	*Int'l*	22
Bam-Bou	*Asian*	22
Banh Mi Bay	*Viet.*	24
Barrica	*Spanish*	25
Black & Blue	*Steak*	19
Brasserie Blanc	*French*	18
NEW Bubbledogs	*Hot Dogs*	18
Busaba Eathai	*Thai*	23
Carluccio's	*Italian*	16
Ciao Bella	*Med.*	23
Cigala	*Spanish*	20
Crazy Bear	*Thai*	20
Dabbous	*Euro.*	26
Draft House	*Int'l*	20
Efes	*Turkish*	22
Elena's L'Etoile	*French/Italian*	20
Fino	*Spanish*	26
NEW Gail's Kitchen	*Euro.*	-
Gaylord	*Indian*	21
Hakkasan	*Chinese*	26
Hare & Tortoise	*Japanese*	22
Honey & Co	*Mideast.*	-
Kaffeine	*Australian/Coffee*	25
NEW Kitchen Table	*Euro.*	-
Lantana	*Australian/Coffee*	24
La Porchetta	*Pizza*	22
Latium	*Italian*	25
Lima	*Peruvian*	23
Malabar Junction	*Indian*	19
Nando's	*Portug.*	18
NEW Newman St.	*British*	-
North Sea	*Seafood*	24
Pescatori	*Italian/Seafood*	22
Pho	*Viet.*	22
Pied à Terre	*French*	28
Ping Pong	*Chinese*	17
Riding House	*Euro.*	21
Roka	*Japanese*	26

Sagar	*Indian/Veg.*	21
Salt Yard	*Italian/Spanish*	24
Sardo	*Italian*	21
Tas	*Turkish*	22
Tortilla	*Mex.*	22
Tsunami	*Japanese*	23
Wahaca	*Mex.*	22
Yalla Yalla	*Lebanese*	24
Zizzi	*Italian*	18

CHARING CROSS/ WESTMINSTER

Albannach	*Scottish*	20
Bank Westminster	*Euro.*	20
Cinnamon Club	*Indian*	26
English Pig	*British*	20
Herman ze German	*German/Hot Dogs*	23
Lupita	*Mex.*	25
Massimo	*Italian/Med.*	21
National Dining Rms.	*British*	20
Prezzo	*Italian*	20
Quirinale	*Italian*	25
Regency Café	*British*	23
Roux/Parliament	*Euro.*	24

CHINATOWN

Chuen Cheng Ku	*Chinese*	20
Empress/Sichuan	*Chinese*	21
Four Seasons	*Chinese*	23
Golden Dragon	*Chinese*	23
Haozhan	*Chinese*	24
Harbour City	*Chinese*	19
Imperial China	*Chinese*	21
Joy King Lau	*Chinese*	21
Leong's Legend	*Taiwanese*	21
Mr. Kong	*Chinese*	21
New World	*Chinese*	20
Plum Valley	*Chinese*	23
Tokyo Diner	*Japanese*	22
Wong Kei	*Chinese*	19

CITY

Alba	*Italian*	22
NEW Angler	*British/Seafood*	-

LOCATIONS

Barbecoa	*BBQ*	23
Barcelona Tapas	*Spanish*	22
Benihana	*Japanese*	20
Bodeans	*Amer./BBQ*	22
Boisdale	*British/Scottish*	22
Bonds	*British*	22
Brasserie Blanc	*French*	18
Bread St. Kitchen	*Euro.*	20
Browns	*British*	19
Burger & Lobster	*Amer.*	23
Café Spice	*Indian*	25
Camino	*Spanish*	22
Caravaggio	*Italian*	19
Chez Gérard	*French*	–
Chilango	*Mex.*	21
Chiswell St. Dining	*British*	22
Cinnamon Kitchen	*Indian*	24
Coq d'Argent	*French*	23
Côte	*French*	18
Don	*Euro.*	23
NEW Duck & Waffle	*British*	20
NEW Fish Market	*Seafood*	–
Gaucho	*Argent./Steak*	22
Goodman	*Steak*	27
Green's	*British/Seafood*	21
NEW Happenstance	*Euro.*	–
Hare & Tortoise	*Japanese*	22
Hawksmoor	*Steak*	26
Haz	*Turkish*	23
NEW HKK	*Chinese*	–
Imperial City	*Chinese*	22
Jamie's Italian	*Italian*	20
Kenza	*Lebanese/Moroccan*	24
K10	*Japanese*	22
L'Anima	*Italian*	25
Leon	*Med.*	20
Le Relais	*French/Steak*	24
Loch Fyne	*Seafood*	22
Lutyens	*Euro./Scan.*	23
Manicomio	*Italian*	18
Marco Pierre White	*Steak*	23
Mercer	*British*	22
Mint Leaf	*Indian*	22
Miyama	*Japanese*	23
NEW New St. Grill	*British*	–
1901	*British*	23

1 Lombard St.	*French*	23
1 Lombard Brass.	*Euro.*	21
Paternoster Chop	*Steak*	22
Ping Pong	*Chinese*	17
Prism	*British*	19
Rhodes 24	*British*	25
NEW SushiSamba	*Brazilian/Japanese*	21
Sweetings	*Seafood*	23
Thai Sq.	*Thai*	19
Tortilla	*Mex.*	22
Tsuru	*Japanese*	22

CLERKENWELL/ FARRINGDON

Amico Bio	*Italian/Veg.*	22
NEW Bird/Smithfield	*British*	–
Bistrot Bruno	*French*	25
Bleeding Heart	*British/French*	23
Burger & Lobster	*Amer.*	23
Caravan	*Int'l*	24
Carluccio's	*Italian*	16
Cellar Gascon	*French*	23
NEW Chabrot Bistrot	*French*	–
Club Gascon	*French*	27
Comptoir Gascon	*French*	25
Cottons	*Carib.*	22
Eagle	*Med.*	24
Gail's	*Bakery*	22
Gaucho	*Argent./Steak*	22
Hix Oyster	*British/Steak*	24
La Porchetta	*Pizza*	22
Le Café/Marché	*French*	25
Little Bay	*Euro.*	21
Medcalf	*British*	22
Modern Pantry	*Int'l*	25
Morgan M	*French*	28
Morito	*African/Spanish*	26
Moro	*African/Spanish*	26
Pho	*Viet.*	22
Polpo	*Italian*	22
Portal	*Portug.*	27
NEW Quality Chop	*British*	–
Rasa	*Indian/Veg.*	24
Smiths/Smithfield	*British*	21
St. John	*British*	26
Sushi Tetsu	*Japanese*	–

Tas | *Turkish* 22

Vinoteca | *Euro.* 23

Vivat Bacchus | *Euro.* 20

COVENT GARDEN

Abeno | *Japanese* 24

Adam St. | *British* 23

Asia de Cuba | *Asian/Cuban* 23

Bali Bali | *Indonesian* 20

NEW Balthazar | *French* 19

Belgo | *Belgian* 21

Bill's Produce | *British/Deli* 19

Brasserie Blanc | *French* 18

Browns | *British* 19

Busaba Eathai | *Thai* 23

Byron | *Burgers* 19

Café des Amis | *French* 18

Cafe Pacifico | *Mex.* 20

Canela | *Brazilian/Portug.* 21

Cantina Laredo | *Mex.* 23

Christopher's | *Amer./Steak* -

Circus | *Asian* 18

Clos Maggiore | *French* 25

Côte | *French* 18

Crazy Bear | *Thai* 20

Delaunay | *Euro.* 21

Diner | *Amer.* 18

Dishoom | *Indian* 23

Fernandez & Wells | *Sandwiches/Spanish* 21

NEW Five Guys | *Burgers/Hot Dogs* -

Food/Thought | *Veg.* 24

Giovanni's | *Italian* 23

Great Queen St. | *British* 24

NEW Green Man | *French* 21

Hawksmoor | *Steak* 26

Hi Sushi | *Japanese* 22

Indigo | *Euro.* 23

Ivy | *British/Euro.* 24

Jamie's Italian | *Italian* 20

Joe Allen | *Amer.* 19

NEW Joe's Southern | *Amer.* -

J. Sheekey | *Seafood* 26

J. Sheekey Oyster | *Seafood* 25

NEW Kaspar's | *Euro./Seafood* -

Kopapa | *Int'l* 22

Kulu Kulu | *Japanese* 22

Ladurée | *Bakery/Sandwiches* 24

L'Atelier/Robuchon | *French* 28

Le Deuxième | *Euro.* 22

Leon | *Med.* 20

Leon De Bruxelles | *Belgian* 19

Les Deux | *French* 19

Loch Fyne | *Seafood* 22

Masala Zone | *Indian* 22

Maxwell's | *Amer.* 19

MEATmarket | *Burgers* 23

Mela | *Indian* 22

Mishkin's | *Jewish* 20

Mon Plaisir | *French* 21

Moti Mahal | *Indian* 25

Nando's | *Portug.* 18

Opera Tavern | *Italian/Spanish* 25

Orso | *Italian* 21

Pix Pintxos | *Spanish* 17

Polpo | *Italian* 22

Porters English | *British* 19

PunJab | *Indian* 23

Real Greek | *Greek* 20

Rock & Sole | *Seafood* 24

Rossopomodoro | *Pizza* 23

Rules | *British* 24

Sagar | *Indian/Veg.* 21

Savoy Grill | *British/French* 24

NEW Shake Shack | *Burgers* -

Simpson's/Strand | *British* 21

Smollensky's | *Amer./Steak* 18

Sofra | *Turkish* 21

Sophie's | *Amer./Steak* 22

Souk | *African* 21

NEW STK | *Steak* -

Suda | *Thai* 23

10 Cases | *Euro.* 23

Terroirs | *Med.* 22

Thai Sq. | *Thai* 19

Tom's Kitchen | *British* 23

Tortilla | *Mex.* 22

Tuttons | *British* 20

Union Jacks | *British/Pizza* 18

Wagamama | *Japanese* 17

Wahaca | *Mex.* 22

HOLBORN

Amico Bio	*Italian/Veg.*	22
Asadal	*Korean*	23
Belgo	*Belgian*	21
Bountiful Cow	*Steak*	22
Brasserie Blanc	*French*	18
Cabana	*Brazilian*	21
Chancery	*Euro.*	24
Chilango	*Mex.*	21
Cigalon	*French*	22
Garufa/Garufin	*Argent./Steak*	26
Gaucho	*Argent./Steak*	22
Hush	*Euro.*	19
Shanghai Blues	*Chinese*	24
28-50 Wine	*French*	21
Union Jacks	*British/Pizza*	18
Vanilla Black	*Veg.*	24
Zizzi	*Italian*	18

MARYLEBONE

Atari-Ya	*Japanese*	26
Aubaine	*French*	18
Beirut Express	*Lebanese*	23
Black & Blue	*Steak*	19
Busaba Eathai	*Thai*	23
Caldesi	*Italian*	18
Canteen	*British*	18
Carluccio's	*Italian*	16
Comptoir Libanais	*Lebanese*	20
Defune	*Japanese*	25
Dinings	*Japanese*	28
Donostia	*Spanish*	24
Efes	*Turkish*	22
Fairuz	*Lebanese*	22
FishWorks	*Seafood*	20
Galvin Bistrot	*French*	25
Golden Hind	*Seafood*	24
Grazing Goat	*British*	20
Iberica	*Spanish*	23
Il Baretto	*Italian*	23
Ishtar	*Turkish*	20
La Fromagerie	*Deli/Sandwiches*	24
La Porte/Indes	*Indian*	22
L'Autre Pied	*Euro.*	25
Leon	*Med.*	20
Le Relais	*French/Steak*	24

Locanda Locatelli	*Italian*	25
NEW Lockhart	*Amer.*	-
Made in Italy	*Pizza*	19
Mandalay	*Burmese*	24
Maroush	*Lebanese*	23
MEATliquor	*Burgers*	23
Nando's	*Portug.*	18
108 Marylebone	*British*	21
Orrery	*French*	23
Özer	*Turkish*	21
NEW Patty & Bun	*Burgers*	21
Phoenix Palace	*Chinese*	23
Ping Pong	*Chinese*	17
Prezzo	*Italian*	20
Providores	*Int'l*	25
Real Greek	*Greek*	20
Reubens	*Deli/Jewish/Kosher*	20
Roti Chai	*Indian*	24
Roux/Landau	*Euro.*	26
Royal China	*Chinese*	23
Royal China Club	*Chinese*	25
Sofra	*Turkish*	21
Strada	*Italian*	17
Texture	*Euro./Scan.*	26
Trishna	*Indian*	26
28-50 Wine	*French*	21
2 Veneti	*Italian*	23
Union Café	*British/Med.*	21
Vapiano	*Italian*	23
Verru	*E Euro./Scan.*	22
Villandry	*Deli/Euro.*	18
Vinoteca	*Euro.*	23
Woodlands	*Indian/Veg.*	23
Zayna	*Indian/Pakistani*	28
Zizzi	*Italian*	18
NEW Zoilo	*Argent.*	-

MAYFAIR

Alain Ducasse	*French*	27
Al Hamra	*Lebanese*	23
Alloro	*Italian*	22
Al Sultan	*Lebanese*	22
Alyn Williams	*Euro.*	23
Amaranto	*Italian*	24
Annabel's	*British/French*	21
Arts Club	*Euro.*	22

Aubaine	*French*	18
Aurelia	*Med.*	22
Automat	*Amer.*	19
Babbo	*Italian*	21
Bellamy's	*French*	24
Benares	*Indian*	25
NEW Bo London	*Chinese*	-
NEW Brasserie Chavot	*French*	-
Browns	*British*	19
Burger & Lobster	*Amer.*	23
Cecconi's	*Italian*	23
China Tang	*Chinese*	21
Chisou	*Japanese*	23
Chor Bizarre	*Indian*	25
C London	*Italian*	23
Corrigan's Mayfair	*British*	25
Cut/45 Park Ln.	*Amer./Steak*	25
Delfino	*Italian*	20
Dorchester	*British*	25
Downtown Mayfair	*Italian*	21
Ed's Easy Diner	*Amer.*	19
El Pirata	*Spanish*	22
Espelette	*French*	25
Flemings Grill	*Euro.*	21
Galvin at Windows	*French*	25
George	*Euro.*	23
Goodman	*Steak*	27
NEW Great British	*British*	-
Greenhouse	*French*	27
Greig's	*Steak*	21
Guinea Grill	*Steak*	24
Hakkasan	*Chinese*	26
Harry's Bar	*Italian*	25
Hélène Darroze	*French*	25
Hibiscus	*French*	25
Hix Mayfair	*British*	25
Hush	*Euro.*	19
Ikeda	*Japanese*	26
JW Steak	*Amer./Steak*	23
Kai Mayfair	*Chinese*	25
Kiku	*Japanese*	24
La Genova	*Italian*	23
Langan's Brass.	*British/French*	21
La Petite Maison	*Med.*	26
Le Boudin Blanc	*French*	24
Le Gavroche	*French*	28

NEW Little Social	*French*	-
Mark's Club	*British/French*	21
Maze	*French*	24
Maze Grill	*Steak*	23
Mews/Mayfair	*British*	19
Miyama	*Japanese*	23
Momo	*Moroccan*	21
Morton's	*Med.*	22
Murano	*Euro./Italian*	26
Nobu Berkeley	*Japanese*	26
Nobu London	*Japanese*	27
Noura	*Lebanese*	22
Novikov	*Asian/Italian*	21
Patara	*Thai*	24
Pescatori	*Italian/Seafood*	22
Pollen St. Social	*British*	25
Prezzo	*Italian*	20
Princess Garden	*Chinese*	24
Rasa	*Indian/Veg.*	24
Sakura	*Japanese*	22
Sartoria	*Italian*	23
Scott's	*Seafood*	26
Sketch/Gallery	*Euro.*	21
Sketch/Lecture	*Euro.*	22
Sketch/Parlour	*British*	21
Sofra	*Turkish*	21
Square	*French*	28
Sumosan	*Japanese*	22
Tamarind	*Indian*	25
Thai Sq.	*Thai*	19
Theo Randall	*Italian*	25
34	*Steak*	23
Truc Vert	*French*	19
Umu	*Japanese*	27
Veeraswamy	*Indian*	24
Wild Honey	*British*	23

PICCADILLY/ ST. JAMES'S

Al Duca	*Italian*	22
Aubaine	*French*	18
Avenue	*British*	20
Balcon	*British/French*	23
Benihana	*Japanese*	20
Bentley's	*British/Seafood*	25
Brumus	*Euro.*	22

Caviar House	*Seafood*	23
Citrus	*Italian*	21
NEW Coya	*Peruvian*	24
Criterion	*Euro.*	21
FishWorks	*Seafood*	20
Fortnum's Fountain	*British*	20
Franco's	*Italian/Med.*	22
Gaucho	*Argent./Steak*	22
Green's	*British/Seafood*	21
Hawksmoor	*Steak*	26
Inamo	*Asian*	19
Ladurée	*Bakery/Sandwiches*	24
Le Caprice	*British/Euro.*	24
Matsuri	*Japanese*	23
Mint Leaf	*Indian*	22
Quaglino's	*Euro.*	21
Ritz	*British/French*	24
Rowley's	*British*	23
Sake No Hana	*Japanese*	25
Seven Park	*British/French*	24
Thai Sq.	*Thai*	19
Wheeler's	*Seafood*	21
Wilton's	*British/Seafood*	26
Wolseley	*Euro.*	23
Yoshino	*Japanese*	24

SOHO

Andrew Edmunds	*Euro.*	24
Aqua Kyoto	*Japanese*	22
Aqua Nueva	*Spanish*	21
Arbutus	*Euro.*	24
Aurora	*Euro.*	24
Balans	*British*	19
Banana Tree	*SE Asian*	21
Barrafina	*Spanish*	28
Barshu	*Chinese*	23
Ba Shan	*Chinese*	24
Bill's Produce	*British/Deli*	19
Bincho	*Japanese*	23
Bob Bob Ricard	*Int'l/Russian*	22
Bocca/Gelupo	*Italian*	25
Bodeans	*Amer./BBQ*	22
NEW Bone Daddies	*Japanese*	21
Brasserie Zédel	*French*	17
Breakfast Club	*Amer./British*	21
NEW BRGR.CO	*Burgers*	-
Brindisa	*Spanish*	23

Burger & Lobster	*Amer.*	23
Busaba Eathai	*Thai*	23
Byron	*Burgers*	19
Café Boheme	*French*	18
Cape Town Fish	*Int'l/Seafood*	23
Cây Tre	*Viet.*	22
Ceviche	*Peruvian*	27
Cha Cha Moon	*Chinese*	18
NEW Clockjack Oven	*American/Chicken*	-
Comptoir Libanais	*Lebanese*	20
Copita	*Spanish*	24
Côte	*French*	18
Dean St.	*British*	22
Dehesa	*Italian/Spanish*	25
Diner	*Amer.*	18
Ducksoup	*Euro.*	21
Ed's Easy Diner	*Amer.*	19
Fernandez & Wells	*Sandwiches/Spanish*	21
NEW Flat Iron	*Steak*	-
Flat White	*Australian/Coffee*	24
Gaby's	*Jewish/Mideast.*	23
Gail's	*Bakery*	22
Gauthier	*French*	28
Gay Hussar	*Hungarian*	21
Giaconda/Dining	*Euro.*	23
Gopal's	*Indian*	19
Gourmet Burger	*Burgers*	18
Groucho Club	*British*	18
Hix	*British*	22
Honest Burgers	*Burgers*	27
Imli Street	*Indian*	22
Inamo	*Asian*	19
Kettner's	*European*	22
Koya	*Japanese*	24
Kulu Kulu	*Japanese*	22
La Bodega Negra	*Mex.*	17
Leon	*Med.*	20
L'Escargot	*French*	25
Little Italy	*Italian*	21
Made in Italy	*Pizza*	19
Masala Zone	*Indian*	22
NEW MASH	*Amer./Steak*	25
Mele e Pere	*Italian*	20
New Mayflower	*Chinese*	24

NOPI | *Asian/Mideast.*	25
NEW 1 Leicester St. | *Euro.*	–
Paramount | *Euro.*	21
Patara | *Thai*	24
Pho | *Viet.*	22
Ping Pong | *Chinese*	17
Pitt Cue Co. | *BBQ*	28
Pix Pintxos | *Spanish*	17
Pizza Express | *Italian/Pizza*	16
Polpo | *Italian*	22
Portrait | *British*	22
Prezzo | *Italian*	20
Princi London | *Bakery/Italian*	24
Quo Vadis | *British*	23
Randall/Aubin | *British/Seafood*	25
Red Fort | *Indian*	23
Rosa's | *Thai*	22
Satsuma | *Japanese*	20
NEW Social Eating Hse. | *British/Int'l*	–
Soho Hse. | *British*	20
Spice Mkt. | *SE Asian*	22
Spuntino | *Amer./Italian*	23
Taro | *Japanese*	24
10 Greek St. | *Euro.*	23
Ten Ten Tei | *Japanese*	25
Thai Sq. | *Thai*	19
Tonkotsu | *Japanese*	–
Vasco & Piero's | *Italian*	23
Viet | *Viet.*	23
Vinoteca | *Euro.*	23
Wahaca | *Mex.*	22
Woodlands | *Indian/Veg.*	23
Wright Brothers | *Seafood*	24
Yalla Yalla | *Lebanese*	24
Yauatcha | *Chinese*	27
Yming | *Chinese*	23

VICTORIA/PIMLICO

About Thyme | *Euro.*	24
NEW A Wong | *Chinese*	–
Browns | *British*	19
Goring Dining Room | *British*	25
Grumbles | *British/French*	19
Kazan | *Turkish*	24
Mango Tree | *Thai*	20
NEW No. 11 Pimlico | *Euro.*	–
Prezzo | *Italian*	20
Quilon | *Indian*	–
NEW Royal Quarter | *Euro.*	–

East London

CANARY WHARF/WAPPING

Amerigo Vespucci | *Italian*	23
Boisdale | *British/Scottish*	22
Browns | *British*	19
Byron | *Burgers*	19
Camino | *Spanish*	22
Canteen | *British*	18
Carluccio's | *Italian*	16
Dockmaster's | *Indian*	22
Feng Sushi | *Japanese*	19
Gaucho | *Argent./Steak*	22
Goodman | *Steak*	27
Gun | *British*	23
Iberica | *Spanish*	23
Il Bordello | *Italian*	25
Jamie's Italian | *Italian*	20
Leon | *Mcd.*	20
Le Relais | *French/Steak*	24
Lotus Floating | *Chinese*	22
Plateau | *French*	21
Quadrato | *Italian*	19
Roka | *Japanese*	26
Royal China | *Chinese*	23
Smollensky's | *Amer./Steak*	18
Sri Nam | *Thai*	21
Tom's Kitchen | *British*	23
Tortilla | *Mex.*	22
Wahaca | *Mex.*	22
Wapping Food | *Euro.*	19

DALSTON/BETHNAL GREEN

A Little/Fancy | *British*	22
Bistrotheque | *French*	21
Buen Ayre | *Argent.*	25
Corner Room | *Euro.*	29
Empress | *British*	23
NEW Lardo | *Italian/Pizza*	–
Mangal Ocakbasi | *Turkish*	–
Nando's | *Portug.*	18
Viajante | *Int'l*	26

LOCATIONS

SHOREDITCH/HOXTON

NEW Beagle	British	–
NEW Beard To Tail	British/Steak	–
Boundary	French	23
Brawn	British/Med.	26
Breakfast Club	Amer./British	21
Brindisa	Spanish	23
Busaba Eathai	Thai	23
NEW Casa Negra	Mex.	–
Cây Tre	Viet.	22
NEW Clove Club	British	–
Diner	Amer.	18
Dishoom	Indian	23
Eyre Brothers	Portug./Spanish	25
Fifteen	British	–
Haché	Burgers	23
Hoxton Grill	Amer.	22
Hoxton Sq.	Tex-Mex	16
Les Trois Garçons	French	23
NEW MEATmission	Burgers	–
Mien Tay	Viet.	24
Pizza East	Pizza	21
Princess of Shoreditch	British	20
Rivington Grill	British	23
Rossopomodoro	Pizza	23
Sedap	Malaysian	26
Song Que	Viet.	25
Stingray/Stringray	Italian	23
Thai Thai	Thai	21
Tramshed	Chicken/Steak	20
Viet Hoa	Viet.	22

SPITALFIELDS/WHITECHAPEL

Barcelona Tapas	Spanish	22
Bevis Marks	Int'l/Kosher	23
Breakfast Club	Amer./British	21
Canteen	British	18
Galvin Chapelle/Café	French	26
Gourmet Burger	Burgers	18
Hawksmoor	Steak	26
Lahore Kebab	Pakistani	25
Las Iguanas	Pan-Latin	21
Leon	Med.	20
Lupita	Mex.	25
Pho	Viet.	22
Poppies Fish	Seafood	22
Real Greek	Greek	20
Rosa's	Thai	22
St. John Bread	British	25
Strada	Italian	17
Tayyabs	Pakistani	25
NEW Upstairs/Ten Bells	British	–
Wagamama	Japanese	17
Whitechapel	Euro.	18

STRATFORD

Balans	British	19
Bumpkin	British	19
Busaba Eathai	Thai	23
Cabana	Brazilian	21
Comptoir Libanais	Lebanese	20
Franco Manca	Pizza	26
Jamie's Italian	Italian	20
Las Iguanas	Pan-Latin	21
Pho	Viet.	22
Rosa's	Thai	22
Tortilla	Mex.	22
Wahaca	Mex.	22

North London

CAMDEN TOWN/CHALK FARM/KENTISH TOWN/PRIMROSE HILL

Belgo	Belgian	21
Bento	Japanese	23
Bull & Last	British	24
Camden Brass.	Euro.	23
Carob Tree	Greek/Med.	23
NEW Chicken Shop	Chicken	–
Cottons	Carib.	22
Diner	Amer.	18
NEW Dirty Burger	Burgers	–
El Parador	Spanish	25
Feng Sushi	Japanese	19
Gilgamesh	Asian	19
NEW Greenberry Café	Int'l	–
Haché	Burgers	23
Hi Sushi	Japanese	22
Kentish Canteen	Int'l	22
L'Absinthe	French	23

La Porchetta	*Pizza*	22	Almeida	*French*	22
Lemonia	*Greek*	21	Antepliler	*Turkish*	26
Made/Camden	*Euro.*	24	Antonio's	*Italian*	23
Masala Zone	*Indian*	22	Banana Tree	*SE Asian*	21
Nando's	*Portug.*	18	Bill's Produce	*British/Deli*	19
Odette's	*Euro.*	25	Blue Legume	*Med.*	22
Pizza East	*Pizza*	21	Breakfast Club	*Amer./British*	21
Poppies Fish	*Seafood*	22	Browns	*British*	19
Rossopomodoro	*Pizza*	23	Byron	*Burgers*	19
Stingray/Stringray	*Italian*	23	Carluccio's	*Italian*	16
Strada	*Italian*	17	Chilango	*Mex.*	21
York/Albany	*British*	20	Diner	*Amer.*	18

GOLDERS GREEN/ FINCHLEY/HENDON/ MILL HILL

Atari-Ya	*Japanese*	26	Duke of Cambridge	*British*	22
Café Japan	*Japanese*	26	Elk/Woods	*Int'l*	21
Good Earth	*Chinese*	25	**NEW** Fish & Chip Shop	*British/Seafood*	–
Green Cottage	*Chinese*	25	Frederick's	*British/Euro.*	23
Leon	*Med.*	20	Gallipoli	*Turkish*	21
Original Lahore	*Pakistani*	23	Garufa/Garufin	*Argent./Steak*	26
Solly's	*Kosher/Mideast.*	20	Gate	*Veg./Vegan*	23
Wagamama	*Japanese*	17	Gourmet Burger	*Burgers*	18
Zizzi	*Italian*	18	Jamie's Italian	*Italian*	20

HAMPSTEAD/ BELSIZE PARK

			Juniper Dining	*Int'l*	28
Artigiano	*Italian*	22	La Fromagerie	*Deli/Sandwiches*	24
Banana Tree	*SE Asian*	21	La Porchetta	*Pizza*	22
Feng Sushi	*Japanese*	19	Le Mercury	*French*	20
Gail's	*Bakery*	22	Masala Zone	*Indian*	22
Gaucho	*Argent./Steak*	22	Mem & Laz	*Med.*	21
Jin Kichi	*Japanese*	27	**NEW** Naamyaa	*Thai*	–
Nando's	*Portug.*	18	Nando's	*Portug.*	18
Nautilus Fish	*Seafood*	26	New Culture Rev.	*Chinese*	20
Old Bull/Bush	*Euro.*	18	Ottolenghi	*Bakery/Med.*	26
Paradise	*Indian*	26	Pasha	*Turkish*	22
Wagamama	*Japanese*	17	Pix Pintxos	*Spanish*	17
Wells	*Euro.*	22	Rodizio Rico	*Brazilian*	20
Woodlands	*Indian/Veg.*	23	Stingray/Stringray	*Italian*	23
XO	*Asian*	20	Strada	*Italian*	17
			Thai Sq.	*Thai*	19
			Tortilla	*Mex.*	22
			Trullo	*Italian*	24
			Wagamama	*Japanese*	17
			Wahaca	*Mex.*	22

ISLINGTON/ HIGHBURY

Afghan Kitchen	*Afghan*	24	**KING'S CROSS/ EUSTON**		
Akari	*Japanese*	24	Camino	*Spanish*	22
Albion	*British*	22	Caravan	*Int'l*	24

LOCATIONS

Chutneys	Indian/Veg.	23
Cocomaya	Bakery	24
Ed's Easy Diner	Amer.	19
Gilbert Scott	British	19
NEW Grain Store	Int'l	-
Mestizo	Mex.	21
NEW Plum + Spilt Milk	British	-
Prezzo	Italian	20
Rotunda	British	19
Shrimpy's	Calif./Mex.	-

STOKE NEWINGTON

Blue Legume	Med.	22
Rasa	Indian/Veg.	24
Yum Yum	Thai	23

STROUD GREEN/ CROUCH END/ HIGHGATE/ MUSWELL HILL

Blue Legume	Med.	22
NEW Chooks	Chicken	-
Côte	French	18
500	Italian	25
Gail's	Bakery	22
La Porchetta	Pizza	22
Pizza Express	Italian/Pizza	16
Strada	Italian	17
Zizzi	Italian	18

South East London

DULWICH/ HONOR OAK

Babur	Indian	27
Barcelona Tapas	Spanish	22
Draft House	Int'l	20
Gourmet Burger	Burgers	18
Palmerston	British	23
Pizza Express	Italian/Pizza	16
Rocca	Italian	24

GREENWICH/ BLACKHEATH/ LEWISHAM

Byron	Burgers	19
Chapters All Day	Euro.	24
Côte	French	18
Jamie's Italian	Italian	20

Las Iguanas	Pan-Latin	21
Nando's	Portug.	18
Old Brewery	British	17
Pizza Express	Italian/Pizza	16
Rivington Grill	British	23
Rodizio Rico	Brazilian	20
Wagamama	Japanese	17
Zizzi	Italian	18

KENNINGTON/ CAMBERWELL/ PECKHAM

Angels/Gypsies	Spanish	25
Dragon Castle	Chinese	22
805	African	24
Ganapati	Indian	26

SOUTHWARK/ BOROUGH/ TOWER BRIDGE

NEW Aqua Shard	British	-
Baltic	E Euro.	23
NEW Bar Tozino	Spanish	-
Bengal Clipper	Indian	21
Black & Blue	Steak	19
Blueprint	Euro.	22
Brindisa	Spanish	23
Browns	British	19
Butlers Wharf	British/Steak	23
Cafe East	Viet.	24
Cantina/Ponte	Italian	19
Champor	Malaysian	22
Constancia	Argent./Steak	25
Del'Aziz	African/Med.	20
Draft House	Int'l	20
Feng Sushi	Japanese	19
Fish	Seafood	23
Gaucho	Argent./Steak	22
Gourmet Burger	Burgers	18
NEW Hutong	Chinese	-
José	Spanish	28
Leon	Med.	20
Le Pont/Tour	French/Seafood	23
Magdalen	Euro.	25
NEW Oblix	Amer.	-
Ping Pong	Chinese	17
Pizarro	Spanish	26

Roast | *British*	25
NEW Story | *British*	-
Tas | *Turkish*	22
Tentazioni | *Italian*	24
Vapiano | *Italian*	23
Village East | *British*	23
Vivat Bacchus | *Euro.*	20
Wagamama | *Japanese*	17
Wright Brothers | *Seafood*	24
Zizzi | *Italian*	18
Zucca | *Italian*	27

South West London

BALHAM/STREATHAM/TOOTING

Gazette | *French*	20
Lahore Kebab | *Pakistani*	25
Lamberts | *British*	28
Pizza Express | *Italian/Pizza*	16
Spice Village | *Indian*	27

BRIXTON

Boqueria | *Spanish*	-
Franco Manca | *Pizza*	26
French/Grace | *British/Mideast.*	-
Honest Burgers | *Burgers*	27
KaoSarn | *Thai*	-
Mama Lan | *Chinese*	-
NEW Salon | *British*	-
NEW Wishbone | *Chicken*	-

CLAPHAM/BATTERSEA/WANDSWORTH

Abbeville | *British*	23
Banana Tree | *SE Asian*	21
NEW Barsito | *Spanish*	-
Belgo | *Belgian*	21
NEW Bistro Union | *British*	-
Bodeans | *Amer./BBQ*	22
Breakfast Club | *Amer./British*	21
Buona Sera | *Italian*	20
Butcher & Grill | *British*	20
Carluccio's | *Italian*	16
Chez Bruce | *British/Med.*	28
Del'Aziz | *African/Med.*	20

Draft House | *Int'l*	20
Ed's Easy Diner | *Amer.*	19
Franco Manca | *Pizza*	26
Gail's | *Bakery*	22
Gazette | *French*	20
Good Earth | *Chinese*	25
Gourmet Burger | *Burgers*	18
Haché | *Burgers*	23
KaoSarn | *Thai*	-
Mama Lan | *Chinese*	-
Mien Tay | *Viet.*	24
Nando's | *Portug.*	18
Osteria Antica | *Italian*	22
Pepper Tree | *Thai*	27
Pizza Express | *Italian/Pizza*	16
Prezzo | *Italian*	20
NEW Rosita/Sherry Bar | *Spanish*	-
Santa Maria | *Argent./Steak*	26
Strada | *Italian*	17
Trinity | *Euro.*	26
Tsunami | *Japanese*	23

PUTNEY/WIMBLEDON/RICHMOND/BARNES

A Cena | *Italian*	25
Annie's | *British*	23
Bill's Produce | *British/Deli*	19
Bingham | *British/Euro.*	24
Butcher & Grill | *British*	20
Carluccio's | *Italian*	16
Enoteca Turi | *Italian*	25
FishWorks | *Seafood*	20
Fox/Grapes | *British*	20
French Table | *French/Med.*	28
Gaucho | *Argent./Steak*	22
Glasshouse | *Euro.*	26
Hare & Tortoise | *Japanese*	22
Light House | *Int'l*	24
Ma Goa | *Indian*	22
Petersham | *Euro.*	23
Petersham Nurseries | *Euro.*	24
Popeseye | *Steak*	24
Strada | *Italian*	17
Thai Sq. | *Thai*	19
Tortilla | *Mex.*	22
Wagamama | *Japanese*	17

LOCATIONS

SOUTH BANK

Canteen	*British*	18
Cantina Vino.	*Int'l*	19
Feng Sushi	*Japanese*	19
Gourmet Burger	*Burgers*	18
Las Iguanas	*Pan-Latin*	21
Oxo Tower	*Euro.*	22
Oxo Tower Brass.	*Asian/Med.*	23
Ping Pong	*Chinese*	17
Real Greek	*Greek*	20
Skylon	*Euro.*	20
Tas	*Turkish*	22
Tate Modern	*British*	19
Tortilla	*Mex.*	22
Tsuru	*Japanese*	22
Wahaca	*Mex.*	22

WATERLOO/ VAUXHALL

Anchor/Hope	*British*	25
Black & Blue	*Steak*	19
Brasserie Blanc	*French*	18
Hot Stuff	*Indian*	25
Meson Don Felipe	*Spanish*	23
R.S.J.	*British*	22
Tas	*Turkish*	22
Wahaca	*Mex.*	22

West London

BAYSWATER/ PADDINGTON

Alounak	*Persian*	23
Al Waha	*Lebanese*	22
Angelus	*French*	25
Banana Tree	*SE Asian*	21
Bombay Palace	*Indian*	24
Byron	*Burgers*	19
Cocomaya	*Bakery*	24
Côte	*French*	18
El Pirata	*Spanish*	22
Four Seasons	*Chinese*	23
Frontline	*British*	23
Goldmine	*Chinese*	25
Halepi	*Greek*	24
Hereford Rd.	*British*	24
Khan's	*Indian*	20

Le Café Anglais	*French*	22
Mandarin Kitchen	*Chinese/Seafood*	25
Masala Zone	*Indian*	22
Nando's	*Portug.*	18
Noor Jahan	*Indian*	23
Pearl Liang	*Chinese*	25
Rodizio Rico	*Brazilian*	20
Royal China	*Chinese*	23
Satay House	*Malaysian*	26
NEW Shiori	*Japanese*	-
Zizzi	*Italian*	18

BELGRAVIA

Amaya	*Indian*	27
NEW Ametsa	*Spanish*	-
Apsleys	*Italian*	26
Baker & Spice	*Bakery/Med.*	21
Beiteddine	*Lebanese*	26
Boisdale	*British/Scottish*	22
Como Lario	*Italian*	21
Daylesford	*Int'l*	21
Hunan	*Chinese/Taiwanese*	27
Il Convivio	*Italian*	23
Ishbilia	*Lebanese*	24
Koffmann's	*French*	27
La Poule au Pot	*French*	22
Marcus Wareing	*French*	27
Memories/China	*Chinese*	23
Mosimann's	*Int'l*	26
Motcombs	*Int'l*	21
Noura	*Lebanese*	22
Oliveto	*Italian*	24
Olivo	*Italian*	22
NEW Olivocarne	*Italian*	-
Olivomare	*Italian/Seafood*	24
One-O-One	*French/Seafood*	22
Orange	*Euro.*	22
Ottolenghi	*Bakery/Med.*	26
Pantechnicon/Dining	*Euro.*	21
Petrus	*French*	28
Salloos	*Pakistani*	24
Santini	*Italian*	20
Thomas Cubitt	*British*	21
Tinello	*Italian*	25
Zafferano	*Italian*	24

CHELSEA

Admiral Codrington | *British/Euro.*	19
Aglio e Olio | *Italian*	22
Baker & Spice | *Bakery/Med.*	21
Benihana | *Japanese*	20
Big Easy | *Amer.*	21
Bluebird | *British*	20
Blue Elephant | *Thai*	24
Botanist | *British*	18
Bumpkin | *British*	19
Buona Sera | *Italian*	20
Busaba Eathai | *Thai*	23
Byron | *Burgers*	19
Caraffini | *Italian*	22
Carluccio's | *Italian*	16
Cheyne Walk | *French*	20
Chutney Mary | *Indian*	25
NEW Colbert | *French*	17
Daphne's | *Italian*	22
Eight Over Eight | *Asian*	23
El Gaucho | *Argent./Steak*	23
Elistano | *Italian*	21
Enterprise | *British*	21
Feng Sushi | *Japanese*	19
Foxtrot Oscar | *British*	19
Gail's | *Bakery*	22
Gaucho | *Argent./Steak*	22
Geales | *Seafood*	20
Haché | *Burgers*	23
La Famiglia | *Italian*	20
Le Cercle | *French*	24
Le Colombier | *French*	23
Lucio | *Italian*	20
Made in Italy | *Pizza*	19
Manicomio | *Italian*	18
Medlar | *Euro./French*	25
New Culture Rev. | *Chinese*	20
Osteria dell'Arancio | *Italian*	22
Painted Heron | *Indian*	24
Pig's Ear | *British/French*	21
Pizza Express | *Italian/Pizza*	16
Poissonnerie/l'Avenue | *French/Seafood*	24
Rasoi Vineet | *Indian*	28
Rest. Gordon Ramsay | *French*	28
Rossopomodoro | *Pizza*	23
Scalini | *Italian*	24
Sophie's | *Amer./Steak*	22
NEW Tartufo | *Euro.*	-
Tom Aikens | *French*	25
Tom's Kitchen | *British*	23
Ziani | *Italian*	24

CHISWICK

Annie's | *British*	23
Charlotte's | *Euro.*	25
Chisou | *Japanese*	23
Côte | *French*	18
Duke of Sussex | *British/Spanish*	22
Franco Manca | *Pizza*	26
Gail's | *Bakery*	22
Hedone | *Euro.*	23
High Road Brass. | *Euro.*	22
La Trompette | *French*	27
Le Vacherin | *French*	24
Michael Nadra | *Euro.*	25
Sam's Brass. | *Euro.*	24
Singapore Gdn. | *Malaysian/Singapor.*	22
Union Jacks | *British/Pizza*	18

EALING/SOUTHALL

Atari-Ya | *Japanese*	26
Carluccio's | *Italian*	16
Charlotte's | *Euro.*	25
Côte | *French*	18
Hare & Tortoise | *Japanese*	22
Spice Village | *Indian*	27
Wagamama | *Japanese*	17

FULHAM

Bodeans | *Amer./BBQ*	22
Côte | *French*	18
Del'Aziz | *African/Med.*	20
Frankie's | *Italian*	17
Fulham/Kensington Wine | *Euro.*	18
Gourmet Burger | *Burgers*	18
Harwood Arms | *British*	27
Mao Tai | *Asian*	25
Rodizio Rico | *Brazilian*	20
Royal China | *Chinese*	23
Sands End | *British*	22
Strada | *Italian*	17

Tendido Cuatro | *Spanish*	19
Wagamama | *Japanese*	17

KENSINGTON/ EARLS COURT

Abingdon | *Euro.*	21
NEW Acciuga | *Italian*	-
Alounak | *Persian*	23
Aubaine | *French*	18
Babylon | *British*	22
Balans | *British*	19
Byron | *Burgers*	19
Churchill Arms | *Thai*	21
Clarke's | *British*	25
Feng Sushi | *Japanese*	19
Ffiona's | *British*	23
Fulham/Kensington Wine | *Euro.*	18
Hare & Tortoise | *Japanese*	22
Il Portico | *Italian*	19
Kitchen W8 | *Euro.*	25
Koi | *Japanese*	21
Launceston Pl. | *British*	25
Locanda Ottoemezzo | *Italian*	25
Maggie Jones's | *British*	21
Masala Zone | *Indian*	22
Memories/China | *Chinese*	23
Min Jiang | *Chinese*	25
Ottolenghi | *Bakery/Med.*	26
Popeseye | *Steak*	24
Prezzo | *Italian*	20
Saf | *Int'l/Vegan*	23
Strada | *Italian*	17
Timo | *Italian*	24
Troubadour | *Int'l*	20
222 Veggie | *Vegan*	24
Yashin Sushi | *Japanese*	28
Zaika | *Indian*	25

KNIGHTSBRIDGE

Bar Boulud | *French*	24
NEW Brompton Asian | *Asian/European*	-
Brompton B&G | *British/Euro.*	20
NEW Buddha-Bar | *Asian*	-
Chabrot Bistro des Amis | *French*	20
Chisou | *Japanese*	23
Cocomaya | *Bakery*	24

Dinner/Heston | *British*	26
Frankie's | *Italian*	17
Good Earth | *Chinese*	25
Haandi | *Indian*	21
Ladurée | *Bakery/Sandwiches*	24
Maroush | *Lebanese*	23
Mr. Chow | *Chinese*	22
NEW Outlaw's | *Seafood*	-
Palm | *Amer./Steak*	22
Patara | *Thai*	24
Racine | *French*	24
Rib Room | *Steak*	24
Sale e Pepe | *Italian*	24
San Lorenzo | *Italian*	21
Season/Fifth Fl. | *Euro.*	21
Signor Sassi | *Italian*	23
Zuma | *Japanese*	27

NOTTING HILL/ LADBROKE GROVE/ HOLLAND PARK

Assaggi | *Italian*	25
Belvedere | *British/French*	21
Black & Blue | *Steak*	19
Books/Cooks | *Int'l*	25
Bumpkin | *British*	19
Chakra | *Indian*	23
Cow | *British*	22
Crazy Homies | *Mex.*	18
Daylesford | *Int'l*	21
Dock Kitchen | *Euro.*	24
E&O | *Asian*	23
NEW Electric Diner | *Amer./French*	-
Feng Sushi | *Japanese*	19
Gail's | *Bakery*	22
Geales | *Seafood*	20
Gourmet Burger | *Burgers*	18
Granger & Co. | *Australian/Int'l*	19
Julie's | *British*	18
Kensington Pl. | *British*	20
Ledbury | *French*	28
Lucky 7 | *Amer.*	18
Malabar | *Indian*	20
Mediterraneo | *Italian*	23
Osteria Basilico | *Italian*	24
Ottolenghi | *Bakery/Med.*	26

Ping Pong | *Chinese*	17
Pizza East | *Pizza*	21
Portobello | *Italian/Pizza*	23
Rossopomodoro | *Pizza*	23
NEW Shed | *British*	-
Taqueria | *Mex.*	24
Tom's Deli | *Deli/Int'l*	24
202 | *Euro.*	19
Zizzi | *Italian*	18

QUEEN'S PARK/ KENSAL GREEN/ KILBURN

Diner | *Amer.*	18
Gail's | *Bakery*	22
Little Bay | *Euro.*	21
Paradise/Kensal | *British*	23
Sushi-Say | *Japanese*	29

SHEPHERD'S BUSH/ HAMMERSMITH

Adams Cafe | *Moroccan/Tunisian*	21
Anglesea Arms | *British*	21
Balans | *British*	19
Busaba Eathai | *Thai*	23
Byron | *Burgers*	19
Cabana | *Brazilian*	21
Comptoir Libanais | *Lebanese*	20
Esarn Kheaw | *Thai*	23
Gate | *Veg./Vegan*	23
Indian Zing | *Indian*	23
Jamie's Italian | *Italian*	20
101 Thai | *Thai*	24
Pho | *Viet.*	22
Princess Victoria | *British*	25
Real Greek | *Greek*	20
River Café | *Italian*	27
Sagar | *Indian/Veg.*	21
Tortilla | *Mex.*	22
Wahaca | *Mex.*	22

SOUTH KENSINGTON

Aubaine | *French*	18
Beirut Express | *Lebanese*	23
Bibendum | *French*	23
Bibendum Oyster | *French/Seafood*	23

Blakes | *Int'l*	20
Bombay Brass. | *Indian*	23
Brindisa | *Spanish*	23
Bumpkin | *British*	19
Byron | *Burgers*	19
Cambio/Tercio | *Spanish*	24
Cassis Bistro | *French/Med.*	22
Comptoir Libanais | *Lebanese*	20
Diner | *Amer.*	18
El Gaucho | *Argent./Steak*	23
Fernandez & Wells | *Sandwiches/Spanish*	21
Kulu Kulu | *Japanese*	22
La Bouchée | *French*	24
La Brasserie | *French*	20
L'Etranger | *French/Japanese*	25
Noor Jahan | *Indian*	23
Patara | *Thai*	24
Rocca | *Italian*	24
Star of India | *Indian*	26
Tendido Cero | *Spanish*	21
Thai Sq. | *Thai*	19

ST JOHN'S WOOD/ MAIDA VALE/ SWISS COTTAGE

Atari-Ya | *Japanese*	26
Baker & Spice | *Bakery/Med.*	21
Banana Tree | *SE Asian*	21
Bradley's | *British/French*	22
Café Med | *Med.*	19
Del'Aziz | *African/Med.*	20
Gail's | *Bakery*	22
L'Aventure | *French*	25
1 Blenheim Terrace | *British*	24
Original Lahore | *Pakistani*	23
Oslo Court | *French*	26
Red Pepper | *Italian/Pizza*	21
Singapore Gdn. | *Malaysian/Singapor.*	22
Warrington | *British*	19

Outside London

Fat Duck | *British*	28
Le Manoir/Quat | *French*	27
Waterside Inn | *French*	29

LOCATIONS

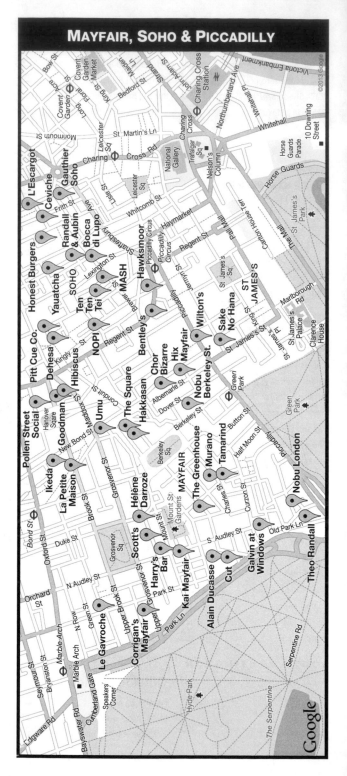

MAYFAIR, SOHO & PICCADILLY

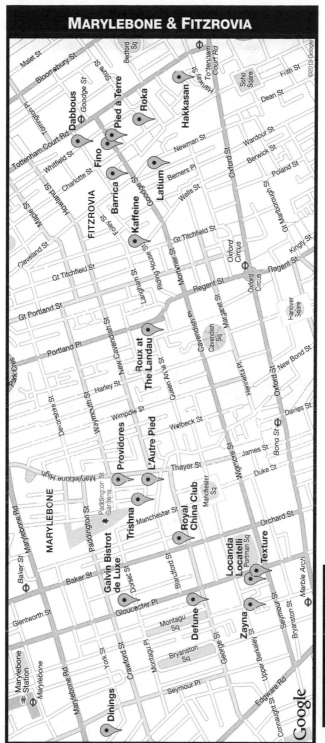

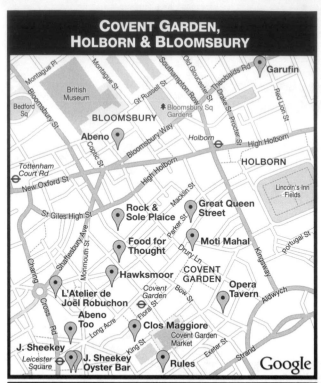

COVENT GARDEN, HOLBORN & BLOOMSBURY

Garufin

British Museum

Bedford Sq

BLOOMSBURY

Bloomsbury Sq Gardens

Holborn

HOLBORN

Abeno

Tottenham Court Rd

New Oxford St

Lincoln's Inn Fields

Rock & Sole Plaice

Great Queen Street

Food for Thought

Moti Mahal

Hawksmoor

COVENT GARDEN

L'Atelier de Joël Robuchon

Covent Garden

Opera Tavern

Abeno Too

Clos Maggiore

J. Sheekey

Covent Garden Market

Leicester Square

J. Sheekey Oyster Bar

Rules

Google

KENSINGTON

Clarke's

Kensington Palace

Ottolenghi

Kensington Palace Green

Kensington Gardens

KENSINGTON

Opera Holland Park

Min Jiang

Zaika

Holland Park

Yashin Sushi

Locanda Ottoemezzo

High St Kensington

Kitchen W8

Launceston Place

Timo

©2013 Google

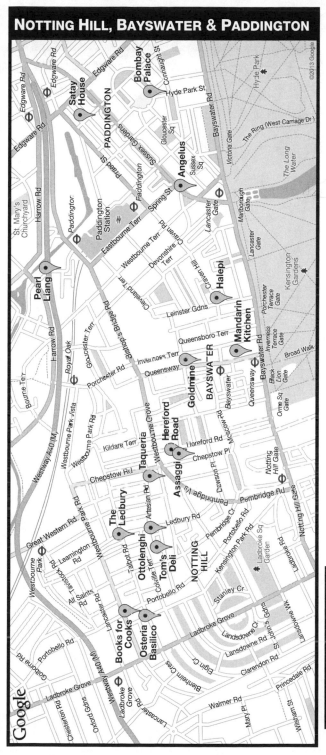

NOTTING HILL, BAYSWATER & PADDINGTON

©2013 Google

Hyde Park

Edgware Rd

Bombay
Palace

Satay
House

PADDINGTON

Hyde Park St

Connaught St

Gloucester
Sq

Bayswater Rd

The Ring (West Carriage Dr)

Victoria Gate

Angelus

Sussex
Sq

The Long
Water

St Mary's
Churchyard

Harrow Rd

Paddington
Station

Eastbourne Terr

Spring St

Westbourne Terr

Devonshire
Terr

Lancaster
Gate

Marlborough
Gate

Lancaster
Gate

Kensington
Gardens

Pearl
Liang

Harrow Rd

Royal Oak

Gloucester Terr

Cleveland Terr

Leinster Gdns

Halepi

Porchester
Terrace
Gate

Bourne Terr

Porchester Rd

Inverness Terr

Queensboro Terr

Mandarin
Kitchen

Inverness
Terrace
Gate

Broad Walk

Westbourne Park Vlla

Westbourne Park Rd

Kildare Terr

Inverness Terr

Queensway

Goldmine

BAYSWATER

Queensway

Bayswater

Black
Lion
Gate

Orme Sq
Gate

Westway A40 (M)

Chepstow Rd

Westbourne Grove

Taqueria

Hereford
Road

Hereford Rd

Chepstow Pl

Moscow Rd

Notting
Hill Gate

Chepstow Rd

Artesian Rd

Assaggi

Dawson Pl

Pembridge Sq

Pembridge Rd

Notting Hill Gate

Great Western Rd

The
Ledbury

Leamington
Rd

Talbot Rd

Ledbury Rd

Ottolenghi

Colville Terr

Tom's
Deli

Pembridge Cr

Portobello Rd

Pembridge Villas

NOTTING
HILL

Kensington Park Rd

Ladbroke Sq
Garden

Ladbroke Rd

Stanley Cr

Westbourne
Park

Tavistock Rd

All Saints
Rd

Lancaster Rd

Portobello Rd

Books for
Cooks

Osteria
Basilico

Ladbroke Grove

Landsdowne Rd

Lansdowne Rd

St John's Gdns

Lansdowne WIk

Colborne Rd

Portobello Rd

Ladbroke Grove

Westway A40 (M)

Blenheim Cres

Elgin Cr

Clarendon Rd

Princedale Rd

Chesterton Rd

Oxford Gdns

Walmer Rd

Mary Pl

Wilsham St

Google

MAPS

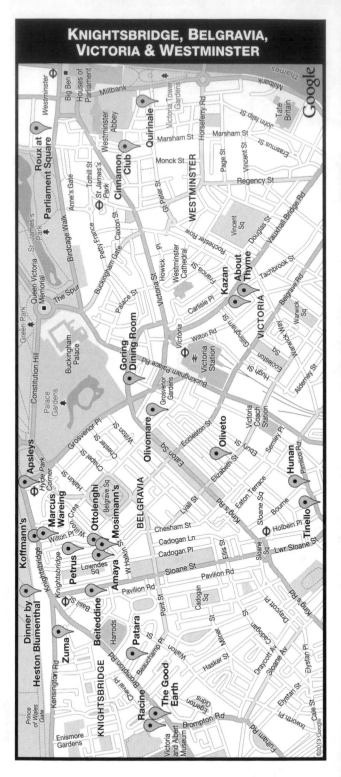

KNIGHTSBRIDGE, BELGRAVIA, VICTORIA & WESTMINSTER

Roux at Parliament Square

Quirinale

Cinnamon Club

Kazan

About Thyme

Goring Dining Room

Apsleys

Marcus Wareing

Olivomare

Oliveto

Hunan

Ottolenghi

Mosimann's

Koffmann's

Petrus

Amaya

Tinello

Dinner by Heston Blumenthal

Beiteddine

Zuma

Patara

Racine

The Good Earth

WESTMINSTER

VICTORIA

BELGRAVIA

KNIGHTSBRIDGE

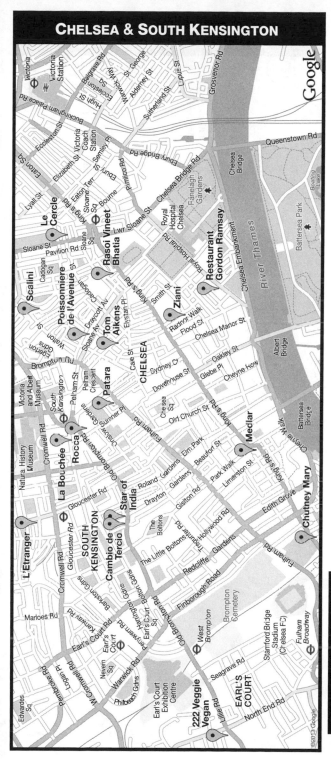

Victoria

Victoria
Station

Belgrave Rd

St. George

Alderney St

Sutherland St

Lupus St

Grosvenor Rd

Google

Hugh St

Warwick Way

St

Eccleston St

Eccleston Sq

Buckingham Palace Rd

Eaton Sq

Victoria
Coach
Station

Ebury Bridge Rd

Semley Pl

Queenstown Rd

Lyall St

Elizabeth St

Ebury St

Sloane Terr

Bourne St

Pimlico Rd

Chelsea Bridge Rd

Ranelagh
Gardens

Chelsea
Bridge

Battersea Park

Boating
Lake

**Le
Cercle**

Sloane St

Eaton Gate

Sloane Sq

Lwr Sloane St

Royal
Hospital
Chelsea

Royal Hospital Rd

**Restaurant
Gordon Ramsay**

River Thames

Chelsea Embankment

Cadogan
Sq

Pavilion Rd

**Rasoi Vineet
Bhatia**

Sloane St

Scalini

Cadogan Gate

Draycott Av

Smith St

Radnor Walk

Ziani

Flood St

Chelsea Manor St

Albert
Bridge

Walton St

**Poissonniere
de l'Avenue**

Sloane Av

Elystan Pl

**Tom
Aikens**

Cae St

CHELSEA

Sydney Ct

Oakley St

Glebe Pl

Cheyne Row

Lygon
Gdns

Bromption Rd

South
Kensington

Pelham St

Pelham
Cres

Patara

Sumner Pl

Onslow Gardens

Fulham Rd

Old Church St

Dovehouse St

Chelsea
Sq

Battersea
Bridge

Victoria
and Albert
Museum

Natural History
Museum

Cromwell Rd

La Bouchée

Rocca

Old Brompton Rd

Gloucester Rd

**Star of
India**

Elm Park
Gardens

Roland Gardens

Beaufort St

Park Walk

Medlar

Cheyne Walk

King's Rd

Drayton
Gardens

Giston Rd

Limerston St

L'Etranger

SOUTH
KENSINGTON

Gloucester Rd

**Cambio de
Tercio**

The
Boltons

The Little Boltons

Redcliffe Gardens

Tregunter Rd

Hollywood Rd

Edith Grove

Chutney Mary

Fulham Rd

Cromwell Rd

Marloes Rd

Kenway Rd

Barkston Gdns

Harrington Gdns

Earl's Court Rd

Bolton Gdns

Finborough Road

Brompton
Cemetery

Stamford Bridge
Stadium
(Chelsea F.C.)

Fulham
Broadway

Edwardes
Sq

Pembroke Pl

W Cromwell Rd

Warwick Rd

Earl's
Court

Nevern
Sq

Philbeach Gdns

Old Brompton Rd

West
Brompton

Seagrave Rd

North End Rd

EARL'S
COURT

MAPS

Earl's Court
Exhibition
Centre

**222 Veggie
Vegan**

Lillie Rd

©2013 Google

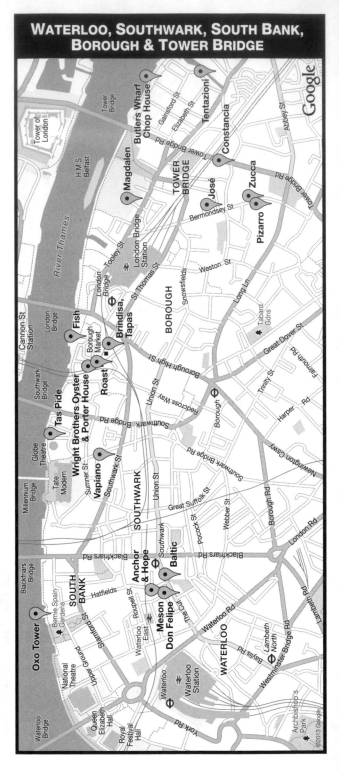

WATERLOO, SOUTHWARK, SOUTH BANK, BOROUGH & TOWER BRIDGE

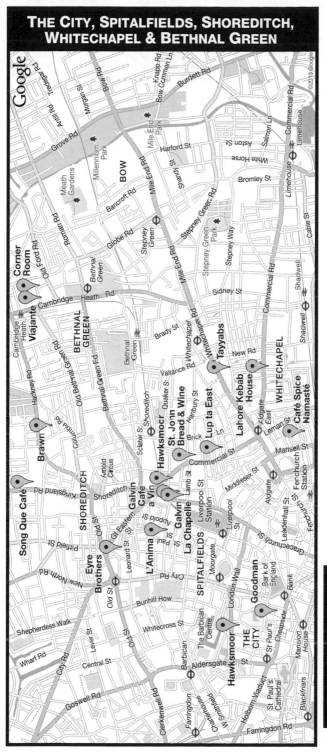

THE CITY, SPITALFIELDS, SHOREDITCH, WHITECHAPEL & BETHNAL GREEN

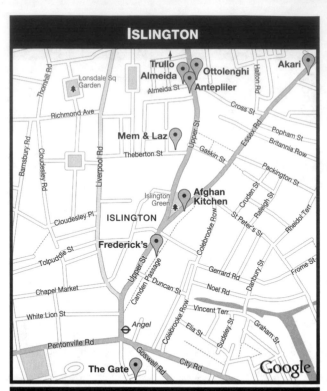

ISLINGTON

- Trullo
- Almeida
- Ottolenghi
- Akari
- Antepliler
- Mem & Laz
- Afghan Kitchen
- Islington Green
- ISLINGTON
- Frederick's
- Angel
- The Gate

Streets: Thornhill Rd, Lonsdale Sq Garden, Almeida St, Halton Rd, Cross St, Richmond Ave, Upper St, Popham St, Britannia Row, Barnsbury Rd, Cloudesley Rd, Liverpool Rd, Theberton St, Gaskin St, Essex Rd, Packington St, Cruden St, Raleigh Rd, St Peter's St, Rheidol Terr, Cloudesley Pl, Colebrooke Row, Frome St, Tolpuddle St, Camden Passage, Gerrard Rd, Danbury St, Chapel Market, Duncan St, Noel Rd, White Lion St, Vincent Terr., Colebrooke Row, Elia St, Sudeley St, Graham St, Pentonville Rd, Goswell Rd, City Rd, Google

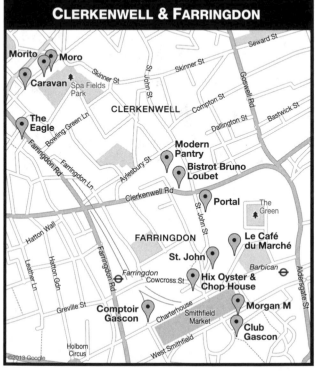

CLERKENWELL & FARRINGDON

- Morito
- Moro
- Caravan
- Spa Fields Park
- CLERKENWELL
- The Eagle
- Modern Pantry
- Bistrot Bruno Loubet
- Portal
- The Green
- Le Café du Marché
- FARRINGDON
- St. John
- Hix Oyster & Chop House
- Comptoir Gascon
- Smithfield Market
- Morgan M
- Club Gascon

Streets: Seward St, Skinner St, St. John St, Goswell Rd, Compton St, Bastwick St, Dallington St, Bowling Green Ln, Farringdon Rd, Farringdon Ln, Aylesbury St, Clerkenwell Rd, Hatton Wall, Barbican, Hatton Gdn, Cowcross St, Leather Ln, Farringdon Rd, Charterhouse, Aldersgate St, Greville St, West Smithfield, Holborn Circus, ©2013 Google